Rethinking Comparison

Qualitative comparative methods – and specifically controlled qualitative comparisons – are central to the study of politics. They are not the only kind of comparison, though, that can help us better understand political processes and outcomes. Yet there are few guides for how to conduct non-controlled comparative research. This volume brings together chapters from more than a dozen leading methods scholars from across the discipline of political science, including positivist and interpretivist scholars, qualitative methodologists, mixed-methods researchers, ethnographers, historians, and statisticians. Their work revolutionizes qualitative research design by diversifying the repertoire of comparative methods available to students of politics, offering readers clear suggestions for what kinds of comparisons might be possible, why they are useful, and how to execute them. By systematically thinking through how we engage in qualitative comparisons and the kinds of insights those comparisons produce, these collected essays create new possibilities to advance what we know about politics.

Erica S. Simmons is Associate Professor of Political Science and International Studies and holds the Department of Political Science Board of Visitors Professorship at the University of Wisconsin–Madison.

Nicholas Rush Smith is Assistant Professor of Political Science at the City University of New York–City College and Senior Research Associate in the Department of Sociology at the University of Johannesburg.

Rethinking Comparison

Innovative Methods for Qualitative Political Inquiry

Edited by

ERICA S. SIMMONS
University of Wisconsin–Madison

NICHOLAS RUSH SMITH
City University of New York–City College

CAMBRIDGE
UNIVERSITY PRESS

University Printing House, Cambridge CB2 8BS, United Kingdom

One Liberty Plaza, 20th Floor, New York, NY 10006, USA

477 Williamstown Road, Port Melbourne, VIC 3207, Australia

314–321, 3rd Floor, Plot 3, Splendor Forum, Jasola District Centre, New Delhi – 110025, India

103 Penang Road, #05–06/07, Visioncrest Commercial, Singapore 238467

Cambridge University Press is part of the University of Cambridge.

It furthers the University's mission by disseminating knowledge in the pursuit of education, learning, and research at the highest international levels of excellence.

www.cambridge.org
Information on this title: www.cambridge.org/9781108832793
DOI: 10.1017/9781108966009

© Cambridge University Press 2021

This publication is in copyright. Subject to statutory exception and to the provisions of relevant collective licensing agreements, no reproduction of any part may take place without the written permission of Cambridge University Press.

First published 2021

A catalogue record for this publication is available from the British Library.

ISBN 978-1-108-83279-3 Hardback
ISBN 978-1-108-96574-3 Paperback

Cambridge University Press has no responsibility for the persistence or accuracy of URLs for external or third-party internet websites referred to in this publication and does not guarantee that any content on such websites is, or will remain, accurate or appropriate.

We dedicate this volume to the memory of Lee Ann Fujii and Kendra Koivu, both of whom were committed to helping us rethink how we see the world.

Contents

List of Figures	*page*	ix
List of Tables		x
List of Contributors		xi
Acknowledgments		xv
1	Rethinking Comparison: An Introduction *Erica S. Simmons and Nicholas Rush Smith*	1
PART I RETHINKING THE BUILDING BLOCKS OF COMPARISON		29
2	Beyond Mill: Why Cross-Case Qualitative Causal Inference Is Weak, and Why We Should Still Compare *Jason Seawright*	31
3	Two Ways to Compare *Frederic Charles Schaffer*	47
4	Unbound Comparison *Nick Cheesman*	64
5	On Casing a Study versus Studying a Case *Joe Soss*	84
6	From Cases to Sites: Studying Global Processes in Comparative Politics *Thea Riofrancos*	107
PART II DEVELOPING NEW APPROACHES TO COMPARISON THROUGH RESEARCH		127
7	Comparing Complex Cases Using Archival Research *Jonathan Obert*	129

8	Composing Comparisons: Studying Configurations of Relations in Social Network Research *Sarah E. Parkinson*	152
9	Against Methodological Nationalism: Seeing Comparisons as Encompassing through the Arab Uprisings *Jillian Schwedler*	172
10	Comparative Analysis for Theory Development *Mala Htun and Francesca R. Jensenius*	190
11	Problems and Possibilities of Comparison across Regime Types: Examples Involving China *Benjamin L. Read*	208
12	Comparisons with an Ethnographic Sensibility: Studies of Protest and Vigilantism *Erica S. Simmons and Nicholas Rush Smith*	231

EPILOGUE 251

13	Theory and Imagination in Comparative Politics: An Interview with Lisa Wedeen *Erica S. Simmons and Nicholas Rush Smith with Lisa Wedeen*	253

Index 275

Figures

7.1 Diffusion of violence in Chicago Race Riot
(July 26–29, 1919) *page* 143
8.1 Militant A's egocentric social network perspective 165

Tables

7.1 Methodological choice and complex comparisons   *page* 138
7.2 Racially motivated violence in the United States (1919)   145

Contributors

Nick Cheesman is Fellow in the Department of Political and Social Change, Australian National University. He is the author of *Opposing the Rule of Law: How Myanmar's Courts Make Law and Order* (Cambridge University Press, 2015), and *Myanmar: A Political Lexicon* (Cambridge Elements, forthcoming). He hosts the "New Books in Interpretive Political and Social Science" podcast on the New Books Network.

Mala Htun is Professor of Political Science, Co–Principal Investigator and Deputy Director of ADVANCE at UNM, and special advisor for inclusion and climate in the School of Engineering at the University of New Mexico. She works on women's rights, social inequalities, and strategies to promote inclusion and diversity. Htun is the author of three books, most recently *The Logics of Gender Justice: State Action on Women's Rights around the World*, coauthored with Laurel Weldon (Cambridge University Press, 2018).

Francesca R. Jensenius is Professor of Political Science at the University of Oslo and Research Professor at the Norwegian Institute of International Affairs (NUPI). She specializes in comparative politics and comparative political economy, with a regional focus on India. She is the author of *Social Justice through Inclusion: The Consequences of Electoral Quotas in India* (Oxford University Press, 2017).

Jonathan Obert is Assistant Professor in Political Science at Amherst College. He is the author of *The Six-Shooter State: Public and Private Violence in American Politics* (Cambridge University Press, 2018) as well as numerous articles on violence, state formation, and American political development.

Sarah E. Parkinson is Aronson Assistant Professor of Political Science and International Studies at Johns Hopkins University. Grounded by social network theory and ethnographic methodologies, her research examines organizational behavior and social change in war- and disaster-affected settings. Parkinson's work focuses predominantly on the Middle East and North Africa; she has conducted extensive fieldwork in Lebanon and Iraq. She received her PhD and MA in political science from the University of Chicago and has held fellowships at Yale University, George Washington University, and the University of Minnesota. Parkinson is also a co-founder of the Advancing Research on Conflict (ARC) Consortium.

Benjamin L. Read is Professor of Politics at the University of California, Santa Cruz. His research has focused on local politics in China and Taiwan, and he also writes about issues and techniques in field research. He is the author of *Roots of the State: Neighborhood Organization and Social Networks in Beijing and Taipei* (Stanford University Press, 2012) and coauthor of *Field Research in Political Science: Practices and Principles* (Cambridge University Press, 2015). He co-edits the Cambridge Elements series in East Asian Politics and Society. His articles have appeared in *Comparative Political Studies*, the *Journal of Conflict Resolution*, the *China Journal*, the *China Quarterly*, and the *Washington Quarterly*, among other journals, and several edited books.

Thea Riofrancos is Associate Professor of Political Science at Providence College and an Andrew Carnegie Fellow (2020–2022). Her research focuses on resource extraction, renewable energy, climate change, green technology, social movements, and the left in Latin America. These themes are explored in her book *Resource Radicals: From Petro-Nationalism to Post-Extractivism in Ecuador* (Duke University Press, 2020) and her co-authored book *A Planet to Win: Why We Need a Green New Deal* (Verso Books, 2019).

Frederic Charles Schaffer is Professor of Political Science at the University of Massachusetts–Amherst. His area of specialization is comparative politics. Substantively, he studies the meaning of democracy, the practice of voting, and the administration of elections. What sets much of his work apart from other empirical research on democracy is a methodological focus on language. By investigating carefully the differing ways in which ordinary people around the world use terms such as "democracy," "politics," or "vote buying" – or their rough equivalents in other languages – he aims to arrive at a fuller appreciation of how they understand and make use of electoral institutions. Professor Schaffer's publications include four books: *Elucidating Social Science Concepts: An Interpretivist Guide* (Routledge, 2016), *The Hidden Costs of Clean Election Reform* (Cornell University Press, 2008), *Elections for Sale: The Causes and Consequences of Vote Buying* (Lynne Rienner Publishers, 2007), and *Democracy in Translation: Understanding Politics in an Unfamiliar Culture* (Cornell University Press, 1998).

List of Contributors

Jillian Schwedler is Professor of Political Science at the City University of New York's Hunter College and the Graduate Center and is Nonresident Senior Fellow at the Crown Center at Brandeis University. She is a member of the editorial committee for *Middle East Law and Governance* (MELG) and was a member of the Board of Directors and the Editorial Committee of the Middle East Research and Information Project (MERIP), publishers of the quarterly *Middle East Report*. She has served as a member of the Board of Directors of the Middle East Studies Association (MESA) of North America and the governing Council of the American Political Science Association. During the spring 2020 semester, she was Visiting Professor and Senior Fulbright Scholar at the Center for Global and International Studies at the University of Salamanca, Spain. Dr. Schwedler's books include the award-winning *Faith in Moderation: Islamist Parties in Jordan and Yemen* (Cambridge University Press, 2006) and (with Laleh Khalili) *Policing and Prisons in the Middle East* (Columbia University Press, 2010). Her articles have appeared in *World Politics, Comparative Politics, Middle East Policy, Middle East Report, Middle East Critique, Journal of Democracy*, and *Social Movement Studies*, among many others. She is currently finalizing a book manuscript titled *Protesting Jordan: Geographies of Power and Dissent* (Stanford University Press, forthcoming).

Jason Seawright is Professor of Political Science at Northwestern University. Professor Seawright's research interests include comparative politics, with an emphasis on comparative political parties and on political behavior as well as methodology, particularly involving multi-method research designs and issues of causal inference. He is the author of *Party-System Collapse: The Roots of Crisis in Peru and Venezuela*. His research has been published in *Political Analysis, Perspectives on Politics, Comparative Political Studies*, and a range of other journals and edited volumes.

Erica S. Simmons is Associate Professor of Political Science and International Studies at the University of Wisconsin–Madison, where she holds the Political Science Department Board of Visitors Professorship. She is the author of *Meaningful Resistance: Market Reforms and the Roots of Social Protest in Latin America* (Cambridge University Press, 2016), which was awarded the 2017 Charles Tilly award for distinguished contribution to scholarship on collective behavior and social movements. She is also the author of numerous articles on contentious politics and qualitative methods. Her work has appeared in *World Politics, Comparative Political Studies, Comparative Politics, PS: Political Science and Politics*, and *Theory and Society*, among others.

Nicholas Rush Smith is Assistant Professor of Political Science at the City University of New York–City College and a Senior Research Associate in the

Department of Sociology at the University of Johannesburg. His primary research interests include democratic politics as seen through the lens of crime and policing in post-apartheid South Africa and on qualitative and ethnographic methods. He is the author of *Contradictions of Democracy: Vigilantism and Rights in Post-Apartheid South Africa* (Oxford University Press, 2019). His work has been published in *African Affairs, American Journal of Sociology, Comparative Politics, Perspectives on Politics, Polity, PS: Political Science and Politics*, and *Qualitative and Multi-Method Research*.

Joe Soss is Cowles Chair for the Study of Public Service at the University of Minnesota, where he holds faculty positions in the Hubert H. Humphrey School of Public Affairs, the Department of Political Science, and the Department of Sociology. His research and teaching explore the interplay of democratic politics, social inequalities, and public policy. He is particularly interested in how practices of governance intersect with relations of domination, oppression, and predation in the United States.

Lisa Wedeen is Mary R. Morton Professor of Political Science and the Co-Director of the Chicago Center for Contemporary Theory at the University of Chicago. She is also Associate Faculty in Anthropology and Co-Editor of the University of Chicago Book Series Studies in Practices of Meaning. Her publications include three books: *Ambiguities of Domination: Politics, Rhetoric, and Symbols in Contemporary Syria* (University of Chicago Press, 1999; with a new preface, 2015); *Peripheral Visions: Publics, Power, and Performance in Yemen* (University of Chicago Press, 2008); and *Authoritarian Apprehensions: Ideology, Judgment, and Mourning in Syria* (University of Chicago Press, 2019), which received the American Political Science Association's Charles Taylor Book Award, sponsored by the Interpretative Methodologies and Methods group, and the APSA's inaugural Middle East and North Africa Politics Section's best book award. She is the recipient of the David Collier Mid-Career Achievement Award and also a fellowship from the National Science Foundation.

Acknowledgments

The idea for this project was born during conversations between the editors near the end of our time in graduate school together and early in our careers as assistant professors at the University of Wisconsin–Madison (Simmons) and at the City University of New York–City College (Smith). We believed that while we had each benefited enormously from learning comparative methods rooted in the Millian paradigm, such methods often sat awkwardly against the political worlds we each confronted during our dissertation and book projects. How to practice comparison outside of controlled methods, though, was something about which we had little insight, even as it was something that we saw regularly in the social science "classics" we read during graduate school. We decided that developing a guide on one potential approach to performing such comparisons would be a useful service for the next generation of graduate students and that it might open the kinds of questions students would feel empowered to ask. We also hoped it might help our colleagues not only understand the methodological logics behind our own work but also encourage them to think differently about possibilities for their own research designs. To that end, we drafted a paper of some initial ideas rooted in our experience as ethnographers, thinking it would be a one-time exercise that might open a conversation within the discipline of political science about comparison beyond its controlled variants. Through our conversations, though, we realized that our own view was limited by the fact that we were trained primarily in ethnographic and comparative historical methods and that scholars outside of these paradigms would have insight on forms of comparison that went beyond our relatively narrow views. In other words, we realized we needed conspirators.

Our first major step in assembling this team was to hold a workshop at the City College of New York in the fall of 2017. Through generous funding supplied by the National Science Foundation (Award #1713769) and the Dean's Office of the Colin Powell School for Civic and Global Leadership, then under the leadership of Dean Vince Boudreau and his chief of staff, Dee

Dee Mozeleski, we were fortunate to bring an extraordinary set of scholars to City College's campus to talk about comparison. We purposefully assembled scholars who saw the world differently from one another – some positivists, others interpretivists; some quantitatively oriented, others qualitatively driven; some comparativists, others Americanists; some theorists, others empiricists – all with the goal of pushing one another to think harder about why the claims we make about the world hold up. Over the course of two days, surprising lines of epistemological agreement emerged, methodological disagreements were clarified, and a sense of joint purpose was formed. We then published an early and abbreviated selection of the papers as part of a symposium on "Rethinking Comparisons" in *Qualitative and Multimethod Research*, while plotting how to expand the work begun at the workshop into the present volume.

Over the many years it has taken this book to come to fruition, we have been fortunate to have received support from a remarkable set of colleagues, some of whom were present at the initial workshop and some of whom offered comments or advice in its wake. The contributors to this volume deserve the first thanks for their seriousness, hard thinking, and patience over several years as we worked to publish this volume. Additionally, Jennifer Cyr, Daragh Grant, Annika Hinze, Murad Idris, Helen Kinsella, Samatha Majic, Zachariah Mampilly, Dipali Mukhopadhyay, Timothy Pachirat, Rachel Schwartz, Peregrine Schwartz-Shea, Dan Slater, Dvora Yanow, and Deborah Yashar all provided comments, shared insights, or presented papers at various points in both our individual research processes and our efforts to produce this volume that sharpened our thinking about comparative methods. Dan Slater and Lisa Wedeen deserve specific mention. Without the inspiration, support, and guidance they provided to both of us while we were graduate students at the University of Chicago, we never would have felt the freedom to question dominant approaches to comparative methods. Audiences at two panels featuring papers from this volume at the 2018 Annual Meeting of the American Political Science Association asked sharp questions that improved several of the papers while making clear the need for a volume like this. Without the hard work of Rachel Schwartz, the original workshop at City College never would have been possible. Coordinating schedules, meals, travel, and lodging for twenty scholars coming from all over the country is no small feat, and Rachel pulled it all off while also contributing a paper herself to the discussion. Without the hard work of Anna Meier, the final manuscript never would have come together. Anna not only copyedited and assembled the final volume but she also chased down contributors (including ourselves) for everything from missing citations to past-due chapters. Linda Benson also served as a superb copyeditor, making sure early on that the prose in our own chapters was intelligible and then joining us in the final stages of the project to copyedit the entire manuscript. Robert Dreesen at Cambridge University Press has been an unfailing advocate for this project since we first brought the idea to

Acknowledgments

him. Comments from two anonymous reviewers with the press improved the manuscript immensely.

Yet, even as we have been fortunate to benefit from the engagement of remarkable scholars, we have also been profoundly saddened by the passing of two wonderful colleagues in the years it has taken to bring this project to light. Lee Ann Fujii and Kendra Koivu contributed remarkable papers, intellectual vitality, and warm spirits at our original workshop at the City College of New York. Their impact on each of us and on the discipline of political science went far beyond the workshop, as each worked to open the sometimes closed intellectual and social spaces of the discipline for us to see the world more fully. For that reason, we dedicate this volume to their memory.

I

Rethinking Comparison

An Introduction

Erica S. Simmons
University of Wisconsin–Madison

Nicholas Rush Smith
City University of New York–City College

Comparative methods have seen a double movement over the past two decades. On the one hand, political scientists point to the "enduring indispensability" of comparative methods, particularly controlled comparative methods (Slater and Ziblatt 2013), to explain political outcomes – an investment that has been deepened amid the increased influence of scholarship that relies on subnational comparison (Giraudy, Moncada, and Snyder 2019) or natural experiments (Dunning 2012) to improve causal inference. On the other hand, in the humanities and humanistic social sciences, comparative methods have come under intense scrutiny. Across these disciplines, particularly with the rise of postcolonial theory, such methods are frequently seen as "old fashioned at best, retrograde at worst" (Felski and Friedman 2013b, 1). Such critiques have gained particular traction because comparative methods were often used to compare "civilizations" through hierarchical, evolutionary social scientific paradigms and were tied to European colonial expansion (see also van der Veer 2016). Therefore, depending on one's vantage and disciplinary training, comparative methods might appear either as an indispensable tool for understanding the world or as intellectually and politically dubious.

Rethinking Comparison appears amid this bifurcated view of the comparative method, tackling some of the challenges raised by both perspectives. To do so, the book asks two fundamental methodological questions: (1) why do we compare what we compare and (2) how do the methodological assumptions we make about why and how we compare shape the knowledge we produce? In the process of addressing these questions, the chapters collectively set out comparative practices that diversify the repertoire of comparative methods available to students of politics while being cognizant of their history as tools to politically and economically dominate (see

Riofrancos, Chapter 6, this volume) or intellectually discipline (see Cheeseman, Chapter 4, this volume; and Wedeen, Chapter 13, this volume).

In pursuing these goals, the volume is intentionally aimed at a broad scholarly audience. Our hope is that the chapters offer tools for scholars of politics regardless of their epistemological or ontological assumptions, regions of interest, or scale of inquiry. Some of the contributors to this volume consider themselves "positivists"; others might use the label "interpretivists." Some compare across regions, others within countries, and others across time. Irrespective of these starting points, they all share a commitment to the importance of a pluralistic approach to comparison. Rooted in this pluralism, the chapters that follow simultaneously allow us to expand our understanding of the world even as we are cognizant that our comparative tools are themselves freighted with complex intellectual and political histories. This commitment is evident in the chapters' pragmatic goal of rethinking how comparison is practiced, their theoretical goal of rethinking why we practice comparison, their disciplinary goal of rethinking who is authorized to compare, and their political goal of rethinking the ends to which we compare.

COMPARISON AND POLITICAL SCIENCE

Our interest in engaging with questions of comparison emerges amid a revival of qualitative methods in the discipline of political science generally and a renewed interest in controlled or paired comparisons specifically.[1] Building on foundational work laying out the value of controlled comparison and the closely related strategies of paired comparisons, subnational comparisons, and natural experiments, this recent work shows how the method can combine the best of both the qualitative and the quantitative traditions.[2] Specifically, controlled comparisons allow scholars to trace out dynamic causal processes while accounting for or negating the effects of possible confounding explanations, ultimately enabling generalizable arguments.[3] Not surprisingly, controlled comparative approaches dominate current best practices in case

---

[1] On qualitative methods in political science generally, see Wedeen 2002; Mahoney and Rueschemeyer 2003; George and Bennett 2005; Gerring 2006; Schatz 2009; Brady and Collier 2010; Mahoney 2010; Ahmed and Sil 2012; Goertz and Mahoney 2012; and Ahram et al. 2018. On controlled or paired comparisons, see Snyder 2001; Tarrow 2010; Dunning 2012; Slater and Ziblatt 2013; Gisselquist 2014; and Giraudy, Moncada, and Snyder 2019.

[2] On controlled comparison, see Przeworski and Teune 1970; Lijphart 1971, 1975; Skocpol and Somers 1980; Brady and Collier 2010; and Slater and Ziblatt 2013. On paired comparison, see Tarrow 2010. On subnational comparisons, see Snyder 2001 and Giraudy, Moncada, and Snyder 2019. On natural experiments, see, e.g., Dunning 2012.

[3] This kind of comparison, often called "most similar with different outcomes" or "most different with similar outcomes," or the method of agreement and the method of difference, continues to reference Mill ([1843] 1882), although scholars often fail to acknowledge Mill's own discussion of the limitations of the approach (for an exception, see George and Bennett 2005). Regardless, what are often invoked as Mill's methods of difference and agreement are ubiquitous in

study political science research. Graduate students and professors alike look to select cases that hold potential alternative explanations constant or leverage variation in initial conditions or outcomes.[4] Indeed, in an article on the value of controlled comparisons, Slater and Ziblatt (2013, 1302) note the "enduring ubiquity" of the strategy in qualitative comparative research.

Contributions (and a Few Critiques) of Controlled Comparisons

Thus, even as qualitative comparative methods – and specifically controlled qualitative comparisons – have come under fire outside of political science, within the discipline, they have been central to some of the most enduring and influential scholarship.[5] Controlled comparisons drive canonical studies of phenomena as varied as the preconditions of social revolution (Skocpol 1979), the effects of social capital on state effectiveness (Putnam 1993), and party system stability and regime type (Collier and Collier 1991). Indeed, controlled comparison is such a dominant force in political science methods training that as two leading methods scholars note, "Nearly all graduate courses on comparative politics commence with a discussion of Mill's methods of 'difference' and 'agreement,'" which serves as the foundation for controlled comparative studies (Slater and Ziblatt 2013, 1302).

We agree that controlled comparisons have important utility for scholars engaging in small-n work. Contemporary scholars have effectively used controlled comparison to shed light on state capacity (Slater 2010), ethnic violence (Wilkinson 2006), and indigenous mobilization (Yashar 2005), just to name a few subjects. Yet, even as controlled comparisons have produced some of our most influential theories of politics, some scholars have noted their limitations. Those working within a quantitative epistemology have argued that research based on controlled comparison has limited ability to generalize (King, Keohane, and Verba 1994; Geddes 2003), a problem that scholars utilizing a mixture of quantitative and qualitative methods have tried to anticipate by implementing "nested" research designs (Lieberman 2005). Scholars working from various qualitative traditions, by contrast, have argued that projects deploying controlled comparisons tend to overemphasize their ability to address confounding explanations while necessarily underemphasizing processes of diffusion (Sewell 1985, 1996a) and interaction (Lieberson 1991, 1994). Still others suggest that controlled comparisons may unintentionally efface context by limiting the importance of people's lived experiences and the

---

qualitative comparative work (for a discussion, see Slater and Ziblatt 2013) and remain central to the ways in which we question and evaluate comparative case research.

[4] The approach to comparison and process tracing that George and Bennett (2005) lay out and the qualitative comparative analysis methods that Ragin (2014) pioneered are important exceptions here.

[5] Slater and Ziblatt (2013) make this point persuasively.

specific meanings they attach to political phenomena (Simmons and Smith 2017).

As an example of these challenges, take subnational comparisons, which scholars have argued are particularly well positioned for controlled comparative approaches because they allow scholars to hold so many potentially confounding variables constant (Snyder 2001; Giraudy, Moncada, and Snyder 2019). As Soifer (2019) carefully shows, however, serious problems emerge when we treat subnational units as independent because drawing appropriate subnational boundaries is challenging and the compound treatment problem plagues even the best subnational studies.[6] The consequence is that even with seemingly ideal subnational comparisons, as with any controlled comparison, it is hard to defend the claim that there is only one relevant difference between units and, therefore, difficult to establish causality in the way that scholars pursuing these comparisons often hope to do (Soifer 2019). Ultimately, the concern is that studies that rely on controlled comparisons may not be as predictive and testable as claimed (Burawoy 1989), pushing scholars to ignore research questions that do not immediately evidence variation that can be explained through logics of control (Ragin 2004, 128).

In this volume, Jason Seawright (Chapter 2) gives us a trenchant critique of the inferential capabilities of controlled comparisons. He does so by applying the comparative method to a class of individuals who would seem comparable and, therefore, about whom it should be easy to make general claims: billionaires. Within the United States, at least, billionaires (particularly politically conservative ones) would seem ideally comparable because they have a common political culture, overlapping social networks, and a shared elite status. Yet, despite these similar characteristics, as Seawright shows, attempts to make general claims about how conservative billionaires engage in politics quickly fall apart, as they have divergent political styles, they fund different kinds of organizations, and they often have varying concrete political goals despite the broadly shared "conservative" label. The problem of comparing billionaires raises a troubling question, though: if controlled comparative methods are of little help in understanding the political practices of such seemingly comparable individuals, how useful are controlled comparative methods for understanding political practices of more complex units of analysis like organizations, social movements, or states?

If political scientists are asking what the value of controlled comparisons is for generalizable causal inference, in the humanities and the humanistic social sciences, scholars have gone much further by questioning the value of comparison in the first place. Specifically, in the wake of postcolonial theory and amid recent demands to decolonize the academy, scholars have examined

---

[6] Giraudy, Moncada, and Snyder (2019, 36) define the compound treatment problem as emerging "when the treatment encompasses multiple explanatory factors, thus making it difficult to pinpoint which factor actually causes the effect."

the historical conditions under which comparative methods emerged and the political ends that they served (see Riofrancos, Chapter 6, this volume). Scholars writing in this tradition have traced the contemporary use of comparative methods to Europe's colonial encounters, seeing such methods as part of the evolutionary theories of civilizational "development" that helped justify colonial domination (see Cheah 1999, 3–4; van der Veer 2016, 1–2).

This dubious history, some scholars argue, means that comparison is always politically suspect. As Radhakrishnan (2013, 16) argues, "Comparisons are never neutral: they are inevitably tendentious, didactic, competitive, and prescriptive." Even further, for scholars in this vein, "Comparisons work only when the 'radical others' have been persuaded or downright coerced into abandoning their 'difference'" (Radhakrishnan 2013, 16). Indeed, for some, this need to create units that can be compared with other like units – say, a state or an ethnic group – makes comparison itself a violent process as the material and discursive conditions from which a unit is created *as* a unit are effaced (Cheah 2013, 178; see also Cheah 1999 and Cheeseman, Chapter 4, this volume). Worse, the material and political conditions under which these units are produced, scholars argue, are never equal (Spivak 2013, 253). So, even as most social scientists may consciously reject evolutionary theories of society and the colonial projects to which they were harnessed, critical scholars argue that this violent past is never fully dead; it continues to haunt present practices of comparison (see Riofrancos, Chapter 6, this volume).

Such haunting takes myriad forms: Parkinson's (Chapter 8, this volume) contribution to this volume offers an excellent example. Studying Palestinian refugee camps in Lebanon, Parkinson quickly found that the organizational dynamics she hoped to understand could not be easily disentangled into independent and dependent variables. Instead, she found that any understanding of the dynamics within the camps needed to be embedded in the historical context that had constructed camps as "camps" that could be compared to one another in the first place. The camps were hardly natural units, after all, given that they were products of violent political processes. Yet, the disciplinary training that most political scientists receive makes such units appear as natural and unproblematic, even as Parkinson discovered in her research that they were anything but.

Beyond Control

While it is important to recognize some of the limitations of controlled comparisons, our primary goal with this volume is *not* to critique controlled comparison (though critiques do inevitably emerge in some of the chapters). Instead, it is to both draw our attention to and better elaborate the logics behind some alternative ways of comparing. Even as controlled comparisons have produced lasting insights and continue to dominate research designs, they are not the only form of comparison that scholars utilize.

Scholars from virtually every subfield of political science have used forms of comparison that are not controlled to make central contributions to our understanding of politics, even as the logics behind these comparisons are rarely elaborated. In political theory, the tradition of systematic but uncontrolled comparison saturates the Western canon. Indeed, Aristotle's consideration of what was the best political regime was arguably the first uncontrolled comparative political science study (see, e.g., Tilly 2010, 8–10). Yet, if creative comparisons undergird the political theory canon, they also show up in both the classics and the cutting edges of modern political science. In American politics, such work ranges from Douglas McAdam's (1982) foundational study of African American political mobilization to Jamila Michener's (2019) recent work on inequality and civil law. In international relations, political sociologist Immanuel Wallerstein (1974) and his followers developed world systems theory to examine the uneven dynamics of capitalist accumulation, while Paul Amar (2013) has more recently studied how free-market economic policies have required novel security arrangements across the globe through a surprising comparison of such practices in Brazil and Egypt.

In comparative politics – the subfield most closely associated with comparative methods – the examples are legion. Foundational works by divergent scholars in the subdiscipline include Samuel Huntington's (1968) canonical study of political order, Benedict Anderson's (1983) classic text on nationalism, and Charles Tilly's (1990) agenda-setting study of state formation. These studies have been read by almost every graduate student at some point and continue to profoundly shape the discipline, despite the fact that they do not rely on controlled comparisons. More recent – yet still highly influential works – by Mahmood Mamdani (1996) on the logics of colonial states across Africa; Doug McAdam, Sidney Tarrow, and Charles Tilly (2001) on the dynamics of contentious politics; James Scott (1998) on high modernist state ideology; and Richard M. Locke and Kathy Thelen (1995) on labor politics – have all used modes of comparison that do not utilize controlled comparative logics. The same is true for some of the most recent work in the subdiscipline including Lisa Wedeen's (2019; see also the Epilogue, Chapter 13, this volume) study of Syrians' desire for autocracy amid the country's civil war, and our own work on social movements in Latin America (Simmons 2016) and vigilantism amid democratic state formation in South Africa (Smith 2019; see also Chapter 12, this volume).

Somehow, though, despite this legacy of classic studies and a profusion of recent scholarship that relies on non-controlled comparison to make claims about politics, surprisingly little methodological guidance is available to graduate students for how to design or execute comparisons that do not rely on control as a central element.[7] Worse, there is little epistemological insight on

---

[7] The works of Tilly (1984); Locke and Thelen (1995); Sewell (1996a, 1996b, 2005); Ragins (2004); Ahram et al. (2018); and Boswell, Corbett, and Rhodes (2019), which we discuss later in the chapter, are important exceptions here.

why such comparisons might be compelling in the first place. As a result, scholars often eschew comparative research designs that are not premised on controlled comparisons, or they shoehorn cases into controlled comparison frameworks that may not fit. And even when scholars do employ a non-controlled comparative approach, they rarely explain the utility of or logic behind the comparisons that they employ or how other scholars might perform similar comparisons. The consequences for our understanding of politics are severe. When we limit the kinds of comparisons we make, we necessarily constrain the kinds of questions we ask, limit the kinds of knowledge we produce, and foreclose our ability to imagine politics differently (Ragin 2004, 128).

Building the Foundations for an Expanded Comparative Method

Scholars within political science have most certainly developed valuable critiques of controlled comparisons, and those outside political science have raised important questions about the goals of comparison as a whole. Yet, social scientists have been less effective in laying out alternative approaches to comparison. The methodological logics behind the comparisons at the heart of their studies are rarely described, even as a wide range of approaches to comparison appears in some of the most influential work across the subfields of political science (see our earlier discussion).

Think, for example, of Benedict Anderson's (1990, but see also 2016) important work comparing ideas of power in Javanese and European political thought. Comparison between Java and Europe violates virtually every tenet of how a controlled comparison should be performed. Anderson writes across different scales (an island versus a continent), different regime types (a monarchy and subsequent dictatorships versus a wide variety of regimes), and different religious traditions (an Islamic system with animist elements versus largely Christian systems). Despite the lack of control, Anderson uses the friction between the conflicting concepts of power to illuminate how ideas inversely structure political practice in both settings. Had Anderson approached the comparison through the logic of control, he would not have been able to generate these insights. At the same time, it is not clear what the epistemology underlying these comparisons is or why they are persuasive or insightful. This explanatory gap leaves graduate students and faculty without the tools to explain why similar research designs will produce important insights.

To be sure, some core methods texts argue that tools like process tracing can "ameliorate the limitations" of the methods of agreement and difference and promise to expand the range of questions political scientists ask (George and Bennett 2005, 214–15). But even in these cases, process tracing is seen as a second-best approach when controlled comparisons are not possible (214–15), given that process tracing often appears as a critical *component* of controlled comparative research designs as opposed to an *alternative* to them (e.g., Luebbert 1991; Htun 2003; Slater 2010).[8] Indeed, absent a controlled comparison, process tracing runs the risk of being labelled as "mere" descriptive inference because it would be unclear how generalizable the processes highlighted in a specific instance are – a critique that it would be hard for any political scientist to withstand, even though descriptive inference has a critical role to play in our explanations of politics (see Wendt 1998).[9]

Even if we were to value the kinds of explanations that emerge from process tracing or descriptive inference equally to causal logics that emerge from controlled comparisons, questions remain about how to pursue projects asking constitutive questions in a comparative fashion. Anderson's work on power in Java and Europe, for example, might be considered a project of descriptive inference in that he gives us two ways to think about concepts of power. Process tracing's focus on causal processes, though, is not appropriate for engaging in this kind of constitutive work given that Anderson is not describing a historical process. And clearly, controlled comparisons would not make sense to justify his project given the wide divergences across context we described earlier. But if the most commonly taught tools in graduate methods courses are not up to the task of helping us produce work like Anderson's, what other options are there?

Fortunately, in the past few years some political scientists have started to develop justifications for alternative modes of comparison. Boswell, Corbett, and Rhodes (2019, 36–39), for instance, argue that scholars might be able to expand the range of comparisons they make if they focus on the similar dilemmas people face across seemingly divergent contexts. As an example, they point to the ways in which both a pensioner in the Isle of Wight and a politician in Palau face major dilemmas in how to navigate the limited transportation options for carrying out their daily tasks (shopping in the case of the pensioner and campaigning in the case of the politician). Although distant in place and experience, Boswell and coauthors argue, comparing shared dilemmas creates opportunities for seeing political and conceptual connections across widely differing contexts that might not be immediately obvious.

Similarly, policy scholars Bartlett and Vavrus (2017) emphasize forms of comparison that look not only to similarities and differences but also to linkages, hierarchies of power, and questions of scale. They describe three, mutually imbricated axes of comparison – vertical, horizontal, and transversal

---

[8] See Slater and Ziblatt (2013, 1304) on this point as well.
[9] Descriptive inference looks different from causal inference insofar as it does not attempt to show that A caused B. Instead, it might explain how B came to be designed the way it is or the conditions that made B possible in the first place. This kind of inference allows us to explain phenomena in the world while not having to make the often-challenging assumptions required by the logics of causal inference (e.g., variable independence). Although they do not necessarily use the term, several of the chapters in this volume make the case that descriptive inference should play a central role in our analysis of politics (see Schaffer, Chapter 3, and Htun and Jensenius, Chapter 10).

comparisons – that situate comparisons not only spatially but also across scales and within historical contexts and relations (on transversal comparison, see also Kazanjian 2016).[10] Engaging in this type of comparison, though, means ridding ourselves of some preexisting ideas about how we think about our cases – to engage in an "unbounding" (Bartlett and Vavrus 2017, 13; see also Cheeseman, Chapter 4, this volume) of our cases so that we can see unexpected connections. Unbounding, Cheeseman argues, leads us to "follow resemblances across a political topography in pursuit of a problematic category or politically salient idea" (this volume, p. 66). Even as we locate our studies in a specific setting, we use that location as a vantage to help us explore the general. Attention to these axes also invites us to think differently about cases in ways that are echoed by Soss (Chapter 5, this volume) and Riofrancos (Chapter 6, this volume). When we focus on the "importance of examining *processes* of sense making as they develop over time, in distinct settings, in relation to systems of power and inequality and in increasingly interconnected conversations with actors who do not sit physically within the circle drawn around the traditional case" (Bartlett and Vavrus 2017, 10–11), we can both see our cases from multiple vantages, as Soss encourages us to do, and situate those cases in the global contexts that Riofrancos emphasizes in her contribution.

Contributors to a recent volume that revives comparative area studies offer a third path out of the binds controlled comparisons can create (Ahram, Köllner, and Sil 2018). Area studies have long been relegated to a second-class status relative to social science disciplines within the academy because of their supposed focus on "mere" description, rather than generalizable theories (see Cheeseman, Chapter 4, this volume). (Note, here, echoes of the critiques of process tracing and descriptive inference we raised earlier in this section.) Comparing across world regions, Köllner, Sil, and Ahram (2018, 4) suggest, is one means of solving this problem by combining the "thick" knowledge of an area specialist with the broad view of a social scientist. As with Locke and Thelen's (1995) work on contextualized comparisons, comparative area studies promise a middle path between the relatively narrow concerns of country experts and the maximizing goals of quantitative social scientists by helping case study researchers identify causal linkages that scholars in both of these other traditions might miss (Köllner et al. 2018, 5). To place area studies within a comparative framework, therefore, is in some sense infringing on disciplinary borders with the goal of balancing "a context-sensitive exploration of phenomena within individual cases with comparative analysis across cases from more than one area so as to develop portable inferences and illuminate

---

[10] A transversal comparison shows a connection between seemingly dissimilar places, time periods, or concepts. Coming from the Latin word *transvertere*, which combines the words for "across" and "to turn," Kazanjian (2016, 7) writes that the concept "means to turn across or athwart, to turn into something else, to turn about, or to overturn. A transverse is thus not simply a line that cuts across, but also an unruly action that undoes what is expected."

the convergence, divergence, or diffusion of practices across regions" (Köllner et al. 2018, 6).

Yet even with these recent efforts to rethink the building blocks of the comparative method, work that relies on non-controlled comparisons is often understood to be extremely risky. Because their logic is not broadly understood, these studies are often reserved for senior scholars with well-established reputations, are published in outlets not necessarily geared toward political scientists such as area studies journals, or are simply dismissed. Such work, therefore, comes with risks – risks that are not borne equally across the profession. For example, in his contribution to this volume, Soss (Chapter 5) writes about some of the risks he has taken in doing non-controlled comparative work throughout his career. Soss asks:

Would the freedom to take this path – and the risks and eventual rewards involved in doing so – have been the same for a more socially and institutionally disadvantaged graduate student? Do scholars today have equal opportunities to take this path, regardless of gender, race, class, sexuality, tenure, or institutional prestige? I think the answer is clearly no. ... The hope in this sort of writing is that we can broaden the ways people think about what is methodologically sound *so that it becomes less risky* to pursue alternative but equally valid ways of knowing and doing. (this volume, p. 101, italics in original)

Taking social location seriously means not only that political scientists need additional tools for designing and executing non-controlled comparisons; scholars also need those tools to become a central part of methods training. In doing this work, we would broaden who has the ability to do this nontraditional work by lowering its risks.

We see *Rethinking Comparison* as an effort to accomplish these goals by building on and expanding existing efforts in three crucial ways. First, *Rethinking Comparison* is deliberately designed to offer logics, tools, and insights for *all* scholars engaged in qualitative political science (and we hope social science generally), regardless of epistemological assumptions. Whereas Boswell et al. (2019) make a crucial contribution to our understanding of how comparison might be practiced by interpretive scholars, we aim to take their work one step further by bringing together scholars working from both positivist and interpretivist epistemologies to make the general case for the value of non-controlled approaches to comparison and, in so doing, bring into the conversation two epistemological communities that are often seen as distinct and irreconcilable. Second, while we are encouraged by efforts to bring comparative area studies back in, not all research projects lend themselves to that particular kind of focus and not all scholars are equipped with deep regional expertise (and we are not arguing that all research questions require this kind of expertise). So, having an expanded range of options for how to compare for a wide range of methods is desirable and, we hope, can help push the comparative area studies effort forward by broadening the range of

Rethinking Comparison

comparative tools available to area studies specialists. Finally, this volume not only allows us to develop multiple approaches to comparison; it also puts them into conversation with one another as part of a single text. The chapters that follow do not offer a unified vision of comparison. Instead, they offer a varied toolkit, allowing scholars to become *bricoleurs*, adopting the best comparative tool for a given project. The more options we have for how to pursue comparison, the better equipped we are to explain and understand why it makes crucial contributions to our understandings of politics, and the more we empower scholars across varied professional positions and substantive interests to pursue non-controlled comparative work.

Thus, even as we recognize the strengths of controlled comparisons, political scientists need to develop epistemological logics for additional strategies of comparative inquiry. This conversation has begun, but there is much work left to do. We need to continue to both add clearly explained and elaborated strategies to our repertoire and strengthen the case for the value of these kinds of comparisons through concrete examples. By elaborating *why* numerous strategies of non-controlled comparisons should be compelling and providing scholars with a vocabulary to describe their approach, the chapters that follow do just that. They provide a foundation for expanding the possibilities for comparative inquiry in political science. Doing so, however, involves rethinking what is to be compared, how to choose those comparisons, and how those comparisons advance our knowledge – objectives to which we turn in the remainder of this introduction.

RETHINKING COMPARISON TO RETHINK POLITICAL SCIENCE

Thus far, we have suggested that a systematic consideration of varied comparative logics beyond Mill's methods can open new pathways for comparative research for scholars old and new – something the chapters in this volume aim to achieve by bringing together work from scholars with varied methodological and epistemological backgrounds to push the boundaries of comparison within the discipline. With the combination of better guidance for how to design and execute non-controlled comparisons and increased understanding of the value of these comparisons among early career and established scholars – both goals that this volume helps us achieve – scholars should feel enabled to tackle new and ambitious comparative projects while having the tools available to explain why their research designs lead to compelling arguments. Furthermore, with this volume we hope not only to enable more scholars to engage in these kinds of comparisons but also to encourage scholars already engaged in non-controlled comparisons to take the time in their own work to think through and articulate the logics behind the comparisons they use. The more we take the time to explain what the logics we use are and why they are compelling, the more we will empower others to tackle these kinds of comparisons as well.

To achieve these goals, the chapters that follow develop logics of comparison that are not motivated by control. The collected chapters achieve this goal by asking and answering foundational questions about comparative methods and their applicability to social science research. For instance, what kinds of questions lend themselves to non-controlled comparisons? How should we think through case selection? What kinds of insights about the world are non-controlled comparisons uniquely positioned to produce? What are potential models for what a non-controlled comparison looks like? Why and how do these approaches contribute to knowledge? By bringing together scholars working in both positivist and interpretivist traditions and asking them to systematically think through how they engage in qualitative comparisons and the insights such comparisons can produce, the collected chapters challenge the conceptual foundations through which we see the political world, create new possibilities to advance what we know about politics, and open our eyes to the political assumptions built into the comparative methods we use – all with the goal of allowing us to see the world differently.

The chapters tackle these challenges by focusing on three central components of the comparative method. First, they ask us to rethink what a case is by challenging dominant conceptions of a case that focus on time or geography and exploring alternative types of cases including, among others, political processes (how things happen),[11] practices (what people do), meanings (how people interact with symbolic systems),[12] and concepts (how people order the world). Second, the chapters expand our notion of what it means to compare. They push political scientists to include attention to the lived experiences of the people they study and how those experiences reorder social worlds. Finally, the chapters expand the explanatory goals of comparison. While most comparative studies in political science emphasize variations in outcomes, these chapters urge scholars to consider comparing variations in political processes, sites, relations, practices, meanings, and concepts. They also push us to think about what it means to generalize an argument (typically the gold standard of explanatory work in political science) by elaborating alternative logics. More foundationally, these chapters ask us to think about how to study political worlds that do not always lend themselves to discrete, fixed outcomes that can easily be identified. In so doing, they push us to acknowledge and

---

[11] To be sure, scholars of contentious politics often focus their attention on political processes. However, when they design these studies to conform to the logics of control, the kinds of dynamics they can explore are severely constrained. Worse, the assumptions required by controlled comparison research designs are difficult to maintain in the study of contentious episodes, as much is contingent on the dynamics of the episode itself, and apparently similar conditions can influence processes in very different ways depending upon such contingent dynamics (see Sewell 1996a). Thus, we would argue that when comparing processes of contention, the limits created by demands for control are particularly constraining and that expanding the repertoire of comparative logics would be particularly valuable for scholars of contentious politics.

[12] See Wedeen (2002).

Rethinking Comparison

embrace ambiguity and develop approaches to studying a world that is often contradictory and incoherent.

By expanding modes of qualitative comparative inquiry, political scientists can both uncover new questions and drive innovations in how we ask questions that have dominated the discipline for decades. Thus, *Rethinking Comparison* encourages us to revisit the kinds of big research questions that animated scholars such as Anderson (1983), Huntington (1968), and Tilly (1990) – scholars whose work is canonical despite their eschewing controlled comparisons. It is often difficult (though certainly not impossible) to tackle ambitious questions about power and governance while looking for cases that meet the standards of controlled comparison. More profoundly, though, as scholars in the humanities who are critical of comparative methods have shown (see Felski and Friedman 2013a), comparisons are not merely reflective of the world and its subjects; they constitute both. It also follows that if we expand how we think about comparison, we can challenge how we see the world and upend the politics of knowledge that shape our understanding of it as a result. We may even be able to upend how politics themselves are practiced, if we are able to imagine them differently (see Schaffer, Chapter 3, this volume). That is what the chapters that follow aim to help us achieve.

RETHINKING WHAT IS COMPARED

While we agree that "the dazzling array of divergences and convergences across nation-states in the modern world ... has long drawn scholars to the craft of comparative politics" (Slater and Ziblatt 2013, 1302), we should challenge ourselves to be open to how we think of the kinds of divergences and convergences that could be brought together in our analyses. Political scientists often talk of "units of analysis" when they study these divergences and convergences – geographical areas, groups of people, and individuals commonly serve as such. In this volume, we challenge scholars to think about the objects they choose not simply as preexisting units waiting to be compared but as dynamic objects being actively created by the researcher. Political phenomena constantly evolve, often in relationship to contingent events in local contexts, implying that the objects of a social scientist's inquiry are never fixed, frozen, or static.

For instance, in his classic *Imagined Communities*, Anderson (1983) wrote about the emergence of nationalism in what he called "Creole states," including the seemingly dissimilar cases of the Spanish American colonies and the future United States (which are often treated as exceptional and not compared with other cases). Writing later, Anderson (2016) described his choice to lump these seemingly dissimilar cases together as "intended to surprise and shock, but also to globalise the study of the history of nationalism." His cases were selected, in other words, not because they could easily control for alternative explanations but because they could illuminate a broader process while making his audience think anew about the cases themselves. His choice of approaching the United States as a certain type of unit of analysis, therefore, had the property of creatively redescribing the colonies and opening up new theories about nationalism.

In this spirit, several chapters in this volume provide tools for scholars to think differently about how to classify, categorize, and redescribe cases.[13] For example, in Chapter 5, Joe Soss addresses this challenge head on by introducing the idea of "casing." When we think about casing our studies, as opposed to studying cases, we embrace the idea that we actively create the objects of our analysis. Soss's chapter highlights the tensions between the purposive, analytic fashion in which political scientists typically think of comparative cases and the dynamic and iterative process of casing that characterizes ethnography and interpretive research. Rather than conceptualizing cases and approaching research sites as predetermined variables and values, Soss proposes a discovery-oriented approach through which scholars can draw on immersive experiences to understand how "a 'case' is something we make – an analytic construct that we develop through our efforts to theorize the phenomena we study" (this volume, p. 85). If we understand our cases as our own constructions, not as real things that exist in the world independent of our ongoing research activities, we acknowledge that our data can be understood from multiple vantage points that are constantly evolving. Identifying what is to be compared through this lens would not only facilitate the more iterative approach that increasingly defines much political science research (e.g., Koivu and Kimball 2015); it would also allow scholars to remain open to new concepts, meanings, processes, and outcomes that may enrich their own studies and contribute to scholarly knowledge more generally.

Sarah Parkinson's contribution to this volume (Chapter 8) also directly engages with the idea that the objects of our analysis are constantly shifting under our feet and need to be rethought at every stage of the research process. Her chapter shows the casing approach at work and demonstrates how it can play a critical role not only in knowledge accumulation but also in the development of new methodological tools. Parkinson takes us through the trajectory of her research on militant organizations' adaptation, describing how it began as a controlled case comparison. She quickly found that the evidence she gathered often contradicted logics of control, independence, causality, and identification that undergird dominant approaches to comparison. Rather, it indicated that complex, relational, often contingent interactions among geographic environment, communities' interpretations of

---

[13] To be sure, many of the chapters in this volume could be discussed under this heading. Htun and Jensenius (Chapter 10) focus on concepts, Seawright (Chapter 2) looks at individuals, and Read (Chapter 11) asks us to think about "foci," etc. We focus our attention here on discussing the chapters that take a broad approach to how we think about what a case is and discuss the other chapters in subsequent sections.

violence, and organizational structures influenced outcomes of interest. Specifically, she found that units she studied – militant organizations – change over time as war disrupts them. To survive, these organizations have to constantly adapt. As a result, rather than taking the "unit" for granted, her work had to assume that the unit changes over time. Parkinson ultimately found that she needed a new language of comparison to make sense of what she was seeing. She drew on the language of neuroscience to introduce the concept of "relational plasticity" – the idea that social relationships, like neurons, are capable of changing content and meaning over time. The brain rewires its neural network in response to traumatic events like stroke to keep functioning (even if with diminished capacity) – just like the organizations Parkinson studied. To understand why one brain or militant group barely survives, a second adapts well, and a third fails, we need to understand their network structures. Borrowing a concept from a seemingly unrelated field and creatively importing it open space for scholars to focus on comparing the structure and content of dynamic systems of relations, rather than of static units, and offer new opportunities for studying organizational change in comparative perspective.

In her contribution to this volume, Thea Riofrancos (Chapter 6) focuses our attention on the dynamic system of relations that Parkinson raises but at a global scale, arguing, "the conventional treatment of case studies ignores their constitutive multiplicity" (this volume, p. 107). Riofrancos proposes that the idea of "siting" them would allow us to capture how places and macroprocesses are co-constitutive. By moving away from the language of "case," we free ourselves from seeing the objects of our analysis as instances of a broader phenomenon and are better equipped to see how they help constitute it. The chapter also empowers us to think differently about the idea of studying a single case – something political scientists are often discouraged from doing as it provides insufficient foundation for generalizable causal inference (for an overview of this view, see Gerring 2004). We often hear scholars address this critique by saying that single cases are never really single, as they are made up of a number of individual observations that we can think of as cases in their own right (e.g., George and Bennett 2005). Riofrancos tackles the challenge from an entirely different perspective, arguing that single cases are not really single, not because of how they can be disaggregated, but because of their position as part of broader processes. These insights offer clear implications for our research designs: if we select our sites based on their role in co-constituting the broader processes that interest us, we can both take a place-based approach to our research and generate important knowledge about how broad macroprocesses are shaping our political worlds.

In this sense, Riofrancos's chapter pushes us to bring systems back into our research designs – something common across several chapters in the volume. Jonathan Obert's contribution (Chapter 7) is notable in this regard (as are Parkinson's [Chapter 8] and Schwedler's [Chapter 9]). For Obert, a basic problem of comparative analysis is that scholars often want to understand complex systems that "involve micro-behavior producing macro-level patterns that in turn shape micro-behavior (and so on)" (this volume, p. 129), meaning that individual cases are often linked to one another at a higher scale of analysis. Therefore, we need to understand complex interdependence within systems to understand outcomes. As an example, Obert points to the challenge of studying race riots in the United States. Such events might seem like separate instances that could be usefully disaggregated as individual cases (and indeed this is typically how they are studied). In fact, such riots are often related – both synchronically, as one riot may "authorize" others in the same historical era, and diachronically, as earlier riots create repertoires for future mass action. How to study such relationships within complex systems presents a problem, though, given that we cannot take individual cases as actual independent instances. Obert offers one possible solution: archival research. He advocates a turn to the archives (and historical explanation generally) because archives have built-in connections across different scales – from the actors involved, through local events impacting actors' decisions, to national or global events that structured interactions at the local level. Archives are (literal) repositories of complex interdependencies that researchers can use to map out systemic adaptations across multiple scales chronologically. In this sense, Obert encourages us to shift *where* we conduct our research to better understand *how* systems impact our objects of study.

RETHINKING HOW COMPARISON IS PRACTICED

If we change *what* we compare based on the suggestions proposed in this volume, we might need to think about whether new tools are necessary for *how* we engage in those comparisons. Typically, political scientists understand the value of comparison to be its ability to help us develop explanations for a given outcome. As a result, we tend to select cases by either looking for variation in the outcome of interest or controlling for alternative explanations. One potential unintended consequence of this drive for control, though, is that scholars may choose simply not to consider potentially illuminating comparisons because they are too different or complex to produce even the illusion of control. Therefore, we need to think differently about what it means to select cases and what the relevant comparisons are. Rather than (possibly artificially) controlling for confounding variables, an expanded approach to comparison could challenge scholars to embrace and exploit tensions presented by complex causal or meaning-making processes. To this end, the contributions in this volume lay out logics that allow us to rethink how we compare across scales, within systems, and across often unrecognized elements of seemingly traditional country case studies.

One way in which the contributors to this volume encourage us to rethink the practice of comparison is by reconsidering the scales at which we compare. In

Rethinking Comparison

their chapters, Jillian Schwedler (Chapter 9) and Thea Riofrancos (Chapter 6) make the case for comparison at a global scale, although in different directions. Schwedler lays out the logic of encompassing comparisons – comparisons that "examine a large process or structure but seek to understand how their relation to the whole structures individual cases" (Schwedler, Chapter 9, this volume, p. 176; also see Tilly 1984, 125–43). Here, the goal is to use broad processes to explain discrete outcomes. Schwedler shows how it is impossible to understand the divergent trajectories of the 2011 Arab uprisings without considering the encompassing security situation in the Middle East in which the states that most successfully countered revolutionary insurrection relied on shared security forces. Because the encompassing security processes affected specific regime outcomes, to treat each uprising and counter-mobilizing effort as independent without seeing its relationship to the encompassing whole would be to misapprehend how some uprisings were stopped.

In her discussion of siting (introduced earlier in this section), Riofrancos reverses this direction of explanation. Her goal is to understand how global processes work through specific sites at which these processes operate. In her current research project, Riofrancos wants to understand the consequences of a large-scale shift to lithium ion batteries as part of the green energy revolution. To do this, she looks at specific sites along lithium's value chain – Chile's Atacama Desert where lithium is mined; Chile's capital, Santiago, where elite networks make deals; Washington, DC, where policy is set; and Chinese factories where lithium ion batteries are produced. For both Schwedler and Riofrancos, then, global processes are paramount for social scientific explanation, whether the process helps us understand specific outcomes or specific sites help us see how broad processes work.

If Schwedler and Riofrancos show us ways to eschew country comparisons, Benjamin Read (Chapter 11) and Mala Htun and Francesca Jensenius (Chapter 10) take the opposite tack and show us new ways to approach these "traditional" comparisons. Read gives us a means to compare dissimilar cases, like Taiwan and China – his primary cases of interest. Often China and Taiwan are taken to be similar given their shared languages and interconnected histories – a view of which Read is skeptical given their manifold differences and the fact that their shared history and China's ongoing territorial claims on Taiwan mean they cannot be taken as independent cases. And, yet, even as these cases fall far short of what is needed to construct a convincing controlled comparison, much can still be learned from comparing across the Taiwan Strait. To do so, Read encourages us to study specific foci – say, similar institutions or comparable processes – across otherwise dissimilar cases.[14] This process, Read shows, allows us to generate insights that would not be possible if we were limited to looking at apparently similar contexts. By

---

[14] This is reminiscent of van der Veer's (2016, 9) suggestion that scholars compare the "fragments of social life."

comparing the same institutional category (in his work, government-structured neighborhood organizations) in dissimilar contexts, we can gain new insights into the substantive phenomena under study, better understand political regimes, and create opportunities for conceptual development. In his own research, Read deftly shows how comparing government-structured neighborhood organizations across these two contexts generates insights into how the regimes themselves operate. Indeed, the distinctiveness of the China-Taiwan dyad is precisely what makes it useful to pursue this kind of foci-driven comparison. When we look at different places in conversation – Read's chapter considers a variety of comparisons involving China, particularly a recent wave of China-India studies – with one another, we may come to understand each of them in ways that would not have been possible without the comparison. Ultimately, by narrowing in on specific foci, Read shows how these kinds of comparisons are not only possible but also crucial to our understanding of politics. As he reminds us, "comparison between unlike political contexts generates new conceptual departures and striking reflections about the very regime types that we commonly take as defining features" (this volume, p. 227).

Where Read pushes us to see different contexts as comparable, Mala Htun and Francesca Jensenius encourage us to learn from the radical differences among cases. Their chapter also offers a clear example not only of how we might go about engaging in cross-regional comparisons (a particularly difficult type of comparison for those seeking to use logics of control) but also of the important contribution such comparisons can make. Htun and Jensenius seek to understand divergent meanings of women's empowerment and how they result in different policies such as family leave in advanced industrial economies. To see such concepts at work, they compare the meanings and implications of women's empowerment in the United States, Japan, and Norway. In their words, the "conceptual comparison" they conducted "made us think differently about the cultural and historical backdrops that shape state action and people's responses and changed our theoretical thinking about how to study the effects of state action on society" (this volume, p. 192). Put differently, the extreme divergence in the meanings of women's empowerment across the cases made concepts and ideas central to their explanation for why these cases have such divergent gender-based policies, something they could not have seen without the differences across the cases. In sum, if some chapters such as Obert's, Parkinson's, Riofrancos's, and Schwedler's give us loci of comparison that fall outside of traditional Millian categories, Read and Htun and Jensenius arguably give us radical re-workings of Mill's methods.

RETHINKING THE PURPOSES OF COMPARISON

Rethinking comparison in ways that challenge how we approach what is to be compared and the methods through which comparisons are designed has potentially revolutionary consequences for how the study of politics is conducted and what we consider the ends of comparing in the first place. In *The Spectre of Comparisons*, for example, Benedict Anderson (1998, 2) describes a moment early in his fieldwork when he encountered the Indonesian leader Sukarno expressing apparent admiration for Hitler as a model nationalist leader. The encounter, Anderson writes, induced "a kind of vertigo" in which, "For the first time in my young life I had been invited to see my Europe as through an inverted telescope." This revelatory moment fundamentally restructured how Anderson understood European politics, but it may also have signaled a shift in what the intellectual purpose of comparing should be. Political scientists typically use comparison to explain variation in or produce generalizable arguments for a given political outcome. By contrast, as with much of Anderson's work, the forms of comparison that some of the following chapters explore are directed toward expanding the conceptual and theoretical categories through which politics are thought about in the first place.

For example, in his contribution to this volume, Fred Schaffer (Chapter 3; see also Schaffer 2015) argues that instead of variation seeking, the goals of comparison might be concept seeking. He outlines two forms of comparison: juxtapositional and perspectival. Juxtapositional comparisons are familiar to political scientists, as they involve placing like things – states, organizations, social movements, revolutions – "side by side to catalog their similarities and differences" (this volume, p. 47). By contrast, perspectival comparisons – where one "compares one kind of thing to a different kind of thing as a way to establish an outside vantage point from which to view one in terms of the other" (this volume, p. 47) – are rarely fronted despite their undeniable importance to our understanding of politics. Examples of such perspectival comparisons include Hobbes's (1996) comparison of the state to a mortal god or Tilly's (1985) claim that the state is like a criminal protection racket. Unlike the variation-seeking goal of juxtapositional comparisons, perspectival comparisons force us to see an object differently, much like a poet might use metaphor to make us see love, life, or death anew. And in its metaphorical qualities, perspectival comparison shows that a comparison is never neutral; comparisons are always political. This is not to suggest that the politics of comparison might be inherently dominating, as we saw some scholars suggest earlier (see Felski and Friedman 2013a). Rather, in making us see the world differently, perspectival comparisons might open our vision to new horizons as they redescribe an otherwise familiar phenomenon. At a minimum, concept-seeking comparisons would provide new tools for political scientists to understand politics beyond the current variation-seeking modes.

Htun and Jensenius (Chapter 10) also push us to rethink the purpose of comparisons, but from an entirely different epistemological perspective. They stress the importance of different types of research designs as being suited to different types of research goals and remind us that we have much to learn from work that does not focus on causal inference as its primary contribution. Htun and Jensenius describe their own research process as initially driven by an interest in the relationship between gender discriminatory laws and women's economic empowerment. They soon found, however, that "empowerment" meant different things in different contexts and that to explore the questions at the heart of their research, they needed to better understand the concept itself. This required a new research design – one that evolved with their theoretical thinking. Htun and Jensenius then developed what they call a "conceptual comparison" leveraging differences in how empowerment is understood in Norway, Japan, and the United States to better understand the concept itself and the political work it might be doing. Here the variation in the outcome drives the case selection but in a way different from the one we are used to in political science. For example, cases (say, party discipline) are not categorized as "high," "medium," or "low" values on a given outcome of interest but rather as varying in type. With this approach, Htun and Jensenius do not think about cases in terms of the presence or absence of an outcome but rather as variation in the substance of an outcome. In each of the cases, "empowerment" has a very different meaning.

In his contribution, Jason Seawright (Chapter 2) also encourages scholars to think about the importance of studies that do not have causal inference as a primary objective. Much of his chapter focuses on the challenges that plague causal inference in controlled comparative studies. But he also leverages the comparison of billionaires introduced earlier in this chapter to show how comparisons, even absent control, make crucial contributions to our knowledge of politics. Echoing Htun and Jensenius, Seawright highlights the role that small-n comparisons can play in concept development and makes the case that they can facilitate measurement by helping us understand the scope of possible outcomes. At the same time, they might also help us better understand what the treatment and control conditions in a particular context might be. Seawright also cautions us to think carefully about how we can offer generalizable insights from small-n comparisons, arguing that the cumulative reiteration across multiple studies and researchers might be the best way to think about how to make generalizable claims. Another way to approach this question is to think about the configuration of causal capacities. Indeed, small-n analysis is uniquely situated to help scholars identify the micro-components of a causal relationship. When we recognize that the same configurations rarely, if ever, repeat (and therefore generalized causal laws or theories are false), then attention to micro-components becomes particularly important. Small-n comparisons can then play a critical role in theory building.

Still, since at least King, Keohane, and Verba's (1994) *Designing Social Inquiry*, generalizability has been the gold standard for political science work. While case studies might provide valuable insight on political concepts or processes in one part of the world, political scientists have long thought to be truly valuable they need to generalize. But if one takes the importance of context and concepts seriously as Schaffer, Htun and Jensenius, and Seawright encourage us to do, this raises a question: how does one make such metaphors intelligible across cultural contexts where words and concepts might have radically different meanings? Put differently, how does one generalize if one assumes difference across context?

In answering this question, some of the chapters push us to rethink how we understand generalization entirely. Specifically, Cheeseman (Chapter 4) and Simmons and Smith (Chapter 12; see also Felski and Friedman 2013b and van de Veer 2016) suggest that scholars consider a logic of translation. Where generalization seeks universal claims, for Cheeseman (this volume, p. 66) translation "provincializes universals" in that it assumes an inherent discordance in exact meaning across space and exposing the contingency of our political concepts.

In an interview that concludes the volume (Chapter 13), Lisa Wedeen offers an ideal example of this process with a discussion of one of the chapters from her book *Peripheral Visions*. In her now-classic analysis of *qat* chews in Yemen, Wedeen (2008; see also this volume, Epilogue) shows that groups often engage in democratic practices, even in the absence of free and fair elections. While few political scientists would have called Yemen democratic during that era, given that the elections that were held tended to produce patently phony results, average Yemenis still engaged in daily debate, discussion, and even mobilization – classic democratic practices that do not rely on elections and may even be deeper forms of democracy than the basic act of voting, given that they can require direct engagement and potential risk. As Wedeen (this volume, p. 265) tells us, "Thinking about the *qat* chews pushed me to reread works in democratic theory." This was particularly the case with her turn to Habermas, whose work on the public sphere was especially relevant to the public discussions Wedeen participated in at *qat* chews. These spaces, though, were not simply Yemeni versions of Habermas's German coffee houses. While there were certain commonalities, important differences between Wedeen's and Habermas's contexts changed the tenor and political effects of public discussions with Yemenis being more consumed with the absence of a functioning state than their German counterparts. To think in terms of translation is to recognize this conceptual variation and to acknowledge that concepts that are seemingly universal are anything but. In this case, while both scholars describe public spheres, they point to differences in their constitutions with differing political effects. Even more, this lack of universality can help us apprehend the wide divergence in political practice across space. Where most political scientists would see early 2000s Yemen as a straightforwardly autocratic place, Wedeen is able to translate the concept of "democracy" onto everyday practices there and then re-translate these practices back onto political scientists' equation of democracy with free and fair elections to show how this equivalence is historically contingent and conceptually impoverished.

In this sense, to prioritize translation over generalization does not necessarily mean that one has to fetishize difference. Rather, as we argue (Chapter 12, this volume), translation can be thought of as a means by which to *bridge* differences in meanings and concepts (see also Cheah 2013, 56–59; Friedman 2013, 39–42; Von Soest and Stroh 2018, 71–73). As with a novel in translation, ideas can travel across physical space and cultural distance. And, as with a novel, one does not assume an exact correspondence when a text is translated into a new language. The same is true of political concepts, practices, and processes. Translation, here, can be understood as the activity of making concepts, practices, or processes comprehensible across space, time, or cultural context, even as we assume that correspondence will not be exact. For example, we describe how findings from our research projects on mobilization in Latin America (Simmons) and vigilantism in South Africa (Smith) translate to other times and places. For Simmons, meaning-making processes around subsistence goods might look very different in different contexts (and around different material goods), but the importance of those goods in constructing community might translate from one time and place or good to another. Smith (2019) shows how some South Africans' concerns about due process rights, which enable popular violence to correct "failures" in existing law, may translate beyond South Africa's border to potentially make practices of vigilantism in new democracies intelligible elsewhere.

As Cheesman (Chapter 4) shows, translation also requires that we locate our work and that we think about method through location as opposed to location through method. To do so, he proposes that we employ "the logic of unbound comparison," an approach that "pushes toward inquiries into general features of human relations: the idea of the state, the moral economy of resistance, or the allures of nationalism" (this volume, p. 65). When we use this approach to think about how the cases we study speak to broader phenomena, we can make different kinds of claims and write about different kinds of practices than is possible when we require representative samples or we hold particular variables constant to conduct our analysis. Cheesman's chapter explores these ideas through attention to the tradition of area studies, drawing on Anderson to argue that area studies invite practitioners to "have somewhere from which to strike out with sufficient confidence to observe phenomena from uncommon angles, and motion toward how many other ways of thinking about how to compare, and of what to compare, might exist" (this volume, p. 68). When we start our studies in a place, our methods follow from that place and must adapt as we move to new levels of analysis and new empirical domains. Cheesman suggests starting with a locus and working toward general categories, letting the locus lead to the concepts. In doing so, we can make general claims about, for example, what impunity and, therefore, the state are made of (Haberkorn 2018) or how nationalism develops (Anderson 1983). By many definitions, these are not causal claims, but they are constitutive – and they are crucial to political science because they help us understand of what politics are made. Equally important, these claims translate to other places by helping us develop foundational concepts while challenging categories and relationships that are often taken for granted.

THE PATH FORWARD

To achieve the goals we have outlined, the volume is divided into two parts. This was not an easy task for us. As is no doubt obvious from the previous discussion, each of the chapters contributes to more than one of the central themes that drive the volume. Given the multiple contributions each chapter makes, dividing the volume along the themes we have outlined – what is compared, the practices of comparison, and the purposes of comparison – would potentially have the consequence of guiding readers to one conclusion from a chapter, while effacing others. So, we chose instead to divide the volume into two, with the first part including chapters that do conceptual work to lay out broad foundations for how to rethink comparison and the second part focusing on more specific strategies for comparative work that emerged from individual research projects and goals.

Part I begins with Seawright's (Chapter 2) discussion of causal inference and controlled comparisons. It then moves on to offer conceptual discussions of different types of comparison, including perspectival and juxtapositional comparisons (Schaffer, Chapter 3) and unbound comparison (Cheeseman, Chapter 4). The final chapters focus on how we think about cases with both Soss (Chapter 5) and Riofrancos (Chapter 6) encouraging us to rethink how we understand what our cases are. Soss presents the idea of nominal case studies, which allows the researcher to understand cases as the products of constant construction and reconstruction during the research process, while Riofrancos encourages us to think about research sites so that the ways in which the global and the local are products of each other can be better understood and explored.

Obert's (Chapter 7) contribution on comparison and archival research kicks off Part II on specific strategies of comparison. Parkinson's (Chapter 8) related discussion of the complexity of comparison in social network research follows. Schwedler (Chapter 9) offers a discussion of encompassing comparisons, reminding us of the importance of placing our research in broader regional and global processes, while Htun and Jensenius (Chapter 10) demonstrate the importance of cross-regional comparisons and the value of studies aimed at concept development. Read (Chapter 11) encourages us to compare places that may look different by designing our comparisons around foci – specific processes, practices, or institutions – that can shed light on broader phenomena. The final chapter in Part II is our own contribution to the volume and brings us back to the research that inspired us to undertake this volume. We discuss the value in bringing an ethnographic sensibility to comparative analysis through the examples of each of our own ethnographic research.

The book concludes with the transcript of a conversation that we had with Lisa Wedeen about how she thinks about comparison and her own work. Wedeen's research inspired not only the editors of this volume but also many of the contributors. She has consistently shown that great studies of politics can come out of research designs that do not fit with mainstream ideas about best practices. But her work rarely includes reflections on the methodological logics that make it as powerful as it is. In this final chapter, we ask her to engage in precisely this kind of reflection. Her thoughts on her own work speak powerfully to the importance of this volume. In particular, in the final section of the conversation, she emphasizes the importance of creativity and imagination in the enterprise of social science research. We hope this volume encourages scholars to use their imaginations to effectively employ the new tools that the contributors offer and to engage in comparisons driven by logics we have not yet begun to consider.

REFERENCES

Ahmed, Amel, and Rudra Sil. 2012. "When Multi-Method Research Subverts Methodological Pluralism – or, Why We Still Need Single-Method Research." *Perspectives on Politics* 10 (4): 935–53.

Ahram, Ariel I., Patrick Köllner, and Rudra Sil, eds. 2018. *Comparative Area Studies: Methodological Rationales and Cross-Regional Applications*. New York: Oxford University Press.

Amar, Paul. 2013. *The Security Archipelago: Human-Security States, Sexuality Politics, and the End of Neoliberalism*. Durham, NC: Duke University Press.

Anderson, Benedict. 1983. *Imagined Communities: Reflections on the Origin and Spread of Nationalism*. London: Verso Books.

1990. *Language and Power: Exploring Political Cultures in Indonesia*. Ithaca, NY: Cornell University Press.

1998. *The Spectre of Comparisons: Nationalism, Southeast Asia, and the World*. London & New York: Verso.

2016. "Frameworks of Comparison." *London Review of Books* 38 (2): 15–18.

Bartlett, Lesley, and Frances Katherine Vavrus. 2017. *Rethinking Case Study Research: A Comparative Approach*. New York: Routledge.

Boswell, John, Jack Corbett, and R. A. W. Rhodes. 2019. *The Art and Craft of Comparison*. New York: Cambridge University Press.

Brady, Henry E., and David Collier. 2010. *Rethinking Social Inquiry: Diverse Tools, Shared Standards*. Lanham, MD: Rowman & Littlefield Publishers.

Burawoy, Michael. 1989. "Two Methods in Search of Science." *Theory and Society* 18 (6): 759–805.

Cheah, Pheng. 1999. "Grounds of Comparison." *Diacritics* 29 (4): 3–18.

2013. "The Material World of Comparison." In *Comparison: Theories, Approaches, Uses*, edited by Rita Felski and Susan Stanford Friedman, 168–90. Baltimore: Johns Hopkins University Press.

Collier, Ruth Berins, and David Collier. 1991. *Shaping the Political Arena*. Princeton, NJ: Princeton University Press.

Dunning, Thad. 2012. *Natural Experiments in the Social Sciences: A Design-Based Approach*. New York: Cambridge University Press.

Felski, Rita, and Susan Stanford Friedman, eds. 2013a. *Comparison: Theories, Approaches, Uses*. Baltimore: Johns Hopkins University Press.

2013b. "Introduction." In *Comparison: Theories, Approaches, Uses*, edited by Rita Felski and Susan Stanford Friedman, 1–12. Baltimore: Johns Hopkins University Press.

Friedman, Susan Stanford. 2013. "Why Not Compare?" In *Comparison: Theories, Approaches, Uses*, edited by Rita Felski and Susan Stanford Friedman, 34–45. Baltimore: Johns Hopkins University Press.

Geddes, Barbara. 2003. *Paradigms and Sand Castles: Theory Building and Research Design in Comparative Politics*. Ann Arbor: University of Michigan Press.

George, Alexander L., and Andrew Bennett. 2005. *Case Studies and Theory Development in the Social Sciences*. Cambridge, MA: MIT Press.

Gerring, John. 2004. "What Is a Case Study and What Is It Good For?" *American Political Science Review* 98 (2): 341–54.

  2006. *Case Study Research: Principles and Practices*. 1st edn. New York: Cambridge University Press.

Giraudy, Agustina, Eduardo Moncada, and Richard Snyder, eds. 2019. *Inside Countries: Subnational Research in Comparative Politics*. New York: Cambridge University Press.

Gisselquist, Rachel M. 2014. "Paired Comparison and Theory Development: Considerations for Case Selection." *PS: Political Science & Politics* 47 (2): 477–84.

Goertz, Gary, and James Mahoney. 2012. *A Tale of Two Cultures: Qualitative and Quantitative Research in the Social Sciences*. Princeton, NJ: Princeton University Press.

Hobbes, Thomas. 1996. *Leviathan*. New York: Cambridge University Press.

Htun, Mala. 2003. *Sex and the State: Abortion, Divorce, and the Family Under Latin American Dictatorships and Democracies*. New York: Cambridge University Press.

Huntington, Samuel P. 1968. *Political Order in Changing Societies*. New Haven, CT: Yale University Press.

Kazanjian, David. 2016. *The Brink of Freedom: Improvising Life in the Nineteenth-Century Atlantic World*. Durham, NC: Duke University Press.

King, Gary, Robert Keohane, and Sidney Verba. 1994. *Designing Social Inquiry: Scientific Inference in Qualitative Research*. Princeton, NJ: Princeton University Press.

Koivu, Kendra L., and Erin K. Damman. 2015. "Qualitative Variations: The Sources of Divergent Qualitative Methodological Approaches." *Quality & Quantity* 49: 2617–32.

Köllner, Patrick, Rudra Sil, and Ariel I. Ahram. 2018. "Comparative Area Studies: What It Is, What It Can Do." In *Comparative Area Studies: Methodological Rationales and Cross-Regional Applications*, edited by Ariel I. Ahram, Patrick Köllner, and Rudra Sil, 3–28. New York: Oxford University Press.

Lieberman, Evan S. 2005. "Nested Analysis as a Mixed-Method Strategy for Comparative Research." *American Political Science Review* 99 (3): 435–52.

Lieberson, Stanley. 1991. "Small N's and Big Conclusions: An Examination of the Reasoning in Comparative Studies Based on a Small Number of Cases." *Social Forces* 70 (2): 307–20.

  1994. "More on the Uneasy Case for Using Mill-Type Methods in Small-N Comparative Studies." *Social Forces* 72 (4): 1225–37.

Lijphart, Arend. 1971. "Comparative Politics and the Comparative Method." *American Political Science Review* 65 (3): 682–93.

  1975. "II. The Comparable-Cases Strategy in Comparative Research." *Comparative Political Studies* 8 (2): 158–77.

Locke, Richard M., and Kathleen Thelen. 1995. "Contextualized Comparisons and the Study of Comparative Labor Politics." *Politics & Society* 23 (3): 337–67.

Mahoney, James. 2010. "After KKV: The New Methodology of Qualitative Research." *World Politics* 62 (1): 120–47.

Mahoney, James, and Dietrich Rueschemeyer. 2003. *Comparative Historical Analysis in the Social Sciences*. New York: Cambridge University Press.

Mamdani, Mahmood. 1996. *Citizen and Subject: Contemporary Africa and the Legacy of Late Colonialism*. Princeton, NJ: Princeton University Press.

McAdam, Doug. 1982. *Political Process and the Development of Black Insurgency, 1930–1970*. Chicago: University of Chicago Press.

McAdam, Doug, Sidney Tarrow, and Charles Tilly. 2001. *Dynamics of Contention*. New York: Cambridge University Press.

Michener, Jamila. 2019. "Power from the Margins: Grassroots Mobilization and Urban Expansions of Civil Legal Rights." *Urban Affairs Review*. OnlineFirst. https://journals.sagepub.com/doi/abs/10.1177/1078087419855677

Mill, John Stuart. [1843]1882. *A System of Logic: Ratiocinative and Inductive*, 8th edn. New York: Harper & Brothers. Original edition, 1843.

Przeworski, Adam, and Henry Teune. 1970. *The Logic of Comparative Social Inquiry*. New York: Wiley-Interscience.

Putnam, Robert D. 1993. *Making Democracy Work: Civic Traditions in Modern Italy*. Princeton, NJ: Princeton University Press.

Radhakrishnan, R. 2013. "Why Compare?" In *Comparison: Theories, Approaches, Uses*, edited by Rita Felski and Susan Stanford Friedman, 15–33. Baltimore: Johns Hopkins University Press.

Ragin, Charles. 2004. "Turning the Tables: How Case-Oriented Research Challenges Variable-Oriented Research." In *Rethinking Social Inquiry: Diverse Tools, Shared Standards*, edited by Henry E. Brady and David Collier. Lanham, MD: Rowman & Littlefield.

2014. *The Comparative Method: Moving Beyond Qualitative and Quantitative Strategies*. Berkeley: University of California Press.

Schaffer, Frederic Charles. 2015. *Elucidating Social Science Concepts: An Interpretivist Guide*. New York: Routledge.

Schatz, Edward, ed. 2009. *Political Ethnography: What Immersion Contributes to the Study of Politics*. Chicago: University of Chicago Press.

Scott, James C. 1998. *Seeing Like a State: How Certain Schemes to Improve the Human Condition Have Failed*. New Haven, CT: Yale University Press.

Sewell, William H. 1985. "Ideologies and Social Revolutions: Reflections on the French Case." *The Journal of Modern History* 57 (1): 57–85.

1996a. "Three Temporalities: Toward an Eventful Sociology." In *The Historic Turn in the Human Sciences*, edited by Terrence J. McDonald, 245–80. Ann Arbor: University of Michigan Press.

1996b. "Historical Events as Transformations of Structures: Inventing Revolution at the Bastille." *Theory and Society* 25 (6): 841–81.

2005. *Logics of History: Social Theory and Social Transformation*. Chicago: University of Chicago Press.

Simmons, Erica S. 2016. *Meaningful Resistance: Market Reforms and the Roots of Social Protest in Latin America*. New York: Cambridge University Press.

Simmons, Erica S., and Nicholas Rush Smith. 2017. "Comparison with an Ethnographic Sensibility." *PS: Political Science & Politics* 50 (1): 126–30.

Skocpol, Theda. 1979. *States and Social Revolutions*. New York: Cambridge University Press.

Skocpol, Theda, and Margaret Somers. 1980. "The Uses of Comparative History in Macrosocial Inquiry." *Comparative Studies in Society and History* 22 (2): 174–97.

Slater, Dan. 2010. *Ordering Power: Contentious Politics and Authoritarian Leviathans in Southeast Asia*. New York: Cambridge University Press.

Slater, Dan, and Daniel Ziblatt. 2013. "The Enduring Indispensability of the Controlled Comparison." *Comparative Political Studies* 46 (10): 1301–27.

Smith, Nicholas Rush. 2019. *Contradictions of Democracy: Vigilantism and Rights in Post-Apartheid South Africa*. New York: Oxford University Press.

Snyder, Richard. 2001. "Scaling Down: The Subnational Comparative Method." *Studies in Comparative International Development* 36 (1): 93–110.

Soifer, Hillel. 2019. "Units of Analysis in Subnational Research." In *Inside Countries: Subnational Research in Comparative Politics*, edited by Augustina Giraudy, Eduardo Moncada, and Richard Snyder, 92–112. Cambridge: Cambridge University Press.

Spivak, Gayatri Chakravorty. 2013. "Rethinking Comparativism." In *Comparison: Theories, Approaches, Uses*, edited by Rita Felski and Susan Stanford Friedman, 253–70. Baltimore: Johns Hopkins University Press.

Tarrow, Sidney. 2010. "The Strategy of Paired Comparison: Toward a Theory of Practice." *Comparative Political Studies* 43 (2): 230–59.

Tilly, Charles. 1984. *Big Structures, Large Processes, Huge Comparisons*. New York: Russell Sage Foundation.

1985. "War Making and State Making as Organized Crime." In *Bringing the State Back In*, edited by Peter Evans, Dietrich Rueschemeyer, and Theda Skocpol. New York: Cambridge University Press.

1990. *Coercion, Capital, and European States, AD 990–1990*. Cambridge, MA: Basil Blackwell.

2010. *Regimes and Repertoires*. Chicago: University of Chicago Press.

van der Veer, Peter. 2016. *The Value of Comparison*. Durham, NC: Duke University Press.

Von Soest, Christian, and Alexander Stroh. 2018. "Comparison across World Regions: Managing Conceptual, Methodological, and Practical Challenges." In *Comparative Area Studies: Methodological Rationales and Cross-Regional Applications*, edited by Ariel I. Ahram, Patrick Köllner, and Rudra Sil, 66–84. New York: Oxford University Press.

Wallerstein, Immanuel Maurice. 1974. *The Modern World-System: Capitalist Agriculture and the Origins of the European World-Economy in the Sixteenth Century*. New York: Academic Press.

Wedeen, Lisa. 2002. "Conceptualizing Culture: Possibilities for Political Science." *American Political Science Review* 96 (4): 713–28.

2008. *Peripheral Visions: Publics, Power, and Performance in Yemen*. Chicago: University of Chicago Press.

2019. *Authoritarian Apprehensions: Ideology, Judgment, and Mourning in Syria*. Chicago: University of Chicago Press.

Wendt, Alexander. 1998. "On Constitution and Causation in International Relations." *Review of International Studies* 24: 101–17.
Wilkinson, Steven I. 2006. *Votes and Violence: Electoral Competition and Ethnic Riots in India*. New York: Cambridge University Press.
Yashar, Deborah J. 2005. *Contesting Citizenship in Latin America: The Rise of Indigenous Movements and the Postliberal Challenge*. New York: Cambridge University Press.

PART I

RETHINKING THE BUILDING BLOCKS OF COMPARISON

2

Beyond Mill

Why Cross-Case Qualitative Causal Inference Is Weak, and Why We Should Still Compare

Jason Seawright
Northwestern University

While qualitative cross-case comparisons were once widespread and respected enough to be described as "the comparative method," the current wave of research on qualitative methods has seen cross-case comparisons fall substantially in esteem. Early criticisms by Geddes (1990) and King, Keohane, and Verba (1994) on the grounds of selection bias have been disputed and no longer receive sustained attention in the qualitative methods literature, but a more recent line of argument has been that qualitative comparison fails for purposes of causal inference. Such arguments emphasize that the assumptions required for causal inference on the basis of qualitative comparisons are simply implausible and also that statistical methods are superior tools for the same purpose. Sekhon (2004) argues that comparisons based on Mill-type methods will always be susceptible to probabilistic alternative hypotheses, which generally cannot be reasonably evaluated using qualitative cross-case comparisons. George and Bennett (2005, 151–79) argue at length that "practically all efforts to make use of the controlled comparison method fail to achieve its strict requirements," and that various within-case qualitative methods are simply more usable than qualitative cross-case comparisons. Collier, Mahoney, and Seawright (2004) characterize many forms of qualitative cross-case comparisons as a form of "intuitive regression" that acts inferentially as a weaker and problem-laden equivalent of statistical analysis. Seawright (2016, 107–9) argues briefly that a potential-outcomes formulation makes evident that qualitative comparisons are exceptionally weak tools for causal inference.

    This recent critical tradition coexists with sustained use of paired and otherwise grouped comparison in qualitative research, as Slater and Ziblatt (2013, 1302–3, 1307–10) demonstrate. Does this juxtaposition of a highly critical stream of methodological research with continued widespread application of the criticized family of methods reflect a failure of methodological training and communication, a principled but perhaps unarticulated objection to the arguments of methodologists, or an applied appreciation for the contributions qualitative comparisons make to goals other than causal inference?

One cannot, of course, readily discern scholars' sometimes unstated motives in making methodological decisions. This chapter argues that the existing critical literature has indeed been insufficiently attentive to the range of justifying assumptions that qualitative scholars might make in thinking about qualitative cross-case comparison, but also that careful consideration reinforces the view that such assumptions are generally implausible. It then goes on to argue that cross-case comparisons in qualitative research have real value for other methodological objectives, value that has not been fully articulated or respected in the existing literature.

COMPARISON FOR CAUSAL INFERENCE

For many contemporary definitions of causation, there is no inherent, logical connection between the method of comparison across cases and the goal of causal inference. Some traditions of thought about causation, dating at least back to David Hume and including a sequence of thinkers up to Baumgartner's (2008) contemporary work, focus on regularities across cases, arguing that causation is just a certain pattern of predictable relationships between variables across a population of cases. Given this kind of definition, it is clear that methods for causal inference would need to rely centrally on comparison. Indeed, it seems that such a view would rule out any methods other than comparison, as any kind of within-case analysis seems to be at most weakly related to the existence of reliable cross-case patterns.

However, influential alternative perspectives regarding the nature of causation are available. Quantitative and statistical thinking about causation in the social sciences is currently dominated by a synthesis of counterfactual- and manipulation-based approaches (Rubin 1974; Holland 1986; Woodward 2003). Here, causation is not inherently about differences across cases, and cross-case comparison is at most a contingent tool for causal inference rather than part of the definitional core of the concept. Instead, causation is ultimately, if perhaps unobservably, about what would have happened within a single case had the treatment (or main independent variable) of interest been manipulated to take on a different value than it in fact did.

That is, causation is always about the difference between what did happen and what would have happened had a particular, well-defined choice been made differently. A common mathematical notation has emerged around this way of thinking. The inherently counterfactual nature of causation in this framework is captured by the creation of multiple versions of the dependent variable for each case. If case i receives the treatment (which is one often arbitrarily chosen value from the range of the main independent variable), then the dependent variable

Beyond Mill 33

that occurs is $Y_{i,T}$, representing the outcome in case *i* if and only if that case receives the treatment. Otherwise (assuming a binary independent variable for simplicity), case *i* receives the control, and the observed value of the outcome is $Y_{i,C}$.

The true causal effect of the main independent variable for case *i*, then, is $Y_{i,T} - Y_{i,C}$. This difference involves two quantities, one of which is observable but one of which cannot be. The impossibility of directly measuring both components of case *i*'s causal effect is the fundamental problem of causal inference (Holland 1986). Given this problem, all conclusions about causation must necessarily rely on assumption-laden inferential methods. Yet, not all assumptions are created equal, and it is well worth exploring the set of possible assumptions that might justify causal inference based on paired (or other qualitative) cross-case comparison.

Differences That Balance within a Group

Qualitative cross-case comparison is sometimes analogized with statistical matching methods for causal inference (Seawright and Gerring 2008; Nielsen 2016). Hence, it is worth looking closely at the assumptions for causal inference made when using these methods. Are they a viable justification for qualitative cross-case comparison?

Matching methods, like most statistical techniques, rely for causal inference on an analogy to experimental research designs (Morgan and Winship 2014). In experiments, the combination of random assignment and the law of large numbers guarantees that the average value of $Y_{i,T}$ in the treatment group will be similar to the average (unobservable) value of $Y_{i,T}$ in the control group. The same logic holds true for $Y_{i,C}$. Hence, the difference between the observed group average values of $Y_{i,T}$ and $Y_{i,C}$ is close to the true causal effect between the two groups.

The comparability of the treatment and control groups within a social science experiment does not arise because each case in the experiment is interchangeable. Individuals, who are usually the cases in experiments, obviously differ from one another in unlimited ways. These differences are accommodated because they balance out on average. Random assignment with large samples guarantees that for every set of people in the treatment group who are unusually sleepy or suspicious, a countervailing set of people in the treatment will be unusually awake or trusting. Causal inference works because the research design statistically balances individual differences within the treatment and control groups. Furthermore, significance testing of various kinds offers a framework for handling the inevitable real-world imbalances that arise in experiments with finite sample sizes.

Matching methods (like regression and many other related techniques) cannot appeal to random assignment to guarantee that differences across cases will balance out within the treatment and control groups. Instead, scholars using matching make a brute-force assumption that after creating group balance across a fixed set of control variables, all other differences will balance out within each group. This assumption is difficult to justify: unmeasured or neglected variables seem to routinely fail to balance. Nonetheless, causal inference is possible with these methods as long as all relevant differences either are included in the set of measured control variables for matching or happen to balance out within the treatment group and within the control group.

This logic, fragile as it is, is all but unavailable to qualitative scholars. In a paired comparison, the treatment and control groups each consist of a single case. Obviously, nothing can "balance out" statistically within a single instance. If the treatment case is, for example, unusually liberal, then the treatment group just is unusually liberal.

When qualitative scholars compare paired sets of cases, such a logic is marginally more viable. There might, for example, be a treatment case that is unusually liberal but that is offset by another treatment case that is unusually conservative to almost exactly the same extent. However, such a procedure requires careful attention and can only realistically work if the total number of differences between cases is small. While it might be possible to handpick a small set of treatment cases in such a way that cases' idiosyncrasies collectively balance each other out on, say, three or four differences, it seems hard to imagine that the same could be done if there were several hundred differences.

Thus, paired comparisons must seek some other justification for causal inference. Small-group qualitative comparisons are likewise obliged unless the cases under comparison are exceptionally simple. Finally, significance testing cannot offer to even mitigate these problems, given that small-n controlled comparisons virtually never feature enough cases for such tests.

Differences That Balance within a Case

How, then, might scholars justify such qualitative comparisons? If, to consider the purest paired-comparison design, the treatment case is just irreducibly different from the control case in ways other than the main independent variable, is causal inference possible?

In a paired comparison, causal inference revolves around $Y_{1,T} - Y_{2,C}$, where case 1 is the treatment case and case 2 is the control. This quantity will correctly describe causal matters for case 1 if $Y_{1,T} - Y_{2,C} = Y_{1,T} - Y_{1,C}$. Thus, the inference requires that $Y_{2,C} = Y_{1,C}$. This is a strikingly stringent requirement: the two cases simply cannot differ from each other in terms of the outcome they would experience under the treatment and under the control. Indeed, while various quantitative approaches to causal inference require assumptions that are difficult to meet or even implausible, this assumption is more restrictive than those required for any widely used quantitative technique. Regression analysis,

Beyond Mill

for example, allows for causal inference in the face of random measurement error or omitted causes that are not confounders; this assumption cannot succeed in the face of either of these problems. Thus, controlled comparison requires the same kind of assumption as regression, but a much stronger version of it.

One assumption that might meet this condition is that the differences between the treatment and control cases balance each other out within each of the two cases. If one unusual feature of case 1 adds, say, three points to $Y_{1,T}$ and $Y_{1,C}$, but the second (and only other) unusual feature subtracts three points, then taken as a whole case 1 poses no problems for causal inference.

Of course, there is no special reason to expect that differences within a case will tend to balance as opposed to accumulate. While it is possible that such cases exist, they must surely be rare.

Differences That Barely Matter

Perhaps the most frequent informally expressed justification for causal inference via qualitative comparison involves the idea that two cases may not be identical, and the distinctive features of each case may not internally balance, but that causal inference will still work if the consequences of the differences are modest enough. Perhaps $Y_{2,C}$ does not equal $Y_{1,C}$, but the causal inference will still be acceptable if $Y_{2,C}$ is very close to $Y_{1,C}$ – a result that will hold if the causal effects of differences between the cases on the outcome of interest are all quite small. What counts as "very close" is relative to the size of the true causal effect: any other differences must have effects that are a tiny fraction of the effect of interest, or the inference will be badly distorted.

This setup can seem reasonable enough. Surely case experts are likely to focus on important differences and may well have the knowledge necessary to pair up broadly similar cases. Nevertheless, this argument results in disturbingly fragile causal inferences. Because the causal inference is only approximately correct if the causal effect in question is large and the effects of all other differences between cases are small, it will only be persuasive to scholars who are already firmly convinced that the main independent variable is the biggest cause of the outcome. Any readers who are instead open to the alternative hypothesis that there are some other causes of comparable importance to the main independent variable cannot avoid worrying that the causal inference is biased by the differences between the cases.

No Differences

Finally, and most starkly, qualitative causal inference will succeed if there are simply no differences between the cases under comparison. If the treatment case and the control case are simply identical in every way that is causally relevant to the outcome, then the causal inference will succeed. This condition, known as "causal homogeneity," seems to capture a common interpretation of what J. S. Mill intended with the method of difference. In some kinds of physical science laboratories, careful procedure can more or less achieve exact interchangeability between a treatment and a control sample, allowing a direct pairwise comparison to support causal inference. It seems self-evidently problematic to identify a pair of human beings, let alone any larger social aggregate or institution, as comparably interchangeable.

BILLIONAIRES AND THE CAUSAL ROLE OF PUBLIC PRESSURE

To illustrate the problems with these four assumptions justifying qualitative comparison for causal inference, consider a paired comparison between two politically conservative American billionaires, David Koch and John Menard Jr.[1] In a broad perspective, these individuals have had an enormous amount in common. They were immersed in the shared political culture of the twenty-first-century United States. They shared an elite socioeconomic position. They had overlapping social networks and quite convergent political views, as evidenced by Menard's participation in a series of seminars sponsored by Koch and his brother.

These and many more similarities notwithstanding, Menard and Koch had crucial differences that matter for understanding American billionaires' participatory strategies. While both Menard and Koch were heavily invested in conservative economic politics, Koch's views received substantially more public attention and indirect defense through his foundations, support for scholarship, and even a handful of public statements. Menard's political perspectives, by contrast, have not been given deliberate public airing – and instead have emerged via investigative journalism and legal action. What explains this contrast in the two billionaires' willingness to engage in stealth politics (Page, Seawright, and Lacombe 2018), that is, participatory strategies that evade public scrutiny and offer little or no deliberative defense of one's policy preferences?

One interesting explanatory possibility is that the difference is accounted for by the extent to which the two billionaires' wealth depends on public-facing businesses and brands. Menard's wealth is founded in the success of his eponymous chain of home improvement stores. As such, publicly visible political action might carry the risk of boycotts or general consumer distaste of a sort that could hurt Menard economically. Koch, by contrast, drew his wealth in substantial part from the energy industry but also from a number of behind-the-scenes investments. Because Koch's wealth mostly came from industries that sell to other industries and depended little on his personal brand, he had limited economic exposure to boycotts or other forms of

---

[1] Material in this section draws on Page, Seawright, and Lacombe (2018). David Koch died in 2019.

consumer rejection. Hence, it may be unsurprising that Koch was willing to participate in more potentially visible ways than Menard: Koch simply had less to lose.

The key issue for this chapter is, of course, not whether this explanation is true or false, but rather whether any of the four assumptions characterized in the previous section are applicable and can justify causal inference with this comparison. It should be immediately clear that the first assumption, that differences will balance within groups, is not applicable. There is only one billionaire within each group – and while it would certainly be possible to expand the analysis to include more billionaires, reaching the sample sizes that would justify use of the law of large numbers essentially precludes qualitative treatment of the comparison.

What of the assumption that differences balance within cases? Even evaluating this assumption would require exceptional prior causal knowledge. Potentially relevant contrasts between Menard and Koch are numerous and varied. The two billionaires differed in terms of family backgrounds, with Koch coming from a successful family with an established (if not yet world-dominant) business while Menard was born to solidly middle-class parents. They differed in birthplaces as well, although perhaps in ways that would only be clear to Midwesterners: Menard was born in Eau Claire, Wisconsin, while Koch came from Wichita, Kansas. They departed substantially in terms of their places of residence and cultural interests. Menard still lives in Wisconsin and has long sponsored a team that competes in the Indy Racing League. Koch, by contrast, lived at 740 Park Avenue in Manhattan and was famous for his substantial philanthropical gifts to support cancer research; the New York and Washington, DC, arts and museum scenes; and a public broadcasting foundation.

Do these and other differences between the billionaires exactly cancel out? While it would be fortuitous if they did, the fact is that even determining the answer would require remarkable prior causal knowledge. Does an affluent as opposed to middle-class origin predispose a billionaire to greater public political visibility, or does the causal effect run in the other direction? Would Koch's philanthropical efforts create connections with Manhattan social life that increase the potential costs of visible political activism, or would philanthropy create a buffer against criticism? The issues involved in even deciding whether the assumption is met are immense and probably, at present, insurmountable.

The exact same challenge destroys any potential applicability of the third assumption, that the differences between these two billionaires barely matter. I might invite the reader to believe that public- versus industry-facing primary sources of wealth have much more powerful effects on political participatory strategy than do social networks, family histories, and so forth. Yet what of the inevitable reader who disagrees? For any reader who sees social networks as potentially as important, the comparison crumbles. A scholar might respond by selecting a comparison between billionaires with similar social networks – but this problem will remain as long as any difference whatsoever persists between the billionaires. At the ultimate limit, imagine a pair of identical twin billionaires raised in the same household and residing in the same condominium building, but with one of them for some reason heavily invested in consumer-facing enterprises and the other not. Even though these hypothetical billionaires are similar to the point of fantasy, it nonetheless remains certain that they will have subtle but potentially relevant differences. Their social networks will not be identical. They will have slightly divergent sets of politically relevant information. Some life experiences will not be shared, and so forth. To claim that these differences *must* have smaller effects on participatory strategies than the public- versus industry-facing contrast is to assert a priori that the causal effect of interest is relatively large. Thus, this assumption becomes uncomfortably close to circular.

Finally, the discussion over the previous paragraphs should absolutely suffice to reject any notion that Menard and Koch are identical in all ways other than whether their businesses face the consumer public. Billionaires are not chemical samples, and there is simply no prospect for interchangeability. Thus, it would seem that prospects for causal inference from a paired comparison between Menard and Koch are grim. One might tinker at the margins by selecting slightly more similar pairs of billionaires, but the basic issues encountered here will persist.

Yet if qualitative comparisons are a hopeless strategy for causal inference about billionaires, prospects are surely grim for virtually any other application of this design in the social sciences. Among the overall population of humans, after all, American billionaires are a remarkably homogeneous group, with similarities in culture, class, and context that are exceptional. Surely other kinds of individual comparisons will suffer from at least the same degree of challenge as was seen in this example. Furthermore, causal inference from comparisons of larger and more complex institutions or collectives will evidently face even more intense problems. Simply put, qualitative comparison appears to have little to offer as a tool of direct causal inference, because the required assumptions are implausible at best in the social sciences.

THE VALUE IN COMPARISON

Of course, it certainly does not follow from this argument that qualitative comparison is useless, or that existing qualitative work featuring controlled comparison needs to be discarded altogether. Rather, the value of comparison arises from goals other than direct causal inference. Here, I will highlight three ways that qualitative comparisons, as in this chapter a comparison between John Menard Jr. and David Koch, make social scientific contributions. Such comparisons are valuable because they sharpen conceptualizations and measurement, allow exploration of the prevalence of a particular arrangement of causal capacities, and provide raw materials for the construction of theories of causal moderation. It makes sense to reread existing studies of this sort along such lines, even perhaps against their authors' intentions – and it is emphatically reasonable to design future qualitative comparisons with these alternative goals in mind.

To begin with, as Slater and Ziblatt (2013, 1312) note, comparison facilitates conceptualization and measurement by providing empirical content and grounding for theoretical contrasts. There is value in using qualitative comparisons to understand the meaning and real scope of possible different outcomes with respect to a dependent variable. As the literature on conceptualization and measurement has emphasized, knowledge of the real contrast space connected with a concept is vital for full understanding and valid measurement. Qualitative comparison can allow inductive discovery related to that contrast space in ways that are hard to replicate with other methods. Likewise, qualitative comparisons are valuable for clarifying of what the treatment and control conditions in a particular theoretical context actually consist.

With respect to the comparison between billionaires, both benefits are evident. Koch is often imagined in the press as a particularly secretive billionaire, perhaps the prototype of stealth politics. Yet in fact a comparison with Menard makes clear that Koch is much closer to the middle of the spectrum in terms of stealth politics. After all, Koch's political views have been explained and defended somewhat directly via his 1980 Libertarian Party vice-presidential campaign, and indirectly through his funding of the Institute for Humane Studies and other organizations. Menard, by contrast, has made no publicly discoverable statements on policy issues, has never run for elected office, and has founded no academic or other institutes for explaining and disseminating sympathetic views. Instead, his political activism has involved campaign contributions and private strategies including disincentivizing union activity in his stores and paying employees to participate in ideologically loaded citizenship training. Thus, while analysts examining Koch's strategies in isolation have tended to regard him as a prototypical case of the secret exercise of political influence, a qualitative comparative perspective clarifies the true range of the outcome variable of interest by demonstrating that billionaires can participate politically in far stealthier ways than those of David Koch.

Likewise, the concept of a billionaire with public-facing assets is, in the abstract, difficult to measure. Nearly all billionaires either (directly or indirectly) own consumer-facing brands or generate products that in some form reach consumers, so it might seem reasonable to regard public facing as a constant for this population. Comparison between Menard and Koch makes clear that this is in fact a domain of substantial difference. It is true that Koch's industrial investments did indeed involve products that eventually connect in one way or another with consumers, and that consumers sometimes find out about more direct investments by the Kochs in consumer products such as the

2017 film *Wonder Woman*. Yet identifying any significant proportion of the products of Koch investments would require substantial research, whereas a motivated consumer could meaningfully express disapproval of Menard's political participation simply by boycotting the chain of stores that carries his name. This contrast makes succinctly clear that, while no billionaire experiences the ideal-typical absence of public facing, the empirical range is such that a clear contrast is present and a meaningful dichotomy can be constructed.

Slater and Ziblatt (2013) argue at length for another advantage of qualitative comparison: providing external validity for causal inferences based on (qualitative or quantitative) single-country analysis. Their argument demonstrates decisively that scholars routinely use qualitative comparison for this purpose, and that such studies are often well received by their respective research communities. Yet there are certain tensions involved in the discussion that result from conceptual messiness related to the idea of external validity.

External validity is sometimes discussed in terms of sample-to-population statistical inference. Here, external validity is a property that holds when a statistic is a good (unbiased and/or consistent, efficient, and so forth) estimate of a population parameter. Thus, for example, a well-executed random sample survey provides an externally valid description of a population as a whole. It is deeply unclear that qualitative comparison could ever provide external validity in this sense: qualitative cases are rarely randomly sampled, and even if they were, it would be exceptional for qualitative analysis to include enough cases to invoke the law of large numbers. Hence, qualitative comparison will generally not provide high-quality estimates of population parameters – nor indeed is it designed to do so. Does a comparison of Menard and Koch generalize to a broader population? Surely the conceptual insights discussed earlier have implications for thinking about other American billionaires, and perhaps about the politics of the affluent in general, but it should be clear that the comparison does not provide statistically valid descriptions across such a population. We have other methods better suited to that goal.

To speak of external validity in the context of qualitative comparison, a reframing is needed. Slater and Ziblatt (2013, 1314) helpfully reformulate the concept: "If an argument deriving from a controlled comparison is stated in terms of general variables and can be shown to shed explanatory light on specific cases outside the original sample, then the original argument can be said to enjoy external validity." Here, external validity becomes a sliding scale: an argument scores higher to the extent that it applies to more cases, and also presumably to the extent that it throws a brighter "explanatory light" on each case.[2]

---

[2] It is unclear how one might evaluate tensions between these two components of external validity, were they to arise. Is an explanation that applies to only a handful of new cases but explains them

Beyond Mill

What does "explanatory light" consist of? By usage in the quoted passage, and by Slater and Ziblatt's (2013) deployment of related terms throughout, "explanatory light" appears to be a relation between an explanation and a case. At one point, they gloss this feature as involving "verisimilitude on causal mechanisms" (1314). Unfortunately, this might have various meanings: highly detailed theories of causal pathways, extensive and persuasive pattern-matching (Campbell 1966) evidence that a given case exemplifies a theorized causal pathway, or evidence justifying an overall causal inference regarding an entire theoretical model's causal correctness vis-à-vis a given case (Waldner 2015), to name a few.

On the supposition that Slater and Ziblatt are referring to causal pathways, that is, sequences of variables with causal linkages that may serve to fill in steps between the treatment and the outcome within a given case, there is another difficulty. Two cases might have very different results even if they experience the same causal pathways in the sense that each is affected by genuine causal linkages from the treatment variable, through one or more shared mediator variables, to the outcome: the size of the causal effects involved in each relation need not be constant across cases and background facts about a given case may render it more or less susceptible to a particular causal effect and thus may change the magnitude of causal patterns without altering their form. Such changes in magnitude should probably be seen as altering the degree to which a theory explains a given case, as would differences in the nature of the observed mediator variables – but such sequential causal inferences are difficult at best. It is not clear that qualitative research is a powerful tool for quantifying series of causal magnitudes, and it is also unclear how one might trade off between magnitudes of effects versus identities of mediators in evaluating explanatory fit.

One further argument has been offered, perhaps most visibly by Yin (2013, 325–27), for the role of cross-case comparisons in something like external validity, this time pivoting around the concept of "analytic generalization," which is "the extraction of a more abstract level of ideas from a set of case study findings – ideas that nevertheless can pertain to newer situations other than the case(s) in the original case study" (325). In other words, the scholar interprets each case (or sometimes each key transition, moment, or causal dynamic within a case) as a representative of a category of other situations and generalizes the patterns within that case to that broader category. Comparison across multiple cases can here stand in for comparison of multiple categories or abstract, generalized types.

While this is an intriguing idea, and analytic generalization of this kind surely represents a worthwhile goal for any researcher, the problem of justifying a typologically oriented analytic generalization is if anything more extreme

---

in depth better or worse than an explanation that applies to many cases but only explains them to a limited extent?

than for simpler and more mechanical ideas of generalization. Specifically, why are we to believe that one or a few cases are typical representatives of the category to which they belong? It seems that only two arguments are available here. First, we may have prior knowledge that the categories in question are highly uniform, or that the cases we are studying are representative of the relevant patterns across the relevant category. Such prior knowledge would necessarily require extensive study of the dynamics of interest across the set of cases within each category. Hence, the work of generalization would already be finished, and the case studies would not in fact contribute toward that goal.

Second, we may lack prior detailed knowledge of the overall pattern within each category. In this scenario, the case study or studies that represent each category would have to carry out the work of justifying a generalization from the case study or studies to the larger population of cases that forms part of a given type. In other words, the problem of justifying a single act of generalization from case studies is replaced with multiple, identical problems for each category of cases within the overall population.

Ultimately, I am unpersuaded that there is value in applying the concept of external validity to qualitative cross-case comparisons. If a causal theory is correct for a given case, then it cannot be made untrue by results in another case, nor can a theory that is false for a given case be made true by its performance in other cases. Consideration of a theory's explanatory value outside the core case or cases of interest is thus a matter neither of statistical generalization nor of testing the theory's validity. Ultimately, scholars should probably think of generalization in case studies the way that they think of generalization in experimental research: as the cumulative result of replication and reiteration across a community of researchers, rather than as a key metric for the quality of an individual study. As Mullinix et al. (2015, 125) argue in discussing generalizability in different kinds of survey experiments, "scientific knowledge advances through replication rather than accepting or rejecting research based on sample-related heuristics."

Contemporary theories of causation provide a helpful set of tools for reframing this issue, in ways that are arguably compatible with, although more extensive than, the potential-outcomes framework adopted earlier (e.g., Cartwright 2009; Seawright 2016, 29–30). Cartwright (2007) in particular pushes us to think of causation as context-specific arrangements of objects, institutions, actors, and so forth in such a way that the well-known capacities of each specific entity interact so as to generate the outcome of interest. Because configurations of entities and their causal capacities just differ across contexts as a brute fact, there is no reason why valid causal arguments should be expected to be universal, or indeed even to be valid more than once. Thus, in Cartwright's view, good causal theories are those that identify relevant entities and correctly describe their causal capacities and arrangements. These micro-components of a causal explanation can be real and theories about their capacities can be true – but because of the prevalence of difference in arrangements across cases,

Beyond Mill

generalized causal theories or laws are false (Cartwright 1983). Rather, the kinds of causal findings that result from an experiment, case study, or most other approaches are true or false relative to some given "nomological machine" or specific arrangement of causal capacities (Pemberton and Cartwright 2014).

From such a position of central concern for entities and their causal capacities, Slater and Ziblatt's concern for external validity can be helpfully re-characterized as understanding the prevalence of the causal capacities central to a theory across a range of cases. In-depth qualitative and/or quantitative analysis of a single case might give us good reason to believe that a particular causal arrangement is operative in that case, and no evidence from other cases need ever trouble that conclusion. Yet, it remains instructive to ask whether there are other cases in which the same entities demonstrate the theorized causal capacities. While a causal explanation can be valid and nonetheless unique to a single case, an obvious gain to credibility occurs when explanations involve common, easily demonstrated capacities that are not unique to the case in question. One might argue in complex ways about whether statistical methods or qualitative comparison is better for this task, but the goal is both reasonable and compelling, and it is immediately obvious that qualitative comparison can at least contribute. A comparison among American billionaires extended along these lines would seek evidence that the new set of actors attends to boycott risks and other costs of publicity, considers political action strategically across multiple behavioral and institutional domains, and avoids being forced to adopt a purely self-interested self-concept. Showing that such dynamics exist – even if the political results are quite different from those found in the cases of Koch or Menard – would reinforce the conceptual and causal narratives driving the case studies in Page, Seawright, and Lacombe (2018).

Of course, social scientists are rarely satisfied to note that one set of cases is simply causally different from another. If causal capacities are arranged one way in a first domain and another way in a second, it is reasonable and perhaps compelling to ask why the domains differ. This kind of second-order problem of causal theory involves the project of understanding relations of causal moderation, that is, the background variable or variables that cause cases to differ in terms of the main theory's network of causal relations and capacities. Building (and perhaps to some extent testing) theories about moderation is in itself a highly valuable goal.

Furthermore, it is easy to interpret much of the use of qualitative comparison in the comparative historical literature in political science and sociology as carrying out (to varying degrees) careful within-case causal inference and then using comparison to structure theory building about moderation. Consider, for example, Collier and Collier's (1991) study of labor, parties, and regimes in early- to mid-twentieth-century Latin America, a classic that serves as one of Slater and Ziblatt's motivating examples. In that study, the treatment variable is labor incorporation (i.e., the inclusion of labor unions as part of the legal political system), and the outcomes involve patterns of party system formation and certain trajectories of regime dynamics. The central argument of the volume is in fact that labor incorporation, a shared event across the eight countries in the study, does *not* have the same effects or activate the same causal dynamics across the region. Instead, Collier and Collier argue that certain background characteristics have a tendency to cause countries to incorporate labor in different ways, and that these different modes of incorporation produce divergent arrangements of causal capacities. The bulk of the study consists of careful within-case analysis that attempts to establish the actual causal effects for each case, and the cross-case comparisons that frame the volume can easily be understood as building a theory of causal moderation (a theory that is in part also tested using the within-case analysis).

For the study of billionaires, the key set of puzzles involves understanding why the shared cause of extreme affluence leads to different patterns of political engagement: (mostly liberal) political speech combined with limited or no financial investment in politics, (mostly conservative) financial contributions combined with little or no political speech, and disengagement from the political arena. For the exploratory purpose of generating new ideas about the sources of these differences in political participatory strategy, closely matched billionaires such as Koch and Menard are not helpful: they both end up in the same category here. As a result, relatively little insight is to be expected into possible causes for differences in strategy; instead, a broadly inductive comparison across deeply dissimilar cases (e.g., the Koch brothers, Menard, Michael Bloomberg, and the Mars family heirs) would be more promising. Once goals other than causal inference are embraced, scholars can thus find themselves freed from the constraints of control and can explore the intellectual fruits of far wilder comparisons.

CONCLUSIONS

This chapter has argued that none of the assumptions that could justify causal inference via paired or more elaborately grouped qualitative comparison is likely to be even remotely plausible in social science applications. Thus, it is a mistake to attempt to justify a qualitative comparative research design by claiming that the design will achieve causal inference via control, correspond with Mill's methods, or even meaningfully rule out a given explanation (which might after all be probabilistic or interact in complex ways with background variables).

Yet, the conclusion is not that qualitative researchers should abandon comparison. Such research designs make real contributions in terms of conceptualization and measurement, exploration of the prevalence of causal capacities, and the building of theories of causal moderation. These contributions all retain their value, independent of the methods used for within-case causal inference. The optimal comparative designs for these purposes should be a lively topic for future research within the qualitative methods community. As this research develops, applied scholars will it is hoped move in the direction of explicit clarity regarding the assumptions behind and contributions of their cross-case comparisons.

REFERENCES

Baumgartner, Michael. 2008. "Regularity Theories Reassessed." *Philosophia* 36 (3): 327–54.
Campbell, Donald T. 1966. "Pattern Matching as an Essential in Distal Knowing." In *The Psychology of Egon Brunswik*, edited by Kenneth R. Hammond, 81–106. New York: Holt, Rinehart and Winston.
Cartwright, Nancy. 1983. *How the Laws of Physics Lie*. Oxford: Oxford University Press.
  2007. *Hunting Causes and Using Them: Approaches in Philosophy and Economics.* Cambridge: Cambridge University Press.
  2009. "How to Do Things with Causes." *Proceedings and Addresses of the American Philosophical Association* 83 (2): 5–22.
Collier, David, James Mahoney, and Jason Seawright. 2004. "Claiming Too Much: Warnings about Selection Bias." In *Rethinking Social Inquiry: Diverse Tools, Shared Standards*, edited by Henry E. Brady and David Collier, 85–102. Lanham, MD: Rowman & Littlefield.
Collier, Ruth Berins, and David Collier. 1991. *Shaping the Political Arena: Critical Junctures, the Labor Movement, and Regime Dynamics in Latin America.* Princeton, NJ: Princeton University Press.
Geddes, Barbara. 1990. "How the Cases You Choose Affect the Answers You Get: Selection Bias in Comparative Politics." *Political Analysis* 2 (1): 131–50.
George, Alexander L., and Andrew Bennett. 2005. *Case Studies and Theory Development in the Social Sciences*. Cambridge, MA: MIT Press.
Holland, Paul W. 1986. "Statistics and Causal Inference." *Journal of the American Statistical Association* 81 (396): 945–60.
King, Gary, Robert Keohane, and Sidney Verba. 1994. *Designing Social Inquiry: Scientific Inference in Qualitative Research*. Princeton, NJ: Princeton University Press.
Morgan, Jana. 2007. "Partisanship During the Collapse of Venezuela's Party System." *Latin American Research Review* 42 (1): 78–98.
Mullinix, Kevin J., Thomas J. Leeper, James N. Druckman, and Jeremy Freese. 2015. "The Generalizability of Survey Experiments." *Journal of Experimental Political Science* 2 (2): 109–38.
Nielsen, Richard A. 2016. "Case Selection via Matching." *Sociological Methods and Research* 45 (3): 569–97.
Page, Benjamin I., Jason Seawright, and Matthew J. Lacombe. 2018. *Billionaires and Stealth Politics*. Chicago: University of Chicago Press.
Pemberton, John, and Nancy Cartwright. 2014. "Ceteris Paribus Laws Need Machines to Generate Them." *Erkenntnis* 79 (10): 1745–58.
Rubin, Donald B. 1974. "Estimating Causal Effects of Treatment in Randomized and Nonrandomized Studies." *Journal of Educational Psychology* 66 (5): 688–701.

Seawright, Jason. 2016. *Multi-Method Social Science: Combining Qualitative and Quantitative Tools*. Cambridge: Cambridge University Press.

Seawright, Jason, and John Gerring. 2008. "Case Selection Techniques in Case Study Research: A Menu of Qualitative and Quantitative Options." *Political Research Quarterly* 61 (2): 294–308.

Slater, Dan, and Daniel Ziblatt. 2013. "The Enduring Indispensability of the Controlled Comparison." *Comparative Political Studies* 46 (10): 1301–27.

Waldner, David. 2015. "What Makes Process Tracing Good? Causal Mechanisms, Causal Inference, and the Completeness Standard in Comparative Politics." In *Process Tracing: From Metaphor to Analytic Tool*, edited by Andrew Bennett and Jeffrey T. Checkel, 126–52. Cambridge: Cambridge University Press.

Woodward, James. 2003. *Making Things Happen: A Theory of Causal Explanation*. Oxford: Oxford University Press.

Yin, Robert K. 2013. "Validity and Generalization in Future Case Study Evaluations." *Evaluation* 19 (3): 321–32.

3

Two Ways to Compare

Frederic Charles Schaffer
University of Massachusetts–Amherst

In taking up the charge of "rethinking comparison," we might gainfully ask a basic, but not-too-often posed, question: What are the different ways to compare?

My aim in posing this question is to bring into clearer view a way of comparing that often goes unnoticed despite being common to the social sciences. Monopolizing the attention of social scientists who write about comparison is what we might call "juxtapositional" comparison: placing like kinds of things side by side to catalog their similarities and differences. But a different way to compare exists, one that is rarely acknowledged in the literature on comparison. We might describe this less recognized form as "perspectival." It compares one kind of thing to a different kind of thing as a way to establish an outside vantage point from which to view one in terms of the other. In shining a light on perspectival comparison, I hope to both show how integral it is to social science and offer insight into how it might be used more thoughtfully. These tasks are important because perspectival comparison not only serves as a basis for juxtapositional comparison; it is also a powerful tool for (re)imagining the social world. To ignore this form of comparison, or to use it unreflectively, is to risk trapping ourselves in a reality that we erroneously take to be fixed and given.

JUXTAPOSITIONAL VS. PERSPECTIVAL COMPARISON

According to the *Oxford English Dictionary*, "compare" derives from the Latin *comparāre*, literally "to pair together, couple, match, bring together." A cursory look at most any grammar book reveals two distinct uses of the English-language term. On the one hand, to compare can mean to bring together and place side by side

---

I thank Erica Simmons and Nick Smith for their valuable feedback on my chapter and for all their work in pulling this volume together. I am also grateful to Derek Beach, Judy Carr, Barbara Cruikshank, Markus Kreuzer, Timothy Pachirat, María Helena Rueda, Lisa Wedeen, and Dvora Yanow for their generous and helpful comments.

similar kinds of things to estimate or catalog their similarities and/or differences.[1] We can thus compare one person with another and describe how they stack up against each other with regard to wit, height, wealth, education, or the like. One can similarly compare one country with another, one revolution with another, or one social movement with another. I propose calling this side-by-side way of comparing "juxtapositional."

On the other hand, to compare can mean to draw an analogy between two different kinds of things, to liken one kind of thing to a different kind of thing. When we compare the moon to Swiss cheese, we show how one kind of thing (the moon) is like a different kind of thing (Swiss cheese). One might similarly compare the moon to a boat that sails across a sea, a parent who tucks a child into bed, or a song that plays in the distance. Sometimes when we compare dissimilar things, the analogy is made explicit by the use of simile (e.g., the moon is *like* a piece of cheese). At other times, the analogy is more hidden or implied and takes the form of metaphor (e.g., the moon *is* a piece of cheese). To speak of politics in terms of carpentry – as Max Weber ([1919] 1946, 128) did when he famously described politics as "a strong and slow boring of hard boards" – is but one example of comparing dissimilar things by means of metaphor.[2]

When we compare dissimilar things, we show the relationship between them. What Kenneth Burke (1941, 421–22) wrote about metaphor holds for comparing dissimilar things more generally: "It brings out the thisness of a that, or the thatness of a this." In comparing the moon to Swiss cheese, we bring out the cheese-like qualities of the moon. In comparing politics to carpentry, Weber brings out the carpenter-like dispositions that someone with the vocation of politics should possess. Because comparing dissimilar things involves bringing out the "thisness of a that, or the thatness of a this," we might say that it establishes, to again borrow from Burke, an outside "perspective" (422). It uses cheese as an outside vantage point from which to view and gain perspective on the moon or carpentry as an outside vantage point from which to

---

[1] Here and elsewhere in this chapter, I use "things" in a colloquial, encompassing sense. The term includes not only material objects but also events, actions, processes, practices, experiences, and so on.

[2] The claim that I advance is only that metaphor involves comparison, that the metaphoric "the moon is a piece of cheese" can be reworded as the simile "the moon is like a piece of cheese" and still make sense (Carston 2002, 358). This is not to argue that simile and metaphor work in precisely the same manner or that every metaphor can be so directly recast into a corresponding simile. For a range of views on how metaphor involves comparison, see Perrine (1971), Ortnoy (1979), Miller (1993), and Fogelin (2011). A contrasting position – held by authors such as Glucksberg and Keysar (1990) and Israel, Harding, and Tobin (2004) – is that at least some metaphors categorize rather than compare. In my judgment, those who hold this position draw a distinction between comparison metaphors and categorization metaphors that is too sharp and artificial. As experimental studies by Bowdle and Gentner (2005) and Rubio-Fernández, Geurts, and Cummins (2017) demonstrate, metaphoric categorization itself involves comparison or builds upon prior comparison.

Two Ways to Compare

view and gain perspective on politics. For this reason, I propose calling this way of comparing "perspectival."[3]

We have, then, two ways to compare. To compare juxtapositionally is to place like kinds of things side by side to catalog their similarities and differences. To compare perspectivally is to draw an analogy between different kinds of things as a way to establish an outside vantage point from which to view one kind of thing in terms of another. When "compare" is used in its juxtapositional sense, we can say either compare "with" or compare "to." When the term is used in its perspectival sense, we more typically say compare "to." When astronomers juxtapositionally compare the moon with planet Earth, they estimate the similarities and differences between the two celestial bodies with regard to mass, diameter, chemical composition, gravitational pull, and the like. When the poet Nicholas Vachel Lindsay (1913) perspectivally compares the moon to a city, he brings out the cityness of the moon, with its "yellow palaces upreared upon a glittering ground."

The difference between the two ways of comparing is also revealed in the popular warning against comparing "apples with oranges" – or "grandmothers with toads," as the saying apparently goes in Serbian. Whatever the language, this idiom admonishes against juxtapositionally comparing things that are deemed to belong to different categories. Such a warning would be wrongly invoked when comparing perspectivally. Indeed, a perspectival comparison *requires* comparing things deemed to belong to different categories – comparing, say, the moon to cheese, or grandmothers to toads.

I repeat "deemed to" because, as we have learned from Nelson Goodman, "anything is in some way like anything else" (1972, 440). Depending on the interests of the person doing the comparing, the same pair of things can be deemed to belong to either the same or different categories. Apple farmers concerned with the yields of assorted varieties of that fruit might deem oranges to belong to a different category that holds little interest to them. For them to juxtapositionally compare apples with oranges might make little sense. Nutritionists, in contrast, may well want to juxtapositionally compare apples with oranges so that they can estimate the vitamin content of various types of fruit that might be included in school lunches. We could also imagine evolutionary biologists taking an interest in comparing juxtapositionally the DNA of toads and grandmothers, or astrobiologists wanting to compare juxtapositionally the molecular compounds present in both cheese and the moon. There is, to repeat, nothing intrinsically similar or dissimilar about any two things. We must be careful, then, not to reify or naturalize our categories: we come *up* with similarities, not

---

[3] I do not call it "metaphoric" because this way of comparing can rest on simile or analogy as well. I resist using "literal" and "figurative" in place of "juxtapositional" and "perspectival" because the distinction between literal and figurative is less clear than might at first appear. Metaphor is typically considered to be a type of figurative language, yet we treat many metaphors as literal. For example, "They constructed a theory" might be taken to be a literal expression, but it is an instance of the theory-as-building metaphor (Lakoff and Johnson 2003, 52–55).

across them. But once we deem things to be similar or dissimilar, to belong to the same or different categories, juxtapositional comparison requires comparing like with like, whereas perspectival comparison requires comparing like to unlike.

JUXTAPOSITIONAL COMPARISON IN THE SOCIAL SCIENCES

Social scientists who offer methodological advice about comparing usually focus their attention on working out how to compare juxtapositionally. Much of this advice comes from scholars operating within the positivist tradition. To ensure that apples are being compared with apples and oranges with oranges, that whatever is being compared actually belongs to the same category, some positivist methodologists develop guidelines for creating categories that are well demarcated, a task that often goes by the name of "concept formation" (see, e.g., Sartori 1970). To increase confidence that the particular cases chosen for study actually belong in those categories, that clear procedures exist to help correctly categorize this piece of fruit as an apple and that piece of fruit as an orange, other positivist methodologists offer guidance on "operationalization" and "measurement" (see, e.g., Schoenberg 1972). To provide reasoned criteria for deciding which particular apples, among the entire universe of apples, are selected for juxtapositional comparison, still others attend to "sampling" or "case selection" (see, e.g., Ebbinghaus 2005).

Advice from interpretivist scholars on how to compare juxtapositionally often differs. Some interpretivists argue that the construction of well-demarcated concepts is not necessary for juxtapositional comparison (see, e.g., Schaffer 2016, 59–64). Other interpretivists offer guidance on case selection that overlaps only partially with the advice given by positivists (see, e.g., Simmons and Smith 2017). Yet others argue that juxtapositional comparison can or should rest not on a selection of cases posited to exist in the world, but rather on a constructive casing of the world (see, e.g., Soss, Chapter 5, this volume). But whatever differences exist in how positivist and interpretivist scholars typically approach juxtapositional comparison, the fact remains that this way of comparing is crucial to both.

Because John Stuart Mill's *Logic of the Moral Sciences* ([1872] 1988) has become a reference point for many social scientists who today write about comparing, it is perhaps worth pointing out that his method of difference and his method of agreement are both modes of juxtapositional comparison. It is not the case that the method of difference is juxtapositional and the method of agreement perspectival. Both of Mill's methods compare things that are deemed to belong to a single category. In his own example, the category was that of "nation." To see whether the wealth of nations is a result of their commercial policies using the method of difference would require, he explained, finding two nations – one rich and one poor – "which agreed in everything except their commercial policy," while the method of agreement would require that the nations "agree in no circumstance whatever, except in having a restrictive system and in being prosperous" (Mill

[1872] 1988, 68, 70). Whether we use the method of difference or agreement, we compare one nation with another. If we were to compare a nation perspectivally, in contrast, we would need to compare it to something we deem to belong to a different category. We might thus perspectivally compare a nation to a family, human body, or melting pot.

Turning our attention to another, more recent, scholarly reference point, it is also the case that the three logics of historical comparison identified by Theda Skocpol and Margaret Somers (1980) are all modes of juxtapositional comparison. Each logic, the authors explain, involves "the juxtaposition of historical cases" (175). The logics differ primarily in the purpose served by comparing juxtapositionally. In macro-causal analysis, the idea is to "mak[e] causal inferences about macro-level structures and processes" (181). In the parallel demonstration of theory, the aim is to "demonstrate that a theory similarly holds good from case to case" (178). In the contrast of contexts, the motive is to "bring out the unique features of each particular case" (178). One might suppose that the contrast of contexts involves perspectival comparison insofar as it involves comparing cases that differ greatly one from the other. But even in this logic, the divergent cases are deemed to belong to the same ontological category, and thus it too is a mode of juxtapositional comparison. Take Clifford Geertz's *Islam Observed* (1971), which Skocpol and Somers present as an exemplar of that logic. In this book, Geertz compares the historical development of Islam in Morocco and Indonesia. Whatever differences he discovers in how Islam developed in each of these two country-contexts, he nonetheless deems both histories to be histories of Islam (Geertz 1971, 4).

Still, Geertz writes that Moroccan Islam and Indonesian Islam "form a kind of commentary on one another's character" (4). This statement might be taken to imply that juxtapositional comparison also offers an outside vantage point, that juxtapositional and perspectival comparisons are less distinct than I have characterized them. Such an interpretation, in my view, would be mistaken. Geertz's comparison does not draw forth the Indonesianness of Moroccan Islam or the Moroccanness of Indonesian Islam. It does not, returning to Burke's formulation, "brin[g] out the thisness of a that, or a thatness of a this" (1941, 421–22). Rather, the commentary of which Geertz speaks is juxtapositional. It highlights the distinctive features of Islam in each country by contrasting one with the other and cataloging their differences.

This point may perhaps be made clearer by turning our attention to another example. Would it make sense to argue that the French Revolution provides a perspective on the Iranian Revolution or vice versa? For sure, juxtapositionally comparing two revolutions can teach us much about their commonalities and differences (and perhaps too about the causes of such commonalities and differences). Put another way, one revolution can furnish, to return to Geertz's language, a "commentary" upon another revolution. It can tell us if one, relative to the other, was quick or drawn-out, peaceful or bloody, secular or religious. But juxtapositional comparison does not equip us to imagine revolution in other terms. It does not make us see revolution as a burning fever or a rational game or a mechanical process – as Brinton (1965, 16–18), Tullock (1971), and McAdam, Tarrow, and Tilly (2001), respectively, invite us to do. Enabling us to "see as" is the job of perspectival comparison. Both juxtaposition and perspective taking are forms of comparison: both involve a "pairing together," as the etymology of "compare" indicates. But whereas juxtapositional comparison brings two apples together to allow one apple to comment upon another apple, so to speak, perspectival comparison brings an apple together with something else to provide a vantage point outside of appledom in terms of which to conceive it.

WHY PERSPECTIVAL COMPARISON IN THE SOCIAL SCIENCES WARRANTS MORE ATTENTION

Working out how to best compare juxtapositionally or why to compare juxtapositionally is a worthy project. Juxtapositional comparison, after all, pervades the social sciences, no doubt because it is a basic mode of human apprehension. Yet we must acknowledge that social scientists (along with everyone else) routinely compare perspectivally as well. Game theorists conceive of politics or economics as games with rules and predictable outcomes. Process tracers think of society as a kind of machine in which various sorts of causal mechanisms are at work. Interpretivists – or at least some of them – liken culture to a web that suspends people in meanings they have spun, to paraphrase Geertz (1973, 5). Sometimes such metaphors are self-consciously crafted and invoked. More often they are implicit and taken for granted and thus go unnoticed. Consequently, perspectival comparison has been the subject of far less methodological reflection in the social science literature on comparing than its juxtapositional cousin.

Perspectival comparison deserves more time in the spotlight for at least four reasons. For one, it often serves as the foundation for juxtapositional comparison. To juxtapositionally compare, say, the causal mechanisms that produced both the French and Iranian Revolutions requires first conceiving of a revolution as an ordered sequence of events produced by processes that are analogous to the operation of parts in a machine. If our thought is not to be guided in unexamined ways, we need to be more attentive to how the perspectival comparisons that we make shape the way we understand the phenomenon in question, frame the way we conceptualize what is going on, guide our choices about those facets of social reality to compare juxtapositionally, and inform how we answer the question, "What should we treat these as cases of?" (Soss, Chapter 5, this volume). One reason why social scientists sometimes fail to notice the perspectival comparisons that lie beneath their inquiries is that such comparisons are in many instances already embedded in the ordinary language that they draw upon to conceptualize their studies.

Two Ways to Compare

A perspectival comparison can seem so obvious and natural that it is not even recognized as a perspectival comparison. Notice, for instance, how I slipped in a perspectival comparison three sentences earlier by likening social reality to a cut gem. Like the multiple polished faces of a diamond, social reality too may be thought of as having facets – an idea that has become so commonplace that it is rarely even noticed as metaphoric.

The second, related, reason why perspectival comparison deserves more time in the limelight is that any similarities generated by means of it are only partial. Politics is like carpentry in some ways *but not others*. A nation is like a human body in some ways *but not others*. Any perspectival comparison channels our attention toward some things and away from others. As Max Black explains:

> Suppose I am set the task of describing a battle in words drawn as largely as possible from the vocabulary of chess. These latter terms determine a system of implications which will proceed to control my description of the battle. The enforced choice of the chess vocabulary will lead some aspects of the battle to be emphasized, others to be neglected. (Black 1962, 41–42)

Perspectival comparisons specify and disregard at the same time. To point out the chessness of battle is to both focus on the move-countermove strategy of battle and take no note of its horror. To point out the carpentryness of politics is to both shed light on the place of passion and perspective in politics and overlook the possibility that politics might not always be a matter of treating people like lumber to be drilled, that it can instead involve people coming together as equals. Adopting the language of Hannah Arendt (1958, 220–30), we might conceive of politics in terms of "action" rather than "making." Social scientists who rely on a given perspectival comparison need to be aware of where that comparison directs attention and what it removes from view if they are not to let the comparison channel their thought in ways that are both unrecognized and unduly constraining. By recognizing the place of perspectival comparison in our thinking, we become more aware of the ways in which particular perspectival comparisons potentially box in our thinking.

The third reason why perspectival comparison merits attention is that it is a powerful tool for making sense of ourselves, our experiences, and our world. To characterize what love "really is," we might compare it to a delicate dance, smoldering fire, wild rollercoaster ride, or even hand-to-hand combat. Our understanding of love takes shape, in part, by means of the multiple perspectival comparisons that we make, by viewing love from not one but many vantage points. As Burke put it more abstractly, "It is by the approach through a variety of perspectives that we establish a character's reality" (1941, 422).[4] If we want to

---

[4] Note that Burke has an expansive understanding of "character." He defines it as "whatever can be thought of as distinct (any thing, pattern, situation, structure, nature, person, object, act, rôle, process, event, etc.)" (1941, 422).

establish what kind of thing, say, modern democracy is, we might perspectivally compare it to a game (see, e.g., Bobbio 1987), a market (see, e.g., Downs 1957), and a theater production (see, e.g., Edelman 1988), among other things. It is by viewing modern democracy from multiple vantage points that we build up a textured understanding of what it is.

We come, finally, to the fourth reason. If perspectival comparison helps establish reality, then making a fresh perspectival comparison can help establish a different reality, can inaugurate new ways of giving sense to the world. When Thomas Hobbes persuaded readers of *Leviathan* to see the state as an "artificial man," he changed their conception of it ([1651] 1998, 7). They came to view the state as both human and a work of artifice, as something that could be engineered by means of social contract. When Paul Samuelson convinced readers of *Foundations of Economic Analysis* to conceive of economics in terms of thermodynamics, they came to see the operation of physical laws, such as Le Chatelier's Principle, at work in the market (1947, 36). Samuelson's imaginative use of analogy, not incidentally, helped secure his place as the "father of modern economics," to quote one historian (Parker 2002, 25). It is a curious fact that while many scholars celebrate metaphoric and analogical reasoning for its contributions to creative scientific thinking (see, e.g., R. Brown 1976; Gross 1990, 21–32; Genter et al. 1997; Dunbar 2000, 53–55; T. Brown 2003), few recognize it as a distinctively comparative approach or conceptualize it as such. To be clear, I am not here claiming to "discover" the importance of metaphoric and analogical reasoning to social science. I am merely pointing out how such reasoning involves comparison making and should thus be incorporated into our accounts of how social scientists compare.

WHAT MAKES FOR A "GOOD" PERSPECTIVAL COMPARISON?

Recognizing perspectival comparison as a distinct and pervasive mode of comparative analysis within the social sciences raises a host of methodological questions. Here let me focus on perhaps the thorniest: Are any perspectival comparisons "true" or at least "better" than others? How one answers this question depends in good part on how one understands the relationship of language to the social world. If one believes that the social world exists independent of language, then perspectival comparisons might be conceived of as models or hypotheses about that independently existing social world that can be tested (see, e.g., Landau 1961, 334–35). Statements like "politics is carpentry" or "society functions like a machine" become propositions that can be verified or falsified through observation of a world taken to be freestanding.

But such a view of how language relates to the social world is, I believe, incorrect. Our social world is built up by the words we use. Battles, politics, nations, and grandmothers do not stand apart from language. As Charles

Two Ways to Compare

Taylor puts it, language is "constitutive" of the social world (1971, 25).[5] This claim should not be taken as a naive argument for linguistic determinism. Taylor clarifies:

> The situation we have here is one in which the vocabulary of a given social dimension is grounded in the shape of social practice in this dimension; that is, the vocabulary wouldn't make sense, couldn't be applied sensibly, where this range of practices didn't prevail. And yet this range of practices couldn't exist without the prevalence of this or some related vocabulary. There is no simple one-way dependence here. We can speak of mutual dependence if we like, but really what this points up is the artificiality of the distinction between social reality and the language of description of that social reality. The language is constitutive of the reality, is essential to its being the kind of reality it is. (24)

Words and the social world, in short, are inseparable.

If the words we use are constitutive of the social world, and if we make comparisons, not find them, then there is no freestanding social world "out there" against which to test statements like "politics is carpentry" or "society functions like a machine." Indeed, it is by means of such perspectival comparisons that we build up our understanding of what that world is. Here we would also do well to remember that the social world is multivalent. We can think of democracy in terms of a game, a market, a theater production, *and many other things besides*. We are not locked into a single perspective (Lakoff 1987, 304–37). Given this polysemy, given the multiple ways that we have of conceiving the social world, how should we think about truth? Philip Wheelwright offers what I take to be sage advice:

> The best we can hope to do is catch partisan glimpses, reasonably diversified, all of them imperfect, but some more suited to one occasion and need, others to another.... The metaphoric and the mythic are needed elements in the intellectual life of an individual and of a community; only, when serious questioning begins, one must deal with the proposed answers not by outright acceptance or rejection but with limited and qualified consideration, murmuring with the Hindu gurus of the Upanishads, "*neti neti*" – "not quite that, not quite that!" (1962, 172–73)

The "goodness" of a particular perspectival comparison depends on the occasion and the need; even so, it can offer only a glimpse of something that is not entirely that. To sharpen Wheelwright's point, we might add that a good perspectival comparison within the social sciences – with its particular occasions and needs – might be one that, among other things, generates deep insight about what the social world is or what takes place within it; while a good social science *use* of perspectival comparison is one that acknowledges that any one comparison, however profound, still only offers a single vantage point among many.

---

[5] See as well Cienki and Yanow (2013, 168–69) and Schaffer (2016, 1–25).

What might count as "deep" insight? Working up an answer to this question requires first recognizing that most, if not all, social science perspectival comparisons are double layered. By this I mean that the perspectival comparisons made by social scientists provide insight into a social reality that is itself built up by means of perspectival comparison. Much of how people ordinarily conceptualize the world, after all, is structured by metaphor. Anglophones, for instance, speak of time in terms of money (something that can be saved, wasted, or budgeted), status in terms of height (upward mobility, peak of a career, climbing the social ladder), ideas in terms of food (that can be meaty, spoon-fed, or half-baked), and so on (Lakoff and Johnson 2003). The perspectival comparisons made by social scientists overlay whole systems of metaphor already baked into the conventional ways in which people speak and think. Anthony Giddens (1977, 12) argued that social science involves a "double hermeneutic" because social science interpretations "concern a 'pre-interpreted' world of lay meanings." Geertz (1973, 9) articulated a similar idea when he wrote that "what we call our data are really our own constructions of other people's constructions of what they and their compatriots are up to." What I am suggesting here is that the same holds true for the perspectival comparisons of social scientists. They are perspectives on other people's perspectives.

I now submit that a good social science perspectival comparison, one that deepens understanding, can perform different tasks, each of which establishes a distinctive relationship between the two layers of perspective. Here I focus on three tasks, what we might call surfacing, extending, and reimagining. I do not think this short list is necessarily exhaustive, but it is a start.

A social science perspectival comparison that *surfaces* makes explicit conventional perspectival comparisons that operate beneath the awareness of those being studied. An exemplary study of this type is *The Family Romance of the French Revolution* by Lynn Hunt (1992). Although Hunt is a historian, her book offers a fine illustration for social scientists of what surfacing can accomplish. Hunt likens the French Revolution to a family romance to show how the revolutionaries collectively but unconsciously imagined power relations and how they sought to replace one kind of national family with another (xiii–xiv, 8). The value of surfacing lies in its ability to draw together diverse manifestations of a metaphor to show their underlying coherence. Or, as Hunt puts it with regard to her own study, it can "help us make sense of evidence that would otherwise remain confounding and mysterious" (xiv). Indeed, she devotes much of her book to showing the connections that run like a hidden thread through an array of sources ranging from paintings to newspapers to pornographic novels.[6]

---

[6] Lakoff (2002, 17) similarly aims to show by surfacing familial metaphors in American politics how seemingly odd collections of liberal and conservative policy positions "fit together."

A social science perspectival comparison that *extends* not only surfaces a conventional perspectival comparison but also explores an unarticulated entailment of that comparison. In *Friction: An Ethnography of Global Connection* (2005), Anna Tsing brilliantly uses perspectival comparison to extend by first surfacing the conventionalized way in which people understand global connections in terms of "motion" and then asking what kinds of "friction" impede that motion. She explains:

> The metaphor of friction suggested itself because of the popularity of stories of a new era of global motion in the 1990s. The flow of goods, ideas, money, and people would henceforth be pervasive and unimpeded. In this imagined global era, motion would proceed entirely without friction. By getting rid of national barriers and autocratic or protective state policies, everyone would have the freedom to travel everywhere. Indeed, motion itself would be experienced as self-actualization, and self-actualization without restraint would oil the machinery of the economy, science, and society.
>
> In fact, motion does not proceed this way at all. How we run depends on what shoes we have to run in. Insufficient funds, late buses, security searches, and informal lines of segregation hold up our travel; railroad tracks and regular airline schedules expedite it but guide its routes. Some of the time, we don't want to go at all, and we leave town only when they've bombed our homes. These kinds of "friction" inflect motion, offering it different meanings. (2005, 5–6)

By looking at the friction of global connections – at "what happens when Japanese traders buy Indonesian trees, when army officers make deals with nature lovers, or when university students sit down with village elders" (3) – Tsing is able to illuminate how such encounters make possible, channel, and disrupt globalizing forces. Put another way, Tsing extends the connection-as-motion metaphor to add nuance to it and thereby show how intellectually generative it can be.

A social science perspectival comparison that *reimagines* offers a new perspectival comparison that departs from and exposes the imaginative limits of a conventional one. A provocative study of this type is John Keane's *Power and Humility: The Future of Monitory Democracy* (2018). Keane surfaces the ways in which people tend to deploy a particular ontological metaphor when talking about democracy, how they often speak of democracy as if it were a container in which activities like deliberation or elections take place (e.g., "*in* a democracy, people have a right to vote"). These democratic containers, he explains, come in different sizes ("small-scale" democracy or "large-scale" democracy) and are located in particular territorial places (democracy in ancient Greece, in America, in a New England town, etc.) (302–309).

The problem, for Keane, is that the container metaphor constrains our democratic imagination in the enmeshed world of the twenty-first century, especially when we think of those containers as sitting within fixed national boundaries. He has in mind, in particular, the ways in which territorial understandings of democracy fail to capture the diverse assemblages of local, non-territorial, and extraterritorial mechanisms that monitor the exercise of power around the globe, mechanisms that range from consumer councils to online petitioning to global watchdog organizations (Keane 2018, 107). Conceptualizing democracy in a way that recognizes the salience of such monitory mechanisms, he argues, "requires a fundamental shift of perspective – a *Gestalt* switch – in the way contemporary democracies are understood" (103). The shift he proposes is to think of democracy in terms of quantum physics, of democracy existing "within the expanding *multiverse* of differently sized, spatially entangled institutions and networks of power that straddle our Earth" (310). Within this multiverse, he explains, "boundary disputes, 'spooky action at a distance' (Einstein), spillover effects, arbitrage pressures and butterfly effects are common. Here-there dialectics are chronic. Things that happen in one place have effects elsewhere, in far-away locations" (302). Keane's purpose in introducing this new quantum metaphor, it bears emphasizing, is to enable us to reconceptualize democracy. In his own words, it is "an exercise in reshaping the democratic imaginary" (315). It is a perspectival comparison that breaks with and shows the constraints of the conventional spatial metaphoric construction of democracy.

Insofar as social science perspectival comparisons that reimagine rest upon comparisons that depart from conventional ones, we might ask where fresh or novel social science perspectival comparisons come from. Acknowledging that comparisons are made, not found and that similarities are created, not encountered, means that no instrument, no machine is capable of unearthing a new perspectival comparison as if some already existing but completely unnoticed similarity were buried in the ground just waiting to be dug up. It would perhaps be more fruitful to ask instead how we might cultivate habits of thought to render moments of imaginative comparison making more rather than less likely to occur. As C. Wright Mills put it, a certain "playfulness of mind" is surely necessary because, like the sociological imagination that he was describing, perspectival comparison has an "unexpected quality ... perhaps because its essence is the combination of ideas that no one expected were combinable" (1959, 211). Such playfulness requires exercising those parts of the brain where the sparks of imagination ignite – trying one's hand at writing poetry, for instance. It also requires nourishing one's thinking with a rich and varied diet. To see the quantum-like qualities of democracy requires knowing something about both quantum mechanics and democracy. Put another way, intellectual nourishment requires gardening outside the walls of the familiar and reading omnivorously beyond the confines of one's discipline.

FRAUGHT PERSPECTIVAL COMPARISONS

However deep and insightful perspectival comparisons may be, their social science use is also prone to generic dangers. One sort of danger arises when social scientists transpose the conventionalized perspectival comparisons of one group of people onto other groups of people who do not share those conventions. The result is often misunderstanding. Consider, for a moment, some of the market metaphors that American English speakers use to talk and think about democracy in their country. They speak of "selling" political ideas, "branding" politicians, "retail" politics, and the like. When a person votes for a candidate after receiving something of material value from, or on behalf of, that candidate, American English speakers conceive of it as a market transaction and call it vote "buying." Many political scientists have embraced this market perspective. When they encounter voters acting in this way, they often see instances of vote buying (Schaffer and Schedler 2007). People in some corners of the world, for sure, share that perspective, as expressions such as *Stimmenkauf* (German), *achat de voix* (French), and *compra de votos* (Spanish) suggest. But people everywhere do not conceptualize election-time offers to be opening moves in market transactions. To many voters in Kenya, electoral handouts communicate a politician's commitment to serve their interests (Kramon 2018, 16). In some areas of Taiwan, voters see offers of cash as token gifts politicians distribute to demonstrate their courtesy and respect (Rigger 1994, 219). In parts of the Philippines, voters view such offers as gestures of caring generosity (Aguilar and Alis 2018, 89–90). To transpose a market mentality onto voters like these would be to misrecognize what they are thinking and doing. It would also render ineffective policies built upon such a transposition – for instance, civic education campaigns intended to convince voters not to "sell" their votes.

These risks are not hypothetical. In Quezon City, the largest city of the Philippines, middle-class civic educators ran ads prior to one election with messages like "Do you love the country or the money?" and "Don't be blinded by money – vote with your conscience." With the implicit accusation that the poor were treating their ballots as commodities, the ads changed the behavior of few lower-class voters. Worse, many money-accepting voters were offended, for they saw themselves as mere recipients of goodwill handouts that did not obligate them to vote in a particular way. By accepting money or voting for a candidate who gave it to them, they did not consider themselves to be acting unpatriotically or without conscience and found such insinuations to be demeaning. In many poor neighborhoods, the reputation of middle-class civic groups took a hit as did their various efforts to ensure a free and fair election. An attempt to improve the quality of democracy, we see, had the opposite effect (Schaffer 2008, 125–49). The takeaway is that conventionalized perspectival comparisons derived from one class's or community's experience may not travel well to other classes or communities. Social scientists – as well as policy makers, civic educators, and the like – should be on guard not to transfer such comparisons indiscriminately.

Another, related, sort of danger attends the social science use of perspectival comparison: the risk of trapping oneself inside a single perspective, of failing to recognize that it offers only one perspective among many. Analytically, the result can be intellectual confinement, an inability or unwillingness to visit other vantage points from which to view the world. This self-entrapment, it bears noting, can be consequential. To see the world from only one perspective is to reify that perspective, to mistake it for a reality that is objectively and stubbornly given. Such reification risks limiting our capacity to see that the world can be conceived otherwise. Instead of stimulating our imagination, social science perspectival comparison can stifle it.

The problem is especially grave when a social science perspectival comparison reflects and reproduces a hierarchy of power that is left unrecognized or unacknowledged. The result is not only reification but also the reification of a world as the powerful prefer to see it (Lakoff and Johnson 2003, 156–60, 236–37). After 9/11, President George W. Bush declared a "war on terror"; in so doing, he chose one metaphor among many to conceptualize the US response to what happened on that day. Rather than conceiving of the response as a war with enemies to be conquered, he might have seen it as an effort to enforce the law, reduce prejudice, or contain a social epidemic, among other possibilities (Kruglanski et al. 2007). In choosing the metaphor of war, he provided a cognitive framework for a slew of laws and policies, the most noteworthy of which brought into existence the Department of Homeland Security and led to the invasions of Iraq and Afghanistan. The war on terror metaphor, by dint of President Bush's position of power, created a new reality, the basic contours of which many social scientists failed to interrogate. Study after study appeared with titles like *Knowing the Enemy: Jihadist Ideology and the War on Terror* (Habeck 2006) and *With Us and Against Us: How America's Partners Help and Hinder the War on Terror* (Tankel 2018). Such scholarship not only accepted uncritically the war on terror metaphor; it contributed to its calcification into an "obvious" US course of action. To disregard or leave unrecognized the play of power in social science perspectival comparison is to hazard political myopia and reinforce the status quo.

CONCLUDING THOUGHTS

Perspectival comparison is foundational to the social sciences. Acknowledging its central role should both expand and complicate our understanding of the ways in which social scientists compare and the constitutive role played by language when they compare. Much of the interesting and politically consequential work begins once we realize that social reality is not given and overt but – to again quote Wheelwright – "latent, subtle, and shy" (1962, 172). Put more prosaically, social reality and our social science understanding of that reality are often metaphorically constructed, typically in ways that we fail to notice, by means of perspectival comparison. To ignore this more hidden form of comparison or to integrate it unreflectively into our research is to flatten our thinking; to recognize and fully leverage it is to build up a textured understanding of the world or to reimagine it altogether. It is high time that we move perspectival comparison out of the shadows.

REFERENCES

Aguilar, Filomeno V., and Grace Joyce P. Alis. 2018. "Brokers Courting Voters: The Alliance System in a Rural Philippine Village." *Philippine Political Science Journal* 39 (2): 73–96.

Arendt, Hannah. 1958. *The Human Condition*. Chicago: University of Chicago Press.

Black, Max. 1962. *Models and Metaphors: Studies in Language and Philosophy*. Ithaca, NY: Cornell University Press.

Bobbio, Norberto. 1987. *The Future of Democracy: A Defence of the Rules of the Game*. Minneapolis: University of Minnesota Press.

Bowdle, Brian F., and Dedre Gentner. 2005. "The Career of Metaphor." *Psychological Review* 112 (1): 193–216.

Brinton, Crane. 1965. *The Anatomy of Revolution, Revised and Expanded Edition*. New York: Vintage.

Brown, Richard H. 1976. "Social Theory as Metaphor: On the Logic of Discovery for the Sciences of Conduct." *Theory and Society* 3(2): 169–97.

Brown, Theodore L. 2003. *Making Truth: Metaphor in Science*. Urbana: University of Illinois Press.

Burke, Kenneth. 1941. "Four Master Tropes." *The Kenyon Review* 3(4): 421–38.

Carston, Robyn. 2002. *Thoughts and Utterances: The Pragmatics of Explicit Communication*. Malden, MA: Blackwell.

Cienki, Alan, and Dvora Yanow. 2013. "Why Metaphor and Other Tropes? Linguistic Approaches to Analyzing Policies and the Political." *Journal of International Relations and Development* 16(2): 167–76.

Downs, Anthony. 1957. *An Economic Theory of Democracy*. New York: Harper & Row.

Dunbar, Kevin. 2000. "How Scientists Think in the Real World: Implications for Science Education." *Journal of Applied Developmental Psychology* 21(1): 49–58.

Ebbinghaus, Bernhard. 2005. "When Less Is More: Selection Problems in Large-N and Small-N Cross-National Comparisons." *International Sociology* 20(2): 133–52.

Edelman, Murray. 1988. *Constructing the Political Spectacle*. Chicago: University of Chicago Press.

Fogelin, Robert J. 2011. *Figuratively Speaking: Revised Edition*. New York: Oxford University Press.

Geertz, Clifford. 1971. *Islam Observed: Religious Development in Morocco and Indonesia*. Chicago: University of Chicago Press.

―――. 1973. *The Interpretation of Cultures*. New York: Basic Books.

Gentner, Dedre, Sarah Brem, Ronald W. Ferguson, and Arthur B. Markman. 1997. "Analogical Reasoning and Conceptual Change: A Case Study of Johannes Kepler." *Journal of the Learning Sciences* 6 (1): 3–40.

Giddens, Anthony. 1977. *Studies in Social and Political Theory*. New York: Basic Books.

Glucksberg, Sam, and Boaz Keysar. 1990. "Understanding Metaphorical Comparisons: Beyond Similarity." *Psychological Review* 97 (1): 3–18.

Goodman, Nelson. 1972. *Problems and Projects*. Indianapolis: Bobbs-Merrill.

Gross, Alan G. 1990. *The Rhetoric of Science*. Cambridge, MA: Harvard University Press.

Habeck, Mary R. 2006. *Knowing the Enemy: Jihadist Ideology and the War on Terror*. New Haven, CT: Yale University Press.

Hobbes, Thomas. [1651] 1998. *Leviathan*. New York: Oxford University Press.
Hunt, Lynn. 1992. *The Family Romance of the French Revolution*. Berkeley: University of California Press.
Israel, Michael, Jennifer Riddle Harding, and Vera Tobin. 2004. "On Simile." In *Language, Culture and Mind*, edited by Michel Achard and Suzanne Kemmer, 123–35. Stanford, CA: CSLI Publications.
Keane, John. 2018. *Power and Humility: The Future of Monitory Democracy*. New York: Cambridge University Press.
Kramon, Eric. 2018. *Money for Votes: The Causes and Consequences of Electoral Clientelism in Africa*. New York: Cambridge University Press.
Kruglanski, Arie W., Martha Crenshaw, Jerrold M. Post, and Jeff Victoroff. 2007. "What Should This Fight Be Called? Metaphors of Counterterrorism and Their Implications." *Psychological Science in the Public Interest* 8 (3): 97–133.
Lakoff, George. 1987. *Women, Fire, and Dangerous Things: What Categories Reveal about the Mind*. Chicago: University of Chicago Press.
   2002. *Moral Politics: How Liberals and Conservatives Think*, 2nd edn. Chicago: University of Chicago Press.
Lakoff, George, and Mark Johnson. 2003. *Metaphors We Live By*, with a new afterword. Chicago: University of Chicago Press.
Landau, Martin. 1961. "On the Use of Metaphor in Political Analysis." *Social Research* 28 (3): 331–53.
Lindsay, Nicholas Vachel. 1913. "The Moon Is Compared to a City." *Poetry: A Magazine of Verse* 2 (4): 122.
McAdam, Doug, Sidney Tarrow, and Charles Tilly. 2001. *Dynamics of Contention*. New York: Cambridge University Press.
Mill, John Stuart. [1872] 1988. *The Logic of the Moral Sciences*. La Salle, IL: Open Court.
Miller, George A. 1993. "Images and Models, Similes and Metaphors." In *Metaphor and Thought*, 2nd edn., edited by Andrew Ortony, 357–400. New York: Cambridge University Press.
Mills, C. Wright. 1959. *The Sociological Imagination*. New York: Oxford University Press.
Ortony, Andrew. 1979. "Beyond Literal Similarity." *Psychological Review* 86 (3): 161–80.
Parker, Randall E. 2002. *Reflections on the Great Depression*. Northampton, MA: Edward Elgar.
Perrine, Laurence. 1971. "Forms of Metaphor." *College English* 33 (2): 125–38.
Rigger, Shelley Elizabeth. 1994. "Machine Politics in the New Taiwan: Institutional Reform and Electoral Strategy in the Republic of China on Taiwan." PhD diss., Harvard University.
Rubio-Fernández, Paula, Bart Geurts, and Chris Cummins. 2017. "Is an Apple Like a Fruit? A Study of Comparison and Categorisation Statements." *Review of Philosophy and Psychology* 8 (2): 367–90.
Samuelson, Paul Anthony. 1947. *Foundations of Economic Analysis*. Cambridge, MA: Harvard University Press.
Sartori, Giovanni. 1970. "Concept Misformation in the Social Sciences." *American Political Science Review* 64 (4): 1033–46.

Schaffer, Frederic Charles. 2008. *The Hidden Costs of Clean Election Reform*. Ithaca, NY: Cornell University Press.
— 2016. *Elucidating Social Science Concepts: An Interpretivist Guide*. New York: Routledge.
Schaffer, Frederic Charles, and Andreas Schedler. 2007. "What Is Vote Buying?" In *Elections for Sale: The Causes and Consequences of Vote Buying*, edited by Frederic Charles Schaffer, 17–30. Boulder, CO: Lynne Rienner.
Schoenberg, Ronald. 1972. "Strategies for Meaningful Comparison." *Sociological Methodology* 4: 1–35.
Simmons, Erica S., and Nicholas Rush Smith. 2017. "Comparison with an Ethnographic Sensibility." *PS: Political Science & Politics* 50 (1): 126–30.
Skocpol, Theda, and Margaret Somers. 1980. "The Uses of Comparative History in Macrosocial Inquiry." *Comparative Studies in Society and History* 22 (2): 174–97.
Tankel, Stephen. 2018. *With Us and Against Us: How America's Partners Help and Hinder the War on Terror*. New York: Columbia University Press.
Taylor, Charles. 1971. "Interpretation and the Sciences of Man." *Review of Metaphysics* 25 (1): 3–51.
Tsing, Anna Lowenhaupt. 2005. *Friction: An Ethnography of Global Connection*. Princeton, NJ: Princeton University Press.
Tullock, Gordon. 1971. "The Paradox of Revolution." *Public Choice* 11 (1): 89–99.
Weber, Max. [1919] 1946. "Politics as a Vocation." In *From Max Weber: Essays in Sociology*, translated and edited by H. H. Gerth and C. Wright Mills, 77–128. New York: Oxford University Press.
Wheelwright, Philip. 1962. *Metaphor and Reality*. Bloomington: Indiana University Press.

4

Unbound Comparison

Nick Cheesman
Australian National University

The comparative method is a cornerstone of political inquiry in today's academy. Its logic of comparison provides a basis, Charles Ragin (2014, 1) writes in introducing his seminal text on the topic, "for making statements about empirical regularities and for evaluating and interpreting cases relative to substantive and theoretical criteria." Typically, these statements pertain to causal relationships between variables inferred from systematic observations of phenomena in different countries or periods.

But is it necessary to designate a method to study politics comparatively? And if it is, need this be some variant on Mill's (1882) system of comparative logic? Not everyone who studies politics as a vocation thinks so. Among them are contributors to this book. Also among them was Benedict Anderson (2018, 130), who late in his life insisted that comparison of the sort he undertook was not a method, but a discursive strategy. Anderson, who taught comparative politics at Cornell, said that he had learned to compare not by being trained in the comparative method but by spending time with like-minded others, being forced to speak and "think more or less comparatively" (1998, 10; see also Aguilar et al. 2011). For this reason, he was more interested in the explanatory potential of juxtaposing cases, and in the possibilities for unanticipated journeys that follow from surprising discoveries, than in scientific rigor.

I wrote this chapter in 2019 while on a fellowship at the Center for Southeast Asian Studies, Kyoto University. I am thankful to Caroline Hau for her careful engagement with it, and for her insights into Ben Anderson's thinking, as well as to Decha Tangseefa, Mario Lopez, Patrick Jory, and the editors for their close reading and thoughtful comments on drafts. I am grateful to colleagues at the center for their generous intellects and spirits, particularly to Yoko Hayami and Nakanishi Yoshihiro, as well as to audience members at a lecture in Kyoto based on the chapter for their questions and suggestions.

For this reason too, write Simmons, Smith, and Schwartz (2018, 3), Anderson's work violated "virtually every tenet of how comparison should be executed." In his first explicitly comparative study, on the idea of power in Javanese culture, Anderson, they note, compared across different scales, regime types, and religious traditions. His comparisons were informal, uncontrolled, and at times empirically off the mark. Yet even scholars who point to errors in the particulars of his work find grounds for comparative engagement. His comparisons triumphed, as James Siegel (2003, 7) has put it, because they allowed a place for "unwonted and even unwanted thoughts" that expressed Anderson's felt need "to reflect Indonesia to an unspecified world."

This manner of comparing as discursive strategy, its reliance on congenital sagacity and serendipitous encounters, on an impulse to compare rather than a design with which to do so, might seem like an anathema to the methods classroom. "Brilliant insights," King, Keohane, and Verba (1994, 16) note acerbically, "can contribute to understanding by yielding interesting new hypotheses, but brilliance is not a method of empirical research." The methodologist has design and technique to offer, not idiosyncrasy or inspiration. But as Anderson demonstrated, good comparison – comparison that forces the inquirer to rethink what they thought they knew and reconsider old questions in new ways – is a matter of both design and inspiration, both technique and idiosyncrasy. It is not just about having an aptitude with certain instruments. It calls for some combination of instrumentation and strategy. So is this combination not method, after all? If so, what kind of method might it be? And what, if not the logic of control, might be the logic that holds it together?

I agree with Anderson that his was a discursive strategy for comparison. That is why in closing this chapter I address strategies for writing comparatively, not as a penultimate step in comparative inquiry, but as an integral part of it. In doing so, I point to the difference between writing *up*, after inquiry is done, and writing *out*, as it goes along. Nevertheless, with Pheng Cheah (2003) I also see the outline of a comparative method in Anderson's discursive strategy: not of *the* comparative method, but *a* method in the classical Latin sense of a way of proceeding. This is method as path, not technique, method as opening, not fetish. It is comparative method in this sense with which this chapter is concerned.

As with any method that defies stepwise how-to summation, this one is not easy to spell out. Here I make an attempt at doing so not by way of Anderson's oft-discussed inverted telescope (e.g., Harootunian 1999), but via the logic of what Anderson (1998, 31) once called "unbound seriality" to arrive at what I refer to as "unbound comparison."

Like other kinds of comparison, the logic of unbound comparison pushes toward inquiries into general features of human relations: the idea of the state, the moral economy of resistance, or the allures of nationalism. But instead of enumerating every case of something, or taking a representative sample of discrete units from a population of cases so as to make inferences about the relations between variables expressed in general terms, the inquirer working by the lights of this method seeks traits that capture the "paradigmatic style" of communities and practices (Cheah 2003, 5). They do not compare like with like. They do not look for replicas of political practices to classify and measure variation among. Instead, they follow resemblances across political topography in pursuit of a problematic category or politically salient idea: through trails of newsprint hot on the heels of nationalism (Anderson 1991, 1998), along the contours of a map in search of a "geo-body" (Thongchai 1994), up a hill following the footprints left by anarchists (Scott 2010). They draw together observations about the idea pursued that cut across different levels of analysis, compare different kinds of units, and rework analytical categories.

This logic of inquiry depends upon a locus for inquiry. The pursuit starts somewhere. The next section of this chapter explains why. It does so with reference to the tradition of area studies with which Anderson is associated, and with his locus: Southeast Asia. But its argument is not limited to any particular area, or area studies generally. Unbound comparison recommends itself to any student of politics who foregrounds locus in the design of their research and who, rather than imposing method on locus, is interested in thinking method through it. The student of politics working thusly treats the locus and logics of comparison as research partners, as intellectual companions, rather than privileging one over the other.

The subsequent section contrasts this type of comparison with bound comparison. It points to some differences between the two that call for different standards in the assessment of research quality. The section thereafter addresses the question of what unbound comparison does that bound comparison does not: namely, it translates political ideas and provincializes universals. The following one shows how writing out comparatively in this research practice is itself a method of comparison. That is to say, to write *out* research results is not to write about how comparison has been done. The writing itself evinces the logic of inquiry that is integral to unbound comparison. It *is* to compare.

While champions of controlled comparison have spoken of its "enduring indispensability" (Slater and Ziblatt 2013), what of unbound comparison? Might we speak of its enduring indispensability as well? The chapter closes with an answer to this question, in the negative.

A VIEW FROM SOMEWHERE

The textbook approach to comparative inquiry begins with the premise that "there are populations of cases (observations) 'out there' waiting for social scientific analysis" (Ragin 1992, 7). The inquirer is supposed to begin, consistent with old traditions in the philosophy of science, with a view from nowhere. They start not with a situated conception of what they want to study but by reconstructing concepts distant from as yet unidentified cases awaiting analysis (see Schaffer 2016). Categories like ethnicity and gender enter the inquiry ostensibly independent of any specific location. The research topic is divorced from research site. Theory is idealized and abstracted so that it is not polluted by value commitments that would introduce biases. Once the inquirer has justified their project and fashioned their ideas into a hypothesis, cases recommend themselves for analysis (see Soss, Chapter 5, this volume).

As everybody knows from daily experience, the view from nowhere does not anywhere exist. Every inquirer into social or political practices has a standpoint. The question is not whether or not one inhabits a certain locus, a specific time and place, but only whether or not one chooses to efface those daily experiences of ethnicity or gender or class or race or age or whatever when designing research. Those who decline to do so must adopt a locus of some sort. When they do, they depart from the textbook approach. At the outset, they have "a view from somewhere" (Emmerson 2014, 554; see also Hutt 2019), from which to work toward other places with vantage points for comparison. They do not privilege the particulars of their locus, but through them ask questions of the general. Sometimes they query the particular-general dichotomy. They toggle between the empirical and theoretical aspects of their work, as Joe Soss (2018; Chapter 5, this volume) has captured it, with an emphasis on locus added, in italics: casing a study *somewhere* rather than studying a case of *something*.

But wait. Is that the sound of Foucault's ghost chuckling once more at his prefatory remarks to *The Order of Things* (2002, xvi)? There Foucault laughed his way through a passage from Borges about a purported ancient Chinese taxonomy of creatures that are "divided into: (a) belonging to the Emperor, (b) embalmed, (c) tame, (d) sucking pigs, (e) sirens, (f) fabulous, (g) stray dogs, (h) included in the present classification, (i) frenzied, (j) innumerable, (k) drawn with a very fine camelhair brush, (l) et cetera." Foucault laughed because the taxonomy confronted him with the limits to his own way of thinking. He did not write it off as stupid or of no interest because of the incompatibility of its classes of creature or because sirens, like cat-dogs and Cartesian rational men, do not yet exist. He laughed because he could not himself think of a schema that classes stray dogs with sirens. There is no locus that can contain these types in stable relations with one another. His laughter was uneasy because the taxonomy has the form but lacks the criteria on which comparative scientific work depends. Comparison hinges on prior classification (see Kalleberg 1966). But the supposed Chinese taxonomy's prior classification prohibits rather than enables comparison. Even if the page can hold stray dogs and sirens in a sequence, no zoo can ever contain them (see Braverman 2013).

So when Foucault laughed, his laughter shattered familiar landmarks of thought with the idea that somewhere else in the world another culture "entirely devoted to the ordering of space" might "not distribute the multiplicity of existing things into any of the categories that make it possible for us to name, speak, and think" (2002, xxi). With that idea, Foucault felt the philosophical ground of *his* order of things begin to shift under his feet. It was not just that this taxonomy denies the possibility of comparing creatures in ancient China. It raises doubts that anyone can classify and compare anything anywhere.

Not long after Borges's Chinese taxonomy was making Foucault giddy, on the other side of the world Benedict Anderson had the experience of hearing then President Sukarno ventriloquizing Hitler at the University of Indonesia. "Come let us build a Third Kingdom," Anderson (1998, 2) quotes him as saying while adopting the Nazi leader's persona for rhetorical purposes: "And in this Third Reich, hey, sisters, you will live happily; hey, brothers, you will live happily; hey, kids, you will live happily; hey, you German patriots, you will see Germany sitting enthroned above all the peoples of the world." Like Foucault, Anderson had a feeling of vertigo. Listening to Sukarno channeling Hitler on the merits of the Third Reich as nationalist project, *his* Hitler seemed to be slipping away. But unlike Foucault, Anderson did not laugh and watch all the landmarks of thought collapse around him in a thunderclap. Instead he decided that he needed some other locus from which to make sense of this experience than that where he had hitherto stood.

Years later, he hit on the trope of the inverted telescope, which produces a kind of double vision that apprehends things "simultaneously close up and from afar" (Anderson 1998, 2). The observer reverses the telescope's direction to see things differently, but they still have a locus. Whereas for Foucault (2002, xviii), Borges "does away with the *site*, the mute ground upon which it is possible for entities to be juxtaposed," Anderson insists that there can and must be grounds for comparison: not to offer a refuge, a site of intellectual safety, but to have somewhere from which to strike out with sufficient confidence to observe phenomena from uncommon angles, and motion toward how many other ways of thinking about how to compare, and of what to compare, might exist.

This is what area studies invite their practitioners to do. Yet area studies have long struggled to persuade social scientific comparativists to take them seriously. The reasons are methodological and political. By some lights, area studies lack discipline with which to compare systematically. For decades, disciplinarians have held that area studies are unscientific. Though social scientists who double as area studies scholars have sought to show otherwise (e.g., Kuhonta, Slater, and Vu 2008; Huotari, Rüland, and Schlehe 2014), criticisms that area studies are insufficiently methodical and inadequately theoretical persist. Political scientists have been especially pugnacious. The gulf between their discipline and area studies, some say, is too great to bridge; the quality of the two, too disparate; the concerns of political science and area studies "fundamentally incommensurate" (Pepinsky 2014, 443). On this account, area studies have been bettered. Their defenders can try to erect barriers to protect inferior research against more efficient academic industries with "a higher standard of product" (Cribb 2006, 54), but in the imaginary marketplace for scholarly knowledge, sooner or later people will stop buying whatever they are peddling.

By other lights, area studies represent an out-dated mode of inquiry, one "increasingly tied to a schema of the world that no longer exists" (Walker and Sakai 2019, 20). Specialized accrual of knowledge about other places and advanced learning of languages will carry on no matter what, area studies' detractors say, but area as political geography or epistemic regime is already in its "afterlife" (Harootunian and Miyoshi 2002). If it was once a useful fiction to aid in creating and organizing knowledge, they say, it is now merely fiction: an empty signifier of places that do not exist.

This chapter does not offer a broad defense of area studies against their critics. That is not its remit. Others have done and will continue to do that (e.g., Szanton 2004; Hornidge and Mielke 2017; Jackson 2019). Instead it takes the criticism of area, or of locus that precedes method, as provocation. Notwithstanding the propensity of critics to sometimes push reasonable points too far, which might speak more loudly to their own insecurities than those of their targets, the questions that they provoke include the following: what is the comparative advantage of finding method in locus, instead of the other way around? And what lessons does Anderson's work offer for students of comparative politics interested in locating their logics of inquiry in loci, rather than put the one before the other? The next section addresses these questions.

COMPARISON BOUND AND UNBOUND

In his essay on the logic of seriality in *The Spectre of Comparisons* (1998), Anderson opposes two types of seriality, one unbound, the other bound. The unbound type he derives from an argument in *Imagined Communities* (1991) about how nationalist ideas spread through the early print media. He argues that serialization allowed for political ideas to have contact with a diverse range of conditions, and to change through it. Newspapers developed a standardized vocabulary for communicating about a range of events occurring worldwide. They came to agree on shared ways for asserting knowledge of events and interpreted facts via categorical series of "quotidian universals" (Anderson 1998, 33).

Through this unbound seriality, nationalists communicated on terms that were intelligible to one another but also sensitive to the peculiarities of the conditions in which each was working. They could articulate their identities intelligibly without adopting a template for what a national identity should look like. This was nationalism's communicative genius. Unbound, the series through which it traveled was pedagogic, but not didactic. Its success depended on its malleability. It set out primary terms on which people made and disputed political appeals but left the details up to them. Of course, many of these terms emerged from colonial state-making projects. It could not have been otherwise. Nationalists were responding to those projects, appropriating, adapting, or rejecting their vernaculars. But this did not make nationalists unwitting replicators of hegemonic ideas. Unbound, the imagination of anticolonial nationalists gave colonial ideas different character and significance, which took them well beyond the boundaries that colonial states had set for them.

Those boundaries had been set through the logic of bound seriality. Anderson associates that type of seriality with the census. It rests on knowledge claims that encompass the entirety of a population, on the idea that each member of the population is an anonymous unit, and on the integrity of each of the bodies of the persons included as "one" unit of some*thing*. Bound seriality is pedagogic and didactic. It instructs its subjects to think of themselves as having a standard set of attributes on which variation can be documented and reported in relation to others (such as age, sex, religion, occupation, income, ethnicity). It reprimands and sometimes punishes those who resist being classed according to its terms: people who confound the rules for classification and comparison by gender or race, for instance.

To recap, both unbound and bound seriality are concerned with an ability to communicate – with the idea of making knowledge claims and assessing those of others according to shared standards. Both are concerned with series that assign names to organize different ideas and enable diverse things to be classed so as to resemble one another. Both rest on comparative logics. Both deploy "a certain power of the imagination that renders apparent what is not" (Foucault 2002, 80), but how they deploy that power and how through it they reveal continuities differ. The practitioner of bound seriality sorts things out, as in the textbook approach to comparison, prior to collecting and assessing data. Method precedes and dictates locus because knowledge claims are like springs that press on method heavily. Ease up on method and the springs will fly out. The person working by the logic of unbound seriality, on the other hand, finds grounds for comparison in dialogue with others, out of choice or necessity. They locate shared understandings and agreed-upon terms for the manner of communicating, about what, and why. Loci anticipate and recommend methods because knowledge claims are loosely wound. As long as they are firmly located, they hold in place.

Both unbound and bound seriality have within them comparative logics, but because their logical criteria are unalike, their standards for the conduct and quality of comparative research diverge. The same goes for bound and unbound comparison. Bound comparison calls for "commonly accepted methodological norms for the conduct of research" toward the goal of descriptive and causal inference (Seawright and Collier 2010, 349). The assumption that valid comparison of mutually exclusive and exhaustive categories across all known cases of some phenomenon is possible rests on these norms. Absent these, bound comparison's knowledge claims cannot stand. Therefore, bound comparison seeks to fix its categories and establish conventions for doing so:

to make rules and train its practitioners to follow them. It functions as a kind of infrastructure into which the inquirer inserts and organizes data with which to compare.

This is not the case for unbound comparison. It also calls for agreement about the standards by which quality in comparative work is assessed, but its results do not rise or fall on the terms set by methodological norms. The logic of unbound comparison pushes categories across different levels of analysis and into empirical domains that call for methodological adaptation. Its practitioner does not presume to know what all the possible relevant cases of a phenomenon for comparison are. It would be counterproductive for them to adopt a research design that would delimit their comparisons in the manner of the bound comparativist.

The steps that unbound comparison takes are not linear, proceeding from the particular to the general, from the concrete to the abstract, in the manner of their bound other. But neither are they willy-nilly. Unbound, comparison does not run all over the place. It is not controlled, but it is not out of control. Chains of ideas and practices lead in some places and not others. The inquirer is alert to branches in the paths they are following, and to telltale signs of salient activity that might take them to the left or the right, higher up or lower down. They have to make choices about which to follow and which to bypass. Many of these they cannot anticipate or plan for, and neither should they try to. They have to prepare as best as they can and make these choices as they go along.

By way of an example, Tyrell Haberkorn (2018) wrote a history of state violence in Thailand to get at the problem of impunity. Contra portrayals of impunity that cast it as an epiphenomenon of state practice that correlates with politically repressive regime types, Haberkorn theorizes it as integral to state formation, analogous to Nicholas Rush Smith's (2019) theorizing of the relation between vigilantism and democratic state formation in South Africa, and allusive to Charles Tilly's (1985) thesis on war making and state making as organized crime. Haberkorn shows how impunity as a category of practice is complicit in the making and remaking of the state. She compares impunity events over time: instances of state violence accompanied by administrative and juridical arrangements for non-accountability. To do so, she did not randomly select from among all the impunity events in Thailand and come up with a representative sample on which to test causal propositions. Instead of locating specific causes of significant outcomes on general variables, she selected specific cases to show the variety of ways whereby the state constitutes and reconstitutes itself through acts of violence, coupled with official interpretations and reinterpretations of those acts and their consequences.

Like Anderson, Haberkorn compares events that relate to different kinds of violence, on different scales, in different periods of time, under different regime types, and at the hands of a variety of state officers and their affiliates. She starts with locus and works toward general categories – impunity, political violence, the state – not to end with them, but then to move back to locus, going to new points of inquiry in the history and territory of Thailand: southern villages circa 1975 where paramilitaries burned alleged communists to death in oil drums; the commercial district of Bangkok where in 2010 soldiers shot dead anti-government protesters; the recurrent behind-closed-doors scenes of bureaucrats discussing how to make impunity possible. In this way she makes inferences about how particular practices of violence in discrete times and places *constitute* the state. Rather than testing a hypothesis to infer causal relationships with which to predict outcomes, her work evinces a desire to articulate what impunity is made of, and in so doing, what the state is.

Unbound comparison is suited to research projects that aim for these kinds of results: constitutive rather than causal, plausible rather than definitive, interpretive rather than positive – projects whose types and typologies do not fall onto research subjects from nowhere but emerge out of somewhere, so as to arrive at contingent generalizations. Area studies are full of projects like these. Their shortcoming, according to authoritative standards for evaluating quality, is that their results do not meet criteria for external validity. And yet, they do travel. Haberkorn casts doubt on a dominant narrative that posits that worldwide impunity is in decline, measured through a trend toward holding political leaders criminally accountable for violations of human rights (Sikkink 2011). Thailand along with most of Asia empirically contradicts this trend. Haberkorn invites her reader to ask whether or not Asia is anomalous, and if so, why. More profoundly, she invites them to rethink the category of impunity and its relation to state formation – to ask whether impunity might not be a different phenomenon in practice from how it is generally conceptualized and if so with what implications (see Cheesman 2019).

This, then, is a tale of two cultures – and of two sets of standards for assessment of quality. Bound comparison aspires to external validity; unbound comparison does not. Nevertheless, it can contribute to larger debates about political phenomena, and it can reach wide audiences. But it needs to be assessed by some other standard or standards than those that conventionally apply. Like what? One alternative standard that recommends itself is trustworthiness (see Yanow and Schwartz-Shea 2012). Unlike reliability or validity, both of which inhere to the research results, trustworthiness is relational: it calls for the reader to take a position in relation to the authored work and to the author. The question is not just whether or not the reader trusts the contents of the work they read. It is also whether or not they trust the author who has written it. Has the author earned their trust? If so, what have they done to earn it?

Haberkorn earns trust through her demonstrated knowledge of the country in which she did her work, and of the constellation of sites there that delivered up evidence that contributed to her results: archival, ethnographic, literary. She earns trust because she shows that she has the trust of the people with whom she works when she does research, much of it painstaking, some of it risky.

She earns trust because of her demonstrated attention to ethics beyond, and perhaps sometimes in defiance of, the standards set by institutional review boards. She also earns trust not through the pretense of objectivity or disinterest in her research site but through the opposite: by acknowledging the political commitments she brings with her to her project, and by examining the implications of these. And she earns trust by spelling out the research procedures, opportunities, and limitations of her inquiries, as well as by acknowledging uncertainties, and certain discomforts, about her results – by having, that is, a respect and "tolerance for ambiguity" that was once characteristic of a classical pragmatist intellectual sensibility in social science (Krygier 2012, 190), as it was of Anderson's work.

WHAT UNBOUND COMPARISON DOES

Unbound comparison does two things that bound comparison does not. First, it translates political ideas; second, and relatedly, it provincializes universals. Both are intellectually and politically important. Intellectually, they invite ways of comparing politics that might not otherwise be possible. Politically, they encourage ways of managing and distributing knowledge that are not insular.

Comparative politics today has little time for translation. Apparently, the comparison of politics does not call for knowledge about contests over meanings of political ideas like good governance and democracy. Observation of phenomena that serve as indicators for good governance or democracy does not require comparativists to know how these terms resonate in different times and places. It suffices for them to tinker with those categories already available to them, acquired from training and inherited by upbringing. They leave it to others to argue about things like divergent meanings of freedom in Myanmar (Wells 2018) or the informalities of authority in Thailand (Tamada 1991).

This is unfortunate, and puzzling. Obviously, political ideas do matter. Yet, when social scientists reconstruct political concepts from their own personal and academic worlds and plonk them down upon the worlds of their research subjects, they close off routes for inquiry into how ideas in the places they study animate political actions. This is not to imply that a comparative study of, say, populist politics that restricts its inquiry to material conditions of inequality, to state revenue and its redistribution, would be unprofitable. But it would certainly be insufficient to account for the causes and constitution of populist upsurges, whose logic is expressed through what Katherine Cramer (2016) has labeled, in her study of rural consciousness in pre-Trump Wisconsin, the politics of resentment.

As Cramer shows, populism is constituted both through material conditions and through how people experience and react to these conditions. To make sense of the latter calls for translation, which brings us back to Thailand. One way that resentment at the repeated removal of elected governments through military and judicial coup in Thailand came to be expressed in the 2000s and 2010s was by reference to *song māttrathān* or "double standards" (see Streckfuss 2012); one set of standards that apply for *'ammāt*, loosely, aristocrats – military, bureaucratic, judicial, and political officialdom affiliated with the monarchy – and the other to *phrai*, commoners or, more exactly, serfs (see Sopranzetti 2017). Any comparative study of populism in Thailand around 2010 would have to work through how via an old vocabulary "a new grammar of representation came into being" (Anderson 1998, 34) and did so to evoke the idea of aspiring engaged citizens dragged down by an antiquated political order and, arguably, to signal the rise of a new class "present at its own making" (Thompson 1966, 9).

This is not to overstate the part that translation can play in comparing populism here with populism there, our politics with theirs. To observe that opponents of elite-pact politics in the 2000s and 2010s wore t-shirts proclaiming themselves *phrai* is no more sufficient to explain populism in Thailand than a materialist account. The point is not to suggest that it would be. It is only to insist that study of populism, whether in the American Midwest or in northeastern Thailand, must take into account both the material conditions that give it impetus and the ideas that give it force. Unbound comparison makes this kind of study possible. It opens up avenues along which to travel so as to connect particulars to generalities, to establish equality but not sameness. Ideas about social hierarchy captured in terms like *'ammāt* and *phrai* are not the same as those that inhere to ideas about class in England or caste in India, for instance, but they are sensible approximations for expressions of collective privilege versus collective disadvantage, recognizable as historical and sociological phenomena comparable to other types and subtypes. The practitioner of unbound comparison is attentive to these approximations: tracking ideas about human relations, and their consequences, from locus and back again, keeping enough space between specificity and generality to ascertain both simultaneously.

Another way of putting this is to say that whereas bound comparison, whose validity depends on the congruence of definition and measure, hinges on one-for-one correspondence, unbound comparison zigzags between political ideas and practices that may seem rather different and unrelated but that on closer inquiry reveal points of similarity and contact. This is why to be taken up with the study of language in the political world of others is not just for language's sake. Nor is it an esoteric search for secret codes with which to unlock so-called native ways of seeing and thinking. Rather, it is to ask how language is translatable for wider social scientific inquiry, and how attention to it expands and deepens political vocabulary generally.

It is also why, against claims that area studies are nothing other than handmaidens of imperial projects old and new, area studies' comparative logic has a counter-imperialist potential. Without a willingness to address the possibilities and impossibilities of translation, universals can but, as Judith

Butler (2000) has pointed out, cross borders through colonial and expansionist logics – today, as they did historically. An all-too-easy rejoinder to this observation is that translation also can be complicit with the logic of colonial expansion, either by extracting knowledge from vernacular sources or as an instrument through which to transfer dominant values. Yes, it can be. But that is not the kind of translation that unbound comparison calls for. Its method of translation opposes translation for colonial domination, and with it the "imperialism of categories" (Rudolph 2005).

To expand on the point: unbound translation is not like an official announcement with no right of a reply. It is like a personal letter, with expectation of an answer. It is translation *as* correspondence, not *for* it. It is reiterative, not linear. In English, it is not so easy to think of translation this way. The Latin preposition, *trans-*, from one to the other, conveys the idea of border crossing between that language over there and this one over here – or rather, from here (English) to there (every other language). In Burmese, on the other hand, the word for translation is *bathapyan,* where the suffix *-pyan* connotes the repeating or rebounding of something: in this case, language, *batha* (from the Pali, *bhasa*). Translation as *bathapyan* invites counter-imperial possibilities, since the idea that repeats or rebounds in another language is not a duplicate, but one that refers back to its other, opening the way to return to and rethink it. It is translation not as colonization but as social relation, not imposed on others but moving alongside them.

None of this is to say that there cannot be unintended consequences of translation, any more or less than anything else worth doing. But it is to say that the logic of unbound comparison calls for effort to translate against the disinclination of Anglophone social science, political science especially, to hear any idiom other than its own, to hew to the position that nobody else is capable "of uttering the universal" (Mbembe 2001, 4). If a social scientific community thinks it unnecessary to translate, then it can only be because its members share a belief that social and political phenomena are all already "comprehensible, knowable and familiar" (Sakai 2006, 73). This is a narcissistic belief, and a demonstrably false one, but also one that the community of believers has to insist upon so as to maintain a belligerent monolingualism.

Happily, narcissism, like monolingualism, is curable. If an antidote to the latter is to listen up, then an antidote to the former is, as Martin Krygier (2005, 24) has put it, "to look around." Anderson did look around, always on guard against his own prejudices and alert to those of his interlocutors. For all that, he still received criticism for giving too much credence to the expansionist logics of his subject, nationalism, and too little to the anticolonial imagination (see Chatterjee 1993). Was his logic of comparison inflected by bias toward the same kinds of imperialist tendencies that unbound comparison, on this account, works against?

In his essay on seriality, Anderson explains why not. As the essay winds from a Muslim communist speechmaker in central Java to the Hungarian Soviet

Republic and back again, Anderson shows how colonial Dutch, Malay, and Javanese words and worlds interpenetrated. The Javanese nationalists took "this world of mankind" (Anderson 1998, 33, quoting Pramoedya Ananta Toer), or more exactly, to keep the ground under our feet, this earth of humankind, in the classical Pali sense of *bumi manusia*, as their domain "no matter how partially they read it." They standardized vocabulary not to render monarchs or administrators or revolutions the same, but to render them comparable along categorical series. When a monarch or king was rendered *radja*, equality, not sameness, was established. With it, the possibility arose "of extracting an infinite number of distinctions between the two" (Sakai 2006, 76).

Unbound comparison opens up this relationship of equality and distinctiveness through attention to language. It has the goal, after Dipesh Chakrabarty (2008; see also Mitchell 2004), of "provincializing" universal ideas: of resituating them to determine how and in what sense they emerge from particular traditions and travel to others, and how they are reshaped by encounters as they go. To provincialize is to dwell in the tensions and contradictions between the norms of one place and those of another. It is to recognize that the political is everywhere constituted through language. It is to shift epistemic dependence from academic circles of esteem onto the people whose activities are the subjects of social scientific inquiry: to treat them as sources of ideas rather than fonts of data.

Provincializing comparison is not against universals like democracy or good governance or the rule of law. It does seek to expose their conceits; the arrogance with which they impose themselves upon others; and the arrogance of claims to have the scientific tools with which to aggregate, measure, evaluate, and produce knowledge about the relation between universals and their universe of cases through bound logics (see Rajah 2014; Merry, Davis, and Kingsbury 2015). At the same time, it resists the contrary urge to relativize ideas to the point that they cease to be meaningful. The rule of law, for instance, must have something to do with the ability of members of a political community to temper arbitrary state power. Take that away from it and it is not just a variant of the rule of law; it ceases to be the same idea at all. Yet how this core of the rule of law is expressed in practice is contingent. Rule of law–like appeals instantiate themselves in different ways, depending on how power is understood and exercised. *Song māttrathān* captures something of the rule of law idea, even if it does not invoke it. It would be wrong to infer from that usage that taxi drivers speeding around Bangkok or street vendors crisscrossing Chiang Mai are incipient Lockeans. But inasmuch as they locate their grievances in arbitrary power secured by wealth and class privileges, they appeal to rule of law–type values that are comparable to political appeals for the rule of law elsewhere. And that suggests that the politics of resentment in Thailand might be similar to their variants in the United States after all.

WRITING OUT, COMPARATIVELY SPEAKING

In his *Social Science Methodology*, John Gerring begins an appended note on style almost apologetically, remarking that although style is not strictly methodological, "it is nonetheless difficult to separate the desiderata of good writing from the desiderata of good argumentation" (2012, 402). His criterion for good writing and argumentation in social science is intelligibility. This is an excellent criterion. Anderson's prose exemplifies it, which is one reason why he reached a wide audience. His writing arrests readers. It pulls them in, taking them on a journey throughout which he motions to the possibilities for comparison and then leads them out again, to revisit their own locus and see it anew. Anderson expands and contracts time so as to compress subject matter or tease it apart. He conjoins observations one after the next, making slender series of links, returning here and there to strengthen one or another connection. It is not just that he is comparing. His writing strategy forces readers to think along with him comparatively, without making them fully aware of how he is doing it, or that they are doing it with him.

Writing comparatively as discursive strategy is not a discrete stage in the research sequence that follows data generation and analysis – conventionally, *writing up* the results of inquiry. Writing up is what the laboratory scientist does. It is not what a comparativist working from a locus does. Against the way of thinking about writing as something that goes on after other work is done, writing comparatively as discursive strategy is about enabling comparisons through writing itself. It is not only about making text more lucid, though lucidity is among its virtues. It is not writing up, but writing *out*: writing as method of inquiry (see Richardson and St. Pierre 2005).

And so this chapter concludes in agreement with Gerring on his criterion of intelligibility. But it does so through a stronger commitment to writing, not merely as a vehicle for effective communication but also as a practice that is immanent to good comparison. This commitment enfolds with the merits of an emphasis on language in unbound comparison, and on the innumerable possible ways of thinking about political phenomena comparatively. It is not just that language skills open up many more opportunities to generate data than would otherwise be the case. It is also that regard for language presents opportunities to think differently about political ideas and practices and, thereby, to write differently about the political world.

To take a leaf once more from the Burmese dictionary, which has many evocative terms for political ideas that pulsate with meanings different from their English equivalents, consider how the English noun *administration* or the verb *to administer*, which originates in French and Anglo-Norman words conveying an idea of looking after something, translates. The corresponding Burmese *ôkchôk* connotes restraint or confinement: the act of lunging at something and binding it in place. If administration in Burmese is proverbially the work of kings, *ôkchôk min lôk*, then it does not invoke an image of a Hobbesian sovereign looming over the commonwealth with sword and crozier, or alternately of Tilly's (1985) nefarious protection racketeer, but of a somewhat malevolent minor deity pouncing upon and holding down what it thinks is rightfully its. This notion of administration chimes with the history of an area from where people have for centuries literally taken to the hills or fled to other polities to avoid onerous state demands on their assets and labor.

Another merit of writing out comparatively is that it puts the writer on guard against parochial figures of speech that inhabit social scientific texts published in English. A political scientist in Michigan or Uppsala can look out the window and write about snowball sampling without common sense leaving the room. If they do so in Mindanao or Oddar Meanchey, then they are being inattentive – both to the weather and to a more sensible and more applicable metaphor for the same method, namely, chain sampling. Similarly, pork barreling is an appropriate coinage for most of the Philippines, where *lechon* is a delicacy and the politics of pork are among late colonialism's enduring American legacies, but not for predominantly Muslim Malaysia, notwithstanding that the kinds of expenditure on political projects that the term denotes occur there too.

The choice of which foods or seasons to compare metaphorically might seem like a trivial point to make, a small issue to sort out at the end of a research project. It is not. This is not simply a matter of how to write more interesting prose and make less jarring comparisons, though these are good reasons to write research out well. Neither is it merely another way of saying that a well-chosen metaphor can invite new ways of thinking about what to compare and how, by offering a different perspective on things, though this is one excellent reason to select and use metaphors carefully (see Schaffer 2018). Metaphors are the basis for humans' conceptual systems of thought (see Lakoff and Johnson 2003). They are bound up in how people observe and experience the world. Like research projects, they do not come from nowhere. They all have loci. The choice is not whether or not to be somewhere metaphorically, but whether to be somewhere metaphorically that is more or less expansive or not, more or less inclusive or not, more or less fitting than somewhere else or not.

When social scientific writing in English typically uses imagery that can but come from a handful of areas in the world, which are often not the areas toward which the writing is directed at all, it turns the reader's gaze away from research site and toward the author. Research that finds the proof of something by eating a pudding or even just compares apples with oranges, rather than mangoes with cashew nuts, betrays a selection bias toward metaphors that inhabit some areas of the world, some cultures, and not others. One or two such metaphors dropped into a book chapter or term paper won't make much difference. But if writing is littered with misplaced or inapt metaphors, then the cumulative effect is to obstruct the path to good comparison. The better suited that metaphors are to a research project, the more systematic and coherent the project will be. And the best guarantee that metaphors will be well suited to

Unbound Comparison

a project is to write things out, to find metaphor in locus, rather than scratch around for figures of speech when writing up.

Lastly, to write for unbound comparison is not to write against parsimony. Unbound comparative writing is not an invitation to run from one subject to the next. To the contrary, it calls for parsimonious statements of problems and hypotheses, even if in addressing them the author may prefer to write "toward difficulty rather than simplification" (Steedly 2013, 69). To write toward difficulty is not to be verbose. Again, take Anderson's *Imagined Communities*. This is a book that makes things hard for its readers. Yet its thesis is captured in a single paragraph that can be summarized as follows: nationality and nationalism are historically specific, modular cultural artifacts that adapt to variegated political and ideological circumstances so as to arouse deep attachments (Anderson 1991, 4). The other 200-or-so pages in the book turn on this point. James Scott's pithy account of his project to place the subsistence ethic "at the center of the analysis of peasant politics" in *The Moral Economy of the Peasant* (1976, 3) does a similar kind of work. So does Barbara Andaya's repositioning of Southeast Asian women in the closing pages of *The Flaming Womb* (2006).

None of these books follows recognizable, narrow paths of comparison, working from concepts to hypotheses, hypotheses to cases, cases to results, results to conclusions; yet, all of them are exemplary in their author's ability to illuminate and explore ideas. Nevertheless, their manner of writing is toward amplitude rather than brevity. Where the terms of debate cannot be taken for granted, sometimes they have to be spelled out. And when so much of this earth of humankind is in a hurry to find the familiar in the strange, sometimes readers have to be forced to slow down and compare gradually, but surely.

CONCLUSION

If Foucault's laughter at Borges's fable shattered all those landmarks of thought that allow us to compare, then Anderson's troubled musings at *el demonio de las comparaciones* (at Anderson 2005, 32, ironically, by his own admission mistranslated as the "spectre of comparisons") do the opposite. They reassemble landscapes by forcing us to think about the other possibilities for comparison that might exist, beyond those that the social sciences conventionally designate. Wonderment at these possibilities makes a locus for comparison worth finding, and unbound comparison worth doing.

As to the question of the dispensability or indispensability of this method or that, whether or not a case for the enduring indispensability of controlled comparison can be made, I do not think any such claim should be made for its unbound other. To insist on the indispensability of a method is to do what the logic of unbound comparison resists: to insist that *this* method is necessary and to imply that *those* are not. Unbound, comparison is neither indispensable nor dispensable. And while more could be said of that, I prefer to conclude by advocating not for its enduring dispensability but for its enduring *desirability*.

Unbound comparison is a method that is freighted with desire: with a yearning for some comparative ground on which to stand, a ledge onto which to crawl and look around, a locus imbricated with comparison's logics. It is also a desirable method, because social inquiry benefits from the kinds of perspectives and juxtapositions that it can provide. And it is desirable because while a locus might not be stable ground, unlike the proverbial Thai buffalo that thinks so highly of itself as to forget that it is standing in mud, the student of politics who adopts a locus does not lose sight of where their legs are planted.

Seeking out some ground upon which to stand before deciding how to proceed is not a foolish idea. Of course, it is always possible to do something foolish once there, wherever that is. The social sciences and area studies are replete with examples of how not to go about comparing things. None has a monopoly on screwing things up. They are, like all human endeavors, only as good as their exponents. But if the social sciences have training in controlled comparison to offer, then unbound comparison recommends itself because its alternative logics invite other ways of inquiring, and of rethinking how to compare and why.

Would social science be better off without comparative methods that adopt logics other than those associated with *the* comparative method? I think not. Those disciplinarians who long for the day of methodological unity, without rule breakers and iconoclasts like Benedict Anderson, should be careful of what they wish for. Inhabited exclusively by methodologists and their ilk, this earth of human inquiry would not only be a comparatively bleak place but also a comparatively impoverished one – a place whose inhabitants might not notice if the ground is moving beneath them after all, or if their feet are made of clay.

REFERENCES

Aguilar, Filomeno, Caroline Hau, Vincente Rafael, and Teresa Tadem. 2011. "Benedict Anderson, Comparatively Speaking: On Area Studies, Theory, and 'Gentlemanly' Polemics." *Philippine Studies* 59 (1): 107–39.

Andaya, Barbara Watson. 2006. *The Flaming Womb: Repositioning Women in Early Modern Southeast Asia*. Honolulu: University of Hawai'i Press.

Anderson, Benedict. 1991. *Imagined Communities: Reflections on the Origin and Spread of Nationalism*, 2nd edn. London: Verso.

  1998. *The Spectre of Comparisons: Nationalism, Southeast Asia, and the World*. London: Verso.

  2005. *Under Three Flags: Anarchism and the Anti-Colonial Imagination*. London: Verso.

  2018. *A Life Beyond Boundaries*. London: Verso.

Braverman, Lisa. 2013. *Zooland: The Institution of Captivity*. Stanford, CA: Stanford University Press.

Butler, Judith. 2000. "Restaging the Universal: Hegemony and the Limits of Formalism." In *Contingency, Hegemony, Universality: Contemporary Dialogues on the Left*, edited by Judith Butler, Ernesto Laclau, and Slavoj Žižek, 11–43. London: Verso.

Chakrabarty, Dipesh. 2008. *Provincializing Europe: Postcolonial Thought and Historical Difference*. Princeton, NJ: Princeton University Press. Orig. edn., 2000.

Chatterjee, Partha. 1993. *The Nation and Its Fragments: Colonial and Postcolonial Histories*. Princeton, NJ: Princeton University Press.

Cheah, Pheng. 2003. "Grounds of Comparison." In *Grounds of Comparison: Around the Work of Benedict Anderson*, edited by Pheng Cheah and Jonathan Culler, 1–20. New York: Routledge.

Cheesman, Nick. 2019. "Routine Impunity as Practice (in Myanmar)." *Human Rights Quarterly* 41 (4): 873–92.

Cramer, Katherine J. 2016. *The Politics of Resentment: Rural Consciousness in Wisconsin and the Rise of Scott Walker*. Chicago: University of Chicago Press.

Cribb, Robert. 2006. "Region, Academic Dynamics, and Promise of Comparativism: Beyond Studying 'Southeast Asia'?" In *Southeast Asian Studies: Debates and New Directions*, edited by Cynthia Chou and Vincent Houben, 45–64. Singapore & Leiden: Institute of Southeast Asian Studies & International Institute for Asian Studies.

Emmerson, Donald K. 2014. "The Spectrum of Comparisons: A Discussion." *Pacific Affairs* 87 (3): 539–56.

Foucault, Michel. 2002. *The Order of Things: An Archaeology of the Human Sciences*. London & New York: Routledge. Orig. edn., 1970.

Gerring, John. 2012. *Social Science Methodology: A Unified Framework*, 2nd edn. New York: Cambridge University Press.

Haberkorn, Tyrell. 2018. *In Plain Sight: Impunity and Human Rights in Thailand*. Madison: University of Wisconsin Press.

Harootunian, Harry. 1999. "Ghostly Comparisons: Anderson's Telescope." *Diacritics* 29 (4): 135–49.

Harootunian, Harry, and Masao Miyoshi. 2002. "Introduction: The 'Afterlife' of Area Studies." In *Learning Places: The Afterlives of Area Studies*, edited by Masao Miyoshi and Harry Harootunian, 1–18. Durham, NC: Duke University Press.

Hornidge, Anna-Katharina, and Katja Mielke. 2017. "Concluding Reflections: The Art of Science Policy for 21st Century Area Studies." In *Area Studies at the Crossroads: Knowledge Production after the Mobility Turn*, edited by Katja Mielke and Anna-Katharina Hornidge, 327–44. New York: Palgrave Macmillan.

Huotari, Mikko, Jürgen Rüland, and Judith Schlehe, eds. 2014. *Methodology and Research Practice in Southeast Asian Studies*. Basingstoke, UK: Palgrave Macmillan.

Hutt, Michael. 2019. "Area Studies and the Importance of 'Somewheres.'" *South East Asia Research* 27 (1): 21–25.

Jackson, Peter A. 2019. "South East Asian Area Studies Beyond Anglo-America: Geopolitical Transitions, the Neoliberal Academy and Spatialized Regimes of Knowledge." *South East Asia Research* 27 (1): 49–73.

Kalleberg, Arthur L. 1966. "The Logic of Comparison: A Methodological Note on the Comparative Study of Political Systems." *World Politics* 19 (1): 69–82.

King, Gary, Robert Keohane, and Sidney Verba. 1994. *Designing Social Inquiry: Scientific Inference in Qualitative Research.* Princeton, NJ: Princeton University Press.

Krygier, Martin. 2005. *Civil Passions: Selected Writings.* Melbourne: Black Inc.

  2012. *Philip Selznick: Ideals in the World.* Stanford, CA: Stanford University Press.

Kuhonta, Erik Martinez, Dan Slater, and Tuong Vu. 2008. "Introduction: The Contributions of Southeast Asian Political Studies." In *Southeast Asia in Political Science: Theory, Region, and Quantitative Analysis*, edited by Erik Martinez Kuhonta, Dan Slater and Tuong Vu, 1–29. Stanford, CA: Stanford University Press.

Lakoff, George, and Mark Johnson. 2003. *Metaphors We Live By.* Chicago: University of Chicago Press.

Mbembe, Achille. 2001. *On the Postcolony.* Berkeley: University of California Press.

Merry, Sally Engle, Kevin E. Davis, and Benedict Kingsbury, eds. 2015. *The Quiet Power of Indicators: Measuring Governance, Corruption, and Rule of Law.* New York: Cambridge University Press.

Mill, John Stuart. 1882. *A System of Logic: Ratiocinative and Inductive*, 8th edn. New York: Harper & Brothers. Orig. edn., 1843.

Mitchell, Timothy. 2004. "The Middle East in the Past and Future of Social Science." In *The Politics of Knowledge: Area Studies and the Disciplines*, edited by David L. Szanton, 74–118. Berkeley: University of California Press.

Pepinsky, Thomas B. 2014. "Context and Method in Southeast Asian Politics." *Pacific Affairs* 87 (3): 441–61.

Ragin, Charles C. 1992. "Introduction: Cases of 'What Is a Case?'." In *What Is a Case? Exploring the Foundations of Social Inquiry*, edited by Charles C. Ragin and Howard Saul Becker, 1–17. New York: Cambridge University Press.

  The Comparative Method: Moving Beyond Qualitative and Quantitative Strategies. Oakland: University of California Press. Orig. edn., 1987. Rpt., 2014.

Rajah, Jothie. 2014. "'Rule of Law' as Transnational Legal Order." In *Transnational Legal Orders*, edited by Terence C. Halliday and Gregory Shaffer, 340–73. New York: Cambridge University Press.

Richardson, Laurel, and Elizabeth Adams St Pierre. 2005. "Writing: A Method of Inquiry." In *The Sage Handbook of Qualitative Research*, edited by Norman K. Denzin and Yvonna S. Lincoln, 959–78. Thousand Oaks, CA: Sage.

Rudolph, Susanne Hoeber. 2005. "The Imperialism of Categories: Situating Knowledge in a Globalizing World." *Perspectives on Politics* 3 (1): 5–14.

Sakai, Naoki. 2006. "Translation." *Theory, Culture & Society* 23 (2–3): 71–86.

Schaffer, Frederic Charles. 2016. *Elucidating Social Science Concepts: An Interpretivist Guide.* New York: Routledge.

  2018. "Two Ways to Compare." *Qualitative and Multi-Method Research* 16 (1): 15–19.

Scott, James C. 1976. *The Moral Economy of the Peasant: Rebellion and Subsistence in Southeast Asia.* New Haven, CT: Yale University Press.

  2010. *The Art of Not Being Governed: An Anarchist History of Upland Southeast Asia.* Singapore: NUS Press. Orig. edn., 2009.

Seawright, Jason, and David Collier. 2010. "Glossary." In *Rethinking Social Inquiry: Diverse Tools, Shared Standards*, edited by Henry E. Brady and David Collier, 313–60. Lanham, MD: Rowman & Littlefield.

Siegel, James T. 2003. "Introduction." In *Southeast Asia Over Three Generations: Essays Presented to Benedict R. O'G Anderson*, edited by James T. Siegel and Audrey R. Kahin, 7–9. Ithaca, NY: Cornell University Press.

Sikkink, Kathryn. 2011. *The Justice Cascade: How Human Rights Prosecutions Are Changing World Politics*. New York: W. W. Norton.

Simmons, Erica S., Nicholas Rush Smith, and Rachel A. Schwartz. 2018. "Rethinking Comparison." *Qualitative and Multi-Method Research* 16 (1): 1–7.

Slater, Dan, and Daniel Ziblatt. 2013. "The Enduring Indispensability of the Controlled Comparison." *Comparative Political Studies* 46 (10): 1301–27.

Smith, Nicholas Rush. 2019. *Contradictions of Democracy: Vigilantism and Rights in Post-Apartheid South Africa*. Oxford: Oxford University Press.

Sopranzetti, Claudio. 2017. *Owners of the Map: Motorcycle Taxi Drivers, Mobility, and Politics in Bangkok*. Berkeley: University of California Press.

Soss, Joe. 2018. "On Casing a Study versus Studying a Case." *Qualitative and Multi-Method Research* 16 (1): 21–27.

Steedly, Mary Margaret. 2013. *Rifle Reports: A Story of Indonesian Independence*. Berkeley: University of California Press.

Streckfuss, David. 2012. "The Strategy of the United Front for Democracy Against Dictatorship on 'Double Standards': A Grand Gesture to History, Justice, and Accountability." In *Bangkok, May 2010: Perspectives on a Divided Thailand*, edited by Michael Montesano, 274–86. Singapore: ISEAS.

Szanton, David L., ed. 2004. *The Politics of Knowledge: Area Studies and the Disciplines*. Berkeley: University of California Press.

Tamada, Yoshifumi. 1991. "*Ittiphon* and *Amnat*: An Informal Aspect of Thai Politics." *Southeast Asian Studies* 28 (4): 455–66.

Thompson, E. P. 1966. *The Making of the English Working Class*. New York: Vintage.

Thongchai, Winichakul. 1994. *Siam Mapped: A History of the Geo-Body of a Nation*. Honolulu: University of Hawai'i Press.

Tilly, Charles. 1985. "War Making and State Making as Organized Crime." In *Bringing the State Back In*, edited by Peter Evans, Dietrich Rueschemeyer, and Theda Skocpol, 169–87. Cambridge: Cambridge University Press.

Walker, Gavin, and Naoki Sakai. 2019. "The End of Area." *Positions* 27 (1): 1–31.

Wells, Tamas. 2018. "Democratic 'Freedom' in Myanmar." *Asian Journal of Political Science* 26 (1): 1–15.

Yanow, Dvora, and Peregrine Schwartz-Shea. 2012. *Interpretive Research Design: Concepts and Processes*. New York: Routledge.

5

On Casing a Study versus Studying a Case

Joe Soss
University of Minnesota

Most methods texts encourage students to define some site or event as a case (noun) that they will go out and study (verb). Cases are defined as "real members of a general conceptual class": They exist "out there," in a sense, before we even arrive. Surveying available cases, researchers are encouraged to ask a series of analytic questions (which ones? how many? how likely? how typical?) and then select in a purposive way to answer a specific research question.

Valuable as it is, this approach has often felt foreign to practitioners of interpretive research. Charles Ragin recounts in his introduction to *What Is a Case?* how his co-editor Howard Becker "persistently pulled the rug out from under" consensus along these lines:

> From his perspective, to begin research with a confident notion of ... what *this* – the research subject – is a case of ... is counterproductive. Strong preconceptions are likely to hamper conceptual development. Researchers probably will not know what their cases are until [later in the process]. What *it* is a case of will coalesce gradually, sometimes catalytically, and the final realization of [how the phenomenon is to be cased] may be the most important part of the interaction between ideas and evidence. (1992, 6)

This sort of discomfort is the impetus for the current chapter. In studies that focus on a particular site or instance, we often choose our starting points for practical or political reasons, or for reasons related to language, culture, funding, or something else. Our research strategies prioritize discovery and embrace changes in research goals and questions. For these and other reasons, we often wind up with an emerging study (noun) that we need to case (verb). As we learn in the field, we repeatedly confront the challenge of how to conceptualize social action on broader analytic terms. Wrestling with what we are studying, we ask: What should I treat this as a case *of*?

In this chapter, I explore a critical yet underappreciated way case study methodologies may differ. "Nominal" approaches to casing, I suggest, offer a valid and vital alternative to the prevailing "realist" model. The realist approach seeks out the real nature of a thing in the world, asking whether it truly qualifies as a member of the class we are sampling from. The nominal approach asks instead how various ways of knowing a thing can generate different kinds of knowledge. Phenomena in the social world do not exist, in this view, as essentially a case of any particular kind. Rather, a "case" is something we make – an analytic construct that we develop through our efforts to theorize the phenomena we study. From a realist perspective, such fluid and uncertain efforts to case a study, pursued in a shifting and ongoing way, may appear ad hoc, suspect, and even "unscientific." Pressures to meet realist standards may dissuade researchers from pursuing strategies more appropriate for their project. At the writing stage, scholars may distort aspects of their study as they try to shoehorn what they have done into the realist model widely accepted as an ideal. By naming and clarifying the nominal approach, my hope is that we can promote a more pluralistic discipline; improve methodological guidance; and advance the goals of honesty, reflexivity, and transparency.

Toward these ends, the present chapter explores how casing operates in many studies as an *ongoing research activity* designed to advance insight, understanding, and explanation. Nominal casings emerge as we strive to make sense of the particular in more abstract terms – to theorize the things we study as instances of something more general. A nominal perspective, I will argue, encourages scholars to approach established casings in their field as products of earlier intellectual and political activity, available and potentially ripe for critique, challenge, and reformulation. In this sense, the nominal approach to casing can be seen as having important roots in critical as well as interpretive traditions of social science inquiry. To elaborate these themes, I begin by clarifying the logics that underlie realist and nominal traditions of case study research. I then draw on my PhD dissertation project and first book to provide a more concrete, detailed, and personal discussion of relevant issues. Finally, the chapter concludes with some reflections on how studies may be cased for comparison.

THE REALIST VIEW

In the social sciences today, most scholars conceive of case studies in a realist manner. In methods texts and faculty advisors' offices, the realist view tends to enjoy a taken-for-granted status. For most, it operates as a kind of common sense, deployed and taught without much reflection on its distinctiveness or felt need to justify its assumptions. It is simply woven, without notice, into matter-of-fact, how-to lessons for good practice in the social sciences.

The realist stance, as Charles Ragin (1992, 8) explains, posits, "there are cases (more or less empirically verifiable as such) 'out there.'" Realism positions the researcher as an outside observer who *identifies and selects* from cases made available by the real world. Classes of cases should be defined to correspond with reality, "carving nature at its joints" to clearly specify boundaries of generalization. Given a well-specified "universe," phenomena either do or do not qualify as a particular sort of thing – a kind of event (e.g., revolution), institution (e.g., slavery), organization (e.g., corporate firm), relation (e.g., colonial), actor (e.g., judge), activity (e.g., deliberation), belief system (e.g., Vedanta theology), or some such. "The relevant question is where the natural boundaries lie," John Gerring (1999, 386) explains, echoing Abraham Kaplan's (1964, 50) view that "what makes a concept significant is that the classification it institutes is one into which things fall, as it were, of themselves."

To employ the field's prevailing language of case *selection* is, in a sense, to adopt this realist position on the relationship between observer and observed. Cases exist in the world, in this view, as objects that correspond to a given category and, thus, as comparable units rightly analyzed together. Researchers choose among cases that exist, independent of the individual observer, as instances of a general social kind. They may do so in larger number for "extensive" (e.g., statistical) analysis or subject a smaller number to "intensive" analysis (Eckstein 1975). A case study, then, to quote John Gerring's (2004, 342) influential definition, is "an intensive study of a single unit for the purpose of understanding a larger class of (similar) units."

From this perspective, sound case-study design requires careful attention to the risks of misclassification. In particular, researchers must avoid any sort of *conceptual stretching* that might distort the boundary of a general class and, thus, extend generalizations across non-comparable instances (Sartori 1970). To avoid this pitfall (i.e., to ensure that concepts travel only to new cases that truly lie within a shared set of scope conditions), some realist texts encourage researchers to make use of different "levels" on a conceptual "ladder of abstraction" (Sartori 1970). Other accounts depart from the assumption of crisp classical categories to accommodate "family resemblance categories" (where varied traits define members of a shared category) and "radial categories" (where subtypes may be needed to preserve the integrity of comparisons) (see, e.g., Collier and Mahon 1993; Collier and Levitsky 1997). In all such variants, the realist stance urges scholars to make sure conceptual boundaries correspond to real-world differences and only comparable-in-reality cases are grouped together for analysis.

Realist case selection, then, is a purposive activity with both theoretical and empirical aspects. A theory in use among scholars covers only cases that fall within its conditions, so little can be gained by selecting a case outside its scope. Among the theory-relevant options, cases should be chosen to leverage differences in predicted outcomes and expectations about how a social phenomenon works. John Gerring provides a concise statement of this perspective, emphasizing the shared logic of case analysis across research traditions:

The case(s) identified for intensive study is[are] chosen from a population and the reasons for this choice hinge upon the way in which it is situated within that population. This is the origin of the terminology – typical, diverse, extreme, et al. It follows that case-selection procedures in case-study research may build upon prior cross-case analysis. ... Sometimes, these principles can be applied in a quantitative framework and sometimes they are limited to a qualitative framework. In either case, the logic of case selection remains quite similar, whether practiced in small-N or large- contexts. (2008, 645–46)

As Gerring suggests, the realist view plays a key role in the logic of controlled comparison (e.g., Przeworski and Teune 1970). In its narrowest multivariate form, realist comparison prizes unit homogeneity, treating cases as equivalent occasions to observe how causal factors covary with an outcome (e.g., Geddes 1990; King, Keohane, and Verba 1994). It is a mistake, though, to imagine that realism appears only in this guise. The realist approach is put to good use in within-case analyses that focus on "process tracing" and "causal process observations" (e.g., George and Bennett 2005; Brady and Collier 2010). It can underwrite efforts to engage the empirical richness of individual cases and build careful generalizations based on case diversity (Slater and Ziblatt 2013). Indeed, theory-relevant cases may be defined in part by their distinctive conjunctions of conditions (e.g., Ragin 2000). Recognizing that factors may combine in multiple ways to yield a given outcome, generalizations may be built cautiously and incrementally, under the assumption that not all cases work in the same way (Goldstone 2003).

None of these deviations from classical categories and multivariate notions of control requires a departure from realist tenets. Indeed, consider how one of the leading texts on process tracing, typological theorizing, and case diversity states the "requirements" a case study must meet to avoid being "nonscientific, noncumulative" and "atheoretical":

First, the investigator should clearly identify the universe – that is, the "class" or "subclass" of events – of which a single case or a group of cases to be studied are instances. Thus, the cases in a given study must all be instances ... of only one phenomenon. ... Second, a well-defined research objective and an appropriate research strategy to achieve that objective should guide the selection and analysis of a single case or several cases within the class or subclass of the phenomenon under investigation. Cases should not be chosen because they are "interesting" or because ample data exist for studying them. (George and Bennett 2005, 68–69)

Researchers can and do select cases for interpretive research in a realist manner. As Simmons and Smith (2019, 343, 352) rightly note, "Meanings, processes, and practices [can function as] the core drivers of case selection. ... [C]ases can ... refer to political processes, meaning-making practices, concepts, or events." Realism can also accommodate discovery in the field. Over the course of a study, one may encounter unexpected features of the case that further specify or revise its status as most or least likely, deviant or typical. Corrective specifications grounded in the observable features of a case are wholly consistent with, and even recommended by, a realist approach (Ragin 2000).

That the prevailing approach *can* be used in these various ways, however, does not mean that it is the only game in town or always best. Neither the method nor the substance of a study should be seen as a reason to dismiss realist case selection out of hand as inappropriate. Rather, the problem lies in the field's elevation of this approach to a status of orthodoxy – a singular canon of correct practice that is violated when researchers deviate from it. In so doing, we deter the pursuit of valid alternatives that, for some projects, may be more fruitful. Perhaps worse, we pressure researchers (especially graduate students) to distort the reporting of their work so that it conforms to the prevailing disciplinary model.

THE NOMINAL VIEW

"Social actions are comments on more than themselves," Clifford Geertz (1973, 23) famously observed: "Where an interpretation comes from does not determine where it can be impelled to go. Small facts speak to large issues, winks to epistemology, or sheep raids to revolution, because they are made to." Needless to say, Geertz is not suggesting that if we are interested in revolutions in general, we should select the local sheep raid as a theory-relevant case and design a study around it. His comment speaks instead to the possibility that we might, as William Blake put it in *Auguries of Innocence*, "see a world in a grain of sand" (see Pachirat 2006). The humble goings-on at a local research site can be framed in broad conceptual terms and impelled to speak to even the largest of scholarly, social, and political questions.

All case studies aim to advance knowledge of the actually existing world. But where the realist approach focuses on the nature of a thing in this world (Is this really a case of X? Does it truly exhibit the defining features of the population?), the nominal approach emphasizes how various ways of conceptualizing it can generate different kinds of knowledge (What can be learned by treating this phenomenon as a case of X?). From a nominal perspective, "casing" is an ongoing research activity in which we seek to advance insight, understanding, and explanation by conceptualizing the particular in more abstract terms, as a specific instance bearing on more general matters.

From this perspective, phenomena in the social world do not exist, inherently and really, as a case of any social (science) kind. They are ambiguous occasions for meaning making, for researchers as much as for the participants who experience them in daily life. Their relationship to general analytic categories is a question worth puzzling over and playing with – and, thus, an opportunity for intellectual creativity. Experienced realities emerge as bona fide *cases* of something only, to echo Geertz, "because they are made to." As Charles Ragin (1992, 10) rightly notes, "At the start of the research, it may not be at all clear that a case can or will be discerned. Constructing cases does not entail determining their limits [as in the realist view], but rather pinpointing and then demonstrating their theoretical significance." A case in this sense is not a found object that happens to fall within the natural boundaries of a conceptual class; it is an analytic construct that we create through our efforts to theorize phenomena under study.

Nominal casing may be pursued at any point in a study, from the planning stages through fieldwork and into the writing process. Across the breadth of a study, the same bit of social action may be cased in different ways for different purposes. Each casing allows the researcher to put the study into dialogue with a different set of empirical phenomena, creating new standpoints for interpretation; new paths for generalization; and new terms for relational, processual, or comparative analysis. Studying a local one-stop center for social services, for example, I may initially case it narrowly as a local instance of a "government welfare agency." Later, I may put it into dialogue with a broader conceptual class defined as "policy-implementing organizations" (which include, for example, some market firms and nonprofit organizations), or I may treat it as one of many "sites of citizen demand making" (a category that looks in a different direction, toward locales such as legislatures, courts, and voting booths). I may start out casing the social transactions at my site in terms of disciplinary power but then reframe them as a kind of interaction ritual where "presentations of self" get negotiated in open-ended ways. Implicitly or explicitly, each casing hails a different set of real-world referents onto the scene (as suitable instances for comparison) and points our generalizing efforts in a different direction.

A study clearly organized under the umbrella of a single conceptual class may, nevertheless, provide opportunities to engage and set aside different casings for different purposes. In general terms, for example, I may conclude that my study should be presented as a case of "domination and legitimation." Within this frame, though, the sections or chapters of my analysis may shift from interpreting social action as a case of "how identity gets constructed through relations of exploitation" to analyzing it as a case of "how hegemony works through game-like logics." Each maneuver positions the study in relation to a different body of knowledge with its own tale to tell about why this thing matters and works in a particular way. Each specifies a different scope of analytic generalization, its own path for insights that travel. As I case my study in various ways, I create new interpretive opportunities by putting the same social action in dialogue with different ideas and empirical sets.

Not all the things we conceptualize in our research rise to the level of a "case." Casing occurs when we use an abstract concept to define a fundamental category and standpoint of analysis. It happens when we frame what we're studying in relation to a general type and forge a dialogue in which instances of a particular type become the basis for insights into one another. On one side, the concepts, theories, and empirical studies that prior scholars have used to illuminate the general type become interpretive resources for making sense of our study. On the other, our empirically grounded insights become grist for interventions that may elaborate, contest, or revise prevailing understandings of a general sort. In casing a study, then, we do more than just place it in an empirical group: we adopt a schema of understanding – a way of knowing – that organizes and guides our analysis.[1]

In this regard, a nominal approach highlights the critical and disruptive potential of casing in a way that the realist view does not. As social science conventions, classes of cases operate as regulative norms and as lenses that naturalize particular understandings of the world. The realist approach encourages researchers to take these terms as given (established and warranted for reasons that correspond to real-world differences) and then to work within their parameters by selecting cases that belong in the conventional class. All else equal, scholars should adopt the concept "within the existing lexicon which, as currently understood, most accurately describes the phenomenon under definition" (Gerring 1999, 368–69).

By contrast, a nominal perspective encourages scholars to approach the established casing of a phenomenon as a product of earlier intellectual and political activity and, thus, as a site for critique, contestation, and reformulation. Social science concepts are often legacies of specific political projects, conflicts, and power relations (see, e.g., Schaffer 2016). What counts, for example, as a *real* religion, democracy, genocide, family, or act of terrorism? Prior to the 1970s, it would have been miraculous for a scholar to select cases of sexual harassment for study because, before the political struggles and consciousness-raising groups of that decade, the term itself did not exist as a conceptual category (Swenson 2017). The commonsense understandings of scientists and other experts have histories. In political science, perhaps especially, concepts that seem obvious often can be traced back to colonial projects, Cold War conflicts, liberation struggles, and the like. When we unreflectively adopt them as a basis for identifying and selecting cases, we incorporate their politics (for good or ill) as an organizing feature of our scholarship (what we include, what we exclude, and how and what we perceive).

By treating the question "what might we imagine this thing to be a case *of*" as contested ground, it is possible to denaturalize these sorts of taken-for-granted understandings in our field. New casings of familiar social kinds, Howard Becker (1998, 6–7) notes, "suggest ways of interfering with the comfortable thought routines academic life promotes and supports. [They] suggest ways to turn things around, to see things differently, in order to create new problems for research, new possibilities for comparing cases and inventing new categories and the like." And insofar as the knowledge we produce matters for the production and governance of subjects in the broader world, as critical

---

[1] On this structuring role of schemas, see Sewell (1992).

theorists suggest, such interventions can have significant implications for power and practice in societies as much as scholarship.

The nominal view does not counsel against purposive selections of where and what to study, nor does it treat casing as an inductive process to be deferred until entering the field. From a nominal perspective, creative efforts to case the study may be central to the research design phase, providing an explicit basis for the selection of where and what to study. This *preliminary casing* is both valuable and provisional. It helps position and focus the initial stages of research, defining the first steps in an ongoing process. A preliminary casing orients the researcher but also stays in play as an object of reflection, critique, and re-specification. If the initial casing persists to the end of our study unaltered, it is not for lack of trying and is in no way a failure.

Unlike the realist view, however, a nominal approach does not treat explicit casing as a requisite element of research design prior to an empirical study. Here, it is important to distinguish casing from positioning within a site. Realist approaches often define sites as cases in the first instance (e.g., a comparative case study of Guatemala and Nicaragua), and base selection on each site's properties in relation to a specific theory and population. Other reasons for selection are acknowledged as secondary at best.[2] From a nominal perspective, however, uncertainty about casing may be embraced as we prioritize other grounds for deciding where and what to study and how to position ourselves at a site. We may go to a site (or focus on a historical event) because we feel called to confront an injustice. We may choose based on our language skills, familiarity with a culture, social contacts, or the ways our identities are likely to be construed. We may be influenced by the body of available evidence, the costs and distances of locales, safety concerns, our ability to live comfortably in a place (and carry out research for a long period), funders' priorities, and much more. In light of such concerns, it may be "best practice" to position ourselves at a site with a reasonably clear sense of our research interests and how to pursue them but with little certainty about what our study will ultimately be a case *of*.

This openness to possible casings should not be confused with entering the field as a *tabula rasa*, devoid of ideas about what kind of case is at hand. Social science disciplines are disciplinary in the Foucauldian sense: we are trained to understand ourselves and others as particular kinds of subjects and to see phenomena in the world as "obviously" being of one kind or another. Our socialization, professional and otherwise, instills a kind of *habitus* that

---

[2] John Gerring (2008, 679), for example, takes up this possibility only after delivering his core prescriptions for case selection – as a secondary consideration that may influence selections *within* the group of cases identified as meeting more primary analytic criteria: "I have also disregarded pragmatic/logistical issues that might affect case selection. Evidently, case selection is often influenced by a researcher's familiarity with the language of a country, a personal entrée into that locale, special access to important data, or funding that covers one archive rather than another."

structures our predispositions to notice, perceive, and classify what we encounter in field or archival research (Brubaker 1993). Thus, nominal casing efforts should always be understood as *reflexive* practices aimed at our existing conceptions of the world – efforts to question and rework elements of our own feel for the kind of social action in play.

Nominal casing, then, should not be misread as an inductive counterpart to allegedly deductive realist procedures. Rather, it entails an evolving dialogue of fieldwork and framework in which site-specific experiences and observations are put into conversation with broader understandings of theory, history, and social structure (Sanjek 1990; Hopper 2003). As we go along, we consider alternative frameworks and try them on for size, thinking about various ways we might move from what we are studying toward larger analytic questions and generalizations. Shifts in casing frequently emerge from an abductive process in which experiences of puzzlement and doubt generate opportunities for reframing social action (Locke, Golden-Biddle, and Feldman 2008; Schwartz-Shea and Yanow 2012). The path to a catalytic moment of re-casing will often be paved by frustrated suspicions that something is just not right about how our framework fits together with our fieldwork. Indeed, one of the most productive suggestions an advisor might make to an exasperated dissertator is, "Maybe you're puzzled by what's happening because you're thinking about it as a case of X, rather than something else entirely."

Re-casing, then, is not so much a shift in research question as a maneuver in our efforts to explain and generalize. When Lisa Wedeen (2007) cases *qat* chews in Yemen as political deliberation in the public sphere, for example, she asserts that these events can yield insights into other instances of deliberation, that the idea of deliberation can illuminate *qat* chews in important ways, and that lessons drawn from a study of *qat* chews can call general theories of deliberative democracy into question, justifying critiques and revisions. When Timothy Pachirat (2011) cases action at a local slaughterhouse as an instance of the general relationship between visibility and power, he immediately declares the relevance of theories associated with figures such as Zygmunt Bauman, Norbert Elias, and Michel Foucault, hailing them onto the scene as explanatory possibilities. When we deem some bit of social action to be a case of the free rider problem – or a case of gender performance, classification struggle, or the productive power of the gaze – we assert something explanatory about how we think it works. Indeed, as Alexander Wendt (1998, 110–11) notes in an essay on "constitutive explanation," our central goal may be to "explain by subsuming observations under a concept [that suggests how a particular thing works] – as opposed to a law, as in the logical-empiricist model of causal explanation."

Wedeen's study of the *qat* chew and Pachirat's study of the slaughterhouse also underscore how nominal casing can encourage scholars to work with established concepts in novel ways. In contrast to realist worries about "conceptual stretching," Wedeen and Pachirat deliberately engage concepts in empirical contexts where, in the common sense of the field, they would seem misplaced. Their scholarly contributions flow directly from the fact that, a priori, few (if any) political scientists would have identified and selected the *qat* chew as a case of democratic deliberation – or the slaughterhouse as a case of politics at all.

BUCKETS, LENSES, AND UNWANTED CLAIMS

On the first day of a required masters-level course, "The Politics of Public Affairs," I ask students to participate in an exercise. I present a series of ten scenarios – for example, a presidential assassination motivated solely by the desire for celebrity, a case of domestic abuse, an individual's decision not to buy groceries from a local business because of its labor practices, a nineteenth-century lynching carried out by white people who held no positions in government, and so on. For each, I ask students to "decide whether, to you, it qualifies as political." Afterward, students discuss the reasons for their disagreements. Some argue that an act is only political if the actor has political intentions. Others say that consequences matter most. Some lean heavily on public-private distinctions or treat the involvement of government as a necessary condition. Others maintain that politics occurs wherever we confront a relationship of power. The students and I also step back to reflect on the politics involved in asserting that an issue is or is not "political," or in claiming that someone has "politicized" an issue.

At the end, I try to wring one last insight from the discussion – a point about how we use concepts in general. We sometimes use concepts like "politics" as *buckets for objects*, asking whether each item rightly belongs inside the container. In this view, some acts are political; others are not. Politics happens in some places but not others, and at certain times but not others. The point of the exercise, from this perspective, is to identify the right kind of fixed boundary, one that can clearly and reliably distinguish the political from the apolitical. At other times, we use concepts like "politics" as *lenses for aspects*. Instead of asking whether X as a whole is political, we ask whether we can see X in new and useful ways by thinking about it from a political perspective.

When we say the family is "political," for example, we may not mean that it is political in exactly the same way as a legislature – with both falling into the same bucket, "as it were, of themselves" (in Kaplan's (1964, 50) phrasing). We may mean instead that whatever else families are and do, they *also* have political dimensions and serve as sites for relations, processes, and actions that can be usefully understood in political terms. By recognizing how a family is political and clarifying its political dimensions, we may be able to develop a far better understanding of the family as a whole and gain new insights into how it operates as a part of the society and polity. Relative to the buckets view, the lenses approach suggests a broader scope of coverage for a course on "the politics of public affairs." It suggests that political analysis can help us understand and explain many things that are conventionally understood in other terms.

Among the scenarios presented in the exercise, one holds special importance for me: a woman, too poor to pay her bills and feed her children, applies for public assistance. Has she engaged in a political act? This is the scenario that stood at the center of my PhD dissertation and first book, *Unwanted Claims* (Soss 2000). The project was built on a nominal approach to casing in which I used the concept of "political participation" as a lens for analyzing citizens' interactions with the welfare state. What difference did it make that I cased welfare claiming and participation in this unconventional way? In what follows, I draw on this project to illuminate some of the practical, professional, and analytic issues surrounding nominal approaches to casing, as I experienced them in the field of political science in the 1990s.

Unwanted Claims is a study of welfare participation in two institutional settings: a stigmatized income-support program for low-income families (Aid to Families with Dependent Children, AFDC) and a program of income support for people with disabilities (Social Security Disability Insurance, SSDI). The linchpin of the study was my decision to analyze people's welfare experiences as cases of political participation. From the outset, it was clear that this move amounted to a violation of the field's stricture against conceptual stretching. Political participation was among the most well-established areas of study in political science, defined and measured according to a clearly bounded set of research sites and behaviors. Welfare claiming was not among them.

Most political scientists took it as obvious that people who apply for benefits at a welfare agency are doing something different from the bona fide acts of political participation that serve as "citizen inputs" in electoral-representative processes. In leading studies and field essays, I found realist explanations for the scope and content of political participation, detailing why such voluntary acts (mostly aimed at selecting or influencing government officials) should not be confused with other activities people might like to think of as "political" in some way. In T. H. Marshall's (1964) influential view of citizenship, welfare claims were exercises of social rights, not political rights. In Milbrath and Goel's (1982, 9) political-systems approach, they were "apolitical outtakes," contrasted with participatory citizen inputs. Joseph LaPalomabara (1978, 167, 188) famously argued that sound generalizations about political participation require "careful and precise empirical denotation [and a] restricted scope of empirical reference"; scholars must avoid the "indiscriminate and undiscriminating extension of concepts" to activities, institutions, and polities that do not truly (empirically) fit pluralist conceptions of liberal democracy. Citizen-initiated claims on the welfare state did not constitute a theory-relevant case suitable for selection.

As I read ethnographies from other disciplines, visited a few welfare agencies, and talked to some recipients myself, however, I became more and more struck by the political relationships political scientists seemed to be overlooking. In my graduate coursework, the main thing I had learned about poor people's political lives was what they lacked: they knew less about politics, they participated less, they were less organized, they got less effective representation, and so on. But at welfare agencies, poor people had direct, ongoing relations with state authorities that seemed far more intense and consequential than most of what I saw going on in middle- and upper-class Americans' lives. At the welfare agency, people made public claims on state allocations and engaged in conflicts over policy-based decisions. The rights and obligations of citizenship ceased to be abstract: they became the basis for explicit conversations and actions and directly experienced changes in people's lives.

The casing of my study came into focus as I connected these observations to various things I was reading. Unlike most political scientists, women of color – activists and scholars like Johnnie Tillmon (1972) and Jacqueline Pope (1989) – had been talking about welfare in terms of politics and power for decades. I read about how the welfare rights movement of the 1960s and 1970s deployed welfare claiming in political ways, with activist scholars such as Frances Fox Piven and Richard Cloward (1966, 1977) theorizing how welfare demands could be used as a political strategy. I also learned from a growing body of work by feminist theorists: Nancy Fraser (1989) wrote about "the politics of needs interpretation" at welfare agencies. Kathleen Jones (1990) argued that the terms of welfare merited serious attention in any effort to imagine or achieve "a woman-friendly polity." Barbara Nelson (1984) suggested that for poor women, the growth of welfare states had expanded the "action repertoire" of democratic citizenship, and Linda Gordon (1994) provided an incisive historical analysis of the political understandings of welfare and citizenship advanced by women in the early twentieth century.

As I read these works alongside participatory-democratic theorists, such as John Dewey and Carole Pateman, I found people talking less about *political participation* (as defined in the political behavior subfield) than about *participation in the political relations of a society*. From this perspective, people experience power relations, governance, and decision processes in schools and workplaces and families and all sorts of other places that are commonly seen as falling outside the bucket of politics. Eventually, traditional arguments in participatory-democratic theory pointed me toward the basic lines of inquiry for my study: welfare claiming could be studied (1) in terms of its political functions, uses, and processes; (2) as an ongoing, structured relationship of power, authority, conflict, and cooperation; and (3) as a productive process that constructs citizens, defines civic positions, and cultivates political dispositions. So, to case my study of welfare in terms of political participation, I *intentionally* stretched the concept.

The result was not persuasive to everyone. My committee members were terrifically supportive and, across countless office visits, pushed me to develop responses to the many objections they could imagine political scientists raising. The search for a realist line of demarcation became a kind of parlor game for us all. If I wanted to move the line, what criteria would I use to relocate it? Was I suggesting that the whole political behavior subfield had been mismeasuring political participation? What if participation scales in survey research incorporated welfare participation and, in so doing, found no inequalities or patterns of exclusion? Was I saying marginalized people participated in politics just as much as everyone else? Lacking a language for nominal casing, our conversations reflected a tension between our feeling that the political-participatory framing "worked" and our sense that the established concept in the field made welfare claiming unavailable for selection as a case of this kind.

Beyond my committee, I encountered stiffer resistance. One senior faculty member commented that for a graduate student going on the political science job market, a study of "what it's like to be on welfare" seemed like "professional suicide." When I was rejected for a dissertation fellowship, one reviewer wrote that I seemed confused about the concept of "political participation," my reliance on feminist writings suggested I had a political agenda, and my qualitative methods seemed too soft to challenge my political commitments. In a book review of *Unwanted Claims* some years later, Lawrence Mead (2001, 676) called it "an abuse of language" to describe and analyze welfare claiming as a case of political participation.

Objections aside, the casing of my study on these terms – born as I drafted the research design and developed throughout my field research – underwrote virtually all of my first book's contributions. Theories of political participation focused my fieldwork, shaping my interview questions and guiding my ethnographic research in disability support groups and a shelter for homeless families. As I pursued a political analysis of people's welfare experiences, I simultaneously treated my study as an opportunity to rethink political participation as a concept and a practice. Themes from participatory-democratic theories eventually supplied the chapter organization for the book.

I began by asking why people pursued welfare benefits. In the (mostly quantitative) literature on "benefit take-up," the answer seemed obvious: applicants needed income for food, housing, clothing, and so on. Because my analysis was focused on political functions and uses, I paid greater attention to how welfare intersected with power relations in the broader society. Emphasizing political agency and autonomy, for example, I analyzed how people mobilized welfare-state powers and resources against relations of oppression and domination in their daily lives. Many women claimed AFDC as a way to escape horrifying domestic abuse situations. SSDI claimants turned to the state as a way to secure independent living and escape vulnerable forms of dependency on family members and institutions (that sometimes resulted in abuse).

I then asked how demands on welfare agencies get generated. Most models of program take-up correlated individual traits and needs with probabilities of seeking benefits. Instead, I investigated welfare claiming as an outcome of processes – such as recruitment and mobilization – that are commonly emphasized in studies of political participation. I found that like other forms of political action, welfare claims depended on the kinds of knowledge, resources, and support available in individuals' social networks. Welfare applicants were *produced* through social and political processes – recruited and assisted by local organizations, mobilized by friends and family. Welfare demands often depended on shared social understandings of a person's situation that made claiming seem legitimate, reasonable, and right.

Moving on to welfare application encounters, I considered how political scientists had studied the institutional conditions of, say, voting – where it would be normal to think about poll taxes, literacy tests, ID requirements, polling locations, and other conditions as barriers that regulate citizens' abilities to advance their political interests, needs, and demands. Comparing SSDI and AFDC, I showed how institutional designs fostered inequalities of political voice and responsiveness across the two programs. In the field, I also expanded my initial focus on barriers to incorporate a greater focus on expressive forms of symbolic politics. The bureaucratic conditions of welfare claiming, I learned, functioned as a kind of "governmental presentation of self," providing the raw materials for clients' interpretations, beliefs, and expectations going forward. Based on a growing sense of the application encounter as an ideological experience of state power, I eventually focused my chapter on what I called "the puzzle of subordination and satisfaction": how could claimants simultaneously feel degraded, belittled, and silenced in such encounters yet come away expressing satisfaction with their caseworkers?

Given my casing, the ongoing experience of welfare participation offered an opportunity to learn about political relations between state authorities and citizens. In the field, I saw how policies could function like institutions, structuring political relations and setting terms for decision making. I analyzed how client-caseworker relationships advanced as an iterative game of power and position, with citizens learning as they went along whether and how to speak up or stay silent in their dealings with state authorities. Power relations structured in different ways produced distinctive patterns of voice, conflict, and quiescence. Yet as active interpreters of their experiences, clients could vary considerably in the lessons they drew from similar encounters in a single program and, thus, in the ways they chose to act in the future.

Finally, to bring my political analysis to a close, I dug deeper into the participatory-democratic claim that citizens are made, not born; citizenship is constructed, in significant part, through personal experiences of participation in relations of authority and power. I developed a political learning explanation for why experiences in two welfare programs had different effects on the ways clients perceived government and oriented themselves toward political action more generally. In retrospect, this turned out to be the most influential part of the book for political scientists.

It is worth asking why. First, it was the part of my study that connected welfare most directly to things political scientists already cared about: voting, trust in government, political efficacy, and so on. Second, the analysis of how AFDC experiences silenced and marginalized poor people (more so than SSDI experiences) fit easily into the field's prevailing narrative of poverty and political engagement. In contrast to the chapters that emphasized the political agency of welfare claimants, this part of my analysis could easily be integrated into existing explanations for poor people's low participation rates, levels of political knowledge and trust, and so on. Third, through sheer luck, my study coincided with the early years of contemporary "policy feedback" studies. I had never heard of this concept when I designed my project and only learned of it in the later writing stages (as an idea mostly in use among historical institutionalists). In the conclusion of an article for the *American Political Science Review* (1999), I took a first stab at connecting the lessons of welfare to budding interests in the various ways policies make politics. The result offered people in the field a way to see my study of welfare as relevant for the study of public opinion, political behavior, and politics more generally without having to directly address the question raised by my casing: whether welfare participation itself could be critically and effectively analyzed as a form of political participation.

In *Unwanted Claims*, I drew on well-established concepts, questions, and modes of analysis. If the study stood out as unusual, it was mostly because field research was so rare in the political behavior subfield, welfare was so far outside the subfield's normal purview, and welfare participants were so routinely thought of as lacking political engagement. Setting aside the question of whether activities at welfare agencies truly belonged in the bucket of political participation (as a realist case available for selection), I adopted political participation as a lens for analyzing aspects of what I encountered in the field. The unconventional casing drew previously hidden social and political dynamics into view – aspects of the phenomenon that had been rendered invisible by apolitical studies of welfare and political science studies that defined genuine cases of political participation in the prevailing realist manner.

When I came up for tenure some years later, an anonymous reviewer wrote that they thought political science should be "embarrassed" by its long failure to recognize welfare participation as a kind of political participation. The comment stood out to me because it resonated with something Howard Becker (1998, 110) had written in *Tricks of the Trade*: "[In many instances, we] try to formulate a definition that includes all the things we think are alike and leaves out those that are different. We are embarrassed if someone can show that something we didn't think belonged in our collection in fact fits the terms of the definition." We define a conceptual class, Becker suggests, so that it aligns with our intuitive sense of what does and does not belong in the bucket of objects. Using the example of "professions," Becker describes how the resulting definition incorporates unstated and often normative assumptions:

On Casing a Study versus Studying a Case

Researchers tried to define a "profession" as a special kind of work, different from other occupations. What they wanted to include ... were such highly respected and well-paid occupations as medicine and law. So they framed their definition by listing the traits that characterized those occupations. ... Invariably, an industrious and clever critic would find an occupation that fit all the definitional requirements (long years of training, a body of esoteric knowledge, state licensing, and so on) but clearly "didn't fit." Plumbing used to be good for this bit of theoretical skullduggery. Plumbers have the attributes included in the standard definition ... [b]ut "everyone knows" that plumbing is not a profession. The seeming paradox arises because the items in the collection the definition is framed to cover have been chosen on the basis of an unacknowledged variable: the social prestige of the occupation. If prestige correlated perfectly with the other criteria, there would be no problem. But it doesn't. (Becker 1998, 110–11)

Becker's observation jibed with an insightful comment I received at one of my job talks: maybe, the questioner suggested, political scientists had known what kinds of behaviors they wanted to study and crafted the definition of political participation to fit the cases themselves. As I returned to my dissertation, it felt increasingly important to highlight how welfare participation actually did fit the realist definition of political participation on its own terms. It had been excluded despite the fact that it met scholars' own criteria for what belonged in the bucket.

While I was finishing my fieldwork, Sidney Verba, Kay Lehman Schlozman, and Henry Brady published their landmark study of political participation, *Voice and Equality* (1995). Remarkably, they had included a measure of welfare participation in the huge survey that formed the basis of their analysis. But why did they only use this measure as a classification variable for determining who participates more versus less; why did they give it no attention as a form of political action in its own right? I looked to their definition for answers: "By *political* participation, we refer simply to activity that has the intent or effect of influencing government action – either directly by affecting the making or implementation of government policy or indirectly by influencing the selection of people who make those policies" (1995, 38). The criteria for getting into the bucket echoed Sidney Verba and Norman Nie's (1972, 2) earlier line of demarcation: "acts that aim at influencing the government, either by affecting the choice of government personnel or by affecting the choices made by government personnel." But welfare claiming is an act aimed at influencing the choices of government personnel; it does have the effect of influencing government action; it fits comfortably into the category of "affecting the ... implementation of government policy." Like the plumber excluded from the study of professions, it seemed that welfare claiming was being set aside not so much because of the relationship between its empirical features and the formal definition but, rather, *despite* it.

Beneath their stated criteria, scholars seemed to be identifying authentic cases of political participation based on unstated normative assumptions (drawn from liberal-democratic ideals) about what kinds of activities are desirable for citizens of a democracy. In the common sense of the field, efforts to vote and contact elected representatives are the kinds of participatory inputs one hopes to find in abundance in a well-functioning democracy. By contrast, as one questioner asked me at a job talk (I am paraphrasing from memory here): *Would we really have a better democracy if everyone signed up for welfare? Should we really celebrate welfare dependency as some kind of participatory civic good?* A variety of other unstated contrasts seemed to be at work as well. Welfare applicants were just expressing personal needs, not public interests. Welfare applications were technical matters of administration, not politics. Voting controls government; welfare puts the individual under government's control. And so on.

Such arguments never seemed to hold up under closer inspection, in my opinion. But the frequency with which they were asked speaks to the powerful commitments scholars often have toward conventional categories in their field. Confronted with what appeared to be an arbitrary exclusion, many responded with efforts to shore up the realist line of demarcation. Even if past definitions had left some criteria unstated, they suggested, we could remedy the problem now. We could specify the correct "edges of the bucket" (that had been there all along) and, thus, explain why welfare participation had been (and should be) rightly excluded. I had no name for it at the time. But in these discussions, I experienced how nominal casing strategies can circle back on realist casing practices, calling taken-for-granted classifications into question and generating valuable discussions about how we engage with the political world. The fact that such reconsiderations did not take root more broadly and publicly in the field points to an important way in which the scholarly impact of *Unwanted Claims* can be seen as quite limited.

A final point is also worth drawing from my experience with this project, and it has to do with the risks of casing a study in unconventional ways. From one perspective, we might see *Unwanted Claims* as a risky path for a graduate student entering the US politics subfield in the 1990s. I do not say this to urge researchers to be brave, and I am certainly not claiming to be personally courageous. Rather, I want to raise a question of social inequality. So long as realist case selection prevails as a singularly valid approach, unconventional casing will continue to be a risky move, particularly for scholars and students who are not well established. As a white man coming from a relatively high-status political science program with recommendation letters from well-known mentors, I enjoyed a privileged position for taking on a certain amount of risk. In fact, I was *encouraged* by many around me to take on these risks as a way of aiming high.

Would the freedom to take this path – and the risks and eventual rewards involved in doing so – have been the same for a more socially and institutionally disadvantaged graduate student? Do scholars today have equal opportunities to take this path, regardless of gender, race, class, sexuality, tenure, or institutional prestige? I think the answer is clearly no. In fact, the injustice involved in this state of affairs is a major reason why I think it is worthwhile to write the kinds of chapters collected in the present volume. The hope in this sort of writing is that we can broaden the ways people think about what is methodologically sound *so that it becomes less risky* to pursue alternative but equally valid ways of knowing and doing. Nominal casing strategies that challenge conventional framings should not be the exclusive province of more privileged scholars. To the contrary, both justice and social science would be well served by a world in which the freedom to pursue such strategies is more readily available to the people who have been most marginalized in the creation of our received concepts.

From a second perspective, though, I would describe the casing of my dissertation as a risk-*reduction* strategy. Political science was the basis of my training and the field in which I hoped to find employment. As I worked on my prospectus, I struggled with how to turn my interests into something that US political scientists in the 1990s would recognize as relevant to their field. In conversations, friends and mentors expressed their concerns that a study of welfare experiences might leave me unable to find a faculty position in political science. In many ways, this material risk defined the focus of my anxiety at the start of the project. Against this backdrop, the decision to use political participation as a casing frame was a semi-desperate attempt to convince people in the field – not just as scholars but also as potential employers – that my work belonged. It was a tactic designed to reduce the risk that I would invest years of work in a dissertation and then find myself "unwanted" in the field.

RETHINKING COMPARISON

How do nominal approaches to casing intersect with the theme of this volume, "rethinking comparison"? Above all, they encourage researchers to be creative in theorizing what they study, staying on the lookout for ways to forge innovative terms of dialogue between empirical instances. As we learn bit by bit in the archives or field, we often discover new ways of connecting what we are studying to other things in the world. Our insights at such moments may or may not take the form of a comparison between equivalent (i.e., homogenous) units. For example, we may suddenly see two highly dissimilar things in a new light, as distinctive variations on a common theme or a shared underlying logic. We may be struck by the insights we glimpse when we put these two seemingly dissimilar instances into conversation with each other. The resulting comparisons can seem, in the common sense of the field, like apples and oranges (or even apples and Slim Jims) because they are things that would be unlikely to appear to us a priori as members of a coherent population suitable for realist sampling.

David Leheny's book *Think Global, Fear Local* (2006) provides a good example. Over the course of repeated trips to Japan, Leheny found himself torn between different ideas for projects. He was working out an analysis of how Japanese authorities were pursuing anti-terrorism efforts but, as he traveled around, he also became appalled (and fascinated) by his local observations of a sex trade centered on schoolgirls – apples and Slim Jims, to be sure. But then Leheny began to notice some common threads of governance connecting the two issues. In both instances, Japanese authorities were turning liberal efforts to establish international norms into bases for expanded state powers and repressive domestic agendas – quite distinct from the intentions of global reformers. By casing the two together, Leheny pursues a comparative analysis on interpretive terms, effectively showing how transnational reform efforts can become articulated with preexisting national discourses, cultural anxieties, and political agendas. In both cases, local scapegoats and targets of social control displaced the original targets of global agreements; repressive state policies found legitimacy in rising pressures to conform to global norms. "In these international efforts," Leheny (2006, 4) concludes, "local fears found political cover; by cracking down on schoolgirls and unleashing the military, Japan was simply observing its international responsibilities."

Scholars who pursue nominal casing strategies sometimes wind up comparing similarities and differences across two or more instances in a fairly conventional manner. But this need not be so. More dialogic approaches are also common. In many studies, for example, scholars use casing strategies as a way to create empirically grounded standpoints for interpretation: their goal is to leverage each case as a perspective for understanding and explaining the other(s). Reflecting on his comparative histories of racism in the United States and South Africa, for example, George Fredrickson (1997, 7) writes: "Historical comparison [operated] not merely as a method or procedure but also [as] an antidote to the parochialism [of my own vision]."

Fredrickson does not position himself as a detached observer outside his cases, inspecting them solely as objects that have similarities and differences. He stresses how his interpretive study of each case focused and organized his perceptions in new ways, ultimately creating a new kind of standpoint for interpreting the other case. Calling it "comparative *perspective* as a tool of analysis" (1997, 7), Fredrickson explains how a case-based interpretive standpoint differs from the application of a theoretical framework or an analysis of empirical similarities and differences. It is a third mode of analysis: using one empirical case to frame and interpret social action in another, and using the resulting dialogue to shed light on cases of this kind in general.

Nominal approaches to casing can also play an important role in supporting more relational modes of analysis. For example, consider a researcher who sets out to compare a thriving community on a hill and a degraded community located in the valley below. Treating the two as independent cases, they aim to isolate the traits that explain different development outcomes. In the field, they begin to learn more about how the community on the hill has enriched itself for decades by exploiting and extracting resources from the valley community.

More and more, the assumption that these are independent cases – equivalent units that one should compare in terms of their separate traits – begins to strike the researcher as an idea that mystifies relations of domination. The hilltop community has achieved its success precisely by pillaging the valley community and pushing it into despair. In response, the researcher may re-case the study, turning a comparative analysis of two instances into a single case study of how extractive relations produce uneven patterns of community development. Instead of being two cases drawn from a "unit-homogeneous" population, the communities are now cased together in terms of their unequal but co-constitutive positions in a single relationship: dominant and subordinate, exploiter and exploited.

Guided by anti- and postcolonial writings, Micol Seigel highlights this dynamic in comparative studies of racial regimes in Brazil and the United States: "This setup discourages attention to exchange between the two, the very exchange postcolonial insight understands as the stuff of subject-formation. ... Comparisons," Seigel (2005, 65) concludes, "obscure the workings of power." In the language of this chapter, Seigel can be seen as urging a particular kind of casing that treats two countries as subjects of a single co-constitutive discourse. The case here is defined by the racial discourse that has constructed each country's experience and identity in relation to the other. By making this analytic move, Seigel argues, we can gain different kinds of insights into how and why race operates as it does, both transnationally and within each country.

An exhaustive review of various ways we might rethink comparison goes well beyond the purpose of this chapter. The few examples I have provided suffice to underscore how nominal casing strategies can expand analytic possibilities. By clarifying the nominal alternative to realism, my hope is that we can see more clearly the potential downsides of pressuring researchers to define their cases at the outset and use them as a basis for nearly every aspect of their research plan. A priori casing is valuable for the purposes of many projects. But deep investments in a casing, prior to entering the field, also carry substantial risks of lock-in and tunnel vision. Settled and enforced case definitions can foreclose insights and constrain research in rigid and undesirable ways. Graduate students who have been pushed in this manner may be particularly likely to experience their casing as an almost-inescapable trap. Having built the entire edifice of a project around a particular casing, and having won a go-ahead from committee members only on this basis, is it any wonder that a dissertator might not relish the prospect of declaring that what they are studying should probably be thought of as a case of something else? Really, who would want to open *that* can of worms?

The nominal alternative is to encourage graduate students to try out different ways of casing their study from the get-go. By advising students to see their preliminary casing as a provisional standpoint, adopted for now as one possibility among many, faculty advisors can legitimate and foster research practices that embrace generative doubt and make casing into an ongoing subject of reflexive critique. In so doing, we can begin to bridge the gap that students encounter as they move from positivist and realist texts on case study design into more interpretive texts that emphasize open-ended processes of discovery and abductive reasoning. Frustrated by confusing tensions between the two, many scholars who pursue interpretive and critical studies avoid the language of case study research altogether. A more fruitful path forward is to be transparent about working within an alternative and equally valid case study tradition, seizing the analytic opportunities that only reflections on general kinds can provide.

REFERENCES

Becker, Howard S. 1998. *Tricks of the Trade: How to Think about Your Research While Doing It*. Chicago: University of Chicago Press.

Brady, Henry E., and David Collier, eds. 2010. *Rethinking Social Inquiry: Diverse Tools, Shared Standards*. Lanham, MD: Rowman & Littlefield.

Brubaker, Rogers. 1993. "Social Theory as Habitus." In *Bourdieu: Critical Perspectives*, edited by Craig J. Calhoun, Edward LiPuma, and Moishe Postones, 212–34. Chicago: University of Chicago Press.

Collier, David, and Steven Levitsky. 1997. "Democracy with Adjectives: Conceptual Innovation in Comparative Research." *World Politics* 49: 430–51.

Collier, David, and James E. Mahon Jr. 1993. "Conceptual 'Stretching' Revisited: Adapting Categories in Comparative Analysis." *American Political Science Review* 87 (4): 845–55.

Eckstein, Harry. 1975. "Case Study and Theory in Political Science." In *Handbook of Political Science*, edited by Fred I. Greenstein and Nelson W. Polsby, 79–138. Reading, MA: Addison-Wesley.

Fraser, Nancy. 1989. *Unruly Practices: Power, Discourse and Gender in Contemporary Social Theory*. Minneapolis: University of Minnesota Press.

Frederickson, George. 1997. *The Comparative Imagination: On the History of Racism, Nationalism, and Social Movements*. Berkeley: University of California Press.

Geddes, Barbara. 1990. "How the Cases You Choose Affect the Answers You Get: Selection Bias in Comparative Politics." *Political Analysis* 2: 131–50.

Geertz, Clifford. 1973. *The Interpretation of Cultures*. New York: Basic Books.

George, Alexander L., and Andrew Bennett. 2005. *Case Studies and Theory Development in the Social Sciences*. Cambridge, MA: MIT Press.

Gerring, John. 1999. "What Makes a Concept Good? A Criterial Framework for Understanding Concept Formation in the Social Sciences." *Polity* 31 (3): 357–93.

 2004. "What Is a Case Study and What Is It Good For?" *American Political Science Review* 98 (2): 341–54.

 2008. "Case Selection for Case-Study Analysis: Qualitative and Quantitative Techniques." In *The Oxford Handbook of Political Methodology*, edited by Janet M. Box-Steffensmeier, Henry E. Brady, and David Collier, 645–84. New York: Oxford University Press.

Goldstone, Jack A. 2003. "Comparative Historical Analysis and Knowledge Accumulation in the Study of Revolutions." In *Comparative Historical Analysis in the Social Sciences*, edited by James Mahoney and Dietrich Rueschemeyer, 41–90. New York: Cambridge University Press.

Gordon, Linda. 1994. *Pitied but Not Entitled: Single Mothers and the History of Welfare*. Cambridge, MA: Harvard University Press.

Hopper, Kim. 2003. *Reckoning with Homelessness*. Ithaca, NY: Cornell University Press.

Jones, Kathleen B. 1990. "Citizenship in a Women-Friendly Polity." *Signs: Journal of Women in Culture and Society* 15 (4): 781–812.

Kaplan, Abraham. 1964. *The Conduct of Inquiry: Methodology for Behavioral Science*. New York: Chandler Publishing Co.

King, Gary, Robert O. Keohane, and Sidney Verba. 1994. *Designing Social Inquiry: Scientific Inference in Qualitative Research*. Princeton, NJ: Princeton University Press.

LaPolambara, Joseph. 1978. "Political Participation as an Analytic Concept in Comparative Perspective." In *The Citizen and Politics: A Comparative Perspective*, edited by Sidney Verba and Lucian Pye, 166–94. New York: Greylock.

Leheny, David. 2006. *Think Global, Fear Local: Sex, Violence, and Anxiety in Contemporary Japan*. Ithaca, NY: Cornell University Press.

Locke, Karen, Karen Golden-Biddle, and Martha S. Feldman. 2008. "Making Doubt Generative: Rethinking the Role of Doubt in the Research Process." *Organization Science* 19 (6): 907–18.

Marshall, T. H. 1964. *Class, Citizenship, and Social Development*. Garden City, NJ: Doubleday.

Mead, Lawrence M. 2001. "Review of Unwanted Claims: The Politics of Participation in the U.S. Welfare System by Joe Soss." *Political Science Quarterly* 116 (4): 675–77.

Milbrath, Lester W., and M. L. Goel. 1982. *Political Participation*, 2nd edn. Lanham, MD: University Press of America.

Nelson, Barbara. 1984. *Making an Issue of Child Abuse: Political Agenda Setting for Social Problems*. Chicago: University of Chicago Press.

Pachirat, Timothy. 2006. "We Call It a Grain of Sand: The Interpretive Orientation and a Human Social Science." In *Interpretation and Method*, edited by Dvora Yanow and Peregrine Schwartz-Shea, 373–79. Armonk, NY: M. E. Sharpe Press.

—— 2011. *Every Twelve Seconds: Industrialized Slaughter and the Politics of Sight*. New Haven, CT: Yale University Press.

Piven, Frances Fox, and Richard A. Cloward. 1966. "The Weight of the Poor: A Strategy to End Poverty." *The Nation*, May 2. www.thenation.com/article/archive/weight-poor-strategy-end-poverty/

—— 1977. *Poor People's Movements: Why They Succeed, How They Fail*. New York: Pantheon Books.

Pope, Jacqueline. 1989. *Biting the Hand that Feeds Them: Organizing Women on Welfare at the Grassroots Level*. New York: Praeger.

Przeworski, Adam, and Henry Teune. 1970. *The Logic of Comparative Social Inquiry*. New York: Wiley & Sons.

Ragin, Charles C. 1992. "Introduction: Cases of What Is a Case?" In *What Is a Case? Exploring the Foundations of Social Inquiry*, edited by Charles C. Ragin and Howard S. Becker, 1–17. New York: Cambridge University Press.

2000. *Fuzzy Set Social Science*. Chicago: University of Chicago Press.
Sanjek, Roger. 1990. *Fieldnotes: The Makings of Anthropology*. Ithaca, NY: Cornell University Press.
Sartori, Giovanni. 1970. "Concept Misformation in Comparative Politics." *American Political Science Review* 64 (4): 1033–53.
Schaffer, Frederic Charles. 2016. *Elucidating Social Science Concepts: An Interpretivist Guide*. New York: Routledge.
Schwartz-Shea, Peregrine, and Dvora Yanow. 2012. *Interpretive Research Design: Concepts and Processes*. New York: Routledge.
Seigel, Micol. 2005. "Beyond Compare: Comparative Method after the Transnational Turn." *Radical History Review* 91: 62–90.
Sewell Jr., William H. 1992. "A Theory of Structure: Duality, Agency, and Transformation." *American Journal of Sociology* 98 (1): 1–29.
Simmons, Erica S., and Nicholas Rush Smith. 2019. "The Case for Comparative Ethnography." *Comparative Politics* 51 (3): 341–59.
Slater, Dan, and Daniel Ziblatt. 2013. "The Enduring Indispensability of Controlled Comparison." *Comparative Political Studies* 46 (10): 1301–27.
Soss, Joe. 1999. "Lessons of Welfare: Policy Design, Political Learning, and Political Action." *American Political Science Review* 93 (2): 363–80.
 2000. *Unwanted Claims: The Politics of Participation in the U.S. Welfare System*. Ann Arbor: University of Michigan Press.
Swenson, Kyle. 2017. "Who Came Up with the Term 'Sexual Harassment?'" *The Washington Post*, November 22. www.washingtonpost.com/news/morning-mix/wp/2017/11/22/who-came-up-with-the-term-sexual-harassment/
Tillmon, Johnnie. 1972. "Welfare Is a Women's Issue." *Ms. Magazine*. https://msmagazine.com/2021/03/25/welfare-is-a-womens-issue-ms-magazine-spring-1972/
Verba, Sidney, and Norman H. Nie. 1972. *Participation in America: Political Democracy and Social Equality*. Chicago: University of Chicago Press.
Verba, Sidney, Kay Lehman Schlozman, and Henry E. Brady. 1995. *Voice and Equality: Civic Voluntarism in American Politics*. Cambridge, MA: Harvard University Press.
Wedeen, Lisa. 2007. "The Politics of Deliberation: $Q\bar{a}t$ Chews as Public Spheres in Yemen." *Public Culture* 19 (1): 59–84.
Wendt, Alexander. 1998. "On Constitution and Causation in International Relations." *Review of International Studies* 24 (5): 101–18.

6

From Cases to Sites
Studying Global Processes in Comparative Politics

Thea Riofrancos
Providence College

As a subfield of political science, comparative politics is often associated with the comparison of two or more independent and bounded cases. A case, in canonical textual definition and graduate student training, slides between two usages: (1) an instance of a more general class of processes or events or (2) a geographically bounded entity, usually a nation-state but sometimes a city, empire, or province. Neither of these usages is adequate. The former presupposes the membership of a particular phenomenon in a predesignated category. The latter imputes a bounded, enduring holism on what are deeply interdependent – and made and unmade – scales of political life.[1] The virtue of immersive inquiry is its potential to generate novel concepts and to classify events and processes in unexpected ways – which unsettles the first idea of a case. And such immersive inquiry often reveals the connections between political dynamics in one locale to dynamics that go beyond the geographic unit under investigation – thus unsettling the second.

Drawing on my research and engaging a range of methodological scholarship, I argue that the conventional treatment of case studies ignores their constitutive multiplicity. Any one event, institution, or process may belong to more than one category of political life. And any one locale is crosscut by, and co-constitutes, dynamics that exceed its geographic boundaries. In light of this multiplicity, I propose "siting" as an alternative to the conventional approach. Siting provides a framework to study global processes in the moments and scenes in which they unfold, drawing our attention to the co-constitution of particular places and macro processes.

My framework builds on Ragin's and Soss's discussions of casing (Ragin 1992; Soss, Chapter 5, this volume). The process of casing brings "operational closure to some problematic relationship between ideas and evidence, theory and data"

---

[1] On scale making, see Riofrancos (2017).

(Ragin 1992, 218). From this perspective, cases are neither self-evident geographic entities nor members of a predetermined class. Like casing, siting entails iterative encounters between empirical and theoretical knowledge. But my framework goes further, transcending the logic of cases altogether. Particular sites offer a view of the general not because they are *cases* of it, but because they are *constitutive* of it – along with many other sites across the world.

For example, the abstract structure we call "global capitalism" can be empirically observed by identifying its constitutive social relations – wage labor, the profit motive, private property, the commodity form – in the particular contexts in which they emerge, are institutionalized, and are contested.[2] As a corollary, we gain analytic and empirical leverage over abstract, global, and *longue durée* processes by conducting research in the sites where they are salient, observable, and conflictual.

In what follows, I first historicize the conventional comparative method, illuminating the conditions under which the comparison of discrete, independent nation-states became the standard of scientific rigor. Understanding this history is essential to appreciate the contribution of siting as an approach to political inquiry. As I show, the development of the comparative method is bound up with the trajectories of global capitalism, imperialism, and geopolitical conflict across the long twentieth century. Yet the conventional approach to comparison effaces its own global context. Siting, therefore, is a way to acknowledge – and analytically leverage – the always global character of political inquiry.

After recounting this intellectual history, I then zoom in on the status of "single cases" within this hegemonic approach to comparative inquiry. So-called single cases are instructive, given their ambivalent status in a field defined by comparison, because they reveal the key assumptions underlying the goals and criteria of research. On the one hand, they are deemed especially suited for key methodological tasks, such as hypothesis generation or explaining unusual but important historical events (Ragin 1992, 127; Brady and Collier 2004, 13–14; Mahoney and Goertz 2006, 240–41). And they are seen as more likely to meet criteria such as conceptual validity (Ragin 1992, 127; Brady and Collier 2004, 13–14; Mahoney and Goertz 2006, 240–41). On the other hand, they are regarded as an insufficient foundation for the conventionally accepted goal of social science inquiry: generalizable causal inferences.[3] I suggest that this

---

[2] For example, see E. P. Thompson's (1966) history of working-class consciousness; E. M. Wood's (1998) account of the capitalist transformation of the English countryside; Karl Polanyi (1944) on the conflictual emergence of "market society"; Eric Williams (1944) on slavery and the development of capitalism; scholars in the tradition of world systems theory who analyze of the violent incorporation of territories as the peripheries of capitalism (Wallerstein 1974; Stern 1988; Svampa 2016); and studies of the privatization of land and commodification of social life in neoliberal Latin America (Silva 2009, 2012; Simmons 2016).

[3] King, Keohane, and Verba (1994) identify causal influence as the goal of inquiry, and, as discussed later, argue that the greater the number of observations – which is distinct from the number of cases, but not unrelated to it – the more confident our inferences (see chaps. 1 and 6).

disciplinary ambivalence is a product of a misconception regarding the nature of single-case studies. Single cases are not "single" but rather marked by constitutive multiplicity.

But I also go further than reconceptualizing the case. As I have discovered in the course of my research, casing remains bound by the assumption that the phenomena we study are valuable only insofar as they serve as examples of something else. Instead, I argue for selecting research sites that are co-constitutive of a broader process of interest. I illustrate the methodological and substantive value of this approach with reference to my research on the global energy transition. I conclude by encouraging graduate students and junior scholars to work against the grain of comparative politics and embrace the intellectual rigor and creative potential of site-specific inquiry.

A GENEALOGY OF THE "COMPARATIVE METHOD"

In methodological handbooks, graduate and undergraduate seminars, and the obligatory methods section in journal articles, the comparative method is presented as a means to the overarching end of social-scientific inquiry: producing inferences that are generalizable across space and time (King, Keohane, and Verba 1994, chaps. 1–3, 6; Gerring 2004, 342; George and Bennett 2005, 6; Mahoney and Goertz 2006, 228; Gerring 2008, 645–46; Collier, Seawright, and Munck 2010, 25).[4] This logic links a number of methodological operations: theorization, conceptualization, operationalization, hypothesis generation, case selection, identification of dependent and independent variables, data collection, data analysis, and hypothesis testing. The hegemonic status of this logic is only reaffirmed by the debates that take place on its terrain, upon which interventions assume that comparison is a route to generalizability and, therefore, that every step of comparative inquiry should be structured to obtain this desideratum. Overlaid on this understanding of the goal of comparative inquiry is a highly simplified understanding of the "scientific method" thought to govern experimental work, wherein the isolation, control, and manipulation of variation is the *sine qua non* of producing general knowledge.

Of course, this goal of using comparison to generalize has a history – a history that is crucial to understand to appreciate the theoretical and empirical value of shifting from a logic of comparing cases to a logic of studying sites.[5] The comparative method carves up the world into discrete cases, abstracts those cases out of their mutually entangled histories, and then brings them into commensurate relation with one another. As I discuss in the

---

[4] In particular, see King, Keohane, and Verba's (1994) statements on pages 38 and 45, where they use the language of "universal applicability" of their standards to interpretivist and historical work; otherwise "our interpretations would remain personal rather than scientific."

[5] I develop this historical account at more length in Riofrancos (2018).

next section, the further disaggregation of cases into "observations," unmoored from their conjunctural interdependency and divorced from historical time, takes this analytic operation to its extreme. For those of us trained in conventional social science, studying the sites that constitute and are constituted by macro processes requires unlearning this mode of inquiry. And the first step in unlearning is reinserting methodology back into history. As it turns out, the comparative logic is itself a product of, and protagonist in, the world-historic processes its application tends to disavow: imperialism, racial capitalism, and geopolitical conflicts. The comparative method, in other words, is itself a fruitful research site to understand the co-constitution of knowledge and power over the long twentieth century.

As a strategy to render social phenomena intelligible (and predictable), the logic of comparative inquiry emerged in the late nineteenth and early twentieth centuries in a trans-Atlantic milieu marked by a series of interrelated macrosocial transformations: capitalist industrialization and the spread of market society, the growth of state bureaucracies, the consolidation of national identities, and imperial conquest and domination. It was this last process that most decisively shaped the origins of the comparative method in sociology. Rather than an internal reflection on the experience of capitalist modernity within the metropole, Victorian-era sociology primarily applied the comparative method externally to the rest of the world – as seen from the synoptic point of view of the "imperial gaze" (Connell 1997, 1524). Sociologists synthesized the data produced by now sprawling colonial administrations (what Raewyn Connell calls "the ethnographical dividend of empire") and ordered the world's societies in terms of their "progress," conceived of in evolutionary and often explicitly racialized terms (Connell 1997, 1520). Meanwhile, as Jessica Blatt's disciplinary history reveals, a racialized understanding of political development constituted the primary concern of early twentieth-century American political science (Blatt 2018, 54). Racialized typologies and the comparisons they enabled issued from Eurocentric "ideal types" against which the rest of the world was less evolved, backward, or deviant (Tilly 1984, chap. 1; Connell 1997; Steinmetz 2004, 381, 387–89; Blatt 2018, 46–76).[6] Thus, the conceptual boundaries of the taken-for-granted unit of comparison – the nation-state – efface the always already global character of both social scientific theory and the imperial states in which they were developed (Bhambra 2016).

During the interwar period, American sociology turned inward (as exemplified by the Chicago School's model of urban sociology) and political science assumed the task of globe-trotting comparison. Under the rubric of modernization theory and armed with ever more sophisticated quantitative

---

[6] See also Fredric Jameson's analysis of the link between uneven capitalist development and conceptual categories that facilitated comparison (namely, the category of the "mode of production") (Jameson 1989, 37–38).

methods, postwar comparative politics aimed for a "total science" of the world's diverse "political systems" (Mitchell 1991, 79). Echoing the nineteenth-century imperial gaze – although now inflected with the sense of uncertainty and urgency that permeated the Cold War–era policy and research establishment – political science sought to expand the territorial reach of its analysis and dutifully enlisted in the battle against communism to export Anglo-American institutions and "civic culture" (Pletsch 1981, 584–85; Mitchell 1991, 79–80; Oren 2003). The geopolitical and conceptual partition of the globe into three worlds further reinforced the contours of Cold War–era political science. The division that structured the world into friend (first), enemy (second), and contested terrain (third) also marked an academic division of labor: anthropologists studied the inescapably unique cultures of the not-yet-modern third world, whereas sociology, economics, and political science studied those countries that could be located somewhere along the teleological trajectory of modernization and therefore conformed in greater or lesser degree to the quasi-natural laws governing modern societies (Pletsch 1981, 579–83). From this comes the mutual opposition between studies that produce knowledge of specific cultural systems ("idiographic") versus those that produced knowledge in the form of generalizable laws ("nomothetic"). This binary is almost exclusively deployed to denigrate the knowledge produced by single-case studies, which are presumed to be inherently "non-explanatory" – no matter that its twin terms are archaic vestiges of nineteenth-century German debates over the status of general theories in social science (Steinmetz 2004, 382–83).

Even as the specific content of modernization theory has ostensibly fallen out of favor, its goal of a "total science" and its positivist epistemology continued to shape the methodological contours of political science, as well as privilege certain objects of research over others. Beginning in the 1970s, in comparative sociology and comparative politics, the search for timeless laws of modernization – themselves a projection of an imagined Western past – gave way to a historical approach to the study of capitalism, the state, regime type, and social revolutions (Sewell 2005, 81–83). A new canon coalesced around Barrington Moore Jr., Theda Skocpol, Charles Tilly, and others, yielding an approach equally defined by its substantive and methodological orientations. For these studies, where the number of cases fell below the threshold for statistical methods, "comparison" became a marker of social scientific rigor (Hall 2003, 379–81; Steinmetz 2004, 373–81). For example, in his influential article in the *American Political Science Review*, Lijphart framed the comparative method as second best to statistical analysis when there are too few cases to perform a regression analysis (Lijphart 1971). Key to what Calhoun (1996) refers to as the gradual "domestication" of historical sociology was the emphasis on comparison (specifically John Stuart Mill's methods of agreement and difference) as a route to generalizable causal inference.[7] Brubaker refers to

---

[7] For a canonical methodological statement, see Skocpol and Somers (1980).

this as the "Skocpolian moment," and its relative success can be seen in the strong association of comparison and conception of the nation-state as the unit of analysis, as well as the understanding of comparison as a distinctive method and logic, rather than a dimension of a variety of logics of inquiry (Brubaker 2003, 3–4).

The hegemonic status of the method of structured comparison is perhaps most apparent in the conventional treatment of single-case studies, which seem to defy the maxim that the more cases, and the more observations, the more generalizable a study's findings. In the next section, I closely read canonical methodological texts and their equally canonical responses. I show that the assumptions underlying the injunction to "increase the n" – in the service of a total science and the political projects it advances – are tenuous. Finally, I present an alternative approach that leverages rather than negates the interconnections between the many specific sites of macro processes.

FROM CASES TO SITES IN COMPARATIVE POLITICS

King, Keohane, and Verba's (1994) *Designing Social Inquiry* – among the most frequently assigned texts in contemporary methodology courses – is a key source of the prevailing assumptions about what single-case studies can (and cannot) be used for. *Designing Social Inquiry* routinely characterizes small-n studies, and single-case studies most acutely, as providing a weak foundation for what they regard as the primary research goal of the comparative method: generalizable descriptive and causal inferences. Indeed, a reasonable interpretation of this text might suggest that single-case studies are entirely unsuited to the tasks of social science. As King, Keohane, and Verba somewhat blithely put it, the imperative to select cases that vary on the dependent variable – and thus to refrain from only selecting case(s) that register a "positive" value on the outcome of interest, whether revolution or democratization – ought to be "so obvious that we would think it hardly needs to be mentioned" (King, Keohane, and Verba 1994, 129). They go as far as to say that without such variation, "*nothing whatsoever can be learned* about the causes of the dependent variable" (129, emphasis added): given the possibility of omitted variable bias, research conducted on a single case is prone to Type II error (false rejection of the null hypothesis) (Gerring and Seawright 2008). In other words, such research is ostensibly biased toward verification. Their advice for addressing the "extreme selection bias" induced by no-variation case selection strategies: "Avoid them!" (Gerring and Seawright 2008, 130).

The way to do so, naturally, is to increase the number of cases. As a graduate student conducting fieldwork on conflict over resource extraction in Ecuador, I cannot count the number of times a well-meaning professor suggested I add additional cases, even if admittedly superficial "shadow cases." But as other methodologists have argued, if the goal is to explain a historically important outcome in a given case, it makes little sense to treat all cases as "equally relevant" and seek out negative values on the outcome in question to maximize variation (Mahoney and Goertz 2006, 239–41). In addition, the condition of equifinality – that there are multiple paths to the "same" outcome, and that these distinct pathways are of analytic interest – suggests that "selecting on the dependent variable" contributes to our understandings of the *processes and mechanisms* by which seemingly identical outcomes emerge (Ragin 1992, 33–35; George and Bennett 2005, 12–13).

More broadly, graduate students and junior scholars constantly face the imperative to increase the number of observations, thus establishing (at least according to the conventional wisdom in the discipline) a solid foundation for descriptive and ultimately causal inference. As King, Keohane, and Verba (1994, 52, 221) make clear, the number of cases does not per se dictate the number of observations, and even a "handful of cases" can contain an "immense" number of observations. Regardless of this immensity, their advice to case study researchers is to unrelentingly increase the "n."[8] And as one makes advances in their research, the discovery of new testable implications of the theory only amplifies the imperative to include more cases: any hypotheses revised in the process of testing *must* be tested on new data.[9]

King, Keohane, and Verba's final chapter, aptly entitled "Increasing the Number of Observations," suggests various means of doing so, organized into two basic categories: new measures and new units. Either the same units can be subjected to new measures, or new units (including at a lower level of aggregation than the initial unit) can be analyzed – or both. Curiously, however, whichever route to generalizability is chosen, *cases* lose their usual integrity and become a mere collection of observations. Indeed, the authors find that the term "case" "has a fairly imprecise definition" and that while the number of cases "may be of some interest for some purposes," only the number of observations is relevant to testing a theory (King, Keohane, and Verba 1994, 52–53). Elsewhere, they emphasize that cases (whether defined as countries or as phenomena such as revolutions, elections, or wars) are not actually what we study: "Rather, we abstract aspects of those phenomena – sets of explanatory and dependent variables – that are specified by our theories; we identify units to which these variables apply; and we make observations of our variables, on the units" (King, Keohane, and Verba 1994, 217–18). This assumes, of course, that all (theoretically relevant) observations are the same insofar as they are equally valuable in the service of inference. In contrast, Brady, Collier, and Seawright (2004, 11–12) distinguish between dataset and causal process observations, noting that case study approaches are particularly well situated to increase the latter (and thus attend to causal complexity and multiple causality).[10]

---

[8] George and Bennett (2005, 17) somewhat humorously refer to this imperative as a product of "our 'bigger is better' culture."

[9] I discuss this rule in more depth later.

[10] For causal complexity and multiple causality, see Ragin 1992, 133–35.

However, King, Keohane, and Verba (1994, 12–14) do distinguish between "old" and "new" observations. They assert that hypotheses, whether based on existing literature or preliminary research, must be developed and then tested on new data. Ditto if any modification of one's theory that makes it more restrictive occurs in the process of research (22). The concern about verification assumes a sharp temporal and conceptual distinction between the generation and validation of hypotheses. Proponents of case studies tend to reproduce this same distinction, which underlies their arguments regarding the unique advantages of such research designs. Methodological textbooks and articles assert that studies of a single or few cases are uniquely suited to maximize research goals other than the validation of hypotheses: conceptual (internal) validity, hypothesis generation, the falsification of deterministic theories, the identification of causal pathways and causal mechanisms, and the modeling of complex causal relationships (Rueschemeyer 2003; George and Bennett 2005; Seawright and Gerring 2008). Given the particular advantages – and, as a corollary, limitations – of case studies, scholars of qualitative methods frame the decision over the number and type of case(s) in terms of a trade-off that hinges on the particular research goals and object of study (Lijphart 1971; George and Bennett 2005; Seawright and Gerring 2008).

To ease this trade-off, scholars are encouraged to take a "strategic" approach to case selection. For example, Seawright and Gerring's typology suggests a "deviant" case to generate new hypotheses and a "typical" case to test existing ones (Gerring and Seawright 2008).[11] On the one hand, such typologies restore integrity and internal complexity to cases. Cases are not merely sets of observations, nor are they "homogenous units": they are qualitatively *different* from one another and therefore exist in distinct relationship to bodies of theories. On the other hand, the language of such labels explicitly reproduces the same statistical logic underlying King, Keohane, and Verba's framework. As George and Bennett (2005, 69) state, the first step of case selection is identifying "the universe – that is, the class or subclass of events – of which a single case or group of cases to be studied are instances."[12]

In addition to reproducing a statistical logic, the very idea of case selection relies on a realist epistemology in which cases self-evidently exist as members of a universe (Ragin 1992; Soss, Chapter 5, this volume).[13] Drawing on Ragin, Soss inverts this logic – which he refers to as "studying a case" – with an approach that foregrounds casing as an activity throughout the research process – "casing a study" (Soss, Chapter 5, this volume). Both Ragin and Soss reject the split temporality of generation and validation of hypotheses in favor of seeing both processes as interwoven throughout research and analysis.

---

[11] See also Flyvbjerg (2001) for a critique of the statistical logic of case selection.
[12] See Gerring (2004, 645–46) for a similar statement.
[13] For further discussion of the point about statistical logic, see Flyvbjerg (2001, 88–90); Small (2004, 6).

At each moment where hypotheses and data meet, there is a reciprocal encounter and an opportunity for casing (Ragin 1992, 217–20; Soss, Chapter 5, this volume). And casing can occur within the bounds of what would generally be considered the case itself, in ways that might lead to the reclassification of the most macro-level unit of analysis. Conceptual innovation within the bounds of the case may result in a new answer to the question: *What is this an instance of?*

The ongoing process of casing also calls into question the case study's ostensible "bias toward verification." As Flyvbjerg argues, "The advantage of the case study is that it can 'close in' on real-life situations and test views directly in relation to phenomena as they unfold in practice [and therefore] it is falsification, not verification, that characterizes the case study" (Flyvbjerg 2006, 235).[14] As recounted in many ethnographies and archival studies, the experience of field research is marked by a constant re-examination of one's preliminary arguments and their conceptual foundations. The process of re-examination can be prompted by, for example, an unforeseen turn of events, the discovery that a previously unknown actor or institution had a pivotal role in a process under study, or learning from fellow academics and intellectuals in the field. This latter type of interaction problematizes the hierarchical binary of analyst and informant: as I have discovered time and again in my fieldwork, my "subjects" were of course themselves "analysts" of their social world, or what Marcus calls "paraethnographers" (Marcus 1995; see also Riles 2000). For interpretive social science more generally, interpretation is both a technique of analysis and, as enacted by the actors we study, a "linchpin of … social life" (Glaeser 2010, xvii).[15] We interpret interpretations, translating "in and out" of the "frames of meaning within which actors orient their conduct" and the "frames of meaning involved in sociological theories" (Garcelon 2005, 17).

For these reasons, the term "single-case study" is a misnomer. A single-case study is constitutively multiple: a case is always *of* more than one kind. The researcher's ongoing attempts to case a study are one way to attend to this multiplicity. A second approach is an analytic process I refer to as "siting." In contrast to the bounded holism that "case" can imply, a *site* is a particular place where we can observe a broader process unfolding. Capitalism, energy systems, indigenous mobilization, the climate crisis, settler colonialism, the supply chains of production and distribution, migration, citizenship and belonging, and resurgent right-wing authoritarianism: all of these processes defy national boundaries, several of them are global in scope, and all can be fruitfully studied

---

[14] For a critique of "verification" as the goal of case study analysis, see Burawoy (2009), who argues that the goal is theoretical reconstruction (or improvement) rather than validation or invalidation of a preexisting theory.

[15] This is what Giddens termed the "double hermeneutic," and what Garcelon rephrased the "double narrativity" of the social sciences. See Garcelon (2005, 17, cf. fn. 68); Giddens (1984, 284; 1987, 30–31); Rabinow (1986).

in particular times and places.[16] If casing continually re-situates a study vis-à-vis other theories, concepts, and empirical studies, then siting offers a different perspective on the relationship between the specific and the general. Instead of seeing those places as particular instances of a more general category – even, as Ragin (1992) and Soss (Chapter 5, this volume) make clear, of multiple general categories simultaneously – we can see them as particularly fertile sites for studying broader structures and processes that spatially and temporally exceed the sites in question. Siting thus rejects the boundedness that the term "case" assumes. In this vein, and referring to his research on ethnic identity in a Transylvanian city, Brubaker writes: "The Cluj project is not a *case study*, but a *place study*. Cluj is not a *unit of analysis* studied in isolation from (or, except tangentially, even in comparison to) other coordinate units. Cluj is rather a *strategic research site* for studying processes that are of more general theoretical interest" (2003, 1, emphasis in original). Studying sites rather than cases is a way to call into question, rather than analytically reinforce, boundedness: "We don't want to *presuppose* that entitativity or groupness by inscribing it into the very terms in which we pose our research questions" (1). Indeed, even cultural anthropologists, whose ethnographic method has long been associated with the focus on a relatively bounded field site, must contend with the increasing interpenetration and co-constitution of the local and the global (Comaroff and Comaroff 2003, 153–58). If the "foundational fiction" of a closed community is no longer theoretically or empirically tenable, the question of comparison reemerges in a different form (153).

One compelling approach to reformulating comparison along these lines includes the research designs that Tilly refers to as "encompassing comparisons." These "select locations within the structure or process and explain similarities or differences among those locations as consequences of their relationships to the whole" (Tilly 1984, 125).[17] Encompassing comparisons leverage rather than disavow global interconnectedness. But they also contain "a great danger": the temptation of functionalist explanations, whereby the outcomes observed in the unit of interest are wholly attributed to that unit's purpose in a larger, organically construed whole (125–26).[18] Encompassing comparisons thus overcomes the pitfalls of conventional comparisons and simultaneously reproduces them at a higher scale. As McMichael points out, encompassing comparisons takes for granted the "systemic unit and unit cases within which historical observation takes place," in effect removing "the unit of analysis from theoretical contention" (McMichael 1990, 389). In other words, this mode of analysis assumes a priori

---

[16] Scholarship in the paradigm of "planetary urbanization" and "global cities" takes a similar approach to the study of multi-scalar and transnational processes. See Brenner (2014); Sassen (2014).
[17] See also Schwedler, Chapter 9, this volume.
[18] For discussion of this risk, see McMichael (1990, especially pp. 388–89).

From Cases to Sites

the systemic logic, geographic contours, and temporal bounds of the whole to which unit cases belong – rather than interrogating how these three features are co-constituted by a multi-scalar, dynamic whole and its many parts. Such an interrogation would entail rethinking the whole as an "emergent totality ... discovered through the mutual conditioning of its parts" (391). What McMichael refers to as "incorporated comparisons" take emergence and co-constitution as their point of departure. Such comparisons can occur in two forms: diachronic – discrete but related moments of a process unfolding over time – and synchronic – a cross-sectional analysis of a snapshot of a social configuration (389).

Sites capture both of these dimensions. Global processes – capitalism, energy systems, migration – develop unevenly across space and time, allowing for myriad opportunities to study the co-constitution of sites and macro processes. In any given locale, a researcher might investigate how the process in question interacts with preexisting political institutions, partisan alignments, social organizations, economic livelihoods, or cultural identities (a spatial "conjuncture" in McMichael's terms). The researcher could also investigate how these locally or nationally territorialized dynamics in turn reshape the unfolding of the global process under study, with consequences beyond the aforementioned local or national scales (a temporal "process" for McMichael). For example, imagine a planned extractive project that would contaminate water, negatively impacting agricultural livelihoods in a particular region of a country. The affected community stages a protest in response, thus imperiling the project's feasibility and causing investors to renegotiate their contract with the national government and/or scout potential locations in other countries with similar resource endowments. Either of these corporate responses could potentially reshape the global political economy and geography of resource extraction – effects amplified by the fact that the company's decision would likely influence the actions of other extractive firms.

Ultimately, the approach of siting leaves it up to the scholar's research questions and goals whether the emphasis is placed on temporal trajectory or spatial conjuncture – or both. In addition, I also contribute to McMichael's approach with concrete advice for selecting and analyzing sites, grounded in my own reflexive process of siting and re-siting my research on the global energy transition. In the remainder of this chapter, I draw on my work on the global energy transition to illustrate the iterative process of siting and conclude with transportable lessons for research projects on other global processes.

SITING AND RE-SITING THE GLOBAL RENEWABLE ENERGY TRANSITION

Climate change is obviously a planetary condition; meanwhile, the energy transition that is required to mitigate the worst emissions scenarios, and their consequences for societies and ecosystems, is often conceived in domestic terms.

But the material infrastructure of a transition from hydrocarbon to renewable energy involves processes of extraction, manufacture, and distribution that exceed national boundaries. Wind turbines, solar panels, and lithium batteries – to name three of the key technologies needed to effectuate an energy transition – are produced and traded via global supply chains.[19] My research centers on the last of these technologies, which is essential for two aspects of the energy transition: powering electric vehicles and storing energy in renewable grids (Riofrancos 2019). Specifically, I trace the socio-environmental consequences and complex political economy of lithium extracted from the salt flats of northern Chile, one of the primary exporters of lithium for the global market. But I do not take this larger unit of analysis – the global market – for granted. Instead, studying the early phase of an emergent and contested set of interlocking markets – lithium, batteries, electric vehicles, and utility-scale storage – reveals the ongoing work of situated actors to transform a natural resource into a commodity, secure financing for extractive projects, forge the links in a complex supply chain, and implement policies to generate demand for green technologies in a world that remains on the precipice of an energy transition with an uncertain future. In such a context, the dynamics at local and national scales – protest, policy making, geological conditions, contract negotiations – co-constitute the larger whole to which they belong.

The first phase of this project consisted of four months of fieldwork, encompassing the nexus of policy making, corporate headquarters, and elite networks in the capital, Santiago, as well as contention over lithium extraction in the Atacama Desert, the sector that affects ecosystems and indigenous communities and exacerbates water scarcity in one of the driest places on Earth. I conducted interviews and ethnographic observation, simultaneously tracking the global market dynamics and conflictual geopolitics of this relatively nascent industry. I initially engaged in the iterative process of casing and re-casing described earlier – but, as I gained more experience and brainstormed with colleagues, I shifted my analytic gaze to identify the lithium sector in Chile not as a *case* of a more general *category* but as the multi-scalar *site* of global *structures and processes*.

At first, my instinct was to treat lithium extraction in Chile as a case of the extractive frontiers of the renewable transition, in a comparative framework that would include Bolivia and Argentina (neighboring countries that also contain significant lithium reserves), as well as such extractive frontiers further afield, from cobalt in the Democratic Republic of Congo to rare-earth mining in Inner Mongolia. However, the more I learned about the global supply

---

[19] For critical social science approaches to the study of supply chains, which trace their intellectual lineage to the "commodity chains" approach of world systems theory (Hopkins and Wallerstein 1986), see, for example, Hopkins and Wallerstein (1986); Bair (2005); Tsing (2009); Cowen (2014); Arboleda (2020). For a recent study of the environmental impacts of green technology supply chains, see Sovacool et al. (2020).

chains of the renewable transition – and the emergent forms of political contention along them – the less I saw my study as one case among many and the more I saw it as a particularly fertile site to interrogate the global renewable energy transition that is underway, unevenly and unequally, around the world.

This shift in perspective brought into view unexpected connections across historical time and spatial scales. From this vantage point, the lithium sector bore the traces of Pinochet's brutal dictatorship (1973–1990), Cold War–era concerns about nuclear development, and more than a century of resource extraction (first sodium nitrate, then copper, and most recently lithium) in northern Chile. Meanwhile, forces beyond Chile's borders played a key role in constructing, and contesting, this nascent sector: lithium companies deciding where to invest; increasing market concentration and interlocking ownership of projects; the growing role of Chinese capital in South America; governments in the United States, Europe, and China vying for control over battery and electric vehicle manufacture and the raw materials needed for each; and indigenous and environmental activists beginning to coordinate their resistance across the Andean plateau that encompasses northern Chile and Argentina and southern Bolivia.

This is not to collapse the local and global, or to assert that states do not matter. Quite the contrary: contract negotiations, environmental and water regulations, labor laws, and the territorial rights of indigenous communities are all deeply shaped by national policy making, and quite relevant to the dynamics under study. But analyzing the contentious development of the lithium sector in Chile as a *site* of a broader process rather than a *case* of a more general category has been illuminating. For example, my close tracking of corporate discourse, via social media and industry news sites alerted me to a new strategy on the part of electric vehicles manufacturers. Concerned about supplies of battery-grade lithium, firms such as Volkswagen, Tesla, and BMW are entering into direct agreements with lithium mining companies. This is in effect a forced "vertical integration" of the supply chain, tightening the links between "upstream" extraction and "downstream" vehicle production. While this ensures firms' access to battery materials, it also generates new risks: if communities protest or workers strike at a lithium mine covered by such an agreement, the effects of the protest will reverberate all the way down the chain, impacting the shop floor of the electric vehicle manufacturer. In other words, vertical integration amplifies the effects of supply disruptions – and gives communities and workers leverage over key chokepoints in the global economy. Mitchell (2011, chap. 1) called this power "sabotage"; in his book *Carbon Democracy*, he demonstrates how early twentieth-century coal workers were able to win major concessions from firms and governments by shutting down industrial economies at the source of the energy that powered them.[20]

---

[20] For additional analysis of supply chain governance and disruption, see Arboleda (2020) and Cowen (2014).

While these dynamics are still quite nascent in the lithium sector, siting encourages attention to precisely such junctures where the local and the global co-constitute. From the indigenous territory and otherworldly salt flats of the Atacama Desert, to the rechargeable battery manufacturing hub in Jiangsu province, China, to Washington, DC, where US government officials meet with electric vehicle manufacturers to ensure the supply of raw materials, lithium offers a window into the uneven, and unequal, contours of the global energy transition.

SELECTING SITES

The reflexive processes of siting and re-siting described earlier offer lessons to scholars embarking on research projects that cut against the grain of conventional comparison. All global structures encompass multiple sites, but some sites are more analytically and methodologically fruitful than others. Although choosing sites is inevitably a trial-and-error process of false leads and unexpected discoveries, I propose three criteria to guide selection: observable, salient, and contentious.

First, the macrostructure ought to be empirically *observable* at the locale and scale in question, whether accessed in documentary form, elicited in interviews with identifiable actors, or observed in real time through participant observation – or, ideally, some combination of the three. Second, the macrostructure ought to be politically *salient* in the chosen context, meaning that it is (or, for historical studies, was) a topic of live interest to situated actors, a subject of policy making or social mobilization, and an area discussed in public fora and disseminated in mass media outlets – and/or among specific "counterpublics" to which the researcher has access.[21] Third, I recommend that sites be chosen where the process in question is the subject of *contention*. The analytic utility of conflict is that it reveals global processes to be the outcome of interventions on the part of actors located in specific sites, driven by complex interests and ideologies, and situated on an asymmetric terrain. In other words, attention to conflict highlights the emergent and dynamic qualities of whole-part relations.

In addition to these three criteria, I suggest that scholars view empirical reality through a bifocal lens. By tacking back and forth between gathering data on specific sites and on the global processes that spatially and temporally exceed them, we can glimpse the global in the local, simultaneously attending to the specific times and places that the global is produced.

In my research on the supply chains of the renewable energy transition, I chose to begin by siting my project in Chile precisely because the dynamics

---

[21] As defined by Fattal, counterpublics are "a subset of publics that stand in conscientious opposition to a dominant ideology and strategically subvert that ideology's construction in public discourse." See Fattal (2018) and also Warner (2002).

From Cases to Sites 121

around lithium – a key component of this transition – are observable, salient, and contentious. In Chile, lithium is a topic of policy making and economic investment. In addition, since successive Chilean governments have taken an interest in promoting lithium development, state actors are willing to discuss this policy arena with a researcher. At the same time, groups more critical of the lithium sector – from labor unions to leftist politicians to indigenous and environmental activists – have staged demonstrations and issued communiqués. Relatedly, lithium extraction has occasioned multiple forms of contention: protests, partisan disputes over policy, debates among market actors as to whether lithium counts as a "commodity," and competition between states vying for control over the electric vehicle supply chain. The observable, salient, and contentious nature of lithium in Chile made it an ideal first site for this research project.

As I move forward, I will select additional sites guided by the same criteria. For example, the US Congress and the Biden administration are currently making moves to expand the extraction and development of "critical minerals" such as lithium within US borders, in a bid to control more of the electric vehicle supply chain. In response, environmental groups are already warning about the effects of extraction in desert regions such as northern Nevada – and investors are eyeing opportunities for expanded domestic manufacturing of batteries and electric cars. For these reasons, specific sites in the United States – Washington, DC, as the location of elite decision making and Western states slated for potential lithium projects – are next on my list to study this emergent global process.

CONCLUSION

Graduate students and junior scholars who do fieldwork-based qualitative work on one or a few cases often encounter doubts about the rigor of their research. They experience pressure to add more cases, including superficial shadow cases, or to combine their qualitative work with statistical or experimental methods. This chapter, along with the other contributions to this volume, ought to inspire intellectual confidence in immersive, interpretive approaches to social scientific inquiry. Contrary to the conventional wisdom, single cases are not prone to verification, merely anecdotal, purely descriptive, or a first step toward a more generalizable analysis. They do not have an "n" of 1. The many scales of social life call into question their status as a single unit. If anything, the experience of fieldwork and subsequent data analysis is one of being overwhelmed by the sheer quantity of observations and the richness and texture of social life. It is the experience of having one's hypotheses or theories constantly questioned and challenged in real time by situated actors. It is the experience of the "aha!" moment of conceptual innovation in the thick of empirical inquiry, and of our prior categories cast into doubt in the ethnographic or archival encounter with the world in all its breathless complexity. Ultimately, the iterative, reflexive process of collecting and analyzing data, of moving back and forth between our field sites and our epistemic communities, does not undermine the more general import of our studies. It bolsters it, strengthening both empirical acumen and analytic leverage by honing our concepts and subjecting them to the constant tests provided by events, interviews, and archives.

In this chapter, I have presented two ways to conceive the constitutive multiplicity of the so-called single-case study: casing and siting. Casing shows that a single case can be many cases simultaneously; siting shows that specific places can distill phenomena that are world-historic in scope and scale but impossible to apprehend all at once in their immense totality. Both analytic operations underscore the rigor of qualitative, site-intensive research. Far from shying away from producing insights about broader structures and processes, the contribution of such studies is precisely how they articulate the complex relationship between the particular and the general.

REFERENCES

Anria, Santiago. 2013. "Social Movements, Party Organization, and Populism: Insights from the Bolivian MAS." *Latin American Politics and Society* 55 (3): 19–46.

Arboleda, Martín. 2020. *Planetary Mine: Territories of Extraction Under Late Capitalism*. New York: Verso.

Bair, Jennifer. 2005. "Global Capitalism and Commodity Chains: Looking Back, Going Forward." *Competition & Change* 9 (2): 153–80.

Bhambra, Gurminder. 2016. "Comparative Historical Sociology and the State: Problems of Method." *Cultural Sociology* 10 (3): 335–51.

Blatt, Jessica. 2018. *Race and the Making of American Political Science*. Philadelphia: University of Pennsylvania Press.

Brady, Henry E., and David Collier, eds. 2004. *Rethinking Social Inquiry: Diverse Tools, Shared Standards*. Lanham, MD: Rowman & Littlefield.

Brady, Henry E., David Collier, and Jason Seawright 2004. "Refocusing the Discussion of Methodology." In *Rethinking Social Inquiry: Diverse Tools, Shared Standards*, edited by Henry E. Brady and David Collier, 3–20. Lanham, MD: Rowman & Littlefield.

Brenner, Neil, ed. 2014. *Implosions/Explosions: Towards a Study of Planetary Urbanization*. Berlin: Jovis.

Brubaker, Rogers. 2003. "Beyond Comparativism?" Department of Sociology, UCLA. www.escholarship.org/uc/item/7t52j73w

Brubaker, Rogers, Margit Feischmidt, Liana Grancea, and Jon Fox. 2008. *Nationalist Politics and Everyday Ethnicity in a Transylvanian Town*. Princeton, NJ: Princeton University Press.

Burawoy, Michael. 2009. *The Extended Case Method: Four Countries, Four Decades, Four Great Transformations, and One Theoretical Tradition*. Berkeley: University of California Press.

Calhoun, Craig. 1996. "The Rise and Domestication of Historical Sociology." In *The Historic Turn in the Human Sciences*, edited by Terrence J. McDonald, 305–38. Ann Arbor: University of Michigan Press.
Clifford, James, and George E. Marcus, eds. 2010. *Writing Culture: The Poetics and Politics of Ethnography, 25th Anniversary Edition*, 2nd edn. Berkeley: University of California Press.
Collier, David, Henry E. Brady, and Jason Seawright. 2010. "A Sea Change in Political Methodology." In *Rethinking Social Inquiry: Diverse Tools, Shared Standards*, 2nd edn., edited by Henry E. Brady and David Collier, 1–10. Lanham, MD: Rowman & Littlefield.
Collier, David, Jason Seawright, and Gerardo L. Munck. 2010. "The Quest for Standards: King, Keohane, and Verba's *Designing Social Inquiry*." In *Rethinking Social Inquiry: Diverse Tools, Shared Standards*, 2nd edn., edited by Henry E. Brady and David Collier, 21–50. Lanham, MD: Rowman & Littlefield.
Comaroff, Jean, and John Comaroff. 2003. "Ethnography on an Awkward Scale: Postcolonial Anthropology and the Violence of Abstraction." *Ethnography* 4 (2): 147–79.
Connell, Raewyn. "Why Is Classical Theory Classical?" *American Journal of Sociology* 102 (6): 1511–57.
Cowen, Deborah. 2014. *The Deadly Life of Logistics: Mapping Violence in Global Trade*. Minneapolis: University of Minnesota Press.
Fattal, Alex. 2018. "Counterpublic." In *The International Encyclopedia of Anthropology*, edited by Hilary Callan, 1–2. Hoboken, NJ: Wiley.
Flyvbjerg, Bent. 2001. *Making Social Science Matter: Why Social Inquiry Fails and How It Can Succeed Again*. New York: Cambridge University Press.
  2006. "Five Misunderstandings about Case-Study Research." *Qualitative Inquiry* 12 (2): 219–45.
Garcelon, Marc. 2005. *Revolutionary Passage from Soviet to Post-Soviet Russia, 1985–2000*. Philadelphia: Temple University Press.
George, Alexander L. and Andrew Bennett. 2005. *Case Studies and Theory Development in the Social Sciences*. Cambridge, MA: MIT Press.
Gerring, John. 2004. "What Is a Case Study and What Is It Good For?" *American Political Science Review* 98 (2): 341–54.
  2008. "Case Selection for Case-Study Analysis: Qualitative and Quantitative Techniques." In *The Oxford Handbook of Political Methodology*, edited by Janet M. Box-Steffensmeier, Henry E. Brady, and David Collier, 645–84. New York: Oxford University Press.
Glaeser, Andreas. 2010. *Political Epistemics: The Secret Police, the Opposition, and the End of East German Socialism*. Chicago: University of Chicago Press.
Giddens, Anthony. 1984. *The Constitution of Society*. Berkeley: University of California Press.
  1987. *Social Theory and Modern Sociology*. Oxford: Polity Press.
Hall, Peter. 2003. "Aligning Ontology and Methodology in Comparative Research." In *Comparative Historical Analysis in the Social Sciences*, edited by James Mahoney and Dietrich Rueschemeyer, 373–404. New York: Cambridge University Press.
Hopkins, Terrance K., and Immanuel Wallerstein. 1986. "Commodity Chains in the World-Economy Prior to 1800." *Review (Fernand Braudel Center)* 10 (1): 157–70.

Jameson, Fredric. 1989. "Marxism and Postmodernism." *New Left Review* 176 (6): 31–45.
King, Gary, Robert Keohane, and Sidney Verba. 1994. *Designing Social Inquiry*. Princeton, NJ: Princeton University Press.
Lijphart, Arend. 1971. "Comparative Politics and the Comparative Method." *American Political Science Review* 65 (3): 682–93.
Mahoney, James, and Gary Goertz. 2006. "A Tale of Two Cultures: Contrasting Quantitative and Qualitative Research." *Political Analysis* 14 (3): 227–49.
Marcus, George E. 1995. "Ethnography in/of the World System: The Emergence of Multi-Sited Ethnography." *Annual Review of Anthropology* 24: 95–117.
McMichael, Philip. 1990. "Incorporating Comparison within a World Historical Perspective: An Alternative Comparative Method." *American Sociological Review* 55 (3): 385–97.
Mitchell, Timothy. 1991. "The Limits of the State: Beyond Statist Approaches and Their Critics." *American Political Science Review* 85 (1): 77–96.
    2011. *Carbon Democracy: Political Power in the Age of Oil*. New York: Verso Books.
Oren, Ido. 2003. *Our Enemies and Us: America's Rivalries and the Making of Political Science*. Ithaca, NY: Cornell University Press.
Plestch, Carl E. 1981. "The Three Worlds, or the Division of Social Scientific Labor, circa 1950–1975." *Comparative Studies in Society and History* 23 (4): 565–90.
Polanyi, Karl. 1944. *The Great Transformation: The Political and Economic Origins of Our Time*. Boston: Beacon Press.
Rabinow, Paul. 1986. "Representations Are Social Facts: Modernity and Post-Modernity in Anthropology." In *Writing Culture: The Poetics and Politics of Ethnography*, edited by James Clifford and George E. Marcus. Berkeley: University of California Press.
Ragin, Charles C. 1992. "'Casing' and the Process of Social Inquiry." In *What Is a Case?: Exploring the Foundations of Social Inquiry*, edited by Charles C. Ragin and Howard S. Becker, 217–26. New York: Cambridge University Press.
Riles, Annelise. 2000. *The Network Inside Out*. Ann Arbor: University of Michigan Press.
Riofrancos, Thea. 2017. "Scaling Democracy: Participation and Resource Extraction in Latin America." *Perspectives on Politics* 15 (3): 678–96.
    2018. "A Genealogy of the Comparative Method." American Political Science Association Annual Meeting, Boston, September 1.
    2019. "Agency, Critique, and Complicity in *The Extractive Zone*." Book Review. https://doi.org/10.1177/0921374019838886
Rueschemeyer, Dietrich. 2003. "Can One or a Few Cases Yield Theoretical Gains?" In *Comparative Historical Analysis in the Social Sciences*, edited by James Mahoney and Dietrich Rueschemeyer, 305–36. New York: Cambridge University Press.
Sassen, Saski. 2014. *Expulsions: Brutality and Complexity in the Global Economy*. Cambridge, MA: Belknap Press.
Schaffer, Frederic C. 1998. *Democracy in Translation: Understanding Politics in an Unfamiliar Culture*. Ithaca, NY: Cornell University Press.
Schatz, Edward, ed. 2009. *Political Ethnography: What Immersion Contributes to the Study of Power*. Chicago: University of Chicago Press.

Seawright, Jason, and John Gerring. 2008. "Case Selection Techniques in Case Study Research: A Menu of Qualitative and Quantitative Options." *Political Research Quarterly* 61 (2): 294–308.

Seawright, Jason, and Gerardo Munck. 2004. "The Quest for Standards: King, Keohane, and Verba's *Designing Social Inquiry*." In *Rethinking Social Inquiry: Diverse Tools, Shared Standards*, edited by Henry E. Brady and David Collier, 33–64. Lanham, MD: Rowman & Littlefield.

Sewell, William H. 2005. *Logics of History: Social Theory and Social Transformation*. Chicago: University of Chicago Press.

Silva, Eduardo. 2009. *Challenging Neoliberalism in Latin America*. New York: Cambridge University Press.

———. 2012. "Exchange Rising? Karl Polanyi and Contentious Politics in Contemporary Latin America." *Latin American Politics and Society* 54 (3): 1–32.

Simmons, Erica S. 2016. *Meaningful Resistance: Market Reforms and the Roots of Social Protest in Latin America*. New York: Cambridge University Press.

Skocpol, Theda, and Margaret Somers. 1980. "The Uses of Comparative History in Macrosocial Inquiry." *Comparative Studies in Society and History* 22 (2): 174–97.

Small, Mario Luis. 2004. "Lost In Translation: How Not to Make Qualitative Research More Scientific." *NSF Qualitative Methods Working Paper*. http://citeseerx.ist.psu.edu/viewdoc/download?doi=10.1.1.500.6807&rep=rep1&type=pdf

Sovacool, Benjamin K., Saleem H. Ali, Morgan Bazilian, Ben Radley, Benoit Nemery, Julia Okatz, and Dustin Mulvaney. 2020. "Sustainable Minerals and Metals for a Low-Carbon Future." *Science* 367 (6473): 30–33.

Steinmetz, George. 2004. "Odious Comparisons: Incommensurability, the Case Study, and 'Small N's' in Sociology." *Sociological Theory* 22 (3): 371–400.

Stern, Steve J. 1988. "Feudalism, Capitalism, and the World-System in the Perspective of Latin America and the Caribbean." *The American Historical Review* 93 (4): 829–72.

Svampa, Maristella. 2016. *Debates Latinoamericanos: Indianismo, Desarrollo, Dependencia, Populismo*. CEDIB, Centro de Documentación e Información Bolivia.

Thompson, Edward Palmer. 1966. *The Making of the English Working Class*. New York: Penguin.

Tilly, Charles. 1984. *Big Structures, Large Processes, Huge Comparisons*. New York: Russell Sage Foundation.

Tsing, Anna. 2009. "Supply Chains and the Human Condition." *Rethinking Marxism*, 21 (2): 148–76.

Wallerstein, Immanuel. 1974. "The Rise and Future Demise of the World Capitalist System: Concepts for Comparative Analysis." *Comparative Studies in Society and History* 16 (4): 387–415.

Warner, Michael. 2002. *Publics and Counterpublics*. Cambridge, MA: Zone Books.

Williams, Eric. 1944. *Capitalism and Slavery*. Chapel Hill: University of North Carolina Press.

Wood, Ellen Meiksins. 1998. "The Agrarian Origins of Capitalism." *Monthly Review* 50: 14–31.

Yengoyan, Aram. 2006. "Introduction: On the Issue of Comparison." In *Modes of Comparison: Theory and Practice*, edited by Aram Yengoyan, 1–29. Ann Arbor: University of Michigan Press.

PART II

DEVELOPING NEW APPROACHES TO COMPARISON
THROUGH RESEARCH

7

Comparing Complex Cases Using Archival Research

Jonathan Obert
Amherst College

Social scientists have long considered the thorny question of how the large-scale phenomena we are frequently interested in explaining can both be produced by and shape behavior at the level of relatively local individual interaction. This question poses a particular problem for comparative analysis. Since we know that the kinds of phenomena we compare are often spatially or temporally related, how do we account for the seeming interdependency of much of social life as well as the fact that our comparisons often involve an implicit and untheorized assumption that those elements operate at the "same" level of analysis (Sewell 2005)? Treating cases as though they are independent and equivalent allows for controlled comparison and, hence, more rigorous causal inference and increased internal validity. However, this priority comes at the serious cost of providing a broad description of the multiple causes affecting an outcome (causal verisimilitude) as well as being unable to translate findings from research settings into the real world (ecological validity). Indeed, it is one of the great ironies of social science research that many of the phenomena we are most interested in understanding – the big, important events such as democratization, state formation, war and so on – are actually the most difficult to study using traditional tools of scientific research.

A major reason for this dilemma is that these types of social phenomena are *complex systems* – that is, they involve micro-behavior producing macro-level patterns that in turn shape micro-behavior (and so on). Social systems such as wars, nations, and institutions are constituted by activity at multiple scales of analysis and involve complex forms of interdependence among various actors, groups, and the sub- and supra-systems making them up. However, precisely because the cases we study are often interdependent at higher-order scales of analysis, traditional controlled comparisons have a difficult time actually identifying causal factors that might be responsible for explaining outcomes we care about. Thus, while on the one hand, we might wish to compare revolutions or wars to each other to help test our explanatory frameworks, we need to also consider the ways in which those events are tied into a larger, macro-historical system.

This chapter suggests one way to address this problem is to use historical archives to disaggregate the temporal and spatial properties of the phenomena we hope to compare while also tracing connections among those disaggregated elements. This allows us to identify the boundaries around subsystems that can be treated as relatively independent (thus allowing them to be compared directly), at the same time identifying the hierarchical connections tying those subsystemic activities together. Archives often present us with a complex assortment of documents, ephemera, images, and other materials, frequently compiled in unsystematic ways or drawn from multiple sources. By *classifying*, *contextualizing*, *layering*, and *linking* archival materials, analysts have an opportunity to think theoretically about how the phenomena they investigate operate at particular temporal and spatial scales. As a result, they can identify comparisons that consider the embedding of local and temporally truncated phenomena in large, slow-moving processes (and vice versa). Other methodologies can be leveraged to explore dependent and multi-level phenomena as well, but archival analysis allows the analyst to juxtapose different spatial and temporal scales simultaneously and to do so from a global rather than a situated perspective.

This chapter will proceed as follows. First, it will argue that social scientists should take seriously the multi-level and interdependent qualities of the historical phenomena we study, arguing that causal identification strategies (particularly controlled case analysis) only alleviate some of the problems these qualities present. Second, situating various research methodologies and their approaches to studying complexity in social life, it will argue that archival historical research offers scholars an opportunity to remedy some of the issues raised in this discussion. Finally, it will provide a short demonstration of how archival practice can enrich our explanations by analyzing the multi-level and interdependent comparative and causal claims in William Tuttle's (1970) important account of the 1919 Chicago race riot.

THE USES AND LIMITS OF CONTROLLED COMPARISON

Social scientists have long known that adopting the scientific model of explanation to address social phenomena is extremely difficult in part because of how we typically link causal reasoning to comparative analysis. Specifically, much social science research attempts to identify whether or not a particular factor can be causally linked to an observable outcome. As a result, studies deploy comparison to isolate and identify whether that independent factor does, indeed, logically contribute to the consequence in question.

Increasingly, social scientific research explicitly addresses the inferential problems involved in identifying causal factors – that is, the logic by which causal claims are made and validated. Since the growth in popularity of the Neyman-Rubin counterfactual model in the past decades, scholars emphasize that the "gold standard" for causal explanation involves randomized controlled trials, in which the only factor systematically related to the outcome of interest among a given sample of comparable cases is an intervention made by the analyst (a treatment).[1] Randomizing who or what gets allocated to the control and treatment groups across a large and representative sample ensures that the effects of any drug, procedure, or test given by the analyst can be isolated from other systematic factors that might explain or influence the outcome (Rubin 1974). Of course, because it is morally or practically impossible to start a war or initiate a process of democratization to test a particular hypothesis, scholars instead turn to "quasi-experimental" techniques to simulate the causal environment of the controlled randomized trial. These design-based inferential strategies include so-called natural experiments, regression discontinuity designs, and the like. Indeed, even more traditional forms of social science research design such as comparative historical analysis and multivariate regression with controls try to help ensure *internal validity* – the notion that the factor in question really does bear a causal relationship to the outcome because of precise ability to control for confounding factors.

At the same time, even when using these techniques, we inevitably run into stumbling blocks. These problems largely arise for two reasons. First, because most social phenomena are deeply complex and multi-dimensional, comparing multiple cases involves invoking many assumptions about whether the objects we are comparing are actually of the same case. Second, because the causes for events inside and across complex systems are themselves nearly impossible to isolate effectively, it can be difficult to understand the overall importance of the causes we do identify in their actual empirical settings.

One problem is the issue of *interdependency*, in which an event or outcome affects subsequent or other spatially related events or outcomes. Interdependency might involve, for instance, complex causal links among various explanatory variables (such as a latent process causing two or more seemingly independent phenomena or feedback loops or confounds in the link between cause and effect), or it might involve a kind of reverse causality, in which a seeming effect (such as a rise in the stock market) actually shapes the hypothesized causal process (such as future expectations of market performance). Interdependency can also take the form of statistical endogeneity, in which some independent variable is correlated with the error term in a model specification, frequently due to omitted variables and unobserved heterogeneity, measurement error, or simultaneity among the dependent and independent variables. Without correcting for these biases,

---

[1] For an excellent description of the logic underlying experimental design in the social sciences, see Dunning (2012, 5–8).

endogeneity makes it difficult for analysts to clearly state that a given factor is causally related to the outcome.

For instance, the problem of interdependence has long characterized the debate over whether or not democratic institutions cause economic development or whether or not development leads to the growth of democracy. Since many factors (such as state formation process or resource endowment) may shape both democratization and development, disentangling the direction of the causal arrow is difficult. Of course, social science scholars have made great strides in using, for instance, instrumental variables or natural experiments to try to identify variables related to the causal factor but not otherwise related to the outcome to tease out these relations (e.g., Acemoglu, Johnson, and Robinson 2001). But even in these accounts, interdependency can make it difficult to make causal arguments through comparison since there always may be unnoticed systematic factors tying those cases together, as well as intrinsic measurement problems (Morck and Yeung 2011). Since we insist on studying things that cannot be experimented on directly through randomization, like democracy and development, we end up leaving our work vulnerable to the charge that we are omitting something important.

Relatedly, interdependency can also pose a problem when a phenomenon of interest itself causes or has some effect on other cases with which we might like to compare it. For example, take the study of social revolutions. Scholars have long debated whether ideology, psychological factors, social structural factors, geopolitics, or micro-level collective mobilization was most responsible for causing epoch-transforming events such as the French, Chinese, or Russian Revolutions (Goldstone 2001). To explain social revolutions in general means to try to identify the factors present in the successful outcomes (actual revolutions) while also trying to distinguish them from factors that might be causally related to revolution but were not present in these cases (though they may have been present in other states that did not undergo revolution). Indeed, this is exactly the path laid out by Theda Skocpol (1979) in her important book, which leverages direct comparisons among France, China, and Russia (as well as the "negative" cases of England, Japan, and Germany) to make the case for a structural account of revolutionary change.

One problem with this procedure, as Skocpol (1979, 39) herself admits, is that the French, Chinese, and Russian Revolutions cannot really be treated as independent cases, in which causal factors exogenous to the events themselves are crucial in explaining their occurrence. Indeed, as Sewell (2005) suggests, as a transformative and novel process, the French Revolution was more than a case: it was an "event," one that fundamentally altered the world in such a way as to make future revolutions both thinkable (through changing ideologies of popular sovereignty and violence) and practically possible (by opening up a new era in nation-state development). In other words, it might be impossible to imagine the Russian and, consequently, the Chinese Revolutions without the French experience. Because these cases are *not* independent – at some level, the French

Revolution has a causal effect on all subsequent world history (even if subtle and imperceptible) – relying on straightforward controlled comparison can be misleading.

In their classic account of the logic of comparative social inquiry, Przeworksi and Teune (1970) argue that the fact that social phenomena are always part of a larger interdependent system is actually an advantage for making generalized theories. Since, in their view, social systems are relatively stable and bounded, it is possible to claim that "behavior of any component of a system is determined by factors intrinsic to the system and ... relatively isolated from influences outside the system" (12). This move, in turn, means that one can redescribe the properties of a given system (such as the "nation" of France) in terms of more general variables (such as *population* or *economy*) to compare it with other, similar systems (other nations).

The problem is that such interdependence is only contained within a system when we isolate particular systemic scales of analysis, such as nations. At a higher order, however, what happens in France in a given historical moment is also shaped by and shapes the behavior of actors in other comparable systems such as those of Russia and China. Instead of allowing us to treat critical social phenomena within a given historical context as isolated, such multiple hierarchical forms of interdependence call to mind the so-called butterfly effect identified by chaos theorists. The butterfly effect gets its name from the fact that because weather systems are so interdependent, a butterfly flapping its wings in some remote area can alter a local air current, setting in motion a chain of events leading to a hurricane many miles away (Hilborn 2004). In a real sense, the butterfly is a necessary condition or cause for the hurricane. But this cause is so enmeshed in a series of complex interactions that it becomes impossible to compare hurricanes to identify this cause specifically.

Of course, meteorologists would never try to explain a hurricane as solely a product of butterfly-induced wind turbulence. But without an explicit way of situating such small events in a larger complex system of physical interactions and relationships – that is, without taking scale into account of our models of weather dynamics – understanding the relative importance of butterflies in actual outcomes is impossible.

Indeed, such complexity creates a problem for the comparative study of many kinds of systems. In his brilliant critique of genetic determinism, Lewontin (2000, 95) notes the following:

Causal claims are usually *ceteris paribus*, but in biology all other things are almost never equal. The natural differences in effects observed among organisms do not usually have sufficient regularity with respect to the natural variation of individual causes because these individually causally relevant variables are each too weak in their effects to dominate the large number of other variables.

Like organisms, real social phenomena are similarly produced through multiple causal pathways linking events in a chain of history. As a result, empirical analysis, particularly of important moments or movements, should account for an irreducible level of interdependence among cases.

Similarly, interdependence among social phenomena means that the causes for large phenomena like revolutions involve, at some level, highly idiosyncratic and contingent phenomena at multiple levels of social life. Thus, Sewell (2005) goes on to show how the very particular historical conditions surrounding the storming of the Bastille in 1789 allowed a relatively small-scale insurgent action to scale up to full-fledged revolutionary crisis. In other words, not only are many of the kinds of phenomena we like to study interlinked, but they are also themselves complex aggregations of various scales of social action.

In part, this is a question of classification. Revolutions, for example, are distinguished from other kinds of violent rebellion like riots or *coups d'états* because of the profound effects they have on the distribution of authority within a nation-state and because of the scale of their popular mobilization (Tilly 2003). At the same time, revolutions are, at a more rudimentary level, constituted by the same kinds of local phenomena as coups and riots: street fights, pitched battles, and so forth. In this sense, revolutions are something more than the sum of their parts: their scale transforms all these small-scale actions into an event with ramifications and dimensions exceeding those of similar phenomena (Goldstone 2001).

Scientists typically use the concept of "emergence" to describe the ways in which micro-level behavior can create macro-patterns that often take on qualitatively different properties as they scale (Holland 2000). In his work on scaling processes, Geoffrey West (2017) has demonstrated how many characteristics of animals, cities, and organizations do not linearly increase with the size of the entity in question: for example, in large cities, the residents produce more patents, pollution, and wealth than we would expect if we simply extracted a trend line from a sample of smaller cities. Similarly, large animals live longer than we would expect simply by extrapolating the lifespans of smaller animals. These returns to scale, which West argues have to do with the advantages network forms of organization offer circulatory systems in animals and infrastructure in cities, reveal that larger entities are not merely aggregates of smaller sub-processes: as Durkheim (1982) revealed years ago in his description of "social facts," they possess qualitatively and quantitatively different properties.

Moreover, the macro-patterns produced by micro-level activity can also provide feedback on and shape that micro-level activity in an effectively exogenous or independent way. Cities and large organisms not only aggregate micro-processes differently; they also affect the evolution of those processes over time by creating new physical or social environments through which those processes operate. This notion – *coevolution* – is a fundamental attribute of many social phenomena as well (Padgett and Powell 2012). Thus, many scholars of institutions and organizations implicitly argue that such entities are worth studying precisely because they have a seemingly independent effect on the way actors behave, even as it is the activity of those agents that makes institutions and organizations "real" to begin with.

Emergence and coevolution arise because many social phenomena are simultaneously micro and macro – that is, they are multi-level. Indeed, the multi-level quality of social processes has as serious an implication for comparative analysis as interdependence. Since the phenomena we are interested in studying cannot always simply be derived by a straightforward aggregation of individual behavior. In addition, since those entities are seen as worthy of comparison and explanation on their own terms, we must be careful to consider not only whether our comparisons are able to control for possible causal variation but also to identify the specific level at which those comparisons are being deployed. Indeed, unless we specify the level at which we are making our comparisons and attend for the ways multiple scales together constitute cases of some social phenomenon, even sophisticated causal identification strategies are limited in actually explaining outcomes of interest (Kocher and Monteiro 2016).

Again, take social revolutions. As emergent phenomena, revolutions do not merely aggregate collective violence; they also fundamentally change the nature of authority in a state. Moreover, as examples of coevolution, revolutions often concatenate from small-scale street battles or conflictual interaction (such as the storming of the Bastille) while cascading into a larger, coherent social project that informs the interests and desires of participants. Coevolution and emergence allow us to treat revolutions as coherent social entities (or systems) worthy of explanation.

At the same time, if we compare social revolutions to explain them, we must be careful to distinguish levels of comparison. Even when separated by decades, revolutions are interdependent, leading us to try to use techniques such as natural experiments or instrumental variables to tease out specific factors that might be absent in different cases from those that are present to control for them. But as multi-level phenomena – that is, simultaneously combining local interpersonal fights and rebellion, city- or region-wide patterns of violent conflict, and national-level alterations in the distribution of political authority – at what level are those specific factors actually operating? And what role do they then play in the causal model we propose?

We might, for instance, follow Sewell (2005) in noting that the particular historically contingent uprising at the Bastille was able to scale up to the level of a revolution because of local factors like where the event happened (Paris), how the king responded (by fleeing the city), and how the symbolism of the Bastille allowed it to become a focal point for otherwise disparate opposition to the Old Regime. These factors are historically local and unlikely to ever replay in their exact sequence in other revolutions, even as they had crucial effects on the overall social structure of France at the time. However, it is precisely these local and contingent factors that are also likely to be most independent of events happening elsewhere. That is, the storming of the Bastille *itself* is unlikely to have any direct causal relationship to other local catalytic revolutionary activity in Russia or China, for instance, even as the French Revolution *as a whole* was, indeed, causal for later revolutions. In identifying comparisons, it is worth thinking about which parts of the entities we are comparing are actually comparable in a controlled setting and which are actually related to macro-level phenomena (like capitalism or modernity) linking those entities together within a larger system.

This point is very similar to that made by Lewontin (2000), as noted earlier. Like trying to trace every biological operation to genes, thereby ignoring the ways in which environment and organism coevolve, the problem with isolating a single social indicator and using it as a proxy for a whole social phenomenon is that single elements only reflect a small part of the emergent entity that is actually of interest. Without carefully considering how these elements both contribute to the whole and operate in relation to one another, however, simple controlled comparison cannot provide adequate leverage in accounting for causal differences.

In short, the multi-level (emergent and coevoluntionary) and interdependent characteristics of much of social life make straightforward comparisons a difficult proposition for social scientists. While controlled comparisons can be helpful in shedding light on questions of causal inference and internal validity, these benefits often come at the cost of *causal verisimilitude* – the ability for a comparison to reveal a fuller range of true causal relationships at play – and *ecological validity* – the ability of a particular identified causal effect to also operate in the natural world outside a particular (often experimental) controlled comparison.[2]

ADDRESSING INTERDEPENDENT AND MULTI-LEVEL COMPARISONS

Social scientists are, of course, very aware of the difficulties involved in controlled comparison and have designed many techniques to cope with them. Statistically minded scholars spend much time addressing the problem of keeping units of analysis consistent in observational analysis or modeling individual from group observation – the well-known ecological fallacy – while techniques like multi-level modeling help account for different groupings of data within the same analytic framework. Much formal rational choice modeling, in turn, focuses on identifying specific mechanisms operating at a particular unit of analysis as well as trying to trace the relationships between micro-foundations and macro-patterns (even as much of this research remains methodologically individualist in orientation). Network and spatial analyses take seriously the interdependence of observations, and multi-method research designs often combine micro-analysis of particular

---

[2] An important body of research in the comparative historical analytic tradition uses controlled comparisons not to establish causality but rather to help eliminate alternatives and provide a framework through which to identify mechanisms. See Hall (2003) for a review.

cases with statistical analysis of cross-sectional or time series data. Comparative historical analysts and others use process tracing, sequence analysis, and qualitative forms of comparative inquiry like QCA to examine complex causal processes like equifinality (many possible distinct causes having a similar outcome) and conjunctural causation (effects requiring multiple causes). All of these efforts are attempts to address the problems of verisimilitude and ecological validity in comparative analysis.

At the same time, we lack a unified framework for understanding how more fundamental methodological choices might affect our ability to disaggregate the multi-level and dependent qualities of social life. In complex systems (such as, for instance, the human body), many of the sub-components (such as organs and cells) can be studied on their own terms, without paying much attention to the overall system in which they are embedded. Herbert Simon (1996, 171) calls these "nearly decomposable systems" in which "the details of components can often be ignored while studying their interactions in the whole systems," while, in turn, "the short-run behavior of the individual subsystems can often be described in detail while ignoring the (slower) interactions among subsystems." Since the elements of systems are simultaneously bounded into subsystems and arranged in hierarchies according to scale (e.g., multiple organs and their connections together make a larger entity known as the body), we must therefore identify which elements of a given case are actually decomposable into smaller scale units of analysis (and therefore comparable) and which are interdependent.

To return to the example of the butterfly effect, Holland (2000) notes that even though accurately describing every component of a dynamic, nonlinear system like weather is impossible, "because meteorologists do *not* know the value of all the relevant variables, they do not work at a level of detail, or over time spans, in which chaos would be relevant." Instead, he argues, "the key to deeper understanding, as with weather prediction, is to determine the level of detail and the relevant mechanisms" needed to accurately describe weather with a broad brush (44).

Using this as a guide, I suggest classifying methodological choices based on the breadth of perspective through which they identify and verify mechanisms as well as how well they are able to embed those mechanisms in multiple temporal and spatial scales. Table 7.1 presents these classifications. Such a typology is only a heuristic, meant to capture broad generalizations for how to think about comparative analytic choice; undoubtedly, hybrid, multi-method, and computational approaches bridge these classificatory boundaries. Nevertheless, this provides at least a first cut at understanding how the causal logics of our methodological sources address the problems of mechanism and scale.

Experimental designs, for example, are usually very good at comparing *situated* mechanisms. Within the ambit of the controlled environment, that is, an experimental design can identify how a causal factor operates, usually

TABLE 7.1 *Methodological choice and complex comparisons*

		Perspective on Mechanisms	
		Situated	Global
Approach to Scale	Ordered	Experiments	Large-N Empirical Analysis
	Simultaneous	Formal Rational Choice Modeling; Comparative Statics	Agent-Based Models; Network Analysis; Archival Analysis

at the level of the individual. At the same time, most experiments have a difficult time accounting for the multi-level nature of social phenomena, precisely because they are designed to isolate those mechanisms in particular contexts rather than link them across scales. In this sense, they provide an *ordered* approach to considering levels of analysis by only examining one scale at a time. In turn, most cross-sectional and time-series statistical modeling of observational data compares multiple mechanisms at once, including those involving groups, individuals, communities, and so forth. In this sense, rather than a situated perspective, such modeling involves global comparisons. Similar to experimental designs, though, even when it deploys hierarchical controls, observational statistical analysis is usually designed to produce correlative comparisons at a particular scale of analysis – dependent variables involve a particular level of analysis rather than chaining small-scale and large-scale phenomena, for example. It too is ordered.

Some approaches – such as much formal rational choice modeling – instead try to model the links between micro- and macro-level phenomena explicitly, with the goal of allowing the analyst to compare multi-scalar phenomena like tipping points, collective action, and so forth. In this sense, these approaches adopt a *simultaneous* analysis of scale. Also, much like experiments, with a few important exceptions (e.g., Bacharach 2006), many formal rational choice models are ultimately only interested in describing mechanisms emerging from individual, rational behavior. In this sense, one only compares mechanisms that are situated rather than thinking about how multiple sorts of actors and agents might coproduce social phenomena.

Scholars have also proposed techniques such as agent-based modeling or multiple network analysis designed to compare the operation of multiple mechanisms across cases and to juxtapose different scales of analysis directly. However, while there are important exceptions (e.g., Padgett and Powell 2012), these approaches are frequently used for exploratory and theory-building purposes, rather than for analyzing historical, empirical cases.

One of the oldest methodological choices – historical archival research – is surprisingly one of the best options when it comes to comparing actual empirical examples of complex cases usually because of structural factors involved in such work rather than the preferences of the researcher: archives frequently include a wide variety of materials, including letters, reports, notes, photographs, ephemera, and objects, frequently compiled in unsystematic ways. This very non-systematicity requires the analyst to situate and link those materials to interpret them.[3]

THE ADVANTAGES OF ARCHIVES: A FRAMEWORK

I suggest that any user of historical primary material must perform at least four tasks that also serve as a conduit to taking a global perspective on comparing mechanisms and juxtaposing multiple scales of analysis simultaneously. This is not to say most users of historical archives actually engage in these activities. Indeed, one of the hallmarks of traditional historical scholarship is deep focus on a particular historical event, individual, or phenomenon rather than a comparative one. At the same time, comparative social scientists have much to learn, I argue, from using primary material in an analytic way.

The most basic task any archival research process requires is *classification*. Scholars almost always process and sort archival objects into groups sharing a given characteristic. Archives are often pre-classified by archivists or collectors into record groups or collections, albeit to varying degrees. Within a given repository, for example, collections might range from being well-inventoried selections of material from a clear provenance (e.g., government documents) to relatively scattershot collections of uncertain origin (e.g., personal papers). However, scholars almost always need to refit this classification to serve their own ends. This allows them to create what Zerubavel (1996) has termed an "island of meaning," a way of suppressing individual difference and forging uniformity in service of cognitive organization. When examining a series of letters, for example, a researcher might classify by date, topic, provenance, sender/recipient, or some combination of these to address some specific questions or identify some particular chain of events. In turn, scholars also typically classify the materials they review across collections or archives, grouping materials that are institutionally segmented.

Classifying is essential in any research process, but archival classifying provides some intriguing advantages for scholars examining multi-level and interdependent cases. Some archival material (such as letter collections) can be "high bandwidth," including information about specific events or people, as well as reflections on larger macro-level phenomena, like wars or elections. Scholars attempting to classify this material must think through how the

---

[3] For an insightful discussion of the pleasures and complexities of archival inquiry, see Farge (2013).

multiple forms of social life captured in the archival document are situated at the level of the output they hope to produce (usually historical narrative).

Another, related task is *contextualizing* archival materials – that is, situating their production and reception in particular places and times. Contextualizing is also common in a variety of research designs; however, because of the frequently obscure processes by which many archival collections were gathered in the first place, as well as the frequently scattershot way in which the materials within those collections are organized, archival researchers inevitably focus much attention on the task of identifying the provenance for particular documents, people, allusions, and events found in those materials.

Like classifying, contextualizing archival materials is an important way to examine complex social phenomena. By trying to situate often cryptic materials (such as scraps of ephemera, undated account books, etc.) in a time and place, and to interpret what a particular document was and meant, scholars engage in a form of theorizing about the entity producing the text; how the document might have circulated; and, most crucially, why it was preserved and others, perhaps, were not. This, in turn, draws scholars to identify that different archival objects possess their own scales of analysis – personal journals or family documents shed light on different kinds of mechanisms and agents than do published reports or reprinted photographs.

Scholars working with historical archives also frequently engage in another task: *layering*. To produce a coherent account of a given social phenomenon, researchers often see the documents and texts they find in the archives as pieces (or layers) added onto an underlying structure of existing historical scholarship. These pieces might revise or alter that existing scholarship, but archival work always involves a kind of dialogue between secondary interpretations and primary materials. Not only do scholars use existing works as roadmaps to archival collections, they also try to make novel contributions by examining overlooked or unused sources. Moreover, since layering involves aggregating, disaggregating, or uncovering archival evidence in relation to other texts, it also entails the researcher in a process of rethinking the overall phenomenon of interest in light of specific evidentiary discoveries. With each new archival finding – a letter containing an unknown detail or a pattern of events revealed by a statistical summary of previously scattered data – historical researchers inevitably identify the ways these new archival layers alter the conceptualization and measurement of the case they study.

A final task for archival researchers is *linking* materials together to forge an actual historical analysis. Because archival collections must be organized and interpreted to become part of the scholarly conversation, researchers frequently find themselves connecting pieces of evidence from different contexts to produce an evidentiary basis for their arguments. Linking evidence (whether or not archival) is particularly crucial in examining the multi-level and interdependent nature of historical cases. Gaining purchase on the ways in which multiple mechanisms operate together means drawing connections across different cases, reducing social complexity, and identifying multiple resolutions through which to analyze the evidence. That is, archival work requires embedding evidence from a variety of materials together in often-uneasy ways; massive government reports make different claims than those of newspapers because the conditions of their production differ. Analysts trying to link these materials often find themselves zooming between big-picture and close-up analyses, allowing for multiple perspectives on the scales of social action involved in the making of a given occurrence or fact.

Classifying, contextualizing, layering, and linking are not merely techniques for processing archival materials. They also are essential in comparing those materials across cases and contexts to gain theoretical insights. Classifying archival material also means situating particular islands of meaning in a larger ocean of historical evidence; contextualizing involves thinking about seemingly unrelated micro- and macro-processes that might condition a particular case (or, conversely, be absent from that case); layering involves tying a particular case to a larger edifice of scholarly interpretations of similar and different cases; and linking involves direct comparisons and reductions among pieces of evidence and, potentially, different cases to create an actual analysis.

In this sense, even when it putatively deals with a single case, archival work requires scholars to think hard about how the complex social phenomena they study are defined and situated in relation to other historical phenomena. In the words of Ann Laura Stoler (2002), archives are not merely "objects" containing materials to be accessed, they are also "subjects," capable of revealing much about how the producers of these materials thought about and organized their conceptual worlds. Thus, for precisely this reason, archival inquiry can be helpful in identifying a global set of mechanisms and thinking about multiple scales of analysis simultaneously. Engaging the archive as a subject helps us disaggregate and recombine spatial and temporal dimensions of complex social phenomena so as to identify more clearly how comparisons across cases might reveal the relationships among them. It also provides us a way to model complex social cases by giving us an opportunity to think about which elements of cases can be treated as bounded subsystems and the ways in which those bounded subsystems relate to one another hierarchically. I now turn to an examination of William Tuttle's sophisticated account of the Chicago Race Riot of 1919 to demonstrate how archival research can help scholars account for multi-level and interdependent phenomena in a comparative framework.

ARCHIVAL ANALYSIS AND THE CHICAGO RACE RIOT OF 1919

The Chicago Race Riot of 1919 was a key moment in the history of American racial violence. Angered by a fatal attack by a white bystander on a Black boy swimming in a contested zone of a beach in the highly segregated city on the afternoon of July 27, a group of African Americans demanded that a white police officer arrest the man they believed responsible for the attack. Failing to comply with this demand, the white officer instead arrested an African American bystander, leading to rumors about police complicity in the death of the swimmer. This, in turn, sparked a series of conflicts between crowds of African Americans, whites, and police officers, cascading into a general series of brawls and fights. As Tuttle (1970, 8–10) describes it: "Once ignited on July 27, the rioting raged virtually ... uncontrolled for the greater part of five days. Day and night white toughs assaulted blacks, and teenage black mobsters beat white peddlers and merchants in the black belt. As rumors of atrocities circulated throughout the city, members of both races craved violence." By the time the rioting was finally quelled, at least thirty-eight people were dead and hundreds were injured, one of the bloodiest episodes in a summer that witnessed tremendous levels of bloodshed.

Defining "riots" (like their close cousins "revolutions") is fraught with difficulty. In his typology of violent interaction, Tilly (2003, 18) eschews the term completely, arguing that it necessarily "embodies a political judgment" and is rarely used as a term of self-identification. Yet it is precisely because riots involve such political judgments that they take on a "life of their own," capable of shaping other social phenomena (including other riots). Riots are politically integrated and consequential events, treated by participants and audiences as different from "mere" brawls, fights, or lynchings. As a result, they are multi-level and interdependent phenomena. In his work on ethnic rioting, which tries to set out a more encompassing definition, Donald Horowitz (2001, 17–28, 522–24) thus stresses the *process* of rioting, which is intense, intergroup, violence concentrated in time and space. Focusing on this process means that race riots aggregate micro-level violence differently from other macro-level protests and genocides, with the goal of purposively organizing conflict to preserve or unsettle racial social boundaries.

Thus, the Chicago Race Riot itself was made up of many individual acts, but those acts were parts of an integrated spatial and temporal pattern. In his account, Tuttle stresses how the initial impulse of violence diffused outward from the original, concentrated points of contact near the "dead line" (the street separating the highly segregated African American Black belt from white neighborhoods in the south side of the city) to more isolated individual attacks of African Americans and whites in areas controlled by the "other side" in the following days (see Figure 7.1). In particular, Tuttle (1970, 42–43) notes, this was related to police tactics: as the police concentrated in the Black belt, conflict moved into the white neighborhoods surrounding the stockyards. Meanwhile the rumor mill worked overtime, spreading misinformation about the scope and scale of the violence both in the press and among neighbors, friends, and family members. Eventually, the mayor asked the governor (with whom he had an intense political rivalry) for the aid

Comparing Complex Cases Using Archival Research

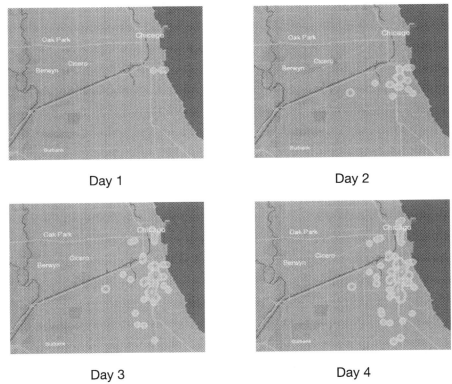

FIGURE 7.1 Diffusion of violence in Chicago Race Riot (July 26–29, 1919)

of the militia. Combined with a couple of rainy days, which forced many of the riot participants indoors, the state guard helped bring an end to the violence.

Tuttle's ability to treat the riot as both an integrated event and as a series of street-level interactions at least partially flowed from the close attention he paid to multiple kinds of archival sources, including interviews, newspaper articles, photographs, military reports, and (most importantly) the report of the Chicago Commission on Race Relations released in the aftermath of the event – *The Negro in Chicago* (1922). In a revealing discussion on his use of sources, Tuttle (1970, 269–89) provides an exhaustive description of how he organized his collections within themes (e.g., labor relations, politics, the Great Migration) as well as by type of resource (e.g., archives, newspapers, bibliographies). This dual scheme allows the reader to reconstruct how Tuttle organized his book (with distinct chapters dedicated to labor, politics, etc.) as well as how he used different sources to different ends (drawing largely on secondary sources for background or context-setting sections of the book and using primary documents for his own reconstruction of the riot itself).

The materials Tuttle used thus explicitly prompted him to *classify* his material by constructing a time line of events involving multiple groups of actors – street gangs, laborers, police officers and officials, and military commanders – acting across several levels of organization. At the same time, he built a narrative *linking* those events into a shared story of a tragic, albeit relatively routine act of violence (an assault upon an African American by a white man defending his "turf") scaling outward through processes of rumor and social mobilization to involve a large section of the city.

The Chicago Riot is thus a clear example of the kinds of complex cases on which this chapter has focused. On the one hand, it (like all social entities) was an aggregation of micro-behavior; on the other hand, the use of the label "riot" by the press and politicians as a shorthand for all the individual acts of violence and the response of the city government to this violence as a large-scale, integrated phenomenon (by, for instance, mobilizing the police and later the militia) directly shaped those very micro-behaviors (Brass 1997). This, in turn, complicates our ability to compare fights or beatings within the riot in any kind of controlled way, since many of those events were directly influenced by the emergence of the multi-level phenomenon of the riot as an integrated social phenomenon.

Tuttle, however, was not only interested in explaining the micro-level of violence in Chicago itself. His archival work also led him to situate the riot at two other levels of analysis. First was a meso-level, national cross-sectional network of towns and cities. As Tuttle points out, the Chicago riot was only one in a large number of racially motivated episodes of violence in 1919: between April and November that year, at least eleven riots took place across the nation in which at least two people were killed for racial reasons, in addition to a large number of other racially motivated violent events (see Table 7.2). In some cities – in particular, Charleston and Washington, DC – the presence of recently demobilized sailors and soldiers (some of whom were African American) meant that local interracial fights quickly scaled into larger confrontations between organized units. In other areas – such as Longview, Texas, and Omaha, Nebraska – riots accompanied vigilante mobilization and attempts at lynching alleged African American criminals. Still other events – in particular the Elaine, Arkansas, and Bogalusa, Louisiana, riots – concerned economic and labor competition.

For Tuttle (1970, 10–14), these events were part of a pattern of violent resistance to the presence of African Americans in those towns and cities most affected by the Great Migration, which brought many Black residents north for the first time. Most significant was the newfound competition over jobs, particularly in midwestern industrial centers and mid-Atlantic cities. African Americans were often hired as temporary scabs or as a low-cost alternative to union labor, leading to resentment on the part of striking workers and presenting a major challenge to unionization efforts. In addition, the movement of African Americans into cities frequently led to shifts in

TABLE 7.2 *Racially motivated violence in the United States (1919)*

Town/City	State	Date	Type of Violence
Millen	GA	April 13	Riot
Warrenton	GA	May 1	Lynching
Philadelphia	PA	May 9	Riot
Charleston	SC	May 11	Riot
San Francisco	CA	May 14	Riot
Vicksburg	MS	May 14	Lynching
Milan	GA	May 24	Riot
New London	CT	May 29	Riot
Ellisville	MS	June 26	Lynching
Annapolis	MD	June 28	Riot
San Francisco	CA	June 30–July 1	Riot
Bisbee	AZ	July 4	Riot
Dublin	GA	July 6	Lynching
Longview	TX	July 11	Riot
Port Arthur	TX	July 14	Riot
New York	NY	July 19	Riot
Washington	DC	July 19–July 23	Riot
Norfolk	VA	July 21	Riot
Newberry	SC	July 26	Lynching
Chicago	IL	July 27–July 31	Riot
Syracuse	NY	July 31	Riot
Lexington	NE	August 5	Riot
Mulberry	FL	August 18	Riot
Cadwell/Ocmulgee	GA	August 26–August 27	Riot
Bogalusa	LA	August 30–August 31	Lynching
Knoxville	TN	August 30	Riot
Jacksonville	FL	September 7	Lynching
New York	NY	September 21	Riot
Omaha	NE	September 28–September 29	Riot
Montgomery	AL	September 30	Lynching
Elaine	AR	September 30–October 1	Riot
Baltimore	MD	October 2	Riot
Gary	IN	October 4	Riot
Monticello	GA	October 7	Lynching
Donora	PA	October 9	Riot
Hubbard	OH	October 10	Riot

(*continued*)

TABLE 7.2 (*continued*)

Town/City	State	Date	Type of Violence
Corbin	KY	October 30	Riot
Macon	GA	November 2	Lynching
Wilmington	DE	November 13	Riot
Bogalusa	LA	November 22	Riot
Lake City	FL	November 29	Lynching

housing values: many whites did not want to live near African Americans or feared the effects of African American neighbors on the values of their properties. Speculators took advantage of this fear to drive prices down, buy properties at a discount, and then rent to African Americans at exorbitant rates. In other areas, white property owners formed housing associations to prevent African Americans from moving into their neighborhoods. In Tuttle's reading, understanding the riot also means situating it in a regional story of interdependent economic and demographic change. Without these meso-level factors, which explain how racial animosity could become so widespread in Chicago to begin with, it is impossible to make sense of how a routine violent interaction could scale to the level of a citywide riot.

How did Tuttle identify this meso level? Partly this was due to the availability of two particular archival resources: newspaper reports and, especially, magazine articles, both of which prompted him to *contextualize* Chicago's experience within the nation and compare it with other areas experiencing racial violence. Newspaper commentators routinely asserted that the events of 1919 were part of an integrated phenomenon of racial conflict (New York Times 1919), while periodicals produced by the National Association for the Advancement of Colored People (in particular, *Crisis* magazine) catalogued and interpreted multiple events across the nation during that year. Tuttle *layered* these findings on an interpretive framework connected to scholarship on the Great Migration, which helped him interpret the local violence as embedded in a larger, structural change in American social life.

Tuttle also, however, situates the Chicago riot at a third level of analysis: a macro-level story about how the global revolutionary movement and social transformations induced by wartime unsettled the racial order in the United States and led to a mass panic (commonly called the "Red Scare") over the threat of radicalism and social disorder. The Red Scare, in turn, "was an extension of the atmosphere of the war, with its cult of patriotism, its generalized climate of violence, and its need for an enemy" (Tuttle 1970, 17).

In other words, it was not simply that street-level violent events were situated in cities and towns undergoing economic and demographic change; those changes were seen as particularly threatening because of the historical conjunctural moment confronting the United States in 1919. The Bolshevik Revolution in Russia, nationalist and revolutionary struggles throughout Eastern Europe, growing disorder and disintegration of the social fabric in Germany and in Western Europe in general, and the presence of a newly militarized American national identity all made violence appear as a much more palatable solution to the problem of localized disorder in Tuttle's (1970, 15–16) view. As African Americans grew increasingly assertive in their willingness to defend themselves and their communities (a phenomenon typically called the growth of the "New Negro" sentiment, emblematic of the increasingly popular resistance rhetoric deployed by figures like W. E. B. DuBois), a generalized middle-class fear of economic radicalism focused on the racialized intransigence of these newly assertive African American voices (Tuttle 1970, 208–22). This was compounded by a growing concern about labor radicalism: for many patriotic Americans, US cities seemed poised on the edge of a generalized revolution. Tuttle's macro-level framework thus allows him to identify the way in which the riot in Chicago was socially constructed as a crucial event in a longer historical process of American race and labor relations.

In constructing this level of analysis, he *layered* his meso- and micro-level findings on sociological literature on racial violence in general, while *contextualizing* his primary material from 1919 to a broader comparison with riots in the 1960s. In his final chapter, which addresses this comparison explicitly, Tuttle (1970, 258–68) was able to *classify* violence in both periods to draw attention to the similarities and differences, arguing that 1960s violence shared with the riots of 1919 similar structural conditions (e.g., rising expectations for African Americans, general social disorder related to warfare) as well as situational and contingent precipitants (e.g., hot weather, a catalytic fight or confrontation). By *linking* his historical material with (at the time) cutting-edge sociological research, Tuttle hoped to craft a longer narrative about the recurrence of racial strife in American life.

THINKING ABOUT COMPLEX COMPARISONS

Does Tuttle's complex and sophisticated analysis of the Chicago riot provide a comparative technique for understanding the causes of race riots? Tuttle, I contend, is able to give us a sophisticated story about specific mechanisms critical to explaining violence in Chicago across multiple levels of analysis simultaneously. He, like Horowitz and Sewell, focuses on the process of collective violence formation – the ways in which micro-level isolated fights intersect with meso-level social cleavages to produce widespread local social mobilization in places affected by rapid demographic and economic change, and how these events were interpreted as elements in a macro-historical moment of national disorder and crisis. In this sense, he does provide an explanatory framework capable of being compared across cases.

At the same time, it makes no sense to directly compare the riot in Chicago with events in, say, Washington, DC, with any hope of controlling for every confounding explanation. Both events were tied up in regional- and national-level phenomena (the Great Migration, demobilization after World War I, etc.) affecting many areas in the country that were, in Tuttle's view, crucial in explaining how a riot could aggregate out of both an otherwise routine fight and a shared background condition. Moreover, it is clear that events in places like Chicago and Washington, DC, did, in fact, help precipitate violence in other cities: news of earlier riots (often carried by national papers like the important African American paper *The Chicago Defender*) likely helped make them "thinkable" for participants in violence elsewhere. Because the riot is a multi-level phenomenon interdependent with other cases with which we might want to compare it, we need to disaggregate these levels of analysis and trace the connections between those different elements instead.

Rather than comparing to control for isolated variables, Tuttle's form of comparison therefore invites us to consider which elements the complex system of a particular riot can be decomposed into subsystems or sub-events and which are related to larger system connections with other riots. The more we can identify particular, bounded subsystems and the hierarchical relations among them, the more confident we can be that we can compare multiple mechanisms operating across different scales of action. Thus, the micro-level story Tuttle presents to explain the precipitating moment of the riot at its base was a simple street fight – a brawl involving members of different racial groups. Such events were relatively common in racially mixed American cities in 1919 and could be treated as a relatively stable subsystem, tied into larger dynamics of city racial hierarchy, but also directly comparable across cases. Indeed, precisely because they are bounded and discrete social events, such fights were neither multi-level nor interdependent across cases.

What made the fight of July 27 different? In Tuttle's estimation, it was the way this particular street fight engaged two other micro-level factors – the brawl took place in a racially contested physical space and a representative of state authority (the police officer) refused to intervene. These other factors are also subsystems, but their particular combination in this case meant that a simple brawl now had the potential to scale to something much larger. It would be fully possible in theory to develop comparisons between cases in other cities like Washington, DC, or Philadelphia that take these micro-level subsystems into consideration and to show how their peculiar juxtaposition provided such enabling conditions.

At the same time, however, as Tuttle reminds us, these micro-level subsystemic mechanisms were embedded in meso-level and macro-level systems that did connect riot events in Chicago to other cities and towns. These connections reveal that part of what made the brawl in Chicago actually scale to the level of a city riot had to do with factors occurring in multiple places at once. Comparing the Chicago riot to other riots in these cases does not mean examining independent cases but instead multiple symptoms of the same underlying social process. This, in turn, might prompt us not to try to compare Chicago's riot to that in Washington, DC, directly to uncover this underlying cause, but rather to compare the *riot system* of 1919 to other moments of collectively violent activity (such as the race riots of the 1960s in many American cities). Of course, even in these comparisons, we are not examining independent events, but merely events that can be bounded into subsystems that, inevitably, at a higher level of historical analysis are themselves causally related.

CONCLUSION

This chapter argues that archival analysis presents us with a highly useful way of demarcating the boundaries around contained and stable subsystemic-level events as well as identifying how these subsystems are themselves connected into larger hierarchical patterns. Classifying and contextualizing archival materials are also ways of grouping and situating events and processes on which we might want to focus analytic energy, drawing boundaries around what I have been calling subsystems (fights, racial geography, etc.) that are comparable and isolable from other subsystems. Conversely, linking materials and layering them in a larger scholarly conversation involves connecting those subsystems into larger narrative structures, situating them in a hierarchy of processes that help us make larger sense of the events and phenomena we care about, revealing the way individual micro-level activities are both shaped by and constitute macro-level patterns.

If we take seriously the need to examine causal mechanisms in a global way and to compare multiple scales of analysis simultaneously, scholars will be much better equipped to address the limits of traditional, variable-bound analysis, which rarely consider the complex nature of social causality. Although not a panacea, archival approaches such as that adopted by William Tuttle can powerfully reveal the way in which multiple factors together help produce real social outcomes.

REFERENCES

Acemoglu, Daron, Simon Johnson, and James A. Robinson. 2001. "The Colonial Origins of Comparative Development: An Empirical Investigation." *American Economic Review* 91 (5): 1369–1401.

Bacharach, Michael. 2006. *Beyond Individual Choice*. Princeton, NJ: Princeton University Press.

Berkowitz, Leonard, and Edward I. Donnerstein. 1982. "External Validity Is More Than Skin Deep: Some Answers to Criticisms of Laboratory Experiments." *American Psychologist* 37 (3): 245–57.

Brass, Paul. 1997. *Theft of an Idol: Text and Context in the Representation of Collective Violence*. Princeton, NJ: Princeton University Press.

Chicago Commission on Race. 1922. *The Negro in Chicago: A Study of Race Relations and a Race Riot*. Chicago: University of Chicago Press.

Coleman, James S. 1990. *Foundations of Social Theory*. Cambridge, MA: Harvard University Press.

Dunning, Thad. 2012. *Natural Experiments in the Social Sciences*. Cambridge: Cambridge University Press.

Durkheim, Emile. 1982. *Rules of Sociological Method*. Edited by Steven Lukes. Translated by W. D. Hall. New York: Free Press.

Farge, Arlette. 2013. *The Allure of the Archives*. Translated by Thomas Scott-Railton. New Haven, CT: Yale University Press.

Goldstone, Jack A. 2001. "Toward a Fourth Generation of Revolutionary Theory." *Annual Review of Political Science* 4 (1): 139–87.

Hall, Peter A. 2003. "Aligning Ontology and Methodology in Comparative Research." In *Comparative Historical Analysis in the Social Sciences*, edited by James Mahoney and Dietrich Rueschemeyer, 373–404. Cambridge: Cambridge University Press.

Hilborn, Robert C. 2004. "Sea Gulls, Butterflies, and Grasshoppers: A Brief History of the Butterfly Effect in Nonlinear Dynamics." *American Journal of Physics* 72 (4): 425–27.

Holland, John H. 2000. *Emergence: From Chaos to Order*. Oxford: Oxford University Press.

Horowitz, Donald L. 2001. *The Deadly Ethnic Riot*. Berkeley: University of California Press.

Kocher, Matthew A., and Nuno P. Monteiro. 2016. "Lines of Demarcation: Causation, Design-Based Inference, and Historical Research." *Perspectives on Politics* 16 (4): 952–75.

Lewontin, Richard C. 2000. *The Triple Helix: Gene, Organism, and Environment*. Cambridge, MA: Harvard University Press.

Morck, Randall, and Bernard Yeung. 2011. "Economics, History, and Causation." *Business History Review* 85 (1): 39–63.

New York Times. 1919. "For Action on Race Riot Peril," October 5, sec. F.

Padgett, John Frederick, and Walter W. Powell, eds. 2012. *The Emergence of Organizations and Markets*. Princeton, NJ: Princeton University Press.

Przeworski, Adam, and Henry Teune. 1970. *The Logic of Comparative Social Inquiry*. New York: Wiley.

Rubin, Donald B. 1974. "Estimating Causal Effects of Treatments in Randomized and Nonrandomized Studies." *Journal of Educational Psychology* 66 (5): 688–701.

Sewell Jr., William H. 2005. *Logics of History: Social Theory and Social Transformation*. Chicago: University of Chicago Press.

Simon, Herbert A. 1996. *The Sciences of the Artificial*, 3rd edn. Cambridge, MA: MIT Press.

Skocpol, Theda. 1979. *States and Social Revolutions: A Comparative Analysis of France, Russia, and China*. Cambridge: Cambridge University Press.

Stoler, Ann Laura. 2002. "Colonial Archives and the Arts of Governance." *Archival Science* 2: 87–109.

Tilly, Charles. 2003. *The Politics of Collective Violence*. Cambridge: Cambridge University Press.

Tuttle, William M. 1970. *Race Riot: Chicago in the Red Summer of 1919*. Champaign: University of Illinois Press.
West, Geoffrey B. 2017. *Scale: The Universal Laws of Growth, Innovation, Sustainability, and the Pace of Life in Organisms, Cities, Economies, and Companies*. New York: Penguin.
Zerubavel, Eviatar. 1996. "Lumping and Splitting: Notes on Social Classification." *Sociological Forum* 11 (3): 421–33.

8

Composing Comparisons

Studying Configurations of Relations in Social Network Research

Sarah E. Parkinson
Johns Hopkins University

Looking back on the initial research design for my book project, the metaphor of butchery comes to mind. However, I do not use the term in the negative sense that most political violence scholars do: that is, to indicate a particularly brutal and uncompromising form of lethal violence. Rather, I hope to evoke the process of carefully carving up a larger body with a preset idea of what makes a proper and desirable cut. As a graduate student of comparative political science who was already quite enmeshed in my field site when I wrote my dissertation proposal, I learned from the discipline that there were obvious ways to divide an overarching country case into appropriate units of comparison. Like ribs or hocks, one could subsequently stack each of these smaller units next to each other and call them "like" things that could be compared over time because they were initially intended to be the same. As a researcher, I simply needed to figure out what the "ribs," "hocks," or "steaks" were for my particular study.

The initial empirical puzzle that motivated my research seemed fairly straightforward. There are twelve officially recognized Palestinian refugee camps in Lebanon. The number of violent incidents between various political factions such as Fatah (a leading Palestinian nationalist organization) or Ansar Allah (a local Palestinian *salafi* organization) varied across those camps, as did the very existence of certain factions. Fatah was present in all camps, but groups such as Ansar Allah were not. Before the Lebanese Civil War (1975–1990), there was little violence between factions in the camps and no *salafi* groups (or political factions that identified as ideologically Islamic). The situation consequently seemed to lend itself to implementing a version of Mill's methods via a modified most-similar-different-outcomes (MSDO) design (George and Bennett 2005). I had ostensibly like units to compare (Palestinian refugee camps), distinct junctures from which to select a starting point for analysis (sometime during the civil war), and clear geographic variation on the outcome of interest. In Joe Soss's (2018) words, I had a noun ("camps") to study as cases or non-cases of postwar violence. In a fall 2008 grant application for dissertation fieldwork, I proposed to study three camps "as representative case studies for distinct patterns of Palestinian politics in Lebanon."[1] Mill's methods provided more than a methodology; they were also a heuristic for looking at the world.

This chapter explores what happened after I took this research design into the field and why this initial design fell apart and, indeed, *needed* to fall apart. Using excerpts from fellowship applications and various iterations of the manuscript, it then traces the trajectories of the post-field intellectual tensions involved with "re-casing" (Soss, Chapter 5, this volume) the work both to better facilitate theory development and to more loyally represent the realities of the spaces where I conducted research. Finally, it outlines a new strategy of network-based comparison based not on comparing preset cases – locales, in this situation – but to casing evolving, geographically distinct *configurations of relationships*. This mechanism-based approach is heavily comparative over time: it relies on the researchers' ability to connect some sort of provocation or stimulus to minute changes in the structure, content, and meaning of networked relations.

This chapter advances a theoretical approach to organizational adaptation and evolution that relies on an explicitly relational (Emirbayer 1997), multiple-network, dynamic approach. Throughout, I argue against the overwhelming disciplinary emphasis on Mill's methods as a heuristic for looking at the world and argue for the inclusion of approaches that embrace the explanatory power of complex rather than linear causality. It first involves recognizing the disciplining power of the "perspectival comparisons" (Schaffer 2018) that undergird MSDO and MDSO (most-different-similar-outcomes) designs: machine processing and medical diagnostics (Collier 2011). These ways of thinking about process were a poor fit for my project: rather than diagnosing a known condition based on symptoms, as Collier's (2011) approach to process tracing encourages, I believed that I was in part trying to study a previously unidentified condition altogether. The resultant tension between what I was attempting to accomplish and the models in existence forced me to rethink the way that both units and causality operated in my project. Exploring neuroscience as a source of perspectival comparison both opened new realms for theorizing and allowed me to think through complex causal processes in ways most existing political science models foreclose. Specifically, theoretical insights from neuroscience help animate the complex causal mechanisms involved in processes of network disruption, reorganization, and repair.

---

[1] International Dissertation Research Fellowship application, November 2008.

COMPOSING RELATIONAL COMPARISONS: FROM MICRO-LEVEL CHANGE TO MACRO-LEVEL PROCESS

In this section, I preview my theoretical and empirical approaches to comparison in social networks, which draw on scholars such as Mustafa Emirbayer (1997) to focus primarily on changing roles and relations rather than on the analysis of static organizational forms. The outcome that I examine is the emergence of new organizational structures, which can be identified by gathering data to reveal new configurations of relations, roles, routines, and practices. This theoretical and empirical strategy thus privileges a method best described as "casing relations." I think of this specific analytic method as acting in the broader service of "composing" comparisons. This perspective became particularly important in my work because the units that I study – local subdivisions of larger militant organizations – *change over time as war disrupts them*. That is, rather than taking the unit for granted, my work expressly breaks down how that unit changes over time. Working in the emergence paradigm in political science, rather than sociology or evolutionary biology where these approaches are well established, expressly challenges standard and broadly understood modes of comparison, which assume static units (e.g., nation-states that remain nation-states throughout the study). However, this assumption does not necessarily apply to the study of complex, dynamic processes, when entire systems may transform, for example, from a guild-based economic system into a partnership system (Padgett and McLean 2006).

Social network theory and analysis are broadly used in international studies research, particularly to examine social movements, advocacy fields, mobilization, and violent organizations (Petersen 2001; Viterna 2006; Wood 2008; Hafner-Burton, Kahler, and Montgomery 2009; Carpenter 2011, 2014; Carpenter and Moore 2014; Staniland 2014; Hadden 2015; Larson and Lewis 2017, 2018). Much research in this realm relies heavily on using large datasets and quantitative analytical tools to identify influential positions in networks, usually operationalized via the core concepts of brokerage, density, or centrality (Pedahzur and Perliger 2006; Siegel 2009; Perliger and Pedahzur 2011; Zech and Gabbay 2016; Gade, Hafez, and Gabbay 2019; Gade et al. 2019; Larson and Lewis 2020). In a rare qualitative example, Paul Staniland's (2012, 2014) work on cohesion and fragmentation in rebel organizations examines specific insurgent organizations as *cases of* network structures. His typology of organizational structures is based on different configurations of horizontal and vertical ties, which in turn produce different outcomes of interest (e.g., cohesion or fragmentation). Some work inductively or abductively cases particular empirical phenomena as processes or configurations of interest. For example, John Padgett and Christopher Ansell (1993) fundamentally case Cosimo d'Medici's position in Florentine society as that of a "robust actor" and d'Medici's associated behavior as "robust action."

Yet, even as such work has become increasingly common in historical or quantitative studies, scholars have yet to extensively leverage the opportunities that immersive – and specifically ethnographic – relational, social network–based approaches present for understanding the relationships among structure, agency, and culture (Emirbayer and Goodwin 1994; McLean 2016). In relational- and network-based casework, configurations of social relations serve as cases. There are two ways to approach them. The first involves a static treatment of networks, where the researcher takes a temporal snapshot of a dynamic social network and examines it as a case of a specific structural configuration of roles and relations. This is often the strategy in archive-, government records-, or print media–based network scholarship. Often, these studies posit network configurations as causing an outcome of interest. For example, Eric Hundman's (2016) study of Chinese soldiers and our (2019) coauthored, comparative work on Chinese and Palestinian officers examine how different configurations of biographical ties facilitate military disobedience. Some approaches present several snapshots of network configurations over time, thus allowing for comparison of network structures. Andrew Papachristos (2009) uses police data to present three network snapshots of gang violence in Chicago and to make claims regarding the relationship of social structure to murder. This technique requires the researcher to carefully collect data on the network nodes (e.g., military officers) and relations of interest (e.g., membership in alumni groups, past participation in regional militias).

By contrast, a second strategy for casing and comparing social networks involves studying how change in social networks *produces* specific configurations of social relations and organizational logics (McLean 2016). Padgett's work with Ansell and with Paul McLean emphasizes how d'Medici's efforts to build political and business alliances via marriage ties created new types of alliances, economic systems, and logics of eliteness (Padgett and Ansell 1993; Padgett and McLean 2006; Padgett 2010). Jonathan Obert's work traces how various violent interactions between gunfighters and private security actors brought about modern policing organizations in the United States (Obert 2014, 2018). My own work has examined how the elimination of particular nodes and ties in wartime Lebanon produced gendered mobilization processes that, in turn, led to the emergence of smuggling, intelligence, and logistics networks (Parkinson 2013) and how gossip networks structure interactions both within and between rebel organizations (Parkinson 2016, 2021). This type of approach, detailed later in this chapter, relies on tracking the work that micro network mechanisms do – such as certain types of nodes or ties forming or disappearing, often via agentive action – and subsequently tracing the emergence of particular network configurations. These mechanisms capture structural features (e.g., the presence or absence of nodes and ties) as well as content (e.g., information sharing between nodes) and nodes' valence (e.g., emotional state or "attractiveness" to other nodes). This mechanism-based approach is heavily comparative over time because it relies on the researchers' ability to connect some sort of provocation or stimulus to minute changes in networked relations.

Rather than deploying commonly used machine-based metaphors that rely on independent variable inputs and mechanistic causal processes, the approach I advocate focuses on contingent, organic complex processes that require a different point of comparative reference. Biological metaphors and phenomena can be carefully employed to open new avenues for political theorizing (Connolly 2002). Though they are often conflated, there is a critical distinction between attributing biological characteristics to social phenomena and invoking biological processes to inspire new trajectories of thought. I aim to do the latter by using three concepts from neuroscience – "plasticity," "activation," and "reconsolidation" – to develop new theoretical foundations for understanding network change and adaptation in social systems. In the following paragraphs, I detail how a perspectival comparison based in neuroscience opens new opportunities for theorizing beyond units and causality and beyond linear processes. After starting with some basic neuroscience, I sketch how I used knowledge of the brain's internal processes to think through the dynamics of network change.

Similarities between social network architectures and brain structure provide compelling opportunities to challenge our ontological assumptions in comparative work in addition to suggesting new approaches to inference. The brain is fundamentally a multiple-network architecture, which is simply to say that it is a system of relationships that vary in their strength, connectedness, and content. In it, layered systems of neurons communicate using electrical signals transmitted through synapses.

Within social systems and organizations, people are assigned roles that have specific tasks and skills associated with them. Neurons, for their part, self-organize and differentiate as they connect to each other, forming task-specific networks known as "cortical maps." Sensory cortical areas of the brain – the areas that process information gathered through taste, touch, smell, sight, and hearing – are divided by sense and are grouped together (i.e., neurons related to each sense are proximate and neurons related to the senses are close to one another) (Buonomano and Merzenich 1998, 151–52). Cortical maps thus resemble scholars' analytical partitioning of different types of social relationships or memberships ties into network domains (Padgett and Ansell 1993; McLean 1998, 2007; Padgett and McLean 2006; White 2008; Padgett and Powell 2012). Organizations within constitutive domains – such as corporations within an economic domain or churches, temples, and mosques in a religious domain – echo sensory partitions of touch, smell, and taste. Relational ties such as finance or communication parallel the varied electro-chemical signals that flow through neural connections.

Neurons' ability to adapt to and compensate for physical injury by forming new neural connections and pathways is referred to as "neuroplasticity"

(Buonomano and Merzenich 1998; Arbib 2002; Doidge 2007). Alvaro Pascual-Leone et al. (2011, 302) explain that "plasticity represents an intrinsic property of the nervous system retained throughout life that enables modification of function and structure in response to environmental demands via the strengthening, weakening, pruning, or adding of synaptic connections and by promoting neurogenesis." Injuries to or destruction of nerves and neurons disrupt cortical maps' functioning. Yet, when the nervous system is damaged, neuroplasticity allows the brain to reroute neural networks and to accomplish the affected maps' tasks in new ways. While this change occurs naturally (e.g., through learning processes), neuroplasticity governs the ways in which the brain responds to sudden, acute damage such as severed nerves/amputations and strokes. Although the brain does not generate replacement neurons, it can reconnect, reorient, strengthen, or weaken the connections between existing synapses. In the event of physical neurological damage, emergent neural maps either augment other cortical areas via new connections or restore old functions by seeding new neural configurations (Doidge 2007, chap. 5).

I argue that leveraging the concept of what I call "relational plasticity" – the idea that social relationships, like neurons, are capable of changing content and meaning over time – opens space for scholars to focus on comparing the structure and content of dynamic systems of relations, rather than of static like or unlike units. In my own work, thinking about militant groups' task-based divisions such as combat units and intelligence apparatuses as comparable to areas of the brain that control senses such as touch and taste created space to consider the complex dynamics of adaptation in a way that allowed more of the parts – relations – to move and change in ways that reflected empirical reality more proximately than mechanical metaphors. As I considered how processes of neural activation and repair to new purposes following injury worked, these processes provided an apt framework for conceptualizing how militants collectively interpret and respond to violence by creating new relationships and taking on new tasks, even in situations where people are dying, disappearing, or demobilizing. I thus came to call a given network map's collective reaction to and interpretation of wartime violence "activation."[2]

---

[2] It is important to note the limitations to the metaphor. People and organizations are, by definition, more complex than neurons. Neurons do not have consciousness, agency, judgment, morals, or emotions. Social network relationships may include infinite types of material or symbolic content, from contracts (Padgett and Ansell 1993) and professional favors (Chang 2011) to violent exchanges (Papachristos 2009; Obert 2014, 2018) and language (Franzosi 1998; Mische and White 1998; McLean 2007; Mische 2007; Parkinson 2016, 2021). Synapses are limited to transmitting electro-chemical signals, even if those signals can vary in their chemical makeup. Thus, one of the core attributes of neuroplasticity – that neurons can only be tasked to one map at one time (referred to as "competitive plasticity") – does not apply to social networks (Doidge 2007, 59–60). Social network relationships, when simplified into network terms, can be unidirectional, bidirectional, or nondirectional. In contrast to social relationships, neural signals

Working through this comparison between social and neurological structures allowed me to clarify how I thought about social relationships; their collective power; the division of labor within larger structures; and the complex, cumulative causal processes that undergirded my theoretical approach. However, the pathway to this point was fraught for two reasons, both related to the near-total permeation of Mill's methods in political science: first, the need to undo some of my own, internal intellectual assumptions regarding comparison and causality and, second, the difficulty involved with portraying work built on complex causality as valid and robust to colleagues focused almost exclusively on linear, variable-based causal models and identification strategies. In the following section, I describe in detail the abductive, field-grounded process – that is, the toggling between theory and empirics – that led me to develop this theoretical approach.

MILL'S METHODS VERSUS PALESTINIAN REALITIES

Since the initial research application described earlier, I have conducted more than eighteen additional months of fieldwork on the project. When I arrived in Lebanon in fall 2009, my pre-dissertation fieldwork provided a foundation from which I continued to explore the history of the camps via ethnographic methods, in-depth interviews, archival work, and camp histories (al-Hajali 2007; Abdullah 2008; Kallam 2008). By the second month, when I was conducting intensive archival work and volunteering in one of the "nonrepresentative" camps (i.e., too small, Christian, and migrant heavy by the initial standards of representativeness I deployed), I had already deduced that the representative approach, that is, with certain camps as cases that represented a larger class, was a nonstarter, mainly because each one was clearly exceptional in several ways that mattered for my work (e.g., one faction dominated in ways it did not elsewhere, it was particularly big, it had recently experienced armed conflict, or it was a Syrian smuggling hub). There would be no way to satisfy the standards of representativeness and non-bias required by many epistemological approaches (Small 2009). It was becoming clear to me that siting my research based on geographic locations would be a nonstarter given the historic specificities of each camp. This recognition also meant that my research design required reconsideration.

Perhaps more interestingly, while conducting field research and participating in local conferences, I repeatedly witnessed members of camp communities challenging other foreign researchers to name their camp most representative: there was a clear politics within camp communities of earning the status of representative. A representative camp, in the contexts where I worked, was not

---

are unidirectional, though they can switch from "upstream" to "downstream." While the brain cannot generate new neurons, social networks can add new members through processes as varied as birth, hiring, or mobilization.

Composing Comparisons

understood as one that was on or close to a statistical trend line produced by a group of interacting variables; rather, it was seen as the one that manifested extremes in a way that refracted aspects of Palestinian life in Lebanon. Thus, the debate centered on places such as 'Ayn al-Hilwa, located in the southern city of Saida, because it had the largest population and more political factions than any other camp (Rougier 2007; Fleifel 2014), thus providing a uniquely complete representation of more of the Palestinian ideological spectrum. Another candidate was Shatila in Beirut, a relatively small camp that is also easily Lebanon's most famous, most studied (or overstudied) (Sukarieh and Tannock 2013), most frequently artistically portrayed, and most visited Palestinian community, mostly due to the 1982 Sabra-Shatila massacre (BBC 2008; Kallam 2008; StudioCamps 2008; Folman 2009; Allan 2013; Al-Hardan 2017). While the version of representativeness voiced by the camps' residents diverges from the ostensibly scientific definition I was attempting to deploy, the debate was deeply instructive in my thinking about what traits could make a camp representative. Specifically, it helped me think of the camps and other Palestinian neighborhoods as geographic spaces that might exhibit or reveal specific political processes of interest (why were there so many different factions in 'Ayn al-Hilwa?) without being representative in the statistical sense of the term.

For even a modified MSDO design to work properly, the camps initially had to be similar to one another across key variables related to my study: they could only really differ on the explanatory variables that I proposed. (The initial factors I hypothesized to be at work were external support, the structure of political competition, and organizational tactics vis-à-vis the population.) The more research that I did, the less that variable-based comparability or control – both necessary for a MSDO design – seemed to be within reach. First of all, the structure of political competition and organizational tactics clearly had a feedback relationship with organizational forms in each camp. They were not independent variables in any sense of the term, and I needed a methodological and ontological approach that allowed me to endogenize the dynamics that I was studying rather than superficially attempt to control for them. I learned that the factions' organizational structures themselves varied geographically; those varied structures produced distinct behaviors and patterns of interaction (not all that surprising). That is, Fatah and its members did not operate the same way in Shatila as it/they did in 'Ayn al-Hilwa (even if the organization had the same national leadership, general history, and external funders).

As I delved further into the archives, it became apparent that the structural differences I noticed across organizations were evident by the end of the Lebanese Civil War (1990). A spatial dynamic was in play. My question became more about why organizations had changed so drastically during the war, but I kept the loose MSDO logic in my mind as I started to explore how experiences of violence had forced militants to renegotiate their professional and personal relationships over the course of the war, giving rise to new logics of organizing.

Two aspects of this initial research design worked in my favor when I later decided to re-case the project. They allowed for later intellectual flexibility in ways that a more stringent MSDO approach may have foreclosed. They also speak to the advantages of ethnographic, or at least intensive, field-based engagement in comparative politics research. First, my planned interviews were heavily focused on organizational dynamics and geared toward parsing webs of relations that influenced how individuals understood and participated in various political processes. Previous fieldwork had allowed me to identify social spaces that might also serve as venues for political debate, meaning that I was interviewing many different populations. As I wrote in that early fellowship application:

First, I will identify community and political leaders within each camp to conduct oral histories. These oral histories will center on political factions' roles and responsibilities in the camps from 1982 until the present. Second, in order to get a broader idea of the factors driving political change in the camps, I will create interview groups centered on social networks connected to central aspects of camp life. Key target groups will include store owners, mosque congregations, religious study circles, and youth groups or sports teams.

When I later re-cased the project, those oral histories and in-depth interviews allowed me to use the same evidentiary material in ways that specifically facilitated intra-organizational and relational comparisons. This was especially true given that I started each interview by asking about people's families – a technique inspired by Padgett's (2010) emphasis on marriage in his scholarship. Because the project had not assumed which spaces were necessarily political, because I focused on developing an experience-based view of life in the camps via oral history, and because I followed my interlocutors' encouragement to "live the reality" (*'aish al-waq'a*) in the camps, I wound up with a more robust picture of network change over time and a thicker representation of complex social structures (see, e.g., Parkinson 2016). The relationships embedded within these structures became the sources for the comparisons that eventually drove the book project. Casting a narrower net by focusing on expressly political organizations such as factions or nongovernmental organizations would have severely constrained this work.

Second, as the preceding paragraph notes, I also pursued a heavily historical project. The initial proposals described interviewing plans geared toward describing the contemporary factional politics of interest. However, gathering extensive data on organizations' histories in Lebanon allowed me to shift the period of the study backward in time when I re-cased it. If it were not for the initial broad, longitudinal interviewing and archival approach that my committee supported, I would never have gathered the evidence that became the core of the book project.

POSTPRODUCTION

Adjusting a research design in the process of conducting the research comes with multiple challenges, including determining which leads to follow, which ones to abandon, and how to develop a viable project from potentially disparate evidentiary material. Extended fieldwork epistemically, ontologically, and empirically upended my original research design. What followed was a several-year period of attempting to reorganize material into a viable project. My old fellowship applications now reveal a process of trying to make sense of the various perspectives that emerged from this process. Immediately following fieldwork, I discarded the "representative camps" approach, favoring instead a comparison between "local divisions of political factions in eight camps in three Lebanese cities (Beirut, Saida, and Sour)" and wrote of my "wartime violence independent variable" that I hypothesized was driving organizational change and, by extension, factional violence.[3] In this design, I was comparing local organizations, across camps, over time; I was still stuck in the compare *things* model. In other words, to use the butchery metaphor, I was pondering a different sort of cut: the unit of analysis had shifted from the refugee camp to organizational units in camps. This approach usefully sold breadth and depth to pre-doctoral fellowships but still did not fully encompass what I was doing analytically. Given the historical nature of my empirical evidence, I already knew that the "things" that I was comparing – subunits of organizations – were not necessarily the same thing – unit – over time, even if they carried the same name (e.g., combat unit).

A fellowship application that I wrote one year after my longest period of fieldwork reflects a project that had moved far away from the MSDO design by ethnographically comparing different types of Palestinian organizations. In this application, I wrote: "In particular, I observed how everyday behaviors – everything from gossip to complaining to religious practice – distinguished members of various social networks – how those practices reproduced or challenged factional affiliations."[4] At this point, I was beginning to focus on network ties and their content – in this case, gossip, complaining, and practice – in a comparative light. This shift was one of the key realizations that pushed me toward the neurological metaphor that helped me build my theory.

By the time I was on the job market, my approach had changed again. The project embraced the idea of comparing organizational and network processes, rather than discrete spaces or even regional divisions of the same militant organizations. I had focused in on how particular repertoires of violence differentially affected networks. However, in describing how my work was sited during presentations and particularly job talks, I found myself relying on the language of some of those discarded models to be legible to political science

---

[3] Order Conflict and Violence program research statement, January 2011.
[4] American Council of Learned Societies research statement, November 2011.

scholars. In the fall of 2011, I had multiple arguments with well-meaning senior scholars about whether or not the 1982 Israeli invasion of Lebanon – the starting point for my study – was an exogenous event that equally treated comparable units of refugee camps. Could I argue that social processes started from equal footing if some camps were 80 percent destroyed and others were 100 percent destroyed? Might the Israel Defense Forces (IDF) have invaded Lebanon because of the underlying social structure or political activities of people in one camp versus another?

Engaging in these discussions elicited both productive and exasperating tensions. The political and human stakes of these comparisons are nontrivial. On one hand, to imply that the 1982 Israeli invasion was exogenous to dynamics in Palestinian refugee camps in Lebanon would be historically inaccurate: the camps were major sites for the organizing and training of Palestinian militant groups. That said, the actual trigger for the IDF's invasion was the fringe Abu Nidal Organization's (not a constituent member of the Palestine Liberation Organization) attempted assassination of the Israeli ambassador to the United Kingdom. It was well known in Israeli policy circles that Minister of Defense Ariel Sharon and other Israeli hawks had long been waiting for such a premise to invade Lebanon, in part because the social and organizational dynamics of Palestinian communities alone did not provide sufficient justification for a full-scale invasion and in part due to the constraints posed by domestic Israeli politics. The invasion was also initially planned as a limited campaign focused primarily on South Lebanon – where only five camps were located and where the majority of Palestinian armed activity against Israel was based – and then controversially expanded in its early days at Sharon's urging to reach Beirut and its Palestinian camps. Did this mean I could call the invasion exogenous? Or exogenous to dynamics in Beirut? When it came to the specific social dynamics that I studied, the invasion was technically exogenous to them, but they were not exactly unrelated. To gloss many of these factors given the historical record would be both scientifically inaccurate and politically loaded.

Arguing about whether or not I could "scientifically" establish a control with the 1982 invasion – because it could be deemed exogenous – given the level of social and physical destruction also seemed to erase the massive human costs of the IDF's invasion of Lebanon. These dynamics, however, were the real focus of my study. The whole point was that the way that wartime violence elicited a crisis in Palestinian organizations, effectively shattered social networks, and started a process of reorganization that created new logics of military organizing. It seemed ridiculous, as such, to ponder whether the 80 percent to 100 percent physical destruction of certain camps was functionally equal social and economic damage. In reality, I heard the question as: "Well, if 20 houses out of 100 were still standing versus no houses out of 100 standing, might people in the 80 percent destroyed camp have been less socially affected?" I was painfully aware that those statistics were in effect only a crude proxy for the damage done to families and communities affected by mass incarceration, the use of incendiary weapons on the refugee camps, and the aerial bombardment of large swaths of Lebanese cities, which resulted in extensive infrastructural damage. Having had hundreds of conversations on the topic, I knew that twenty houses still standing meant little to their inhabitants if they were surrounded by unexploded ordinance and levelled shops, mosques, and homes, left empty by people interred in detention camps.

These inquiries were perfectly legitimate in the context of academic study and were posed to prepare me for inevitable questions at job talks. Because I was unable to articulate what I was doing by using the models taught in the discipline, these questions also had the effect of encouraging me to abandon an approach that centered on the effects of violence on units rather than the effects of violence on relations. It became evident that I did not have the language available to describe an alternative, so I began experimenting with metaphors to convey how I was thinking.

It was during a struggle to finish a workshop paper for a presentation at Yale's Workshop on Order Conflict and Violence in spring 2012 that I almost offhandedly wrote the following:

Combining the idea of violent repertoires with the concept of embedded decision making suggests that individuals who share membership across multiple networks [e.g., faction, family, community] will react to perceived threats in similar ways, empowering select groupings within organizations and driving decision making within organizations. This interaction is akin to the way in which distinct sections of a brain "light up" when exposed to different stimuli; if we think of the militant organization as a human brain, then different "regions" of it will have distinct interpretations of and reactions to the different violent stimuli. Moreover, some stimuli may elicit immediate, instinctual responses, while reacting to others requires time, processing, and conscious decision-making. An organization may be prepared for particular forms of repression, such as enemy forces targeting its leadership, and implement precautionary measures and protocols that call on distinct subsets of the organizational membership (such as a team of bodyguards and a bomb disposal squad). However, unanticipated forms of violence, such as the deliberate massacre of civilians in a particular neighborhood, may activate previously informal subsets of relationships within the organizational body (perhaps by geographic origin or gender), beginning a new process of organizational processing, strategizing, and institutionalization of behavioral norms. Furthermore, several combined tactics could "light up" different sections of the same organization simultaneously, driving multiple adaptive processes.

At this point, I did not know what the formal terms were for these neurological processes, or that neurons could actually change through them. To be frank, I think I likely pulled the metaphor from a medically themed TV show. But something about it resonated. It did not rest on assumptions of exogenous action. Rather, it focused on ties and configurations of relations, it allowed for both individual ties and overarching units to be affected by and respond to environmental factors, and it seemed to represent both organizational routine and the possibility for unpreparedness. I began to explicitly speak in terms of "inputs" and "outputs" rather than "independent" and "dependent" variables to emphasize that I was no longer operating in a framework that assumed linear causality. I added three-dimensional, dynamic sociograms (network diagrams) to PowerPoint presentations so that viewers could see how the project centered relationships and how micro-shifts in social network structures (e.g., ties being cut and reestablished via new connections) scaled up to organizational evolution over time. I spoke about the necessity of endogenizing organizational processes. Above all, I emphasized that my mode of inquiry was systematic and that the approach could easily travel to other settings.

CASING ORGANIZATIONAL CHANGE: THE NITTY-GRITTY

What does the neurology comparison give scholars interested in studying change in social networks? Given a focus on comparing network configurations, it is necessary to have a systematic way of identifying changes to the structure and content of relations. There are two primary ways to case a specific network configuration. The first is to identify a configuration of interest – such as a specific type of organization – and to work backward to determine how that particular system of relations came into being. The other is to gather vast amounts of data and to code it in the hope that patterns emerge. In this section, I elaborate tools that allow researchers to adopt either trajectory. Drawing on my own research on militant organizations and social change in conflict, I specifically use the scenario of war to provide context; however, I expect versions of these mechanisms to travel to other settings. In Figure 8.1, I present a simplified egocentric network representation – that is, a network centered on a singular node, in this case a person – of an individual in a militant organization.

In this sociogram, we view Militant A's social network position from an egocentric perspective, meaning that we are focused explicitly on their relationships with others (alters). Small dotted lines represent Militant A's formal relationships within their militant organization: relational ties link to Militant B and Militant C and all three are bound by constitutive membership ties defined by the rules and skills that accompany membership (solid oval).[5] Elements of these ties are directional and hierarchal, traits that arrows represent. For example, Militant B gives Militant A commands and payments while Militant A issues orders and transfers a salary to Militant C. Individuals D, E, and F are linked to Militant A but are not in their immediate militant network map as defined by constitutive membership ties. Rather, we can think of D and E as Militant A's kin (dashed lines) – and of F as a friend from a social situation, say a religious congregation.

---

[5] Padgett and McLean (2006, 1468–69) developed the concepts of "relational" and "constitutive" ties in their work on Renaissance Florence.

Composing Comparisons 165

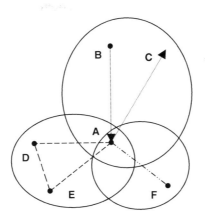

FIGURE 8.1 Militant A's egocentric social network perspective
Note: I thank Roger Petersen for helping me to develop this figure.

The first two mechanisms for evaluating change and facilitating comparison across networks relate to the immediate effects of wartime violence:

1. War can remove nodes (death, functional incapacitation, flight).
2. War can remove ties (block, sever, or empty relational pathways).

Say Militant B is killed (a version of Scenario 1). In war, the loss or incapacitation of individuals through desertion, flight, demobilization, imprisonment, migration, injury, and death (to name a few options) has immediate effects on network maps. To preserve the status quo, Militant A must seek to compensate for this relationship, either by connecting to a preexisting node by forming a new relational tie (i.e., bridging the local structural hole created by Militant B's absence), by altering an existing relational tie to another node (i.e., changing its content), or by bringing a new node into the organizational map to replace the old one and reestablishing the relational tie (i.e., recruitment). However, the environment around Militant A will have changed by the time this adaptation occurs, meaning there is no such thing as an exact 1:1 substitution for the node or its position. Militant B's absence guarantees categorical change because Militant B's presence – personal history, goals, connections, and so on – are co-constituted by the role that they played in their networks.

In Scenario 2, Militants A and B may still be active and available, but the "stuff" that flows through their particular relationship, such as money or communication, cannot flow. Perhaps, for example, they are both under surveillance or militias have constructed checkpoints on the roads that connect their neighborhoods. Militants A and B must find a way to reestablish this relational flow through other nodes and ties. Put differently, they need to operate through at least one broker. When these processes scale to the organizational or domain level – in other words, when a number of similarly connected nodes are simultaneously lost or incapacitated – the macro effects of violent repression can restrict entire organizational subunits and hierarchies from routine functioning. Entire segments of network maps or social structures may be destroyed or cut off.

Wartime violence has six additional potential effects on social systems. Rather than being immediate effects of violence, they involve individual actors' reactions to events:

3. Nodes can join a constitutive or relational network (mobilization, hiring, birth).
4. Nodes can add relational ties between
   a. Previously connected nodes (new content)
   b. Previously unconnected nodes (new tie and new content)
5. Nodes can alter the direction in which content flows through relational ties.
6. The strength/intensity of relational ties can change (quantity of material, frequency of exchange).
7. The temporality associated with ties can change (meetings on Friday rather than Saturday, exchanges occur bimonthly rather than monthly).
8. War can change nodes' valence:
   a. Egocentric focus (focus on the individual, ego, whose network it is) – shifts in ego's personal emotions, motivations, and perceptions
   b. Altercentric focus (focus on others in ego's network) – ego's subjective effect on alters in their network via shifts in their emotions, motivations, and perceptions

Some network effects result from actors' conscious attempts to repair social structures in the shadow of war. To cope with what one might term "first-order" or "material" structural effects of wartime violence (Scenarios 1 and 2), militants can bundle new relational flows into preexisting ties (Scenario 4a). That is, Militants A and B can add flows of material goods or secret information to their previously established financial and communication ties. Or, perhaps upon observing the entry of an occupying force into a country, a previously inactive node moves into a militant organization (a version of Scenario 3). Both of these scenarios would change, for example, the way one would draw an organizational diagram of the group.

Yet wartime violence also has many seemingly invisible effects on organizational structure, in that the material structure of the network – the proverbial steel in the skyscraper (Sewell 1992) or organizational diagram – is not immediately affected. Yet these changes are crucial to shaping both organizational hierarchies and the way that actors understand their roles in them. Scenario 8 – changes in Militant A's emotions, motivations, or perceptions – leaves this material network structure intact. However, the way in which Militant A understands their location within it changes. The experience of war may lead A to perceive new vulnerabilities, experience new feelings, or shift motivations for channeling specific network flows (McLean 1998; Gould 2009, chaps. 1 and 2; Parkinson 2016).[6] Perhaps they originally smuggled guns because their sister asked them to, but experiencing violence firsthand provided new reasons to do (or not do) so. Scenario 8b, in which Militant A's *valence* shifts, provides an altercentric view of war's effect on the individual. Consider the effect of Militant A becoming a collaborator or a dissident who works to observe or undermine Militants B and C via preestablished ties. Militant A is still structurally present in the network, but their subjective effect on the network is now negative when it was previously positive.

Composing relational comparisons requires the scholar to collect and analyze evidence of network change across these eight dimensions, looking for trends in both the incidence of change and its effects. This is all done with the knowledge that multiple network mechanisms can co-occur. In my work, it was a given that someone would have a brother arrested, lose touch with another who fled, have a friend become an informer, and have a teacher recruit them, all in a short period of time. Establishing the periodization of network change – be it regular or according to historically significant dates – is thus essential, especially to determine the amount of data sought.

This analysis can thus be done across time for one set of relations – for example, for one ego, to see how their behavior changes as their personal or organizational network does – or comparison can be done across egos, to see how larger collectivities shift in comparison to each other as egos change in response to their environments. My project, for example, did both. Parts of my work focus on how changes in egos' networks mobilized them into new roles in militant groups. I would speak to a woman who noted particular changes to her egocentric network that resulted from particular repertoires of violence and then linked them to her taking on the role of a smuggler. Other parts of my work focus on the aggregate effect of these dynamics. For example, reconstructing individual women's networks over time and across space allowed me to identify a broader pattern in which the *systematic* mobilization of women as smugglers produced new network maps tasked with clandestine operations, in effect creating an entirely new organizational subdivision. While only one example, it demonstrates that the strategy of composing network comparisons allows scholars to toggle between levels of analysis and to place the unit itself as the outcome of interest, facilitating a nuanced mode of comparison that captures complex social dynamics.

---

[6] Networks may also experience these sorts of processes collectively as a shift in what Deborah Gould terms "emotional habitus," which refers to "a social grouping's collective and only partly conscious emotional dispositions, that is, members' embodies, axiomatic inclinations toward certain feelings and ways of emoting" (Gould 2009, 32–36).

CONCLUSION

Composing network comparisons via the immersive study of roles and relations provides a meaningful way of analyzing organizational evolution. In particular, this approach embraces context specificity, scalability, and generalizability while allowing the scholar to examine both individual- and collective-level outcomes. This chapter has examined the trajectory of a research project on militant organizations' adaptation that began as a classic case comparison and was re-cased into an explicitly network-based comparison of intra-organizational dynamics. In doing so, it has outlined a method of comparison focused primarily on roles, relations, and emergence, rather than on organizational form or behavior. The chapter leverages this individual experience to establish core tenets of a broader approach to studying organizational change in comparative perspective by relying on a neuroscience-based perspectival comparison.

REFERENCES

Abdullah, Hilana. 2008. *Mukhayyam al-Burj al-Shamālī: Hīthu yushīkh ālām (Burj al-Shemali Camp: Where Aging Is Suffering)*. Palestinian Camps Series. Sour (Lebanon): Palestinian Organization for Right of Return (Thabit).

al-Hajali, Ahmad ʿAli. 2007. *Mukhayyam Burj al-Barājna: Zulul al-Mawt wa al-Hayāa (Burj al-Barajna Camp: Shadows of Death and Life)*. Palestinian Camps Series. Sour (Lebanon): Palestinian Organization for Right of Return (Thabit).

Al-Hardan, Anaheed. 2017. "Researching Palestinian Refugees: Who Sets the Agenda?" *Al-Shabaka* (blog). April 27. https://al-shabaka.org/commentaries/researching-palestinian-refugees-sets-agenda/

Allan, Diana. 2013. *Refugees of the Revolution: Experiences of Palestinian Exile*. Stanford, CA: Stanford University Press.

Arbib, Michael A. 2002. *The Handbook of Brain Theory and Neural Networks: Second Edition*. Cambridge, MA: MIT Press.

BBC. 2008. "Shatila Martyrs' Cemetery," May 14, sec. Middle East. http://news.bbc.co.uk/2/hi/middle_east/7392725.stm

Buonomano, Dean V., and Michael M. Merzenich. 1998. "Cortical Plasticity: From Synapses to Maps." *Annual Review of Neuroscience* 21 (1): 149–86.

Carpenter, Charli. 2011. "Vetting the Advocacy Agenda: Network Centrality and the Paradox of Weapons Norms." *International Organization* 65 (1): 69–102.

———. 2014. *"Lost" Causes: Agenda Vetting in Global Issue Networks and the Shaping of Human Security*. Ithaca & London: Cornell University Press.

Carpenter, Daniel, and Colin D. Moore. 2014. "When Canvassers Became Activists: Antislavery Petitioning and the Political Mobilization of American Women." *American Political Science Review* 108 (3): 479–98.

Chang, Kuang-chi. 2011. "A Path to Understanding Guanxi in China's Transitional Economy: Variations on Network Behavior." *Sociological Theory* 29 (4): 315–39.

Collier, David. 2011. "Understanding Process Tracing." *PS: Political Science & Politics* 44 (4): 823–30.

Connolly, William E. 2002. *Neuropolitics*. Minneapolis: University of Minnesota Press.

Doidge, Norman. 2007. *The Brain That Changes Itself: Stories of Personal Triumph from the Frontiers of Brain Science*. New York: Viking.

Emirbayer, Mustafa. 1997. "Manifesto for a Relational Sociology." *American Journal of Sociology* 103 (2): 281–317.

Emirbayer, Mustafa, and Jeff Goodwin. 1994. "Network Analysis, Culture, and the Problem of Agency." *American Journal of Sociology* 99 (6): 1411–54.

Fleifel, Mahdi. 2014. *A World Not Ours: Feature Films | POV | PBS*. www.pbs.org/pov/aworldnotours/full.php

Folman, Ari. 2009. *Waltz With Bashir*. Sony Pictures Classics.

Franzosi, Roberto. 1998. "Narrative Analysis – or Why (and How) Sociologists Should Be Interested in Narrative." *Annual Review of Sociology* 24: 517–54.

Gade, Emily Kalah, Michael Gabbay, Mohammed M. Hafez, and Zane Kelly. 2019. "Networks of Cooperation: Rebel Alliances in Fragmented Civil Wars." *Journal of Conflict Resolution* 63 (9): 2071–97.

Gade, Emily Kalah, Mohammed M. Hafez, and Michael Gabbay. 2019. "Fratricide in Rebel Movements: A Network Analysis of Syrian Militant Infighting." *Journal of Peace Research* 56 (3): 321–35.

George, Alexander L., and Andrew Bennett. 2005. *Case Studies and Theory Development in the Social Sciences*. Cambridge, MA: MIT Press.

Gould, Deborah B. 2009. *Moving Politics: Emotion and ACT UP's Fight against AIDS*. Chicago: University of Chicago Press.

Hadden, Jennifer. 2015. *Networks in Contention: The Divisive Politics of Climate Change*. Cambridge: Cambridge University Press.

Hafner-Burton, Emilie M., Miles Kahler, and Alexander H. Montgomery. 2009. "Network Analysis for International Relations." *International Organization* 63 (3): 559–92.

Hundman, Eric. 2016. "Networks and Loyalties: The Social Roots of Military Disobedience in the Sino-French War." PhD diss. University of Chicago.

Hundman, Eric, and Sarah E. Parkinson. 2019. "Rogues, Degenerates, and Heroes: Disobedience as Politics in Military Organizations." *European Journal of International Relations* 25 (3): 645–71.

Kallam, Mahmud Abdullah. 2008. *Mukhayyam Shātilā: Al-Jaraāh Wa-l-Kifaāh (Shatila Camp: The Surgeon and the Struggle)*. Palestinian Camps Series. Sour (Lebanon): Palestinian Organization for Right of Return (Thabit).

Larson, Jennifer M., and Janet I. Lewis. 2017. "Ethnic Networks." *American Journal of Political Science* 61 (2): 350–64.

  2018. "Rumors, Kinship Networks, and Rebel Group Formation." *International Organization* 72 (4): 871–903.

  2020. "Measuring Networks in the Field." *Political Science Research and Methods* 8 (1): 123–35.

McLean, Paul D. 1998. "A Frame Analysis of Favor Seeking in the Renaissance: Agency, Networks, and Political Culture." *American Journal of Sociology* 104 (1): 51–91.

  2007. *The Art of the Network: Strategic Interaction and Patronage in Renaissance Florence*. Durham, NC: Duke University Press.

  2016. *Culture in Networks*. Cambridge, UK & Malden, MA: Polity.

Mische, Ann. 2007. *Partisan Publics: Communication and Contention across Brazilian Youth Activist Networks.* Princeton, NJ: Princeton University Press.

Mische, Ann, and Harrison White. 1998. "Between Conversation and Situation: Public Switching Dynamics across Network Domains." *Social Research* 65 (3): 695–724.

Obert, Jonathan. 2014. "The Six-Shooter Marketplace: 19th-Century Gunfighting as Violence Expertise." *Studies in American Political Development* 28 (1): 49–79.

2018. *The Six-Shooter State: Public and Private Violence in American Politics.* Rpt. edn. Cambridge, UK & New York: Cambridge University Press.

Padgett, John F. 2010. "Open Elite? Social Mobility, Marriage, and Family in Florence, 1282–1494." *Renaissance Quarterly* 63 (2): 357–411.

Padgett, John F., and Christopher K. Ansell. 1993. "Robust Action and the Rise of the Medici, 1400–1434." *American Journal of Sociology* 98 (6): 1259–1319.

Padgett, John F., and Paul D. McLean. 2006. "Organizational Invention and Elite Transformation: The Birth of Partnership Systems in Renaissance Florence." *American Journal of Sociology* 111 (5): 1463–568.

Papachristos, Andrew V. 2009. "Murder by Structure: Dominance Relations and the Social Structure of Gang Homicide." *American Journal of Sociology* 115 (1): 74–128.

Parkinson, Sarah E. 2013. "Organizing Rebellion: Rethinking High-Risk Mobilization and Social Networks in War." *American Political Science Review* 107 (3): 418–32.

2016. "Money Talks: Discourse, Networks, and Structure in Militant Organizations." *Perspectives on Politics* 14 (4): 976–94.

2021. "Practical Ideology in Militant Organizations." *World Politics* 73 (1): 52–81.

Pascual-Leone, Alvaro, Catarina Freitas, Lindsay Oberman, Jared Horvath, Mark Halko, Mark Eldaief, Shahid Bashir, et al. 2011. "Characterizing Brain Cortical Plasticity and Network Dynamics Across the Age-Span in Health and Disease with TMS-EEG and TMS-FMRI." *Brain Topography* 24 (3): 302–15.

Pedahzur, Ami, and Arie Perliger. 2006. "The Changing Nature of Suicide Attacks: A Social Network Perspective." *Social Forces* 84 (4): 1987–2008.

Perliger, Arie, and Ami Pedahzur. 2011. "Social Network Analysis in the Study of Terrorism and Political Violence." *PS: Political Science & Politics* 44 (1): 45–50.

Petersen, Roger D. 2001. *Resistance and Rebellion: Lessons from Eastern Europe.* Cambridge: Cambridge University Press.

Rougier, Bernard. 2007. *Everyday Jihad: The Rise of Militant Islam among Palestinians in Lebanon.* Cambridge, MA: Harvard University Press.

Schaffer, Frederic Charles. 2018. "Two Ways to Compare." *Qualitative and Multi-Method Research* 16 (1): 15–20.

Sewell, William H. 1992. "A Theory of Structure: Duality, Agency, and Transformation." *American Journal of Sociology* 98 (1): 1–29.

Siegel, David A. 2009. "Social Networks and Collective Action." *American Journal of Political Science* 53 (1): 122–38.

Small, Mario Luis. 2009. "'How Many Cases Do I Need?': On Science and the Logic of Case Selection in Field-Based Research." *Ethnography* 10 (1): 5–38.

Soss, Joe. 2018. "On Casing a Study versus Studying a Case." *Qualitative and Multi-Method Research* 16 (1): 21–27.

Staniland, Paul. 2012. "Organizing Insurgency: Networks, Resources, and Rebellion in South Asia." *International Security* 37 (1): 142–77.

2014. *Networks of Rebellion: Explaining Insurgent Cohesion and Collapse*. Ithaca, NY: Cornell University Press.

StudioCamps. 2008. *Ahlan Wa Sahlan Fi Shatila Mudafukez (Welcome to Shatila Mudfakez)*. Shatila: StudioCamps. www.youtube.com/watch?v=Uvu-hrtc4LE&feature=youtube_gdata_player

Sukarieh, Mayssoun, and Stuart Tannock. 2013. "On the Problem of Over-Researched Communities: The Case of the Shatila Palestinian Refugee Camp in Lebanon." *Sociology* 47 (3): 494–508.

Viterna, Jocelyn. 2006. "Pulled, Pushed, and Persuaded: Explaining Women's Mobilization into the Salvadoran Guerrilla Army." *American Journal of Sociology* 112 (1): 1–45.

Wood, Elisabeth Jean. 2008. "The Social Processes of Civil War: The Wartime Transformation of Social Networks." *Annual Review of Political Science* 11: 539–61.

Zech, Steven T., and Michael Gabbay. 2016. "Social Network Analysis in the Study of Terrorism and Insurgency: From Organization to Politics." *International Studies Review* 18 (2): 214–43.

9

Against Methodological Nationalism
Seeing Comparisons as Encompassing through the Arab Uprisings

Jillian Schwedler
City University of New York–Hunter College

On July 13, 2011, Micah White and Kalle Lasn of the anti-corporate *Adbusters* magazine published a short manifesto, "Tactical Briefing: Shift in Revolutionary Tactics."[1] They sent the text to an email list of 90,000 friends of the magazine, launching the campaign widely credited as the origin of the Occupy Wall Street movement and its hundreds of encampments across the United States, which began on September 17, 2011. The manifesto began as follows:

> Alright you 90,000 redeemers, rebels and radicals out there,
>
> A worldwide shift in revolutionary tactics is underway right now that bodes well for the future. The spirit of this fresh tactic, a fusion of Tahrir with the acampadas of Spain, is captured in this quote:
>
> "The antiglobalization movement was the first step on the road. Back then our model was to attack the system like a pack of wolves. There was an alpha male, a wolf who led the pack, and those who followed behind. Now the model has evolved. Today we are one big swarm of people."
>
> Raimundo Viejo, Pompeu Fabra University, Barcelona, Spain (emphasis in original)

The organizers and many of the tens of thousands of participants in the Occupy movement viewed themselves as joining a global uprising against corporate power and greed that had – among other ill effects – diminished the substance of democracy (in the United States as well as globally),

---

I am grateful to Erica Simmons and Nick Smith for organizing the workshop that inspired me to more fully articulate my earlier critiques of methodological nationalism surrounding studies of the Arab uprisings. They, and the participants at the workshop provided exceptionally helpful suggestions and critiques. I also benefited tremendously from detailed comments from Laryssa Chomiak, Janine Astrid Clark, F. Gregory Gause, III, Pete W. Moore, and Curtis R. Ryan. All remaining blunders are my own.

[1] The full manifesto is available at www.elvey.com/63DZ1nIDl_files/mainframe.html

propped up dictatorships, and produced the greatest level of income inequality in human history. Occupy was the latest manifestation of a global justice movement that had waxed and waned over the years and included such actions as the Battle of Seattle and the annual World Social Forum. Scholars writing about Occupy acknowledge that protesters globally often saw their actions in common – "one big swarm of people." But most analyses of the protests that took place in 2011 around the globe only nod to the simultaneity of the protests without theorizing the very connections invoked by protesters.[2]

The field of comparative politics has long emphasized in-depth or paired case studies over attention to global connections, institutions, or processes.[3] What might case-centric comparative analyses lack? My argument is that case-centered analyses per se are problematic primarily when they treat individual cases (usually countries) as bounded entities whose politics can be largely explained by what is found inside: the history and characteristics of the regime, the state of the economy, the dominant ideas circulating, the nature of the opposition, and so on. Few if any serious scholars, of course, would argue that external factors are irrelevant to understanding domestic politics – foreign interventions, migration and refugee flows, and regional and global rivalries, to give just a few examples, all shape domestic politics and receive considerable scholarly attention. But many of these studies remain inward looking, with many analyses structured around in-depth studies of a single case or else explaining variations across a set of otherwise discrete cases. Larger processes and structures are the purview of scholars of international relations.

A large portion of the scholarship on the Arab uprisings is exemplary of such analytic conventions and thus can bring into view what might be overlooked. The Arab uprisings – what many Anglophone journalists, policy makers, and some scholars call the "Arab Spring"[4] – are a set of protest movements that

---

[2] For example, see Gitlin (2012), who is typical in acknowledging Occupy Wall Street as inspired by movements elsewhere but largely containing the analysis at the national level.

[3] In recent years, the rise of large-N analyses has led some quantitative comparativists to dismiss case studies as largely empirical and not theoretical. Qualitative comparativists have pushed back, publishing a range of works both defending case studies and articulating the theories and methodologies behind them. Many of the classic readings in comparative politics are single-case studies or structured comparisons, including work, for example, by such diverse comparativists as Theda Skocpol, Lisa Wedeen, Barrington Moore, James C. Scott, and Robert Putnam.

[4] Scholars of the Middle East largely favor "Arab uprisings" to "Arab Spring," for two reasons. First, "Arab Spring" emerged among Western journalists and was never widely used in Arabic (*al-rabi`i al-arabi*); second, "spring" is not an analytic category, whereas "uprisings" more precisely labels a range of mobilizations from smaller sustained protests to revolutionary mobilization. The editors of this volume proposed in a personal communication, however, that "maybe journalists are right to call it the Arab Spring and academics are wrong to call them the Arab Uprisings ... the language of Spring forefronts the connection among the uprisings, while the language of Uprising nationally separates them. Spring is inclusive and connective while Uprisings linguistically points to separate, discrete events." I disagree, as "spring" marks less a set of connected events than

broke out across much of the Middle East in 2011. They began in southern Tunisia in December 2010 with the self-immolation of a produce cart vendor and spread across that country over the next weeks until, on January 14, 2011, when the autocratic president, Ben Ali, fled the country – sealing the "success" of Tunisia's Jasmine Revolution.[5] The Tunisian example inspired others across the region to take to the streets and demand substantive political changes, often calling for the fall of the regime. Nearly every state in the Middle East was affected, although not all states saw the protests reach revolutionary levels of mobilization.

The two puzzles that many scholars have sought to explain are (1) why the protests began and spread and when and how they did (and not earlier, when similar conditions of repression and economic hardship seemed to exist) and (2) why some of the uprisings escalated to revolutionary levels while others were contained.[6] For the first question, the scholarly literature often borrows from the language of the sciences, whereby the uprisings spread geographically through contagion or diffusion.[7] Few analyses, however, offer theoretical explanations so much as descriptions of the spatial and temporal spread.

The second question – why only some of the uprisings turned revolutionary – has dominated the scholarly literature on the uprisings. These studies probe the dynamics and trajectories of the protests within individual states to understand their divergent paths. Utilizing a kind of methodological or epistemological nationalism, the analytic focus is on explaining variation across cases, that is, across individual states.[8] Why was only Tunisia's uprising successful in bringing

---

a season, a kind of simultaneity across the region that does not really improve on the way "Arab uprisings of 2011" suggests a collection of cases without saying much about connections between them. Francophone scholarship, however, prefers *printemps arabes* (Arab Spring) over *soulevements arabes* (Arab uprisings).

[5] Tunisia's revolution was only briefly called the "Jasmine Revolution" inside Tunisia. Tunisians in the country's vast interior rejected the term because jasmine flourishes only along the (wealthier) coastal regions – a symbolic class critique that a revolution cannot be accomplished only by the wealthier classes. I mention it here because it appears in many conventional analyses of the unfolding of the uprisings, as this passage aims to capture.

[6] I do not wish to suggest that all single or structured comparative studies of the uprisings focus on these two questions, only that versions of them have dominated the literature. A handful of studies have examined the international political economy of the uprisings or delved into other internal political dynamics of the uprisings. For example, Lisa Wedeen's study of cultural production before and during Syria's uprising and war, *Authoritarian Apprehensions: Ideology, Judgement, and Mourning in Syria* (2019), examines the ideological investments that enable a considerable portion of the population to maintain its allegiance to the al-Asad regime despite its seemingly undeniable atrocities.

[7] See, for example, Patel et al. (2014). Yet the interchangeability of these metaphors is problematic because diffusion and contagion are different processes. In diffusion, the element is thinned or weakened as it spreads, as in a drop of ink into water. In contagion, the element loses no strength as it infects a new host, and it may even strengthen as it infects ever-wider populations.

[8] Wimmer and Schiller (2003) present an excellent critique of methodological nationalism.

about lasting regime change?[9] Why did the uprisings in Libya and Syria descend into civil war? Was Egypt's uprising a revolution, a coup, or a combination of both? Many of these analyses are driven by an underlying normative concern that any transition, whether revolutionary or gradual, should be a democratic transition. When a massive mobilization fails to realize that end, scholars want to understand why. To answer these kinds of questions, many scholars structure their comparisons around identifying and explaining variations between cases.[10] States are sorted into columns, perhaps divided between those that witnessed a mass uprising and those that did not, or between those that saw democratic transitions and those that did not.[11] This kind of typological theorizing seeks to identify potential explanatory variables – differences among the cases that might explain the divergent trajectories. It also reinforces the idea of states as largely stand-alone units, even as foreign actors, institutions, and other factors may play a role. Exemplary of this approach is the volume by Jason Brownlee, Tarek Masoud, and Andrew Reynolds (2015), which asks why some uprisings led to regime reform while others led to repression.

In such variation-finding analyses, explanatory variables include regime type, repressive capacities, and economic factors (e.g., unemployment or inequality), all of which are aggregated to the national or state level. Most such explanatory variables are also largely internal to each state, and the observed outcomes are seen as determined by those domestic factors – again largely distinct from other cases. Yet both state and non-state actors during the uprisings in 2011 were clearly making decisions informed by the dynamics of the other uprisings and how those regimes responded to them. Where external or foreign factors are recognized as playing a role, those factors are still largely examined on a state-by-state basis: for example, foreign intervention in Libya differed from foreign intervention in Syria. The relationships between the cases as well as their relations to the same (or different) external factors or larger structures and processes are seldom explicitly addressed and often entirely overlooked.

[9] I have written elsewhere about the perils of characterizing all the uprisings, except possibly Tunisia's, as failed uprisings, and particularly the problem of ignoring the protests that continue on smaller scales across the region. Our analytic frameworks can do political work when we declare this or that uprising as failed or even nonexistent, even as protesters and other citizens struggle to hold on to that moment of possibility for a different future. See Schwedler (2015).
[10] One common approach, based on the work of John Stuart Mill, is to adopt either a most-similar or most-different design, whereby cases are selected based on either similar features but different outcomes, or vice versa. See Mill ([1843] 2002).
[11] Some comparative studies do acknowledge that Jordan, Morocco, Saudi Arabia, Sudan, Palestine, Kuwait, and nearly every state in the region did see an increase in protests during the period of the uprisings, often with tens of thousands of people in the streets. Even when those protests are acknowledged, however, the analytic framework tends to uphold the methodological nationalist framework, that is, seeking to explain why large-scale uprisings occurred in some countries but not others.

The Arab uprisings thus provide an opportunity to construct a comparative analysis that moves beyond the focus on individual case studies or variation finding across cases. Indeed, I argue that understanding the trajectories of the uprisings in Egypt, Jordan, and Bahrain – three examples examined in this chapter – is only possibly by examining where these countries are located in distinct regional and US-centered global security arrangements. What might be gained by an alternative comparative framework that seeks to bring those connections into focus? As Sewell (2005) reminds us, cases are never fully separate, because events in one case can and do impact events and decisions in other cases. For an alternative comparative methodology, I revisit Charles Tilly's (1984) notion of encompassing comparisons – an approach that aims to understand how individual cases are structured by their relationship to some larger process(es), institution(s), or entity(ies), to which other cases are also connected. The next two sections define encompassing comparisons and then demonstrate how an encompassing comparison of the Arab uprisings could provide a richer and more compelling explanation for one of the most recurrent comparative questions – why only some uprisings escalated to revolutionary levels, and why so few brought regime change. The cases of Bahrain, Egypt, and Jordan, I show, are not cases of, respectively, a crushed uprising, a revolution followed by a counterrevolution, and a mass movement that never turned revolutionary. As stand-alone cases, these broad descriptions are apt. But taken together, a much different picture of mobilization and repression across the region begins to emerge, one that depends on the relationship of each of those individual states to larger regional and global processes and structures. In the final section, I respond to an imaginary interlocutor who might rightly ask how we know which large structure or process is most important.

ENCOMPASSING COMPARISONS

The core insight behind an encompassing comparison is that individual cases are not only connected to larger structures and processes, but that other cases are also connected to those same larger structures and processes. Even more, precisely how each case is connected to those larger structures or processes can have observable political effects across some or all of the other cases. In his handbook on comparative methodology, *Big Structures, Large Processes, Huge Comparisons*, Tilly (1984) describes what he sees as four broad types of comparative analysis. The two most common are *individualizing comparisons* (a single-case study that emphasizes the historic particularities of that case, even as secondary comparisons are explored) and *variation-finding structured comparisons* (including but not limited to most-similar and most-different systems designs) across two or more selected cases. Less common are *universalizing comparisons* (a single-case study that emphasizes similarities with other cases) and *encompassing comparisons*.

Encompassing comparisons examine a large process or structure but seek to understand how their relation to the whole structures individual cases (1984, 125–43). As Tilly puts it:

> Encompassing comparisons begin with a large structure or process. They select locations within the structure or process and explain similarities or differences among those locations as a consequence of their relationship to the whole. In everyday life, people use encompassing comparisons all the time: explaining the difference between two children's behavior by their orders of birth, attributing the characteristics of communities to their varying connections with a nearby metropolis, accounting for the behavior of executives in terms of their positions in the firm's organization chart. (125)

These larger structures and processes, it should be emphasized, can shape the individual cases in profound ways, but they are never determinative. Strict parenting, for example, will not necessarily affect individual children in the same way. Nor is parenting unaffected by the behavior of children: a troublesome child's behavior can influence how the parent treats even the best-behaved child in that family. Thus, one way that encompassing comparisons differ from variation-finding comparisons is that they are dialectic. Although they address similarities and differences across component cases or parts, those parts are always understood to be related to some larger processes or structures (singular or multiple); they are never treated as self-contained or stand-alone cases. And multiple individual cases can be differently connected to multiple larger processes or structures – such as the global economy, securitization and military networks, international financial institutions, and so on. Key to such analyses is identifying which larger process(es) or structure(s) advance our understanding of the individual cases as well as the whole.

In the case of the Arab uprisings, an encompassing comparison can move us beyond the success/fail approach to protests to recognize how even uprisings that failed – that is, those that did not bring regime change or democratic transition – affected political processes and outcomes both internal and external to that case. The goal is to explain not only the dynamics and trajectories of individual cases but to do so while attending to multiple connections to larger processes and structures and in the context of other individual cases that are also connected, in various ways, to those (and possibly other) larger processes and structures. And, indeed, we want to identify how the individual cases affected those larger processes and structures. The next section briefly examines the Arab uprisings in Bahrain, Egypt, and Jordan to illustrate how an encompassing comparison can at times prove more insightful and provide compelling answers to the very questions driving variation-finding comparisons, especially those that adhere to methodologically nationalist frameworks.[12]

---

[12] A few studies of the uprisings do adopt such an approach, particularly those concerned with political economy – often but not exclusively from a Marxist or neo-Marxist perspective – and

LOCATING THE ARAB UPRISINGS IN ENCOMPASSING COMPARISONS

Some dynamics of the Arab uprisings immediately call for analyses that look beyond domestic factors. While scholars have long recognized that foreign actors are deeply involved in regional domestic politics, most states in the region are connected to multiple foreign powers and international agencies, such as the US government (and its military-industrial complex), the World Bank, the International Monetary Fund, and Gulf capital and investment firms – to name just a few. How are we to understand the role of those powers and relations within individual countries as well as across the region as whole, and which of these are influential in particular cases? How are regimes, economic elites, militaries, activists, and so on connected to international alliances, regional and global economic regimes, surveillance and security networks, flows of aid, and weapons sales? Similarly, how are the protests related to one another? How essential was the outcome of Tunisia (the departure of Ben Ali) to the protests elsewhere and to the ouster of Mubarak just weeks after Ben Ali? Arguably, rapid escalation of events in Tunisia and Egypt made the impossible – the rapid fall of repressive regimes across the region – seem for both protesters and regimes to be suddenly within reach. An encompassing comparison would still examine distinct processes within a national setting and how they were affected by larger processes or structure, but would also explore whether any of those larger processes or structures were in turn unsettled by the protests, and whether the uprisings led to adjustments and reconfigurations of those larger processes. Such a comparison can also address how meanings change across time and space. Ben Ali's ouster, for example, was not a static event that moved Tunisia from one analytic column to another; rather, it entailed a complex set of shifting practices and processes that unfolded in sped-up time and became saturated with symbolism – of possibilities as well as warnings – that have shifted and worked differently at different times and places. Two such structures that will come to the fore in this exploratory analysis are the Saudi-Gulf-US security arrangements and a larger US-centered global security arrangement. In Egypt, for example, US-Egyptian military relations remained strong during the uprising, and foreign direct investment around mega construction projects halted during the uprising resumed only months later. These security arrangements are not the only encompassing structures or processes connected to the uprisings. The Iranian-Russian security

---

colonial and postcolonial politics. For example, John Chalcraft's *Popular Politics in the Making of the Modern Middle East* (2016), Charles Tripp's *The Power and the People: Paths of Resistance in the Middle East* (2013), and Adam Hanieh's *Lineages of Revolt: Issues of Contemporary Capitalism in the Middle East* (2013) all offer analyses that anchor the uprisings in temporalities of decades-long processes (such as capitalism and colonialism) and do not treat individual states in isolation. Paul Amar (2013) provides an excellent example of such a comparative framework that could be described as encompassing in Tilly's (1984) sense, although his focus is not the uprisings.

arrangement, for example, is certainly influential, particularly for countries like Syria, Lebanon, and Iraq. Turkey also has had a growing role in regional security in recent years. In this chapter, I focus only on the Saudi-Gulf-US security arrangement and the US-centered global security arrangement to illustrate the significant analytic traction that can be gained through the adoption of an encompassing comparison of the Arab uprisings.

Bahrain

Bahrainis were directly inspired by the uprisings in Tunisia and Egypt, mounting a solidarity protest in front of the Egyptian embassy on February 4, 2011. They turned their anger toward their own regime with a February 14 "Day of Rage" – borrowing language used in other uprisings across the region. That protest saw massive turnout, coming as it did just three days after the fall of Egypt's president Hosni Mubarak. Bahrainis also borrowed the slogan adopted in Tunisia, which was borrowed from a well-known verse written in 1933 by a Tunisian poet that appeared in textbooks and was known across the Arab world: "The people want the fall of the regime!" As Egyptian activists noted, the slogan was particularly striking because it contained no metaphor (Colla 2012). Just as Egyptians adopted the slogan to connect their actions with the Tunisian revolution (which brought about the fall of the Ben Ali regime on January 14, 2011), so did Bahrainis and later protesters elsewhere in the Arab world. They signaled seeing themselves as participating in something larger even as they directed their claims toward their own regime.

In the capital of Manama, the Pearl Roundabout intersection quickly became the symbolic center of the uprising, a kind of Tahrir Square for Bahraini citizens, even as significant protests continued in multiple locations. The protests were not sectarian – Sunni and Shi'i protesters stood together, even drawing attention to the fact in their placards, chants, and social media postings.[13] After an effort to disperse the crowds on February 17 left seventeen protesters dead, the regime – which was divided on how to respond to the protests – eased its response and allowed protesters to gather in multiple locations. That changed with a decision in mid-March to deploy the Peninsula Shield Force (PSF), a military force created by the Gulf Cooperation Council (GCC) to provide joint security for all GCC members (Bahrain, Kuwait, Oman, Saudi Arabia, Qatar,[14] and the United Arab Emirates [UAE]). On March 16–17, 2011, Saudi and Emirati contingents in the PSF entered Bahrain via a causeway, proving

---

[13] Al-Jazeera produced a remarkable documentary about the uprising, *Bahrain: Shouting in the Dark*. Its film crew was on the ground for several months, documenting what was happening at protests and inside hospitals, even as the regime took to the air to advance a false counter-narrative.

[14] Following a dispute between Saudi Arabia and the Emirates, on the one hand, and Qatar, on the other, the Saudis severed diplomatic ties with Qatar and placed a ban on trade with the nation in June 2017.

cover while the Bahraini forces moved to violently disperse the protesters; hundreds of protesters were killed and thousands were injured.[15] The US assistant secretary for human rights was in Manama meeting with the crown prince when the Saudi and Emirati troops arrived. The ruling Al Khalifa family was split on how to deal with the mobilization, but the arrival of the Saudi and Emirati troops basically decided the fight in favor of the hard-liners, who had invited them. Press reports at the time said that the Saudis did not inform the United States of the decision, because they were angry with President Barak Obama for "abandoning" Egypt's ousted President Mubarak.

While Bahraini forces violently broke up protests and dismantled the camp at the Pearl Roundabout, hundreds of plain-clothed *baltajiyya* – thugs drawn, in this instance, from police forces across the Arab region[16] – beat Bahraini protesters and sought to incite sectarian tensions among the protesters where little had existed. Al-Jazeera documented that these thugs were agents of foreign police forces. In Jordan, rumors spread that the country's *gendarmerie* received a bonus for assisting in the crushing of the Bahrain protests. Bahrain had for years been recruiting Sunnis, particularly from Jordan and Pakistan, into the security forces, giving them and their families citizenship. The Bahraini regime then launched a months-long campaign to portray protesters as Iranian-backed Shi'i militants arrived in Bahrain to attack the minority Sunni community – building on a regime narrative already years in the making. The state-controlled media spread falsehoods about sectarian violence even in the face of documentary evidence to the contrary. Finally, the regime used social media to crowd-source identifying individual protesters, who were arrested, tortured, and sometimes murdered.

An individualizing comparative study of Bahrain's uprising would focus on explaining the trajectory of the uprising and regime response: early massive mobilization that is brutally crushed by the regime. A variation-finding structured comparison would analyze that trajectory alongside one or more of the other uprisings, with the primary analytic objective to identify the variables that explain the uprisings' differing trajectories and outcomes. One might sensibly conclude, for example, that whereas no foreign power intervened in the uprisings in Tunisia or Egypt, Saudi and Emirati forces provided cover that facilitated Bahrain's violent repression of the protesters. But here an encompassing comparison provides additional insights without which our

---

[15] Oman and Qatar did not participate; Kuwait only sent a ship to "help guard the coast."

[16] *Baltajiyya* has emerged across the region as a generic term for pro-regime thugs who harass and beat protesters, break up protests, and basically do the dirty work for the police while providing the regime with plausible deniability (because the thugs are not in uniform and thus cannot be proven to be organized by government officials). In Bahrain, these thugs were not the usual hyper-loyalist nationals but rather included foreign nationals from neighboring Arab states; protesters' widespread suspicions that they were not Bahraini were confirmed when identity cards for foreign police agencies were discovered on dozens who were admitted to hospitals for injuries. See the Al-Jazeera documentary *Bahrain: Shouting in the Dark*.

Against Methodological Nationalism

understanding is incomplete at best. Bahrain was not only a part of a regional security alliance that arrived to aid the regime, but troops from Arab countries outside of the GCC also sent support. Even more, the Saudi and Emirati troops included Pakistani and African mercenaries, riding (with their Gulf counterparts) in tanks and bearing weapons that Saudi Arabia and the Emiratis had purchased from the United States. Saudi Arabia in particular has long relied heavily on foreign mercenaries, as in the ongoing Yemen war where Colombian and Sudanese fighters join Pakistanis in donning Saudi uniforms.

The United States has an oversized presence in Bahrain, which is home to the US Fifth Fleet and Naval Central Command – the primary US base for naval and marine activities and the primary US force that polices the Persian Gulf.[17] But the United States was apparently unaware that Saudi and Emirati troops had been invited to provide cover for the violent Bahrain response. This lack of awareness suggests that the US-centered security arrangement in the region overlaps with but is distinct from a specific regional security arrangement. The outsized role played by Gulf states in the US-centered security arrangement in the region, however, does explain Washington's muted response to the brutal repression of the uprising. The Saudi and Emirati move supporting Bahraini hard-liners intent on crushing the uprising also marked a shift in regional security arrangements, in which Saudi Arabia, the UAE, and Qatar would all play expanded roles in the next few years – although not necessarily in coordination or cooperation with one another.[18]

Thus, while a comparative approach might view the Bahraini uprising as a case of a regime receiving outside aid to crush a domestic challenge to its rule, an encompassing comparison would map Bahrain's location in a number of larger structures or processes. First, the protesters viewed their uprising in connection with uprisings elsewhere in the Arab world. From their slogans to their desire to emulate the peaceful tactics that brought down the ruling regimes in Egypt and Tunisia, they drew not only inspiration but also their tactics from fellow protesters across the region. Second, Bahrain tapped into not only the Gulf regional security alliance but also connections with Sunni regimes elsewhere in the region, notably Jordan – with whose *gendarmerie* it had already established close relations. While these regional security alliances were forged among regimes that all had close relations with the United States, the major US intervention here was Washington's muted response.

Third, that virtual US silence opened the door for dramatically escalated Gulf intervention into the domestic affairs of other Arab nations over the next year. These interventions included funding multiple foreign forces to travel to fight on

---

[17] Naval Central Command, or NAVCENT, in Bahrain, played a central role in the Iraq War in Operation Iraqi Freedom, Operation Enduring Freedom, and Operation New Dawn.
[18] Indeed, by 2015 Saudi and Emirati relations with Qatar had soured over the latter's support of moderate Muslim Brotherhood organizations in the region, which the former both strongly opposed (but especially the UAE).

one side or another in Syria – turning that civil war into an arena where domestic struggles became blurred with regional rivalries. One major rivalry was between Iran and Saudi Arabia, but differences over whether to support the Muslim Brotherhood in Syria and elsewhere in the region saw the emergence of two new camps: Turkey and Qatar supporting the Brotherhood and Saudi Arabia and the UAE opposing it. While these new regional security alliances emerged, the GCC (which at the time included all of the Gulf states) intervened in Yemen's uprising to force its plan for Yemen's president Ali Abdullah Salih to resign and a handpicked alternative to be elected president by referendum.

The GCC Initiative in Yemen, as it is known, hijacked that uprising from the Yemeni protesters – most of whom were not affiliated with the established political parties – to seize the opportunity to shape Yemen's political future in a GCC-friendly way, that is, to prevent a democracy from emerging and put reconstruction in the control of Gulf powers and their allied businesses (construction, port building, and so on). When that process faltered in 2014–2015, the GCC again intervened in Yemeni domestic disputes by launching a military campaign in March 2015. That campaign, Operation Decisive Storm, was led primarily by Saudi Arabia and the UAE but was executed in partnership with the United States. The ongoing war in Yemen represents an imbrication of two larger structures: the Saudi-Emirati security alliance and the US-centered regional security alliance. US weapons dominate the fighting on both sides: besides the weapons sold to GCC states, the United States provided weapons to the Yemeni government that are now in the hands of multiple fighting factions. But the United States also provided immediate assistance by flying refueling missions with Saudi aircraft on bombing missions throughout much of the war – stopping only under pressure from Congress. And the United States continues to provide intelligence to Saudi Arabia in particular.

The uprising in Bahrain, along with the Saudi, Emirati, and US responses to it, brings into view the regional and global arrangements that made possible Bahrain's violent repression of its peaceful protesters. Those regional and global responses set in motion a shift in regional security alliances, including more assertive Saudi, Emirati, and Qatar interventions across the region – as well as a split between the Saudis and Emiratis and Qatar. Although Bahrain's uprising seems wholly disconnected to that of Egypt, an encompassing comparison shows how Saudi intervention – and, again, US non-action – significantly affected the ultimate fate of Egypt's January 25 Revolution.

Egypt

Egypt's uprising has been the subject of more books and articles than any of the other Arab uprisings; Tunisia is a close second. As the story goes, a number of progressive Egyptian youth groups – including April 6, We Are All Khalid Saeed, and Kifaya – were inspired by the Tunisian uprising and called for a protest on Police Day, January 25, 2011, against widespread police brutality. The organizers hoped that 10,000 Egyptians might turn out that day, but as many as ten times that number took to the streets across Egypt. After eighteen days of protest and numerous police efforts to clear Tahrir Square – the roundabout intersection in Cairo that became the center of the revolution – the military elite forced Hosni Mubarak to resign his position as president. The next year, 2012, brought a new constitution and Muslim Brotherhood victories in the parliamentary and presidential elections, where Mohammad Morsi became Egypt's first democratically elected president. But Egyptians fearful of Brotherhood rule raised alarm about Morsi seizing power for the presidency, and tens of thousands began protesting in spring 2013. By midsummer, the army launched a coup to remove Morsi and the Brotherhood from power, appointing General El Sisi as interim president until a new election could be held. El Sisi quickly consolidated his power and has since made Egypt more repressive than it had been under Mubarak.

In this individualizing comparative approach, Egypt's uprising is the story of a revolutionary mobilization that led to a coup – the army removing the president from office – followed by a transition period and then a countercoup. But the trajectory and outcome of Egypt's uprising were not determined solely by what took place in Egypt. Egypt's military has close relations with its US counterpart. Even as the Muslim Brotherhood took power in 2012, the Supreme Council of the Armed Forces (SCAF) made clear that relations with the United States were not to change. After Israel, Egypt is the largest recipient of US military aid globally. Egypt also receives tremendous development aid from the United States and other donor countries, and it is beholden to a series of agreements with the International Monetary Fund.

Egypt did not experience a social revolution – one in which established economic hierarchies are overturned or at least reconfigured. While many protesters were calling for just such an outcome, the revolution/coup went forward only because certain structures and relationships larger than the Egyptian state – notably military alliances, peace treaties, and patterns of foreign investment key to the US-centered regional security arrangement – were taken off the table. When the SCAF forced Mubarak's resignation and took control of Egypt's "transition," it portrayed itself as protector of the revolution while guaranteeing its own assets would remain safe. Indeed, the military in Egypt functions like a corporation, owning land, major industries, and even shopping malls, so controlling the transition enabled it to direct attention to political institutions while forfending against substantive social or economic changes that would hurt its own interests as well as the interests of its regional and international allies. As the SCAF under El Sisi's leadership turned to undermine the Morsi regime in 2013, those foreign agencies did not raise concerns because they prized their relationships and investments with the army over a democratic transition.

And just as Saudi Arabia's regional reach extended into Syria and Yemen (and elsewhere) in the wake of the uprisings, so did it deepen relations with

Egypt under El Sisi. Given their animosity toward the Muslim Brotherhood across the region, Saudi Arabia and the UAE poured aid into Egypt to support the El Sisi coup and rescue Egypt's flailing economy, including by providing much-needed cash to pay salaries. Military relations between Egypt and Saudi Arabia deepened, strengthening both the new Saudi-dominated regional security arrangement and the US-centered security arrangement in the region. In April 2016, El Sisi declared that two Egyptian islands in the Straights of Tiran (at the entrance to the Gulf of Aqaba) – Sanafir and Tiran – were actually located within Saudi territorial waters. That declaration sparked outrage among Egyptians who viewed the move as tantamount to selling parts of Egypt to Saudi Arabia in exchange for direct cash infusions and substantial regional aid. The deal between the two regimes includes the eventual construction of a causeway over the two islands that will connect the mainland of Saudi Arabia with that of Egypt. Thus, the trajectory and fate of Egypt's uprising cannot be fully grasped outside of an understanding of Saudi Arabia's changed role toward more direct intervention in domestic politics in the region, including in Bahrain, Syria, and Yemen. An encompassing comparison brings into view how these regional and global security arrangements play a direct role in the domestic repressive capacities of states like Bahrain, Egypt, and Jordan – to which we now turn.

Jordan

Scholars have devoted far less attention to Jordan's uprising, in part because its protesters, which peaked at tens of thousands (out of a country of 7 million), demanded only reform and not the fall of the regime. Analyses of Jordan's uprising note that it started on January 7, 2011, in Dhiban, a town outside of Amman that had seen an increase in labor activism in the preceding three years (Ryan 2018; Phillips 2019). Large protests broke out in the capital weekly from January 14 until late February. In addition to the established political parties and labor and syndicate activists, a new sector of activism emerged, broadly described as the Hirak (movement). Not a single movement, the Hirak were a series of (initially) youth-led groups drawn from supposedly regime-loyalist areas. But the regime began to make concessions to various factions and aggressively lobbied the loyalist areas to diminish the impact of the protests, which it did by late spring. Subsequent waves of protests emerged periodically, including massive anti-austerity protests in November 2012 that were put down with relative violence to how Jordan normally polices protests. Four prime ministers were appointed and sacked within a year, and a new electoral law and elections in 2013 saw a fairly quick return to politics as usual for Jordan.

Like Egypt, Jordan's political stability is critical to the US-centered regional security arrangement. Egypt and Jordan were the first two Arab states to establish full diplomatic relations with Israel and to grant that state full recognition. (The UAE announced full normalization with Israel in July 2020, and Saudi Arabia is expected to follow suit in the near future.) Jordan shares a large border with Israel, along with the Jordan River Valley, one of Israel's major sources of water. With Washington's unwavering commitment to Israeli sovereignty and security, Jordan – a state with few natural resources or industries to drive its economy – has survived largely as a semi-rentier state reliant on foreign aid. Pete Moore (2014) goes so far as to characterize Jordan as a US protectorate, one that is effectively unable to make budgetary decisions without approval from Washington. Indeed, the US prerogative over Jordan is at times fully transparent. In July 2015, for example, US Secretary of Defense Ashton Carter landed at a Jordanian air base without a civilian Jordanian official waiting to greet him. The move was an embarrassing (for Jordan) violation of protocol, but one that also revealed the extent to which the kingdom is beholden to US largess (Moore 2018).

Unlike Bahrain, however, foreign troops did not have to enter Jordan to put down the protests, which only briefly reached revolutionary levels (even as they refrained from revolutionary demands). Saudi Arabia and the United States poured aid into Jordan to bolster its economy and allow the government to pay salaries to supposed regime loyalists from East Bank–dominated governorates; in the region, only Israel receives more total aid from the United States than does Jordan (Egypt receives the second-most military aid). Gulf investments in Jordan increased over the next years, with Jordan's security services closely allied with those in the Gulf, particularly with those of Bahrain. As noted earlier, Jordan sent a contingent of several hundred members of its *gendarmerie* to help crush the Bahraini uprising. The Bahraini regime urged the GCC to consider inviting Jordan to join the Gulf security alliance, despite not being a Gulf country. The idea was floated but membership was never formally extended. Saudi funding to Jordan increased precipitously, however, part of the Saudi effort to extend its regional security arrangement deeper into other Sunni-dominated states, ostensibly to balance Iranian influence in countries with significant Shi'i populations, like those in Syria, Lebanon, Yemen, and Iraq.

Here again, an encompassing comparison reveals Jordan not merely as a case of a failed uprising but also as a state tied to – and desperately dependent on – US and Saudi largess. Domestically, Jordan's uprising never became revolutionary because its citizens wanted reforms but not the fall of the regime. But the stability of the regime is largely a function of its importance to the regional agendas of foreign actors and thus its connections to both Saudi regional security arrangements and those of the United States. Indeed, Jordan is more than a recipient of aid from these states. It is deeply connected to both regional and global security arrangements, including through three centers in which Jordanian and US military officers train regional and international *gendarmeries* and counterterrorism forces on Jordanian soil.

CONCLUSION

A variation-finding comparison of these three cases – Bahrain, Egypt, and Jordan – might well recognize the role of US and Saudi intervention into each one's domestic politics. No serious scholar examines a country as if it exists in a vacuum, so the argument here is not to suggest that such analyses are unaware of the role of foreign actors. But an encompassing comparison does more than examine foreign factors or variables. It attends to the larger structures and processes to which individual cases (here, states) are connected, and the ways in which other cases are also (albeit perhaps differently) connected. In terms of the uprisings, Egypt, Jordan, and Bahrain are all part of the US-centered security arrangements, and thus saw US and Saudi policies – Saudi Arabia being key to US interests in the region – that strengthened the existing regimes and US partners (i.e., various militaries and security forces). Those US and Saudi policies were not always carried out in coordination; indeed, following Saudi Arabia's intervention into the Bahraini uprising, it pursued its own agenda to expand its reach across the region, including with significant direct or indirect interventions into Syria and Yemen. Rather than viewing the uprisings as interruptions to authoritarian politics-as-usual in a number of cases across the region, an encompassing comparison shows instead shifts in the larger structures of security arrangements regionally and the maintenance of the US-centered regional alliances and priorities.

The cases of the uprisings in Bahrain, Egypt, and Jordan show the ways in which each is connected to multiple and sometimes imbricating regional and global structures. The protesters saw themselves as part of something larger, learning and borrowing from one another – just as the regimes striving to maintain their rule learned and borrowed from one another's tactics. Each of the three regimes is an important regional ally of the United States, and each is closely connected to Gulf political aspirations, particularly those of Saudi Arabia. Egypt and Jordan are both also beholden to agreements with the International Monetary Fund and World Bank, and both maintain peace treaties with Israel. But these factors operated differently in each of the cases. Indeed, the fate of each of these three uprisings – their trajectories, possibilities, and outcomes – can only be fully understood by examining the relation of each to the larger structures, and the relationship of other countries to those larger structures as well. Just as protesters were inspired by the mobilizations (and early successes) of uprisings elsewhere in the region – and globally groups like Occupy were inspired by the Arab uprisings – counterrevolutionary forces frequently learned from other regime responses and at times directly assisted one another. International financial organizations watched in horror, concerned only that the existing neoliberal economic regimes – which vary considerably across cases – remain intact. Without understanding these global connections and the ways in which these individual cases are tied to one another, no one can fully understand the trajectory of any individual uprising.

Against Methodological Nationalism

In short, many individualizing and variation-finding comparisons – and not only in studies of the Arab uprisings – risk scholars asking questions and producing knowledge that does not reflect reality. Epistemologically, an encompassing comparison is a move away from an analysis based on the identification of explanatory variables and toward telling a rich story of complex connections and power relations. More than simply adding background, it involves embedding the local within larger connections, processes, structures, and historical time lines of the sort that also move away from thinking in terms of outcomes.

How Does One Determine the Right Encompassing Comparison?

In constructing an encompassing comparison, what big structure or large process – to return to Tilly's (1984) language – should be brought into view? The answer is that there is no final or superstructure above all others to which the individual cases should be related. As these three examples from the Arab uprisings show, multiple structures or processes may come into view, such as the US-centered regional security arrangement but also the shifting Gulf engagements across the region. Bahrain is a member of the GCC and shares much in common with its neighboring Gulf monarchies, while Egypt and Jordan have distinct profiles to offer as regional and global partners. Egypt and Jordan are also connected differently to international processes of finance, aid, and debt than is Bahrain, whose wealth comes not from its own oil (which has long run out) but from the profits of an oil field shared by agreement with Saudi Arabia. The larger structures or processes that come into view will depend, as always, on the research topic at hand. The larger point is that encompassing comparisons are desirable for examining events such as the Arab uprisings because the move beyond methodological nationalism brings into view a broad range of factors that shaped (and were shaped by) the trajectory and outcome of those events.

Finally, encompassing comparisons push us methodologically toward explanations that can provide a more accurate and nuanced understanding of politics than variable-based causal models can provide. In the case of the Arab uprisings, this means moving away from models that seek to explain the success or fail approach of individual cases to an understanding of politics that is more dialectic. Even failed protests can sometimes dramatically shape political processes and outcomes, even if they do not always unsettle those in power. Some studies of the Arab uprisings have indeed sought to bring these dynamics into view. In addition to the neo-Marxist explanations footnoted earlier (see n. 9), scholars have examined, for example, shifting patterns of war and intervention following the uprisings (Lynch 2017) and how globalization is connected to authoritarianism (Bogaert 2018). Encompassing comparisons, and the epistemological turn they entail, can do a better job of illuminating these dynamics and, indeed, offer richer and more accurate explanations for some of the very questions posed in more conventional comparative analyses.

REFERENCES

Amar, Paul. 2013. *The Security Archipelago: Human-Security States, Sexuality Politics, and the End of Neoliberalism.* Durham, NC: Duke University Press.

Bogaert, Koenraad. 2018. *Globalized Authoritarianism: Megaprojects, Slums, and Class Relations in Urban Morocco.* Minneapolis: University of Minnesota Press.

Brownlee, Jason, Tarek Masoud, and Andrew Reynolds. 2015. *The Arab Spring: Pathways of Repression and Reform.* New York: Oxford University Press.

Chakrabarti, Debashis. 2013. "Quest for Arab Spring Chromosomes in OWS Protests." *Humanities and Social Sciences Reviews* 2 (3): 175–82.

Chalcraft, John. 2016. *Popular Politics in the Making of the Modern Middle East.* New York: Cambridge University Press.

Colla, Elliott. 2012. "The People Want." *Middle East Report*, no. 263 (Summer). www.jstor.org/stable/i40079958

Gitlin, Todd. 2012. *Occupy Nation: The Roots, the Spirit, and the Promise of Occupy Wall Street.* New York: It Books.

Hanieh, Adam. 2013. *Lineages of Revolt: Issues of Contemporary Capitalism in the Middle East.* Chicago: Haymarket Books.

Kumar, Nils. 2018. *The Tea Party, Occupy Wall Street, and the Great Recession.* New York: Palgrave Macmillan.

Lynch, Marc. 2017. *The New Arab Wars: Uprisings and Anarchy in the Middle East.* Washington, DC: PublicAffairs.

Mill, John Stuart. [1843] 2002. *A System of Logic.* Honolulu, HI: University Press of the Pacific.

Moore, Pete W. 2014. "The Arab Bank and Washington's Protectorate in the Levant," *Middle East Report Online*, September 25. https://merip.org/2014/09/the-arab-bank-and-washingtons-protectorate-in-the-levant/

    2018. "The Fiscal Politics of Rebellious Jordan," *Middle East Report Online*, June 21. – merip.org/2018/06/the-fiscal-politics-of-rebellious-jordan/

Navarro, Pablo Pérez. 2018. "'Where Is My Tribe'? Queer Activism in the Occupy Movements." *InterAlia. A Journal of Queer Studies* 13: 90–102.

Patel, David, Valerie Bunce, and Sharon Wolchik. 2014. "Diffusions and Demonstrations." In *The Arab Uprisings Explained*, edited by Marc Lynch, 55–74. New York: Columbia University Press.

Phillips, Colfax. 2019. "Dhiban as Barometer of Jordan's Rural Discontent," *Middle East Report*, 291–92: 15–19.

Ryan, Curtis R. 2018. *Jordan and the Arab Uprisings: Regime Security and Politics Beyond the State.* New York: Columbia University Press.

Schwedler, Jillian. 2015. "Comparative Politics and the Arab Uprisings." *Middle East Law and Governance* 7 (1): 141–52.

Sewell, William H., Jr. 2005. *Logics of History: Social Theory and Social Transformation.* Chicago: University of Chicago Press.

Tilly, Charles. 1984. *Big Structures, Large Processes, Huge Comparisons.* New York: Russell Sage.

Tripp, Charles. 2013. *The Power and the People: Paths of Resistance in the Middle East.* New York: Cambridge University Press.

Wedeen, Lisa. 2019. *Authoritarian Apprehensions: Ideology, Judgement, and Mourning in Syria*. Chicago: University of Chicago Press.

Wimmer, Andreas, and Nina Glick Schiller. 2003. "Methodological Nationalism, the Social Sciences, and the Study of Migration: An Essay in Historical Epistemology." *The International Migration Review* 37 (3): 576–610.

10

Comparative Analysis for Theory Development

Mala Htun
University of New Mexico

Francesca R. Jensenius
University of Oslo/Norwegian Institute of International Affairs

Comparison is an essential part of political science, particularly so for theory development. Comparing enables us to discover what is unusual and what is more widely shared, requires that we clearly define and operationalize our concepts, and sharpens awareness of the assumptions that underlie our theories. It even changes what questions we ask. We compare because it helps us produce good theory.

By comparison, we refer to two practices that Fred Schaffer (Chapter 3, this volume) calls "juxtapositional" and "perspectival" comparison. Comparison involves putting two or more institutions, processes, groups, events, contexts, individuals, or other units side by side – juxtaposing them – to identify similar and dissimilar features. Comparing may also involve analyzing an entity from the standpoint or the perspective of another entity. The act of comparing serves multiple goals, including developing theoretical arguments, identifying key variables, exploring scope conditions, and probing mechanisms (cf. Eckstein 1975). However, as the introduction (Chapter 1) to this volume points out, our field's most widely taught qualitative methods texts tend to orient research designs toward only one of comparison's varied purposes: testing causal theories via controlled comparisons across a small number of cases. As this suggests, a discrepancy exists between the types of research designs scholars typically teach and the type of research they actually conduct.

In this chapter, we identify and dispel five misperceptions about comparative research design that we have encountered among our students and are likely to be more widely held. These misperceptions pertain to the goal, nature, logic, and justifications of comparative research design.

First, in contrast with the belief that the primary goal of comparative research is to test theories, we hold that comparative research has multiple goals besides theory testing, such as theory development, exploration of mechanisms, and so forth, and that we therefore need different types of comparative research design for different projects. Our rule of thumb is that a comparative study should be designed in a way that creates interesting variation in whatever we seek to learn more about.

Second, rather than proceeding as if a research project has to have only one static research design – as is implied in the practice of pre-registering or publicly posting a research plan on a verified service[1] – we argue that research designs should evolve as projects evolve and that different parts of a project may need different designs.

The third misperception is that qualitative projects must be shoehorned into a narrow understanding of a case study. However, as Soss (Chapter 5, this volume) argues, we tend not to know what our study is a case of until we are advanced in the research. We propose that projects aimed at theory development select diverse *contexts* to *explore* ideas rather than *cases* to *test* ideas.

Fourth, in contrast with the view that theory derives primarily from experiencing epiphanies, identifying holes in existing literature, or closely scrutinizing single experiences or cases, we reaffirm the central role of comparative research in developing new theory.

The final misperception we tackle is the idea that it is "unscientific" to take personal or practical concerns into account when choosing what to study. We argue that it is methodologically appropriate and theoretically beneficial to incorporate such concerns into research design. In fact, denying the human element reduces transparency (Koivu and Hinze 2017). Like Koivu and Hinze, we argue that incorporating personal and practical concerns may reveal a universe of possibilities for case selection and serve to complement theoretical and methodological criteria.

To be sure, none of these arguments is new. We are reiterating perspectives that are vital to our own methodological understanding but that are scattered across the literature and rarely emphasized, and not often taught, as part of training in research methods.

After analyzing and pushing beyond the five misperceptions we have encountered, we discuss how the five arguments pertain to the evolution of one of our own ongoing projects on women's empowerment. Our study started out as a cross-national study of the relationship between gender discriminatory laws and women's economic empowerment; however, as our research progressed, new questions emerged. Among other areas, we became interested in how the concept of "empowerment" has different meanings and implications in different parts of the world. As a result, different research designs became more appropriate.

To probe the concept's differing reference points and boundaries, we conducted fieldwork in three contexts: Norway, Japan, and the United States.

---

[1] See, e.g., "Preregistration of Research Plans" at www.psychologicalscience.org/publications/psychological_science/preregistration

These countries are not cases for us – understood as specific instances of a clearly defined class of events (George and Bennett 2005) – but contexts that provide interesting variation in the key concept we wish to learn more about. Our "conceptual comparison" across three very different contexts does not allow us to draw causal inferences about the associations between state action and societal outcomes. But the conceptual comparison has made us think differently about the cultural and historical backdrops that shape state action and people's responses and changed our theoretical thinking about *how* to study the effects of state action on society. Finally, we offer examples of how our multicultural research team has enabled us to build local knowledge and leverage insider and outsider advantages across different study sites. Our experiences are suggestive of a potentially liberating approach to research design for qualitative comparative politics.

FIVE MISPERCEPTIONS ABOUT RESEARCH DESIGN FOR QUALITATIVE COMPARATIVE STUDIES

1 Aligning Your Design to Your Goal, Which Does Not Have to Be Theory Testing

The publication of *Designing Social Inquiry* in 1994 (King, Keohane, and Verba 1994, henceforth KKV) cast a long shadow over the methodological training received by graduate students. The book stimulated important discussions about research design and scientific rigor and offers useful advice. It focuses primarily on how to use observational data to make descriptive or causal inferences. The main takeaway message is that a larger N is better and that it is difficult to draw causal conclusions from the comparison of a small number of observations. For small-N research, the book promotes controlled comparisons, preferably with observations selected on the explanatory variable. KKV refer to researchers with goals besides inference as "interpretivists" (King, Keohane, and Verba 1994, 37), and the book has little guidance to offer in terms of research design for their studies. In fact, as the authors clarify in a symposium on their work, their original goal was to provide guidance on research designed to evaluate theories, not to develop them (King, Keohane, and Verba 1995, 475).

As this suggests, KKV assume that the goal of most scholars conducting comparative work is to test theories about causal relationships among variables, and they offer research design advice accordingly. Many later books on qualitative methods for political science follow KKV by focusing overwhelmingly on comparative research designs aimed at theory testing, either explicitly (e.g., Gerring 2001; Brady and Collier 2010) or more implicitly. For example, George and Bennett (2005, 151) argue that case studies in general are good for fostering new hypotheses, but they refer to comparative research designs as "case study methods that attempt to approximate the conditions of scientific experiments," which affirms KKV's idea that comparison is geared toward causal inference.

Widely taught textbooks thus emphasize controlled comparisons across small numbers of units, or variations of Mill's methods of agreement and difference (see Mill 1884; Teune and Przeworski 1970). By engaging with these texts, many students acquire the misperception that theory testing is the primary goal of comparative studies. And methods texts insist that research designs aimed at testing theories should be carefully designed to avoid endogeneity and various forms of bias, leading us to the recommendation of controlled comparisons. However, controlled comparisons are not the only way to design comparative research, as this volume argues. In fact, controlled comparisons are arguably a terrible way to test causal arguments (Seawright, Chapter 2, this volume).

Though methods texts focus on designs for theory testing, a large share of empirical studies using comparative methods are aimed primarily at theory development. As a result, as George and Bennett (2005, 10) point out, there is a lack of alignment between the goal presumed by methods texts and the actual goal of students conducting comparative work. In contrast to theory testing, which is presented as rigorous and transparent, texts tend to portray theory development as a more casual or idiosyncratic process, usually happening through the study of single country experiences, and as a "lesser cousin" to the real work of theory testing. The methods training students receive may thus seem irrelevant or even prevent students from developing an appropriate research design, as they try to force their projects into a design that is inappropriate for their research goals (see also Soss, Chapter 5, this volume).

Since there is little concrete advice about how to conduct research aimed at theory development, people may assume that they do not need to think rigorously about design. This is not the case! We should reflect on and defend our research design for theory development in a similar way as research designs aimed at theory testing. Scholars should *always* think carefully about how to best design their study to achieve their particular goal, whether that is interpreting, building causal intuition, elaborating concepts, identifying patterns of regularity, exploring mechanisms, or something else.

How do you design a study to fit the varied and different goals of comparative research? Existing literature offers few recommendations about how to select observations for theory development. As Levy (2008) points out, most texts recommend picking cases that are extreme or deviant with respect to the main dependent or independent variables (see also Van Evera 1997). If you have a clear sense of what those variables are, selecting extreme or deviant observations makes sense. But many people engaged in the early stages of projects aimed at theory development may not know what their main variables are. In fact, a great deal of qualitative work occurs *prior* to gathering information related to relevant variables. And even if you do have a sense of key variables, it is often counterproductive to follow this strategy unless the goal is to observe whether different values in the explanatory variables are associated with different outcomes on the outcome variable. You are better off with a design more precisely aligned to your research goal.

Gerring (2011, 41) includes a comparative design that is not aimed at testing causal theories in his overview of case selection strategies and criteria. When the goal is primarily descriptive inference, he recommends selecting a diverse set of cases based on their descriptive features. This is sound advice, but it is not so clear how to apply it to the many different goals of studies aimed at theory development, including identifying possible variables, developing concepts, probing causal mechanisms, exploring scope conditions, and so on.

Taking inspiration from both Levy (2008) and Gerring (2011), we propose a more general approach: select units for your study that offer *interesting variation in whatever you wish to understand more about*, including possibly key variables, concepts, mechanisms, or scope conditions. This variation is what will provide all the benefits of a comparative design and yield insights that can enhance your understanding and clarify exactly what you are studying. In other words, you should select objects of study that differ in whatever phenomenon you aim to learn about. For example, if your goal is to understand the politics of racial identity, you should look at contexts where racial identities assume different forms. If your interest is to assess the scope conditions of an argument, you should look for places where you think it is more and less likely that the argument will hold. When probing for mechanisms of an observed pattern, you should pick cases where your suspected mechanisms may or may not be in place. And when you want to understand more about the meaning of a concept in different circumstances (like the example we give later), you select contexts where your main concept of interest ("empowerment" in our case) seems to be understood and deployed by social actors in different ways.

Choosing to observe units that display interesting variation in whatever we want to know more about might, in practice, actually bring us back to controlled comparison, as selecting potential dependent or independent variables is one way of creating interesting variation. In fact, as Van Evera (1997, 68) points out, controlled comparison can be great for theory development if one has a fairly good idea about key variables. The central difference is that the purpose of this selection strategy is not to draw causal conclusions based on the study of two or more units – which, as Seawright (Chapter 2, this volume) makes very clear, is a poor way of trying to make causal inferences – but to gain comparative insight and develop your theoretical thinking.

2 Variation and Iteration in Research Design

The second misperception of comparative studies we often encounter is the idea that a research project needs to have one static research design. In recent years, growing emphasis on the importance of rigor and transparency in research and a trend toward pre-registration of empirical studies have helped reinforce this notion. For research aimed at testing clearly laid out theoretical claims, transparency and pre-registration can help prevent p-hacking and constrain scholars tempted to adjust their research question after the fact to conform to the patterns they actually found. Yet the trend toward pre-registration, which presumes a fixed design, is not a helpful approach for all types of research, nor for all parts of a research project. Different components of a project, for example, might have different goals, require different designs, and involve comparing different things.

Since different parts of a study play different roles, it is acceptable that they are designed differently. Even if your overarching goal is to develop a causal argument, you probably do not want to design the part of your study that probes mechanisms as a quasi-experiment. Collier, Mahoney, and Seawright (2004, 101) defend "no-variance designs," which involve the comparison of units with the same value on the dependent variable. Though Geddes (1990), King, Keohane, and Verba (1995), and others warn against this type of design, Collier, Mahoney, and Seawright (2004) hold that a no-variance may help frame the analytic problem, suggest causal ideas, refine conceptualization and measurement, including stimulating the creation of typologies – theory development – as well as allow for valuable descriptive inferences and provide exploratory tests of the developed arguments.

What is more, a research design can and should evolve with the theoretical thinking. If your theoretical thinking changes, so should your research design. George and Bennett (2005, 73) note that one might need "some iteration" in the process of designing and implementing qualitative research. This is an understatement. Very often, researchers start out with a research design based on their theoretical priors; however, as they start conducting their work, their understanding of key concepts, important variables, possible observable implications of arguments, and even what the research question should be, changes. This is partly because of the realities of fieldwork. As McKeown (2004, 164) notes, during fieldwork we often find that some of our key assumptions going into the study are wrong, that the data-gathering techniques we envisioned are not feasible, or that people we thought would be key informants are actually irrelevant. Changes are also simply a part of the intellectual process of discovery, and the path to knowledge is rarely as straightforward as published articles and books make it seem. As Lund (2014, 231) puts it, "The orderliness of one's method is easier to establish in hindsight as futile detours can be erased to make it look more coherent and neat than it felt and was at the time."

In summary, it is important to start out with a plan and to provide a sensible justification for that plan, and it is also fine to modify that plan as one learns more. An overly static approach may stifle the intellectual contributions from a project focused primarily on theory development.

3 Selecting Contexts Not Cases

In our experience, many students struggle with the idea that their qualitative studies have to fit into the framework of cases and case studies, and that a case selection has to be defended on the basis of variation in key variables. The standard questions "what is this a case *of*?" and "aren't you selecting on your dependent variable?" often result in a moment of existential crisis and the realization that providing a clear answer to skeptics is not so easy.

Confusion arises partly from contradictory usage of the term "case" in different texts and even within the same text. A common understanding is that cases can be understood as specific instances of a clearly defined class of events (George and Bennett 2005, 17) – the French Revolution is a case of a revolution, while the adoption of the Colombian constitution of 1991 is a case of a massive legal change. Yet as Eckstein (1975, 85) explains, a study of six elections in England can be a study of $N = 1$, $N = 6$, or $N = 120,000,000$, depending on whether the subject of study is electoral systems, elections, or voters. To avoid confusion, Eckstein suggests using the term "case" to refer to a phenomenon for which only a single measure is made. King, Keohane, and Verba (1994, 52–53) observe, however, that Eckstein's solution goes against common usage. They suggest using "observation" to refer to a single measure and "case" more loosely to refer to a single unit for which a large number of observations are usually made.

If your goal is to test a theory, you must be clear about what your case (or unit of analysis) is and what universe of cases (or units) you are selecting from. If your goal is to develop a theory, however, clarity in defining cases is not as important. In fact, at the beginning of a research project, we may not be sure what our case is, or how to define the universe of relevant cases (see Ragin and Becker 1992). We often choose to study something because it seems inherently interesting and important, even if it is not entirely clear what it is a case of.

How then should we talk about the work that we do? Levy (2008, 2) defines a case study as an "attempt to understand and interpret a spatially and temporally bounded set of events." Levy's definition comes close to the way that many qualitative researchers seem to use the term. However, it does not provide a solution to the main challenge. Do we know, and are we able to define, the nature, most salient elements, and boundaries of the set of events *before* we undertake a study, or do we know this only *during* or *after* we are progressing in our research?

As Soss (Chapter 5, this volume) suggests, we are in a position to identify what our study is a case of – how it fits into existing theory and understanding – only after we have already done a significant amount of research. Soss calls this process "casing a study." Indeed, gaining awareness of what the object under study is a case of, and how it fits into existing bodies of knowledge, is a central part of the research process itself. That is why, as Van Evera (1997, 78) says eloquently, decisions on case selection are premature before you know what you want to know.

We propose that people think of selecting contexts rather than cases when they engage in theory development or when it is unclear what the research is a case of, or what the relevant universe of cases is. *Context selection* may be a particularly productive strategy if the goal of the project (or a part of the project) is to get a sense of relevant variables, understand more about a certain concept (as in our study of empowerment), explore the scope conditions of an argument, probe for mechanisms, or even figure out what research questions are worth asking.

4 The Sources of Theoretical Inspiration

The fourth misperception we often encounter among students is the notion that theory development comes mainly from moments of inspiration, the discovery of inconsistencies in the literature, or fieldwork in a single case. To be sure, epiphanies and the like may be great potential routes to theory development. And Seawright and Gerring (2008) provide an excellent overview of how single-case studies can be used to generate theoretical insights. Yet comparative analysis also plays an important role in theory development: it helps generate hypotheses (Lijphart 1971, 691), improve conceptualization and measurement (Collier, Mahoney, and Seawright 2004, 100), and identify antecedent conditions for theories (Van Evera 1997, 55).

In our experience, comparative fieldwork is useful to develop theoretical intuition, a more precise understanding of which questions to ask, which concepts and variables are important, how they may hang together under what circumstances, and what the phenomenon under study is a case of. When trying to understand something new, it may be hard to grasp what is interesting and unique about the circumstances unless you have a good point of comparison (see Schaffer, Chapter 3, this volume, on perspectival comparison). As mentioned earlier, exploring the same phenomenon across multiple contexts helps identify which features are important. When you look at one context from the perspective of other contexts, some things stand out and others do not. Things that people take for granted in one place are seen as shocking in another.

Comparative racial politics provides an example of the theoretical payoff of comparative work. To many people raised in the United States, the U.S. system of racial identity seems normal and obvious. But when we look at how American society classifies people racially – who it considers Asian, Black, or white, for example – from the perspective of Brazil or Colombia, the US system seems anomalous. The "one drop rule" governing US racial classifications – according to which mixed people are classified in the subordinate, nonwhite group – is unique (Nobles 2000).

Observing the logic and mechanisms of racial classification from the perspective of different countries in the Americas helps identify key theoretical features of a system of racial identity that can guide further comparison. Is racial classification based on descent or on appearance? Are mixed people classified with the subordinate status group, or are they included in intermediate categories? Is it only the government and census or other social organizations – hospitals, workplaces, schools, universities – that identify and organize people by racial identity (Htun 2016a)? Race, as Brubaker, Loveman, and Stamatov (2004, 47) point out, is not a "thing in the world" but a "way of seeing the world." These ways of seeing vary over time and across contexts.

Comparative work aimed at theory development starts out with theoretical intuitions and ideas – perhaps even with fairly strong conjectures – but these may change as the project progresses. By contrast, comparative work intent on theory testing tends to establish the parameters of comparison ahead of time and risks missing important dimensions of variation. For example, large comparative datasets on ethnic diversity established by scholars such as Fearon (2003) presume that ethnic identity is based primarily on descent and classify groups accordingly to generate data about fractionalization and outcomes such as economic performance. Yet in most of Latin America, ethnic identity, as well as racial identity, is based not on descent but on appearance and behavior. Though 44 percent of Peruvians stated in the Project on Race and Ethnicity in Latin America's (PERLA) survey that they had an indigenous ancestor, only 20 percent identified with one of the country's indigenous groups, and only 10 percent identified with the category "indigenous" (Sulmont and Callirgos 2014, 149–53). This example suggests that we should know about history and contextual specificity of the concepts guiding our investigation before we use them to structure comparative research.

5 Balancing Theoretical and Practical Concerns

Finally, we turn to the question of how to balance theoretical and practical concerns in research design. Koivu and Hinze (2017) argue that most methods texts ignore or downplay the human elements that guide case selection, such as language skills, funding, local knowledge, data access, networks, or a passionate interest in the topic of study. Methods texts, advisors, colleagues, and peers often give the impression that our motivation for picking cases to study should be based on theoretical concerns alone. Many people therefore deem it unprofessional to allow – and to admit they allow – personal or logistical reasons to factor into case (or context) selection.

Yet prioritizing methodological rigor over the human element diminishes transparency. Koivu and Hinze (2017) suggest that researchers make explicit their logistical constraints (such as language knowledge) and complement these reasons with theoretical criteria when designing research and sharing research designs.[2] Indeed, transparency about the researcher's position vis-à-vis the research has always been a key element of interpretivist work (Pachirat 2015).

The human element is not just a limitation on our work but is more importantly an *asset* that we can leverage for deeper insights and better theory. Even KKV (1994, 37) admit the importance of knowing a great deal about a culture and context prior to formulating research questions, though they mention this only in the context of interpretivists doing fieldwork. Prior knowledge is critical not just for interpretivist work but also for most research, and certainly for most theory development. How can someone with little knowledge of a context say something important and persuasive about it? Yet studying the same place, or the place you are from, again and again because of ease of access and cultural comfort may limit your insights. The ideal, in our minds, is to find a good balance between theoretical and practical considerations. We should not default to the same locality or ignore the value of language skills, contextual knowledge, or other personal or practical experiences.

Both insider and outsider perspectives have their benefits. When you are conducting fieldwork, the insider perspective may be necessary to understand nuances in people's actions and responses, as well as unstated norms and assumptions. At the same time, there are advantages to having an outsider's perspective, which facilitates what Schaffer calls a perspectival comparison. Outsiders ask fresh questions and often notice things that insiders take for granted. As we discuss in the next section, one approach for gaining both an insider and an outsider perspective in the same study is to form multicultural or multinational research teams.

AN EVOLVING RESEARCH PROJECT ON EMPOWERMENT

In one of our ongoing research projects, we aim to understand more about the effects – and limitations – of different types of state action to promote women's empowerment. As a result of our prior research, we were somewhat disenchanted with research focused on top-down laws and policies alone. Work by Htun and Weldon (2018) on the "rights revolution" for women, for example, left unanswered whether policy changes on violence against women, equality in the family, or public support for caregiving actually produced changes in behavior and attitudes on the ground. Jensenius's work on marginalized communities in India shows that despite decades of quotas in politics, educational institutions, and jobs and a slew of programs aimed at improving their socioeconomic status, historically stigmatized groups are still disadvantaged both socially and economically (Jensenius 2017). These

---

[2] It also masks power hierarchies in our discipline and the types of financial and other personal constraints – partners, children, parents, health issues – that affect the type of research we are able to conduct.

combined experiences make it clear that participation in political parties and elected office, formal laws ensuring equal rights, and other state efforts to change entrenched social inequalities may be necessary but are far from sufficient to deliver inclusion and justice to disadvantaged groups.

Under what conditions do legal changes actually promote empowerment? Existing research has shown that a principal driver of women's empowerment is their economic agency – their disposition and capacity to make autonomous economic choices. Economic agency and control over resources enables women to contest oppressive gender norms and change gender relations from the ground up (Okin 1989; Agarwal 1994, 1997; Kabeer 1999, 2012; Iversen and Rosenbluth 2006; United Nations 2015). As these studies suggest, to the extent that legal changes remove restrictions on women's agency, we might expect them to induce greater empowerment.

To explore this expectation, we worked with the Women, Business, and the Law dataset developed by the World Bank, which includes information about a large variety of legal provisions in 173 economies (World Bank 2015). Following the multidimensional approach to gender outlined in Htun and Weldon (2018), we developed indices on constraining and enabling laws, including restrictions on women's legal capacity, discrimination in the workplace, and the extent to which the state promotes work-life balance (Htun, Jensenius, and Nelson-Nuñez 2019). Using these indices, we explored the correlation between legal variation and multiple macro-level indicators of women's economic agency: access to bank accounts, participation in firm ownership, participation in the labor force, share of women workers in the informal sector, and the gender wage gap. This analysis reveals, not surprisingly, that countries with fewer restrictions on women's legal capacity tend to have higher numbers of women with bank accounts, more firms where women participate as owners, and higher female labor force participation (Htun, Jensenius, and Nelson-Nuñez 2019). However, the great variation in women's agency among countries with similar legal environments makes it clear that laws tell only a small part of the story. A great deal of action shaping patterns of women's agency takes place within countries and is hard to see when we conduct studies across countries. We needed to conduct within-country research to understand this variation better.

Our cross-country work thus led us toward a different line of investigation, focused on understanding more about the effects of legal changes and policy interventions on attitudes, behaviors, and norms within countries. We wrote a paper on the relationship between violence against women legislation on social norms in Mexico (Htun and Jensenius forthcoming) and an article on public attitudes toward gender equality in Myanmar (Htun and Jensenius 2020). But our research orientation toward the law-practice relationship also raised new questions. Contexts in which progressive laws and access to resources foster women's economic empowerment still face many challenges. Across the Global North, where attitudes tend to support equality, wealthy, elite women suffer from sexual harassment and abuse, less pay for the same work, biased and discriminatory treatment, a glass ceiling blocking their rise to leadership, and trouble juggling the demands of family and care work. Moreover, there are many ideas of what an empowered life looks like, and considerable inequality among women along the lines of class, race, ability, and other differences. The Covid-19 pandemic made inequalities among women worse.

If enduring discrimination and harassment and persisting inequalities among women characterize women's experiences in so-called empowered societies, is empowerment so great after all? And if this is not empowerment, what is it? Does empowerment imply that women occupy the same roles as men? That households conform to a dual-income, co-participation in care work model? Or is empowerment about everyone having the choice to do what they want, even if it means that some people conform to restrictive and traditional gender roles? If empowerment is not about promoting equality, why do we care about legal reform, political participation, social mobilization, and other mechanisms to promote it? These questions led us to decide that we wanted to do more work on the concept of "empowerment," what it means in different contexts, and how these different ideas animate the ways that states and societies put empowerment into practice. In other words, although our overarching research interest is to study the role of the state in bringing about empowerment, this particular part of our research aims to understand more about variation in the *meaning* of empowerment, since these different meanings may shape state interventions and their effects.

COMPARING TO EXPLORE THE BOUNDARIES OF A CONCEPT

To explore differences in the meaning of women's empowerment – which may or may not matter for the main causal patterns we are interested in – we chose a comparative approach. We decided to take a deeper look at three wealthy countries that have relatively few formal restrictions on women's legal capacity, little state-sanctioned discrimination in the workplace, and many women who appear to be fairly empowered economically, but with seemingly different discourses about empowerment: Norway, Japan, and the United States. Each country holds a particular appeal. Following much of the gender and politics literature, Htun had long seen Norway as the "paradise" of gender equality, due to its extensive social provisions, relatively high degree of class equality, and the widespread commitment of virtually all political actors to gender justice (Leira 1992). The United States is compelling due to its many puzzles and contradictions, including a stratification of gender equality by class and race (Putnam 2016; Michener and Brower 2020) and inconsistent progress toward gender justice by issue area (Htun and Weldon 2018). Japan stands out among the rich countries for the resilience of traditional social norms in the face of policy and rhetorical changes to promote women's labor force participation, men's caregiving, and greater work-life balance for all (Estévez-Abe 2013; Nemoto 2016).

Some people may say our study resembles a controlled comparison of similarly placed countries that differ in their state approach to empowerment. However, we did not choose to study these three countries because we wanted to make a causal argument about the effects of one state's approach compared with the others'. Nor do we believe they are similar in all other ways besides their legal approach to the empowerment of women. Following the framework of Gerring (2017, 41), the case selection strategy that most resembles our approach is the analysis of a set of cases that are diverse with respect to their descriptive features.

However, since our goal is theory development, and to understand more about the empowerment concept in particular, we sought interesting variations in how empowerment seems to be understood and used them to inform our theoretical thinking. The cases in our study are not units from a well-defined universe of a class of events. We picked them because they are vastly different contexts that, viewed from the vantage point of one another (Schaffer's perspectival comparison), furnish insights into women's empowerment. We did not choose our diverse contexts on the basis of values on a single descriptive feature. Our prior knowledge of the many characteristics of these countries made us think that they would provide us with informative stories and enriching perspectives about the content and boundaries of the empowerment concept. As such, our choices fit uneasily within a common framework describing different types of case selection. In short, we do not think of this study as a comparative case study, but rather as a perspectival and juxtapositional comparison of a concept across three contexts.

Each context we study in this project has helped bring out particular and unique features of the others, while revealing connections within contexts we thought we already knew well. By conducting fieldwork in each context, we have gained a better sense of the nature and degree of social contestation over women's empowerment. We have seen how gender, class, and race equality relate to one another in different ways. We have learned that people's views on women's empowerment are connected to their views of the good life, as well as how they evaluate the proper role of the state in citizen's lives and as a mechanism for social coordination. We have traced the connection between government goals vis-à-vis women's liberation and other state priorities and observed how these goals sometimes compete and sometimes complement one another. In addition, the fieldwork has alerted us to our own cultural biases related to women, gender, the state, and the economy.

MULTICULTURAL RESEARCH TEAMS AND COLLABORATIVE FIELDWORK

Our selection of three contexts was not based purely on theoretical concerns. We also consciously designed our study to maximize our insider and outsider advantages. In the United States, we focused on New Mexico, where Htun has spent much of her life. Jensenius has spent considerable time in the United States but is quite unfamiliar with the New Mexico context, and her accent makes it evident that she is a foreigner. In Norway, we worked in Oslo, which was a new context for Htun but where Jensenius grew up. In Tokyo, Jensenius was clearly an outsider, Htun was somewhat more acculturated due to a one-year fellowship in 2006–2007, and we recruited a PhD student from Yokohama, Melanie Sayuri Dominguez, as a collaborator.

By conducting fieldwork collaboratively in 2016, 2017, and 2018, we could leverage both an insider and an outsider advantage in real time. As insiders, we had easier access to sources, command of the native language, and greater understanding of subtle cultural cues. As outsiders, we were able to pose out-of-the-box questions and notice patterns and particularities that an insider rarely thinks of.

Including both insider and outsider perspectives on the same team, at the same time, allowed us to push further in interviews and in participant observation situations than we would have been able to do on our own. It made us familiar with the narratives that people commonly choose to share with dissimilar others, while allowing us to achieve a level of intimacy that made respondents more open and candid as the conversation progressed.

What is more, this research technique helped us become more aware of and challenge some of the cultural biases that shape our research. We were, for instance, fascinated to discover the extent to which Norwegians (including Jensenius) take the role of the state for granted when it comes to upholding a common image of the good life and structuring people's lives. Htun, while enamored with the generous welfare policies for working parents, reacted intuitively with more skepticism to the ways in which the state's one-size-fits-all policy solutions limit individual choice. Meanwhile, Jensenius questioned the ideal of a leaning-in form of feminism that Htun takes more for granted, as well as the dichotomous choice – between career and care work – many women face. For Jensenius, an ideal of empowerment that implies outsourcing care work to other women, such as low-income immigrant women, seemed unattractive and unjust.

In summary, constructing a multicultural research team allowed us to leverage both insider and outsider perspectives to elicit features of experiences, narratives, processes, and other things that we would not have been able to notice on our own. These insights have now come to inform the way we approach our larger study of the state's role in promoting women's equality.

CONCLUDING THOUGHTS

Since the publication of KKV's *Designing Social Inquiry* in 1994, much of the research design advice passed to graduate students as part of their methodological training has presumed that their general goal is to test theories about a causal relationship among variables. It is critical to design research aimed at theory testing carefully to avoid bias. However, empirical studies involving the in-depth comparison of a few cases or contexts often have the goal of theory development rather than theory testing. And theory development consists of many different stages and parts, including building intuition and contextual knowledge, conceptualizing and operationalizing key variables, exploring causal mechanisms, identifying scope conditions of arguments, gaining insight from deviant cases, and so on. In our view, comparing generates important perspectives for all of these stages and parts, and we therefore need to think carefully about research designs for multiple aspects of a project. There is no one-size-fits-all solution, but rather some practical rules: align your research design with your research goals, be explicit about the choices you make, and aim to capture some interesting variation in whatever you want to understand better.

Clarity and transparency about these thought processes will help others see the source of your insights, most of which will likely stem from systematic research and not epiphanies. What is more, scholars do not need to know everything about their study in advance, and so research designs may evolve as thinking develops. It can be rigorous, transparent, and scientific to learn as you go along. In the final analysis, comparing is useful for almost any part of a research project. Comparative work helps open your mind and extend your horizons. Let its insights enrich your theory.

REFERENCES

Agarwal, Bina. 1994. *A Field of One's Own: Gender and Land Rights in South Asia.* Cambridge: Cambridge University Press.
  1997. "'Bargaining' and Gender Relations: Within and Beyond the Household." *Feminist Economics* 3 (1): 1–51.
Brady, Henry E., and David Collier, eds. 2010. *Rethinking Social Inquiry: Diverse Tools, Shared Standards.* Lanham, MD: Rowman & Littlefield.
Brubaker, Rogers, Mara Loveman, and Peter Stamatov. 2004. "Ethnicity as Cognition." *Theory and Society* 33 (1): 31–64.
Collier, David, Joe Mahoney, and Jason Seawright. 2004. "Claiming Too Much: Warnings about Selection Bias." In *Rethinking Social Inquiry: Diverse Tools, Shared Standards*, edited by Henry E. Brady and David Collier, 85–102. Lanham, MD: Rowman & Littlefield.
Eckstein, Harry. 1975. "Case Studies and Theory in Political Science." In *Handbook of Political Science*, edited by Fred I. Greenstein and Nelson W. Polsby, 79–138. Reading, MA: Addison-Wesley.
Estévez-Abe, Margarita. 2013. "An International Comparison of Gender Equality: Why Is the Japanese Gender Gap So Persistent." *Japan Labor Review* 10 (2): 82–100.
Fearon, James D. 2003. "Ethnic and Cultural Diversity by Country." *Journal of Economic Growth*, 8 (2): 195–222.

Fraser, Nancy. 2016. "Contradictions of Capitalism and Care." *New Left Review* 100: 99–117.
Geddes, Barbara. 1990. "How the Cases You Choose Affect the Answers You Get: Selection Bias in Comparative Politics." *Political Analysis* 2: 131–50.
George, Alexander L., and Andrew Bennett. 2005. *Case Studies and Theory Development in the Social Sciences*. Cambridge, MA: MIT Press.
Gerring, John. 2001. *Social Science Methodology: A Criterial Framework*. New York: Cambridge University Press.
  2011. *Social Science Methodology: A Unified Framework*. New York: Cambridge University Press.
  2017. *Case Study Research: Principles and Practices*. Cambridge: Cambridge University Press.
Htun, Mala. 2016a. "Emergence of an Organized Politics of Race in Latin America." In *The Double Bind: The Politics of Racial and Class Inequalities in the Americas*, edited by Juliet Hooker and Alvin Tillery, 35–45. Report of the APSA Task Force on Race and Class in the Americas. Washington, DC: American Political Science Association.
  2016b. *Inclusion Without Representation in Latin America: Gender Quotas and Ethnic Reservations*. New York: Cambridge University Press.
Htun, Mala, Francesca R. Jensenius, and Jami Nelson-Nuñez. 2019. "Gender-Discriminatory Laws and Women's Economic Agency." *Social Politics: International Studies in Gender, State & Society* 26 (2): 193–222.
Htun, Mala, and Francesca R. Jensenius. Forthcoming. "Violence Against Women Legislation and Changes in Social Norms in Mexico." *World Politics*.
  2020. "Political Change, Women's Rights, and Public Opinion on Gender Equality in Myanmar." *The European Journal of Development Research* 32 (4): 1–25.
Htun, Mala, and S. Laurel Weldon. 2018. *The Logics of Gender Justice: State Action on Women's Rights Around the World*. New York: Cambridge University Press.
Iversen, Torben, and Frances Rosenbluth. 2008. "Work and Power: The Connection between Female Labor Force Participation and Female Political Representation." *Annual Review of Political Science* 11: 479–95.
Jensenius, Francesca R. 2017. *Social Justice through Inclusion: The Consequences of Electoral Quotas in India*. Oxford: Oxford University Press.
Kabeer, Naila. 1999. "Resources, Agency, Achievements: Reflections on the Measurement of Women's Empowerment." *Development and Change* 30 (3): 435–64.
  2012. "Women's Economic Empowerment and Inclusive Growth: Labour Markets and Enterprise Development." *International Development Research Centre* 44 (10): 1–70.
King, Gary, Robert Keohane, and Sidney Verba. 1994. *Designing Social Inquiry: Scientific Inference in Qualitative Research*. Princeton, NJ: Princeton University Press.
  1995. "The Importance of Research Design in Political Science." *American Political Science Review* 89 (2): 475–81.
Koivu, Kendra L. and Annika Marlen Hinze. 2017. "Cases of Convenience? The Divergence of Theory from Practice in Case Selection in Qualitative and Mixed-Methods Research." *PS: Political Science & Politics* 50 (4): 1023–27.

Leira, Arnlaug. 1992. *Welfare States and Working Mothers: The Scandinavian Experience.* Cambridge: Cambridge University Press.

Levy, Jack. 2008. "Case Studies: Types, Designs, and Logics of Inference." *Conflict Management and Peace Science* 25 (1): 1–18.

Lijphart, Arend. 1971. "Comparative Politics and the Comparative Method." *American Political Science Review* 65 (3): 682–93.

Lund, Christian. 2014. "Of What Is This a Case? Analytical Movements in Qualitative Social Science Research." *Human Organization* 73 (3): 224–34.

McKeown, Timothy J. 2004. "Case Studies and the Limits of the Quantitative Worldview." In *Rethinking Social Inquiry: Diverse Tools, Shared Standards*, edited by Henry E. Brady and David Collier, 139–67. Lanham, MD: Rowman & Littlefield.

Michener, Jamila, and Margaret Teresa Brower. 2020. "What's Policy Got to Do with It? Race, Gender & Economic Inequality in the United States." *Daedalus* 149 (1): 100–118.

Mill, John S. (1884). *A System of Logic, Ratiocinative and Inductive: Being a Connected View of the Principles of Evidence and the Methods of Scientific Investigation* (Vol. 1). Harlow, UK: Longmans, Green.

Nemoto, Kumiko. 2016. *Too Few Women at the Top: The Persistence of Inequality in Japan.* Ithaca, NY: Cornell University Press.

Nobles, Melissa. 2000. *Shades of Citizenship: Race and the Census in Modern Politics.* Stanford, CA: Stanford University Press.

Okin, Susan Moller. 1989. *Justice, Gender, and the Family.* New York: Basic Books.

Panda, Pradeep, and Bina Agarwal. 2005. "Marital Violence, Human Development and Women's Property Status in India." *World Development* 33 (5): 823–50.

Putnam, Robert D. 2016. *Our Kids: The American Dream in Crisis.* New York: Simon & Schuster.

Ragin, Charles C. 2004. "Turning the Tables: How Case-Oriented Research Challenges." In *Rethinking Social Inquiry: Diverse Tools, Shared Standards*, edited by Henry E. Brady and David Collier, 123–38. Lanham, MD: Rowman & Littlefield.

Ragin, Charles C., and Howard S. Becker, eds. 1992. *What Is a Case? Exploring the Foundations of Social Inquiry.* Cambridge: Cambridge University Press.

Rosenbluth, Frances M. 2006. *The Political Economy of Japan's Low Fertility.* Stanford, CA: Stanford University Press.

Seawright, Jason, and John Gerring. 2008. "Case Selection Techniques in Case Study Research." *Political Research Quarterly* 61 (2): 294–308.

Sulmont, David, and Juan Carlos Calligros. 2014. "¿El país de todas las sangres? Race and Ethnicity in Contemporary Peru." In *Pigmentocracies: Ethnicity, Race, and Color in Latin America*, edited by Edward Telles, 126–71. Chapel Hill: University of North Carolina Press.

Telles, Edward, René D. Flores, and Fernando Urrea-Giraldo. 2015. "Pigmentocracies: Educational Inequality, Skin Color and Census Ethnoracial Identification in Eight Latin American Countries." *Research in Social Stratification and Mobility* 40: 39–58.

Teune, Henry, and Adam Przeworski. 1970. *The Logic of Comparative Social Inquiry.* New York: Wiley-Interscience.

United Nations. 2015. "Progress of the World's Women 2015–2016: Transforming Economies, Realizing Rights." http://progress.unwomen.org/en/2015/
Van Evera, S. 1997. *Guide to Methods for Students of Political Science*. Ithaca, NY: Cornell University Press.
World Bank. 2015. "Women, Business, and the Law 2016: Getting to Equal." Washington, DC: World Bank.

11

Problems and Possibilities of Comparison across Regime Types

Examples Involving China

Benjamin L. Read
University of California, Santa Cruz

"The unconscious thinker does not ask himself why he is comparing; and this neglect goes to explain why so much comparative work provides extensions of knowledge, but hardly a strategy for acquiring and validating new knowledge." So alleged Giovanni Sartori (1970, 1035) in his oft-cited article on concepts in comparative politics. He was certainly right that the question of why we compare bears conscious consideration and discussion, because the rationales are "not intuitively evident," at least not necessarily so. This is particularly true when it comes to comparisons between fundamentally dissimilar political systems, especially across contrasting regime types. The purpose of this chapter is to reconsider such comparisons, the very type of comparison that Sartori criticized as prone to conceptual stretching and other offenses.

The brunt of the critique from Sartori and like-minded scholars fell on efforts to compare democracies and communist systems, particularly the Soviet Union and its satellite states. Much has changed in the fifty-odd years since those writings (not least the practice of using male pronouns to refer to thinkers in general). Today it is China, led by an ideologically retooled Communist Party and powered by a dynamic engine of economic growth, that has assumed the mantle of the world's most significant nondemocratic regime model. Thus, it seems appropriate to focus on recent comparisons involving China. Much research on the politics of the People's Republic of China (PRC) – like mainstream research on American politics – stays within the country's geographic borders. In such work, very reasonably, comparison to other

---

This chapter is a substantially rewritten and expanded version of Read (2018a). I thank Erica S. Simmons and Nicholas Rush Smith for leading the Rethinking Comparison project, which spurred these thoughts, and all participants at the October 2017 workshop at The City College of New York. I am also grateful for thoughts and comments from Kent Eaton, Mark W. Frazier, Elizabeth J. Perry, Juan Diego Prieto, and participants in the May 30, 2019, comparative and global politics workshop at UC Santa Cruz.

places and regions is more implicit, or the reference point is general theories of authoritarian politics.[1]

And yet, over the years, scholars of politics and other social scientists have pursued many comparisons between China and other political systems, as Mark Frazier (2018) thoroughly surveyed in a recent overview. Frazier and William Hurst (2017) as well, vigorously advocate for more such research, and, indeed, a burst of energy and initiative is driving a wave of cross-national comparisons involving China. So, it is to our advantage to revisit some of the questions that such comparisons pose – focusing here on the seemingly problematic subcategory of cross-regime-type studies. Specifically, when is it reasonable to pursue such comparisons, and what is their purpose? Why, indeed, are we comparing in this way?

As Sartori's invocation of "new knowledge" suggests, this is an epistemological question. For him, the purpose of comparison – of comparative politics as an enterprise – was "a systematic testing, against as many cases as possible, of sets of hypotheses, generalizations and laws of the 'if ... then' type" (1970, 1035). Without discounting these goals, the fruits of cross-regime-type comparisons are by no means limited to the generation and testing of hypotheses and laws, as other chapters in this volume also attest. Further, while we might guess that such comparisons take the form of most-different-systems designs (Mill's Method of Agreement) – that is, positing two cases that have nothing in common save a shared X linked to a shared Y – the examples reviewed here rarely and only partially follow that pattern. Many of their contributions take other forms entirely.

The main themes of this chapter are as follows: Sartori usefully cautioned against comparing unlike entities, yet his advice was overly confining. Meaningful studies can be set up in ways that do not pose problems of conceptual stretching. In the past ten or fifteen years, scholars have productively compared a wide-ranging selection of phenomena in authoritarian China, from welfare policy to social movements to local political economy, with their counterparts in democratic regimes. Indeed, often gaps or disjunctures between substantially dissimilar political systems provide opportunities for innovation, even if they complicate Mill-style comparison or require quite different modes of analysis.

Producing such a study requires two distinctive analytical steps. The researcher first must *set up the comparison*, providing an overview of the two or more country-level cases that accounts for all the relevant ways in which they differ while also building an argument for shared features that make it meaningful to examine the two in relation to each other. Second, the researcher must *establish a specific focus of comparison*, which is not

---

[1] It should go without saying that the PRC's complexity, distinctiveness, and importance provide ample justification for such China-centered inquiry and, as scholars have long argued and as Lily Tsai (2017) has elaborated in detail, such work can contribute to general social science theory building in many ways.

necessarily a dependent variable but a feature manifested across the cases that the research will examine closely. I give examples of two kinds of foci: a comparable institution and a comparable process, issue, or conundrum.

I assert that such projects can generate intellectual payoffs in at least four ways. In the first instance, and most obviously, they generate findings about the specific *substantive phenomenon* under study by investigating it in widely varying political circumstances. Second, they provide insights on *the broader political regimes themselves*, the context in which the empirical subject is embedded, often highlighting ways in which these regimes behave that run contrary to what we might expect. Third, such studies provide opportunities for *conceptual development* by elaborating on and exploring the phenomena that are shared across contrasting political systems, explaining how they follow divergent or surprisingly parallel tracks. Finally, such comparisons make innovative contributions by *framing* a topic of study, specifying its universe of cases, and scrutinizing the gains and problems of bringing material from disparate contexts into a common category. I argue that these, not merely logics of control, are among the most important benefits of cross-regime comparative research that employs in-depth, qualitative analysis.[2]

Such comparisons are not always feasible or useful; I do not believe that "anything goes." There are such things as phenomena that are only superficially related to one another, that cannot be treated as comparable without willfully ignoring essential facts. When appropriately posed, however, cross-regime studies hold the promise of new thought-provoking theoretical and conceptual departures. These kinds of benefits may not be foreseeable in advance; rather, they may emerge only through the process of comparison itself.

COMPARISON ACROSS DISSIMILAR POLITICAL SYSTEMS

I start by acknowledging that cross-regime-type studies are not the most common subtype of cross-national comparison. As political scientists, we often compare among cases that fit more or less comfortably within a category, precisely to achieve controlled comparison through a most-similar-systems design. Thus, a study might be framed as "in modernizing agrarian bureaucracies" or "in transitional democracies" or "in late industrializers." China has been the subject of many studies involving controlled comparisons in the most-similar-systems mode. These follow a particular pattern and, as the following two sets of examples show, have typically had a very specific payoff: explaining notable divergences between China and counterparts.

---

[2] Here I am not considering research in which quantitative data points from China are combined with those from other countries. Such studies raise all the same questions, but qualitative research tends to delve more deeply into issues and problems of comparison and thus lends itself more readily to the discussion at hand.

Problems and Possibilities of Comparison across Regime Types   211

First, given that the PRC borrowed institutions that were pioneered by the Soviet Union and emulated from Poland to Vietnam, one line of research has explored comparisons with other state socialist regimes. In these most-similar-systems comparisons, the point has often been to understand why China diverged from its peers, for instance, by pursuing a Maoist ideological variant (Schwartz 1951) or undertaking sweeping market reforms (Walder 2016). For the past three decades, the biggest question has been why, unlike many counterparts, China's ruling party avoided collapse in 1989–1991 and instead resiliently rebuilt its control, with scholars weighing the roles of structural conditions, institutions, and leadership choices (Pei 1994; Walder 1995; Bernstein 2013; Dimitrov 2013).

Second, a somewhat parallel line of most-similar-systems comparison pairs China with Taiwan – in other words, with the Republic of China (ROC) state. The ROC preceded the PRC in governing much of the Chinese mainland before its 1949 defeat in the civil war. At that point, it retreated to Taiwan, an island it had only acquired after the end of World War II. Taiwan is hardly the mirror image of China, given disparities such as its relatively small size, legacies of Japan's fifty-year colonial rule, and the gulf that separates 1940s-era arrivals from the mainland (and their descendants) from those whose ancestral connection to China dates back centuries. Still, a number of studies have considered the two an "experimentally ideal" pairing (Gilley 2008, 1) or close to it. They base this on the Chinese cultural and linguistic heritage shared by most of Taiwan's population, as well as resemblances between China's ruling party and Taiwan's Kuomintang, particularly prior to the latter's relinquishing authoritarian control and accepting democracy in the late 1980s and the 1990s. Most-similar-systems studies in this vein have addressed many topics, including regime consolidation (Strauss 2019) and rural development (Looney 2020) but have trained special attention on the question of why Taiwan democratized while the mainland did not. In so doing, they have explored contrasts in the ruling parties (Dickson 1997; Wong 2008), business groups (Solinger 2008), critical episodes of protest (Wright 2001), and elections (Cheng and Lin 2008).[3]

All these studies fit more or less comfortably into the pattern of most-similar-systems research designs. What kinds of problems might a researcher encounter when stepping outside this common template and comparing dissimilar political systems? Some readily apparent stumbling blocks include the possibility that data is unavailable or incommensurate in one or more of the cases to be compared. Another is that inquiry across highly dissimilar systems might merely confirm the obvious rather than turning up anything interesting.

---

[3] I consider such comparisons in "China-Taiwan Comparisons: Still Promising Though Not 'Ideal,'" Workshop on Chinese Politics, Harvard University, revised February 23, 2018. https://benread.net/publications/ReadBenjaminL_2018_China-Taiwan_Comparisons.pdf

A subtler set of problems could be called "concept incompatibility," bringing us to Sartori. In his classic article, as Schaffer (Chapter 3, this volume) also points out in discussing juxtapositional comparisons, Sartori cautioned against comparing systems that are fundamentally dissimilar. Things that one would compare must belong "to the same genus, species, or sub-species – in short to the same class," he wrote (1970, 1036). He linked this to his conception of the very purpose of comparative politics, which he saw as "a method of control" in testing hypotheses.[4] Going beyond such "taxonomical requisites of comparability" is precisely what he says leads to "conceptual stretching," which generations of political scientists came to recognize as a cardinal sin. Sartori went on to criticize examples of such hyper-elongation, including what he considered flawed applications of the terms "pluralism" and "participation," rooted in Western democracies to non-Western, nondemocratic polities. So too, concepts like "mobilization" "originate from a totalitarian context," and applying them to the West presents a fallacy of "reversed extrapolation" (1970, 1035, 1036, 1050–52).

Sartori's article, as well as related critiques in the same era (e.g., LaPalombara 1975), reacted against a tendency in structural-functionalist theorizing to paper over deep differences in an effort to apply universal political abstractions. They inveighed against equating practices or institutions that have superficial similarities yet actually work in profoundly different ways.

Sartori's taxonomical metaphor, with its injunction against comparing across genera, may have seemed like a prudent corrective to problematic scholarly trends in 1970, yet it appears too confining today. We now confront a world all the more replete with complexity, including hybrid regimes and democratic backsliding; some countries shift regime types repeatedly.[5] More generally, his skepticism that *any* category might travel effectively from the West to Africa or South-East Asia now seems excessive, even essentializing. Both Sartori and LaPalombara questioned whether political participation could happen in communist regimes, yet certain forms of participation, including grassroots protests, are frequent in today's China. While Sartori objected to using the term "mobilization" in democracies, it is now well accepted that individuals do not always engage in democratic political action purely on their own initiative; rather, they are driven to act by friends, organizations, inspiring leaders, and so forth.[6] One can simultaneously note this and also bear in mind a vital distinction in kind between this and the type of ruling party

---

[4] We should assess hypotheses and other generalizations against "all cases," Sartori wrote, but those should be all cases within the relevant taxonomical class.
[5] I thank Juan Diego Prieto for suggesting this point.
[6] Among many works that come to mind, consider Disch (2011), García Bedolla and Michelson (2012), and Han (2014) on mobilization in democracies and Fu (2018) on civil society groups mobilizing within China despite state repression.

Problems and Possibilities of Comparison across Regime Types

orchestration that, in autocracies, compels people to cast ballots in sham elections and the like.

The key point here is that we can investigate related phenomena across contrasting political systems without losing sight of nuances, frictions, and the possibility that they have radically different meanings. Taking conceptual fit and context seriously will not necessarily lead us to conclude that any comparison of dissimilar regime types is ill conceived. On the contrary, these strengths of qualitative work are precisely what enable us to learn from cross-regime-type comparisons. By assessing conceptual fit with care and attention to context, we guard against thoughtlessly and misleadingly assimilating unlike things, a danger that Sartori was right to warn against.

SETTING UP THE COMPARISON

If the aim is to set up a comparison across highly different systems in such a conscious and sensitive fashion, how does one proceed? Making the case for some degree of comparability despite stark contrasts is a crucial part of an investigator's task in such research. Usually, this begins with (in one form or another) a sketch of the broad contrasts as well as similarities between the political contexts that are to be juxtaposed. This acknowledges the gap between the systems, the distance that the analysis to follow will span, while also anchoring that analysis in an overall frame of reference that contains some shared landmarks.

The introductory chapter to Duara and Perry's (2018b) edited volume on China and India provides a well-elaborated and apt example. The coeditors begin by acknowledging that their project is "fraught with methodological challenges," noting that the two countries "not only have vastly different political systems; their social systems are also markedly divergent" (2018a, 1). They observe that social fault lines between the two do not exactly line up, centering as they do on caste, language, and religion in India and more on factors like class and the coastal/inland divide in China. They write: "The divergent foundational events of the two states – a massive social and political revolution in China and a more gradual transition from colonialism in India, along with the very different political institutions to which these events gave rise – have generated strikingly different trajectories over the last 65 years" (1–2).

From there, they pivot to compiling a broad case why the two "Asian giants" nonetheless deserve much more side-by-side comparison than they have previously received. Both saw uprisings in the mid-nineteenth century in response to disruptions wrought by British imperialism. Both saw moderate reform movements give way in the early twentieth century to more radical nationalists, who ultimately sparked mass movements (under Gandhi and Mao respectively) that generated the Republic of India and the PRC in close succession. The two states' ideological tenets differed substantially, yet they faced similar developmental challenges: "Both states inherited societies where over 80 percent of the population was rural, agricultural, and largely illiterate" (6). Both sought industrial development and pursued import substitution strategies while borrowing in various ways from the Soviet model of planning and state control. Later, first China and then India substantially liberalized and embraced new strategies for development that gave wider play to market forces, and thereafter they experienced parallel pressures from globalization. Meanwhile, each saw a rise in popular movements based on rights claims. In this way, convergent developments that each state experienced in its own way established a framework of parallel temporalities, from nation building to neoliberalism.

The authors establish this framework not to advance any particular argument but to make the general case for comparability – and a new mode of study, "convergent comparison" – within which the book's eight chapters stake out more specific lines of inquiry. (I discuss later examples from these chapters and from related China-India comparisons.) It shows, for instance, that some of what can appear as unbridgeable incompatibilities are actually similar processes happening in somewhat different ways, or at different points in time. And it suggests that regime differences – the kind that Sartori took as specifying absolute typological boundaries – in some ways mask broader parallels. The point is to establish rationales for juxtaposing the two country cases and to specify broad patterns of disjuncture and affinity in light of which particular connections can be examined. All such comparisons must include such a rationale, even if not always articulated at such length and with such historical sweep.

ESTABLISHING A SPECIFIC FOCUS OF COMPARISON

Having laid out broad relationships among the regime-level systems, a further step is to argue for a focal point for the comparison, to single out one particular thing shared by two dissimilar political systems on which an analytic lens will be trained. Scholars identify, somewhere within these messy, complex entities, some particular dimension or aspect or arena of politics. This is common in many forms of comparative study, where attention focuses on particular processes or units (Tilly 1984, chap. 4). In cross-regime comparisons, this likely entails an explicit or implicit argument that the thing in question follows its own distinct rules and patterns in ways that make sense across the disparate cases. Next, I consider two broad kinds of foci.

A Comparable Institution

Institutions that exist in some clearly identifiable form in both cases provide one viable focus for cross-regime-type comparison. Nara Dillon (2018) took the welfare states of China and India as the object of comparison – specifically, one

Problems and Possibilities of Comparison across Regime Types 215

component thereof: cash transfers to the elderly. In Kellee Tsai's (2016) research, also on China and India, it is the developmental aspects of local governments and their relationships with internationally mobile, entrepreneurial diasporas. Weller et al. (2017) studied religious organizations engaged in charitable activity in China, Taiwan, and Malaysia. More specifically, their book examines the operations and political interactions of the Tzu Chi Foundation as a primary case but also activities of other Buddhist as well as Christian, Daoist, and other groups.[7] We can see in each of these cases a quite tangible institutional referent underpinning the comparison.

William Hurst's (2018) study of China and Indonesia takes as its subject the "legal regime," that is, "a system or framework of rules governing some physical territory or discrete realm of action that is at least in principle rooted in some sort of law" (21). A legal regime defines "how easy or difficult it is for social groups or individual or organized interests to gain political influence or power and how readily and in what manner nonjudicial state institutions or empowered actors intervene in legal institutions' handling of specific cases" (14). Somewhat more abstract than other subjects considered here, this directs attention to questions of whether and how state officials and others outside the legal system itself interfere with the workings of legal institutions.

A project of my own focused on government-structured neighborhood organizations across China and Taiwan (Read 2012). In the former, my subject was the Residents' Committees (RCs; *jumin weiyuanhui*) that the Chinese state has maintained since the early 1950s.[8] In the latter, it was the state-sponsored neighborhood offices (*li bangongchu*) that date to the Kuomintang's arrival in the mid-1940s. The two institutions have a number of things in common. Both are part of a nationwide network that covers all urban space.[9] While organizational details vary somewhat by locality, they are mandated in national law and correspond to a unified template. A neighborhood has no choice about having such an office. In both countries, the offices handle a wide range of responsibilities. They serve as what might be called all-purpose contact points for state agencies at the community level, for instance, helping the welfare bureaucracy determine households' eligibility for assistance programs by drawing on their local knowledge of residents' circumstances. They also field a seemingly endless variety of queries and demands from their constituents. That both organizations are highly structured by official policies and practices and organizationally connected to

---

[7] While the authors of this study are anthropologists, unlike most of the other authors referenced in this chapter, their book's sustained focus on regime context and political relationships, among other qualities, makes it relevant for comparative politics.

[8] The project involved comparisons at multiple levels: among residents within a neighborhood, among neighborhoods (with different kinds of leaders, housing, and demographics), and among cities. Here I focus on the cross-national dimension.

[9] In China and Taiwan alike, these organizations have rural counterparts.

the state facilitates the comparison. Comparisons to more pluralistic settings are harder.[10]

Taiwan's institutions certainly had significant differences from China's. Taiwan's neighborhoods have but a single leader, a warden (*lizhang*), who is partnered with a civil servant (*liganshi*). China's RCs, as their name indicates, are larger committees of three to seven people and have become parts of even larger community (*shequ*) organizations. The two variants differ dramatically in how their leaders are chosen. Taiwan's wardens are selected in open, fair, and usually competitive elections every four years, whereas triennial elections for China's RCs are heavily stage-managed. Also, while neighborhood bodies in both places cooperate closely with the police, in China the police do not merely fight crime but also tamp down and root out dissent. In Taiwan, much more than in China, residents are free to organize independent community groups of their choice. Moreover, while neighborhood Chinese Communist Party (CCP) committees embody China's firm insistence on the CCP's monopoly of political organization, in Taiwan, neighborhood leaders can affiliate with any political party (or run as independents, as many do).

A Comparable Process, Issue, or Conundrum

In other studies, the focus centers not on a shared institution but on a comparable sociopolitical process, issue, or conundrum. Zhang's (2013) analysis of the politics of urban preservation provides a good example. Her book examines a problem faced by Beijing, Chicago, and Paris: which old buildings to protect in the name of historical preservation and which to bulldoze in the name of progress and urban revitalization. The specific topics of controversy vary – in Beijing, ancient city gates and neighborhoods once occupied by the Manchu elite; in Chicago, houses, businesses, and churches in immigrant and African American communities; in Paris, safeguarded sectors, the historic market of Les Halles, and thousands of heritage buildings – but the dilemma itself is very much the same in each case. Later work by Zhang examines another distinct urban issue, slum redevelopment and governance, in Beijing, Mumbai, and São Paulo (Zhang 2020).

Mark Frazier's (2019) comparison of Shanghai and Mumbai spotlights protest and claim making. Differences between these cities notwithstanding, he writes, "one can find observable similarities in ... contentious claims over the distribution of urban resources and calls for recognition" (10). Both experienced remarkably parallel episodes of strikes, social movements, and rebellion in 1919, the interwar period, and 1966, for example. With contention as the outcome, Frazier also draws parallels between causal factors

---

[10] One article compares Shanghai's RCs to Los Angeles's neighborhood councils. This results in some astute observations but mainly a catalog of structural contrasts (Chen, Cooper, and Sun 2009).

that span these two coastal centers of textile manufacturing: specifically, "the civic spaces, commercial districts, courtrooms, factories, roads, and even housing types that are the settings in which urban residents experience abstractions such as imperialism, capitalism, gentrification, or neoliberalism" (6). Kevin O'Brien and Lianjiang Li's (1996, 2006) influential work on "rightful resistance," a concept derived from rural China, also looks outside of China for comparative examples, including democratic Norway and the United States as well as apartheid-era South Africa. Manjusha Nair (2018), in turn, finds the concept of "rightful resistance" useful in explaining protest in rural India as well as rural China. In both contexts, whether or not the overall political regime is democratic, members of the village population, despite deep subordination, engage in contention and make claims based on a sense of what the state justly owes them.

In the subfield of international relations, some scholars, such as structural realists, entirely discount regime types and all other features of domestic politics. Others take domestic politics more seriously and identify parallel political processes or dynamics that span different political systems and affect states' behavior in the international realm. An example is Thomas J. Christensen's *Useful Adversaries* (1996), which remarkably compares the United States and China from 1947 to 1958. He argues that in both countries, leaders stoked low-level conflicts to rally the public for long-term security strategies, and that such frictions can spiral into unwanted wars, such as the Korean War.

Another study concerning the domestic politics of foreign policy is Dorothy Solinger's *States' Gains, Labor's Losses* (2009). This book examines France, Mexico, and China, three countries that "would normally not be analyzed together," as she writes, given that they were "a democracy with its multiparty system; a regime that was authoritarian with an overarching, dominant party during the time when the pivotal events unfolded, a regime that later became 'semi-authoritarian' and finally democratizing; and a post-totalitarian government yet ruled by a communist party" (9). What brings them under a common tent in her study, first, is the choice that each made to engage with international trade agreements, triggering job losses, despite long-standing pro-labor commitments. A second focus is the extent to which labor subsequently won compensation in each.

Selecting and Defending Focal Points for Comparison

Do these studies commit taxonomical errors, in Sartori's terms? While I do not claim that any of them is beyond reproach, least of all my own, I argue that the general answer is no. Whether the focus of comparison is labor unions, or urban preservation, or protest, the objects of these studies hold up as having a meaningful coherence even across very different political contexts. To be worthy of comparison, the institutions or processes in question need not be exactly alike but must support conversation across the cases from which defensible new insights and perspectives can be gleaned. This is not happenstance or automatically true of any comparison. Rather, in making decisions about how to approach the points of focus that connect the cases, authors must avoid conceptual incompatibility as well as stating the trivially obvious. To blithely take Beijing's neighborhood elections at face value, for example, would indeed conflate categories and risk stretching concepts beyond meaning. Or, to give another example, comparing China's and Taiwan's community institutions in terms of their relationship with political parties might well produce little or no new insight; they differ just as we would expect of organizations in a single-party authoritarian regime and a pluralized democracy. It is when we think of them in terms of the role that they play in ordinary people's lives as intermediaries between state and society that a more productive comparison emerges.

As we have seen, in cross-regime-type studies, the focus of comparison may be somewhat isolated from other aspects of the political system, or at least not wholly reducible to it. It is likely to stand at some remove from the very things that define regime-level variation, such as elections or other processes through which key state officials obtain their positions. While not impossible, comparisons along such lines would run higher risks of simply describing obvious contrasts or violating Sartori's prohibition against assimilating fundamentally unlike things. Happily, many aspects of politics remain available for viable comparison. As this brief review has suggested, at minimum these can include a broad spectrum of public policy issues, state-society relationships, political processes within and around particular institutions (such as judiciaries), and outside institutional channels (such as protests). The workings of both national-level states and perhaps particularly subnational states and local governments hold comparative potential.

PURPOSES AND BENEFITS OF COMPARISON

Explaining Substantive Phenomena and Their Implications

The most obvious purpose of comparison across regime type is to learn new things about the substantive phenomenon at hand. The key questions from this perspective are whether, how, and why it varies in considerably different contexts. Outcomes can be of interest if they turn out not to differ across the cases or if they do, especially for unexpected reasons. The research explains the patterns observed, which may take the form of a puzzle to be solved. The outcome or dependent variable may be important for its intrinsic significance or for implications that follow from it, things on which it sheds light.

Zhang's (2013) book is a good example of a study that places most emphasis on the substantive outcome that it explains – patterns of urban preservation and

Problems and Possibilities of Comparison across Regime Types 219

obstacles to preservation in three large cities located in three very different countries. Her comparative study yields the principal findings that "fragmentation" characterizes the politics of urban preservation in each city, and that this fragmentation takes different forms in Beijing, Chicago, and Paris. In Beijing, it is "the functional segmentation among various municipal agencies"; in Chicago, "landmark designation and zoning [are] controlled by aldermen and [are] territorially fragmented along ward boundaries"; and in Paris, "urban preservation is increasingly subject to the intergovernmental fragmentation between the national government and the Paris municipality" (148). The fact that two of the cities fall under democratic regimes, seemingly in stark contrast to Beijing, turns out to matter relatively little in Zhang's account. Preservation has its own particular dynamics, forces, and trade-offs, and the point of the comparison is to explicate these. The book reaches findings of practical importance; for instance, preservation is "more likely to be implemented if it is within the boundaries of single jurisdictions and less likely so if it crosses multiple jurisdictions" (148). Zhang also finds that intergovernmental fragmentation, the pattern seen in Paris where the national government and municipal government jostle over jurisdiction, hampers preservation less than the other forms of fragmentation (149).

In Solinger's (2008) comparative study of China, France, and Mexico, the intrinsic importance of workers' fate under globalization – the question of whether labor retains any power in its relationships with states and international economic forces – motivates the project. Her two-stage study first explains the three states' decisions to join the World Trade Organization, the European Union, and the North American Free Trade Agreement, respectively. It then looks at the extent to which workers won state compensation for the disruptions of employment relations that ensued. Paradoxically, Mexico and France had stronger labor unions, yet this strength ended up merely leading to deeper labor repression in the former and disillusionment and passivity in the face of fragmentation and competitive squabbling in the latter. By contrast, the very weakness of the CCP-controlled official union left workers free to engage in widespread protests, which ultimately wrung new forms of welfare programs from the state. As Solinger notes, this provides perspective on the nature of unions' connections – their "terms of attachment" – to states and to their members.

In my research on state-backed neighborhood organizations in China and Taiwan, I might have expected that their facilitation of administrative and policing work would be strongly and universally disliked in China, in particular, given the repressive nature of that state. This was not the case, providing one aspect of a puzzle. Thus, I undertook the task of explaining variation in residents' opinions of and interactions with these organizations in both Beijing and Taipei. Surprisingly, residents of Beijing and Taipei had many similar patterns of opinions and perceptions of their neighborhood leaders. Those who did not like them or found them unimportant or irrelevant did so for the same types of reasons. For instance, young, childless professionals whose lives had little connection with the neighborhood often felt this way. On the other hand, those with more favorable views (often, for instance, elderly residents or those with businesses in the community) looked to neighborhood leaders for help with similar kinds of problems and often appreciated their keeping an eye on the locality. I traced this to, first, the similar webs of interpersonal networks that linked people with their community chiefs through various kinds of social structures, activities, and services and, second, to a shared and widely prevalent vision of the state's appropriate role as being closely and intimately cooperative. People's perceptions of these liaisons to the government serve as a window on patterns of state-society relationships.

Up to a point, these comparisons could be thought of as applying a logic of control, partialing out regime-level differences. But to say that these studies control for regime type would oversimplify and miss much about how they work. The significance of the overall political system is more complex than a democracy/autocracy binary – as seen, for instance, in the complicated state-union relationships Solinger (2009) examines, or the nested municipal-national relationships seen in Zhang's accounts of Beijing and Paris. As well, the overall political system is not neatly accounted for and removed from the analysis. The broader environment conditions every aspect of the research. And sometimes it does so in ways that are surprising with respect to general expectations for regime types, as in Solinger's study, where it is in the most authoritarian case, China, that workers end up having not the least but the most latitude for protest and thus win the greatest concessions. This brings us to the next point.

Insights on Political Regimes

Even if the primary purpose of a given cross-regime-type comparison is to study some quite specific substantive phenomenon, rather than the broader political system in which this phenomenon is embedded, such comparisons typically provide insights into the overall regimes in question. We learn about democracy through studying authoritarian regimes, and vice versa. Often what stands out are counterintuitive findings that depart from what is expected for a given regime type.

In Duara and Perry (2018b), the themes of India manifesting tendencies other than what might be associated with democracy and China not acting like a stereotypical autocracy come through loud and clear. Indeed, the book's title, *Beyond Regimes*, signals the central point that "distinctions in regime type ('democracy' versus 'dictatorship') alone offer little insight into critical differences and similarities between the Asian giants in terms of either policies or performance" (ix). Thus, a chapter on education finds that China's university system boasts substantial autonomy, innovation, and openness to international partnerships (among other features), while India's fares poorly on these scores and others (Kapur and Perry 2018). In terms of their educational systems in general, the countries confound any expectation that a universal franchise ought to lead to universal education, or that autocracies cater to a narrow elite (Kapur and Perry 2018, 213).[11] Selina Ho's comparison of public goods provision in China and India similarly takes China's superior performance in delivering drinking water to urban residents as grounds for reflection on their respective political regimes and the social contracts on which, in her telling, they rest (Ho 2019). Investigating the state's dispossession of rural land, Lynette Ong (2020) is struck as much by similarities as by differences between India and China; though poor farmers are better able to mobilize in the former, they do not necessarily prevail against dominant social groups that support land acquisition policies. In short, contrasting outcomes are not necessarily the result of regime differences and do not necessarily follow patterns predicted by common theories. As well, many similarities crosscut the seeming opposites, a result of responses to similar pressures, imperatives, and forces.

Weller et al. (2017) also point out instances where the countries in their study play contrary to type. They note that despite the CCP's atheism, the Taiwan-based Buddhist charity Tzu Chi was able to build a large headquarters, including a medical building, on the Chinese city of Suzhou's "most expensive piece of land, a generous gift from the municipal government" (55) and received other forms of welcome as well. This parallels the way in which Tzu Chi received state assistance in Taiwan, most notably when, during the island's authoritarian period, President Chiang Ching-kuo helped the group acquire land for its first hospital (54). While observing that China imposes political constraints on the group's work, Weller et al. (2017) conclude, "democracies do not necessarily provide more support for NGOs than authoritarian regimes" (57).

As pointed out earlier, comparisons of the kind discussed here do not focus on the very things that define regime-level differences. It is by investigating other phenomena that they provide valuable comparative perspectives on the regimes themselves. There is, perhaps, some danger in such work of overemphasizing the counterintuitive, spotlighting the "man bites dog" story and not the stories of all the dogs that unremarkably sink teeth into people. Still, it provides a useful corrective: it complicates our understanding of the world. It ensures that we do not become overly fixated on the idea that everything that we study follows patterns defined by regime categories.

---

[11] In fairness, the authors also acknowledge facts that are more in keeping with prevalent ideas about regime categories, such as the CCP's close control over appointments to university leadership and the tightening of political strictures under President Xi Jinping (Kapur and Perry 2018, 232–33).

Concept Development

By their nature, comparisons among highly dissimilar political systems practically require the researcher to confront deep conceptual issues – and qualitative research has an important role to play in so doing. If, as Gary Goertz (2006) writes, "a concept involves a theoretical and empirical analysis of the object or phenomenon referred to by the word" (4), it is natural that those working at and around conceptual boundaries will carry out much analytical work. As Schaffer (2015) illustrates, to fix the meaning of a given concept within even one society, let alone multiple contexts, can be fraught with problems of one-sidedness and universalism and implicated in power relationships. Whether one adopts the former's necessary and sufficient condition approach, or the latter's bottom-up elucidation, or some other method, the need for careful attention to concepts in such research is clear.

Comparison across dissimilar systems often provides opportunities for conceptual innovation and development even as it poses risks of "stretching." Far-reaching comparisons can, of course, draw on existing conceptual definitions, but I argue that they are relatively more likely to create opportunities for new departures. This need not, and should not, take the form of haphazardly extending concepts to places where they do not fit. Rather, it can mean defining or discovering categories of empirical phenomena that differ from what is already known and accepted – whether or not they are so novel as to constitute "unidentified political objects" (Jourde 2009, 201). These might be tangible, such as a particular type of organizational structure, or intangible, such as a kind of dynamic within a social movement.

Kellee Tsai (2016) gives special emphasis to the conceptual fruits of her research, spanning China and India, on the developmental role of local states and entrepreneurial diasporas. She extends the usually domestic-centered concept of "state-society relations" to encompass transnational migrants and diasporic communities, the actors who drive cross-border informal finance in Wenzhou and Surat and tech-sector start-ups in Zhongguancun and Bangalore. She also enriches Albert Hirschman's (1970) "exit, voice, and loyalty" typology, noting: "Migration (exit) may not be permanent, but even when it is, remaining abroad does not preclude deep-rooted identity (local and/or national loyalty), or meaningful impact on homeland affairs (voice)" (Tsai 2016, 336).[12] The result of her study is a conception of "cosmopolitan capitalism," in which local rather than national developmental states join with globally mobile populations to pursue distinctive and dynamic patterns of growth.

Weller et al.'s (2017) comparison of the charitable role of religious organizations across three political settings and regimes generates numerous

---

[12] Jonathan Fox (2007, chap. 10) separately makes related points in research involving comparison across the United States-Mexico border.

memorable concepts. Rather than employing the established but Western-centric term "faith-based organizations," they find that "engaged religion" better suits specifically Chinese groups, which do not necessarily take NGO-like forms and for whom faith per se is not central (17). In their relationships with host governments of various persuasions, these groups take part in a process of "political merit-making," from which they obtain space to operate and perhaps influence, while the state receives legitimation (59). The lay volunteers who participate in their projects do so in a process of "civic selving," constituting themselves as "a generous and loving self, resonating with cosmopolitan ideas about a universal and unbounded good" (14). The enterprise as a whole, pioneered by Tzu Chi and emulated by other Buddhist groups, constitutes "industrialized philanthropy," a term that captures its massive scale and systematized processes of accounting and media publicity, among other dimensions (2).

In my China-Taiwan study, the very process of working across systemic differences rooted in parallel but divergent histories forced me to re-confront the conceptual question, "What is this a case *of*?" Originally, I thought of the RCs as mass organizations, common in all communist systems. What became clear through the process of reframing, however, was that, in fact, this topic was one of broader relevance found not merely in the cases of China and Taiwan but also in a diverse set of political systems. I conceptualized the state-backed neighborhood organizations that I studied as instances of a phenomenon I called "administrative grassroots engagement," institutions "in which states create, sponsor, and manage networks of organizations at the most local of levels that facilitate governance and policing by building personal relationships with members of society" (Read 2012, 3–4). This category emerged from an extended process of research: conducting more than twenty months of immersive fieldwork in China and Taiwan, reading widely, working with other scholars, making a field research trip to a third country, and ultimately coediting a book on related cases (Read and Pekkanen 2009).

Such possibilities for innovation should be recognized as an important part of what cross-system comparison accomplishes. (The reader will note a kinship with the casing process discussed by Soss, Chapter 5, this volume, and with the points on conceptual development in Htun and Jensenius, Chapter 10, this volume.)

Scoping and Framing the Comparison

Particularly when considering widely varying political systems, decisions about the scope and framing of the comparison can require substantial research and be consequential contributions in themselves. In the course of designing a cross-national comparative project (not necessarily at the beginning), the researcher establishes a universe of relevant cases – which may constitute a novel and unfamiliar set. Much methodological advice (e.g., Seawright and Gerring 2008) addresses the question of how to select cases once that universe has been defined, but the prior step may be more a matter of creative perceptiveness than of following rules and prescriptions. In Zhang's book, for example, the mere juxtaposition of Beijing with, say, Chicago is itself a startling and intellectually disruptive act for readers accustomed to thinking of these places in completely different theoretical contexts. As with framing processes more generally, these decisions create an "interpretive schemata that simplifies and condenses the 'world out there' by selectively punctuating and encoding objects, situations, events, experiences, and sequences of actions" (Snow and Benford 1992, 135). Having done this, the researcher scrutinizes the crucial attributes that include certain cases in a common set and exclude others. These characteristics, on which so much hinges, require ongoing evaluation in relation to the purpose and justification for the comparison.

As discussed earlier, Duara and Perry (2018b) began their edited volume on China and India with a coauthored chapter that drew out common themes in the two countries' development over the past century and a half. Looked at one way, this provided justification for the comparisons laid out in the respective chapters that followed. But the end result is more than this. One could easily see China and India as simply belonging to incommensurate categories, the gulf between them too wide to provide for much dialogue beyond tale-of-the-tape measures like annual growth in population or GDP. But their volume, including the introduction as well as the framing mechanisms in each of the eight substantive chapters, stands to change the way we look upon these two ancient states. Whether at the level of city pairs such as Shanghai and Bombay, or developments in social policy, or social movements, the book makes a strong and novel argument that each deserves to be looked at in light of the other. Though these chapters' individual findings might of course be rebutted or contradicted, the broader act of putting the two countries within a common spotlight seems likely to have lasting consequences for future research agendas. Something similar could be said about Hurst's (2018) comparison of China and Indonesia, two countries that generally figure in different kinds of scholarly conversations, divergent as they are not just in current regime type but in colonial history, demographics, religion, and other respects. Indeed, Hurst writes that his is "the first side-by-side comparison" of the two (249). The book's act of reframing truly encourages us to think about these countries in novel ways.

In the course of studying the form of state-society engagement that I found in the neighborhoods of China and Taiwan, I became aware that what I was studying could be found in other countries as well, including Japan, South Korea, Vietnam, Singapore, and Indonesia. These contexts span a range from autocracies to democracies: regime type seems less important than having a certain kind of statist and corporatist orientation in which the state proactively structures and draws upon grassroots institutions. Exploring the boundaries and background of this conceptual category brought into focus the historical connections that link certain key cases. Some are fairly well known among specialists, such as imperial China's *bao-jia*, an institution that organized households into clusters and large groups, each with a designated leader, mainly for purposes of security. At the same time, not all variants can be traced to direct historical predecessors, nor is the phenomenon entirely confined to East and Southeast Asia. Framing the comparison in a new way enabled different and deeper forms of conceptual work than would have been possible in a single-country study. For example, while administrative grassroots institutions are always distinct from autonomous civil society groups, they pursue related activities and, in some ways, mimic the functions, activities, and rewards of voluntary groups. So, too, while the organizations in question overlap and have some commonalities with Gregory Kasza's (1995) administered mass organizations, they also buck this categorization in various ways, from the voluntary nature of citizens' participation to their persistence in political systems that have transitioned from authoritarian to democratic regimes. They thus hold a number of conceptual surprises.

The point here is to emphasize the important aspects of comparison that involve framing the cases and defining the subject under study. Bringing together a set of units across unfamiliar lines, the researcher makes a contribution by encouraging readers to look at the political universe in new ways, very much as in the perspectival comparisons that Schaffer (Chapter 3, this volume) eloquently discusses. This cuts across boundaries that Sartori sought to harden rather than relax.

Innovations through framing and concept development are separate things and need not co-occur in the same project, yet the two are related. As we shift focus away from the familiar and toward less-similar cases, our attention is drawn to conceptual aspects of the cases that went unnoticed or seemed unimportant in other perspectives. ("Unlike the other cases, Indonesia never had A and instead had B, yet it is similar to the others in terms of C, and I wonder if that operates through the same mechanism.") At the same time, spotlighting different features of the concepts may catalyze efforts to find related, heretofore unexamined, cases that share those features. ("I wonder if Malaysia has something like that.")

CONCLUSION

It is no accident that a new wave of cross-regime-type research involving China is emerging; the reasons for it are many. China's political system, whatever its future fate, has diverged enough from its state-socialist brethren to demand study from new perspectives, not merely as a variety of communism. It has shown enough staying power and dynamism to be considered as a fairly stable comparative referent in itself, not merely as an ephemeral case of transition. And its very distinctiveness provides important opportunities to observe political phenomena in a different context from what is found elsewhere. As seen by the various case pairings and comparative foci in the works reviewed here, many different aspects of Chinese politics shed light on counterparts elsewhere (and vice versa), from protests to urban preservation, from state-society relations to legal regimes. With China not merely embracing but also pioneering new technologies from social media to digital surveillance and globalizing rapidly through flows of people, goods, capital, and knowledge, such opportunities will no doubt continue to increase.[13]

The methodological lessons here are not, I am sure, confined to research involving China but have more general applicability. Comparing things that are embedded within fundamentally different political systems is hard. In addition to the ordinary challenges of cross-national comparison – possible language differences, spreading one's time and effort across different locales, asymmetries in the researcher's degree of expertise and extent of local contacts, and so on – such studies confront special issues that are very much related to the pitfalls Sartori identified. The point is not that all comparisons are equally valid or illuminating. There is indeed such a thing as conceptual stretching.

Still, comparison across regime types presents far more constructive possibilities than Sartori acknowledged. His critique should not deter us from considering ambitious and creative juxtapositions. Comparison across dissimilar systems does not necessarily mean committing errors of conceptual incompatibility or blurring categories to the point of meaninglessness. The key to avoiding trouble is not to confine oneself only to comparing political systems of the same species. Rather, it lies in remaining aware of the full meanings and contextual dependencies of concepts one is working with, staying alive to the danger that the comparison is putting square pegs in round holes. It requires a combination of thoughtful caution and initiative.[14]

Though it is of course not possible to spell out all the things that one might learn through comparative projects of the sort considered here, I have tried to categorize some major kinds of contributions that they can make. While comparing across systems that are quite unlike each other in many respects, such studies only sometimes and partially take the form of classical Millian most-different-systems analyses, which isolate common causal factors that explain a shared outcome.[15] My China-Taiwan study could in part be read this way, as could Christensen's China-US comparison. In other cases like

---

[13] I thank Elizabeth Perry for suggesting this point.

[14] Boswell, Corbett, and Rhodes's (2019) stimulating book also makes an argument for unorthodox comparisons, including those across "species," though along somewhat different lines from those of this chapter. For example, by privileging "decentered explanations" based on "the contingent beliefs and actions of individuals" in varied social settings, it downplays the importance of context a priori in ways I would not (1, 4).

[15] Among a sample of journal articles examined by Koivu and Hinze (2017), about 10 percent invoked a "least similar systems" logic (1025).

Zhang's or Kapur and Perry's, however, difference is what is explained. And often the value comes from things other than explaining convergence or divergence. More commonly, comparison between unlike political contexts generates new conceptual departures and striking reflections about the very regime types that we commonly take as defining features. And often, a large part of the payoff comes from creating new juxtapositions, from capturing aspects of politics within a novel kind of framework.

Finding novelty while avoiding stretching is facilitated by up-close, in-the-field analysis. It is no accident that almost all of the examples discussed earlier involved substantial field research by the authors.[16] Immersion, whether in textual evidence or in field sites, gives researchers continual opportunities to sharpen their sense of how best to conceptualize the political world (Kapiszewski, MacLean, and Read 2015, 20–26). Without it, identifying the common basis for comparison might be far from obvious, much less justifying it. A comparison framed around widely differing places could ring hollow unless supported by deep understanding of the respective locales. The sparks of insight upon which novel concepts are built or the reflections on how comparison sheds light on a country's overall political regime are likely to draw upon the kind of nuanced understanding that more or less requires experience on the ground. One needs this kind of understanding to navigate between the errors of a taxonomical stay-in-your-lane rigidity on the one hand and pell-mell conceptual conflation on the other.

REFERENCES

Bernstein, Thomas P. 2013. "Resilience and Collapse in China and the Soviet Union." In *Why Communism Did Not Collapse: Understanding Authoritarian Regime Resilience in Asia and Europe*, edited by Martin K. Dimitrov, 40–63. Cambridge: Cambridge University Press.

Boswell, John, Jack Corbett, and R. A. W. Rhodes. 2019. *The Art and Craft of Comparison*. Cambridge: Cambridge University Press.

Chen, Bin, Terry L. Cooper, and Rong Sun. 2009. "Spontaneous or Constructed? Neighborhood Governance Reforms in Los Angeles and Shanghai." *Public Administration Review* 69: S108–15.

Cheng, Tun-jen, and Gang Lin. 2008. "Competitive Elections: Experience in Taiwan and Recent Developments in China." In *Political Change in China: Comparisons with Taiwan*, edited by Bruce Gilley and Larry Diamond, 163–83. Boulder, CO: Lynn Rienner.

Christensen, Thomas J. 1996. *Useful Adversaries: Grand Strategy, Domestic Mobilization, and Sino-American Conflict, 1947–1958*. Princeton, NJ: Princeton University Press.

---

[16] The exception is Christensen's book, which is based on deep immersion in historical documents and archives.

Dickson, Bruce J. 1997. *Democratization in China and Taiwan: The Adaptability of Leninist Parties*. New York: Oxford University Press.

Dillon, Nara. 2018. "Parallel Trajectories: The Development of the Welfare State in China and India." In *Beyond Regimes: China and India Compared*, edited by Prasenjit Duara and Elizabeth J. Perry, 173–207. Cambridge, MA: Harvard University, Asia Center.

Dimitrov, Martin K. 2013. "Understanding Communist Collapse and Resilience." In *Why Communism Did Not Collapse: Understanding Authoritarian Regime Resilience in Asia and Europe*, edited by Martin K. Dimitrov, 3–39. Cambridge: Cambridge University Press.

Disch, Lisa. 2011. "Toward a Mobilization Conception of Democratic Representation." *American Political Science Review* 105 (1): 100–114.

Duara, Prasenjit, and Elizabeth J. Perry. 2018a. "Beyond Regimes: An Introduction." In *Beyond Regimes: China and India Compared*, edited by Prasenjit Duara and Elizabeth J. Perry, 1–27. Cambridge, MA: Harvard University, Asia Center.

  2018b. *Beyond Regimes: China and India Compared*. Cambridge, MA: Harvard University, Asia Center.

Frazier, Mark W. 2018. "China and the Challenges of Comparison." In *The SAGE Handbook of Contemporary China*, edited by Weiping Wu and Mark W. Frazier, 1227–44. Thousand Oaks, CA: SAGE.

  2019. *The Power of Place: Contentious Politics in Twentieth-Century Shanghai and Bombay*. New York: Cambridge University Press.

Fox, Jonathan. 2007. *Accountability Politics: Power and Voice in Rural Mexico*. Oxford: Oxford University Press.

Fu, Diana. 2018. *Mobilizing without the Masses: Control and Contention in China*. Cambridge: Cambridge University Press.

García Bedolla, Lisa, and Melissa R. Michelson. 2012. *Mobilizing Inclusion: Transforming the Electorate through Get-out-the-Vote Campaigns*. New Haven, CT: Yale University Press.

Gilley, Bruce. 2008. "Comparing and Rethinking Political Change in China and Taiwan." In *Political Change in China: Comparisons with Taiwan*, edited by Bruce Gilley and Larry Diamond, 1–23. Boulder, CO: Lynn Rienner.

Goertz, Gary. 2006. *Social Science Concepts: A User's Guide*. Princeton, NJ: Princeton University Press.

Han, Hahrie. 2014. *How Organizations Develop Activists: Civic Associations and Leadership in the 21st Century*. Oxford: Oxford University Press.

Hirschman, Albert O. 1970. *Exit, Voice, and Loyalty: Responses to Decline in Firms, Organizations, and States*. Cambridge, MA: Harvard University Press.

Ho, Selina. 2019. *Thirsty Cities: Social Contracts and Public Goods Provision in China and India*. New York: Cambridge University Press.

Hurst, William. 2017. "Treating What Ails the Study of Chinese Politics." *Chinoiresie* (blog), September 15, 2017. www.chinoiresie.info/treating-what-ails-the-study-of-chinese-politics/

  2018. *Ruling before the Law: The Politics of Legal Regimes in China and Indonesia*. New York: Cambridge University Press.

Jourde, Cédric. 2009. "The Ethnographic Sensibility: Overlooked Authoritarian Dynamics and Islamic Ambivalences in West Africa." In *Political Ethnography:*

What Immersion Contributes to the Study of Power, edited by Edward Schatz, 201–16. Chicago: University of Chicago Press.

Kapiszewski, Diana, Lauren M. MacLean, and Benjamin L. Read. 2015. *Field Research in Political Science: Practices and Principles*. Cambridge: Cambridge University Press.

Kapur, Devesh, and Elizabeth J. Perry. 2018. "Higher Education Reform in China and India: The Role of the State." In *Beyond Regimes: China and India Compared*, edited by Prasenjit Duara and Elizabeth J. Perry, 208–53. Cambridge, MA: Harvard University, Asia Center.

Kasza, Gregory J. 1995. *The Conscription Society: Administered Mass Organizations*. New Haven, CT: Yale University Press.

Koivu, Kendra L., and Annika Marlen Hinze. 2017. "Cases of Convenience? The Divergence of Theory from Practice in Case Selection in Qualitative and Mixed-Methods Research." *PS: Political Science & Politics* 50 (4): 1023–27.

LaPalombara, Joseph. 1975. "Monoliths or Plural Systems: Through Conceptual Lenses Darkly." *Studies in Comparative Communism* 8 (3): 305–32.

Looney, Kristen E. 2020. *Mobilizing for Development: The Modernization of Rural East Asia*. Ithaca, NY: Cornell University Press.

Nair, Manjusha. 2018. "State-Embedded Villages: Rural Protests and Rights Awareness in India and China." In *Beyond Regimes: China and India Compared*, edited by Prasenjit Duara and Elizabeth J. Perry, 143–70. Cambridge, MA: Harvard University, Asia Center.

O'Brien, Kevin J. 1996. "Rightful Resistance." *World Politics* 49 (1): 31–55.

O'Brien, Kevin J., and Lianjiang Li. 2006. *Rightful Resistance in Rural China*. Cambridge: Cambridge University Press.

Ong, Lynette H. 2020. "'Land Grabbing' in an Autocracy and a Multi-Party Democracy: China and India Compared." *Journal of Contemporary Asia* 50 (3): 361–79.

Pei, Minxin. 1994. *From Reform to Revolution: The Demise of Communism in China and the Soviet Union*. Cambridge, MA: Harvard University Press.

Read, Benjamin L. 2012. *Roots of the State: Neighborhood Organization and Social Networks in Beijing and Taipei*. Stanford, CA: Stanford University Press.

———. 2018a. "Problems and Possibilities of Comparison across Regime Types." *QMMR: Qualitative and Multi-Method Research* 16 (1): 33–38.

———. 2018b. "Serial Interviews: When and Why to Talk to Someone More than Once." *International Journal of Qualitative Methods* 17 (1): 1–10.

Read, Benjamin L., and Robert Pekkanen, eds. 2009. *Local Organizations and Urban Governance in East and Southeast Asia: Straddling State and Society*. Milton Park, Abingdon, Oxon: Routledge.

Sartori, Giovanni. 1970. "Concept Misformation in Comparative Politics." *American Political Science Review* 64 (4): 1033–53.

Schaffer, Frederic Charles. 2015. *Elucidating Social Science Concepts: An Interpretivist Guide*. New York: Routledge.

Schwartz, Benjamin I. 1951. *Chinese Communism and the Rise of Mao*. Cambridge, MA: Harvard University Press.

Seawright, Jason, and John Gerring. 2008. "Case Selection Techniques in Case Study Research: A Menu of Qualitative and Quantitative Options." *Political Research Quarterly* 61 (2): 294–308.

Snow, David A., and Robert D. Benford. 1992. "Master Frames and Cycles of Protest." In *Frontiers in Social Movement Theory*, 133–55. New Haven, CT: Yale University Press.

Solinger, Dorothy J. 2008. "Business Groups: For or against the Regime?" In *Political Change in China: Comparisons with Taiwan*, edited by Bruce Gilley and Larry Diamond, 95–114. Boulder, CO: Lynn Rienner.

2009. *States' Gains, Labor's Losses: China, France, and Mexico Choose Global Liaisons, 1980–2000*. Ithaca, NY: Cornell University Press.

Strauss, Julia C. 2019. *State Formation in China and Taiwan: Bureaucracy, Campaign, and Performance*. Cambridge: Cambridge University Press.

Tilly, Charles. 1984. *Big Structures, Large Processes, Huge Comparisons*. New York: Russell Sage Foundation.

Tsai, Kellee S. 2016. "Cosmopolitan Capitalism: Local State-Society Relations in China and India." *The Journal of Asian Studies* 75 (2): 335–61.

Tsai, Lily L. 2017. "Bringing in China: Insights for Building Comparative Political Theory." *Comparative Political Studies* 50 (3): 295–328.

Walder, Andrew G., ed. 1995. *The Waning of the Communist State: Economic Origins of Political Decline in China and Hungary*. Berkeley: University of California Press.

2016. "Bending the Arc of Chinese History: The Cultural Revolution's Paradoxical Legacy." *The China Quarterly* 227: 613–31.

Weller, Robert P., C. Julia Huang, Keping Wu, and Lizhu Fan. 2017. *Religion and Charity: The Social Life of Goodness in Chinese Societies*. Cambridge: Cambridge University Press.

Wong, Joseph. 2008. "Maintaining KMT Dominance: Party Adaptation in Authoritarian and Democratic Taiwan." In *Political Transitions in Dominant Party Systems: Learning to Lose*, edited by Edward Friedman and Joseph Wong, 57–74. Abingdon, Oxon & New York: Routledge.

Wright, Teresa. 2001. *The Perils of Protest: State Repression and Student Activism in China and Taiwan*. Honolulu: University of Hawaiʻi Press.

Zhang, Yue. 2013. *The Fragmented Politics of Urban Preservation: Beijing, Chicago, and Paris*. Globalization and Community, Vol. 22. Minneapolis: University of Minnesota Press.

2020. "The Urban Turn in Comparative Politics: Cities as the Anchor of Cross-Nation, Cross-Regime Comparison." *APSA Comparative Politics Newsletter* 30 (1): 13–22.

12

Comparisons with an Ethnographic Sensibility
Studies of Protest and Vigilantism

Erica S. Simmons
University of Wisconsin–Madison

Nicholas Rush Smith
City University of New York–City College

To what extent can an ethnographic sensibility enhance comparison? Recent years have seen a renewed interest in controlled comparisons in qualitative research designs within political science (e.g., McAdam, Tarrow, and Tilly 2001; Dunning 2012; Slater and Ziblatt 2013; Gisselquist 2014; Giraudy, Moncada, and Snyder 2019). Broadly, the recent work on controlled comparison – an approach that emphasizes case selection based on either contrasting outcomes in spite of similar potentially explanatory characteristics or similar outcomes in spite of contrasting potentially explanatory characteristics – suggests that the method combines the best of both the qualitative and the quantitative traditions. Controlled comparisons are useful, this literature argues, because they allow scholars to trace out dynamic political processes while accounting for the effects of possible confounding explanations. Such methodological moves, however, do not come without costs. In particular, this approach to case selection often leads researchers to de-emphasize the critical role that meaning making plays in political processes.

We argue that approaching comparison with an "ethnographic sensibility" (Pader 2006; Schatz 2009) – that is, being sensitive to how informants make sense of their worlds and incorporating meaning into our analyses – can strengthen comparative qualitative research. Adopting an ethnographic sensibility would enhance the quality of scholarly arguments by incorporating the processes through which actors ascribe meanings to their lived experiences and the political processes in which they are enmeshed. Because social science

---

This paper draws from two short, previously published papers (Simmons and Smith 2015, 2017) to elaborate arguments that could not be made in the abbreviated versions due to space constraints. Many thanks to Dipali Mukopadhayay for her comments on a draft presented at the Annual Meeting of the American Political Science Association in August 2018.

arguments often involve accounts of individual actors' interests, ideas, or impressions, it is imperative to place such cognitive arguments in a broader cultural context. Adopting an ethnographic sensibility requires attention not only to that context but also to the political and social meanings that make that context intelligible. This approach builds on scholarly efforts to embrace complexity in historical analysis (see Slater and Simmons 2010). However, it pushes us beyond the methods of difference and agreement that continue to guide much qualitative comparative work (for a discussion, see Slater and Ziblatt 2013) by asking scholars to make the complex meanings that often shape politics the object of inquiry – something that is rarely done even in the best recent qualitative comparative work.

To compare with an ethnographic sensibility also changes the goal of comparison. The goal of most quantitative or controlled comparative methods is to develop either "generalizable" arguments or arguments that "travel" or are "portable" to other contexts; that is, the goal is to find patterns of politics that are mechanistically produced across broadly similar political contexts. By contrast, we advocate for a different goal for comparative research: *translation*. As we explain in greater depth later in this chapter, the logic of translation does not assume mechanistic reproduction. Instead, much like with linguistic translation, the goal of comparing for translation is to develop ideas that are intelligible or recognizable in a different context, even as the context will change the ways in which an idea or political practice is interpreted or enacted.

To illustrate these arguments, this chapter utilizes two recent research projects that approach comparison with an ethnographic sensibility: a comparison of anti-market protests in Bolivia and Mexico and a comparative analysis of vigilantism in South Africa. In the case of anti-market protests, the chapter shows how the meanings grievances take on play a critical role in social movement origins and dynamics. By bringing an ethnographic sensibility to the comparison, the analysis of Bolivia and Mexico challenges dominant assumptions in the social movements field. Specifically, a large body of literature had argued that while grievances are important in social movements, we could take the presence of a grievance as essentially given and therefore ignore it for explanatory purposes. However, the Bolivia-Mexico comparison shows that the literature had failed to theorize *how* grievances matter. To show that understanding the meaning of grievances is the key to understanding the relationship between grievances and mobilization, comparative work is required. But it only reveals the dynamics at work when meaning making plays a central role in the comparison. Thus, comparison with an ethnographic sensibility shows how the meanings with which different grievances are imbued can play a critical role in the mobilization process. This argument is then translatable in a number of different ways. At the most general level, it invites us to think about how meaning making around grievances might matter to mobilization. But as we will show, it also develops more specific insights that

Comparisons with an Ethnographic Sensibility 233

might shed light on everything from the role of daily practices in producing mobilizing identifications to the ways in which insecurities might be heightened in neoliberal economies.

The second case – a comparative analysis of vigilantism in South Africa – reveals other strengths of comparing with an ethnographic sensibility: the ability to complicate intuitive explanations for political phenomena and refine categories of analysis. The South African subnational case comparison presented here explores the relationship between crime and vigilantism. While both intuition and a large body of research suggest that high crime rates lead to vigilantism, initial research revealed that South African townships with widely differing crime rates experienced vigilantism. This suggested that crime was at best a partial and potentially a misleading explanation for vigilantism. Yet during the course of research, interlocutors frequently cited crime as a concern. Considering this talk of crime in relation to actual crime rates suggests that something about the social *meaning* of crime – as opposed to its mere presence or relative intensity – connected crime and vigilantism. Adopting an ethnographic sensibility allowed the researcher to examine a common, intuitive explanation that was incomplete and to place a static variable (crime rates) into a rich, meaning-laden context, which included socially understood crimes like witchcraft that were not subject to prosecution through the courts. Even more, as we discuss in greater detail later, the poor fit between existing theories of vigilantism and patterns of violence common across cases suggested that commonly held ideas about state effectiveness and state failure translated poorly into local contexts, allowing Smith (2019) to challenge how political scientists think of such concepts in the first place.

This chapter is divided into four sections. First, we discuss what we mean by an ethnographic sensibility and how such a sensibility can productively contribute to comparative research. Second, we argue that an ethnographic sensibility encourages three core shifts in how scholars think about comparison. By recognizing the limits of our abilities to control in comparative research designs, appreciating the ways meaning enhances comparative analyses, and focusing on processes as the object of comparison, an ethnographic sensibility allows scholars to think differently about how and what they compare. Third, we describe how comparing with an ethnographic sensibility shifts the goal of comparison from a logic of generalizability to one of translation. Finally, to show the analytical use of meaning for comparative research designs, the chapter describes two research projects employing such a design. These examples illustrate the value of comparison with an ethnographic sensibility for comparative political inquiry more generally.

EMBRACING AN ETHNOGRAPHIC SENSIBILITY

When scholars adopt an ethnographic sensibility, they pay attention to how people make sense of their worlds; they seek to "glean the meanings that the people under study attribute to their social and political reality" (Schatz 2009, 5). The approach requires that scholars attend to how an individual's perceptions of the world are embedded in their interactions with others, commit to understanding the work that language and other symbols do, and are open to incoherence and instability as part of explanatory frameworks.

An ethnographic sensibility has informed the ways that political scientists study everything from civil war violence (Wood 2003), to the formation of public opinion (Walsh 2009), to compliance under authoritarian regimes (Wedeen 1999). Scholars often explore these topics through ethnographic research rooted in participant observation. However, in spite of dominant assumptions in the field, the embrace of an ethnographic sensibility need not be – and is not – limited to the domain of ethnographers. Nor does an ethnographic sensibility require the long-term immersion in field sites or participant observation methods typical of anthropologists (see Pader 2006; Schatz 2009), though both may be beneficial. Scholars can develop understandings of the social processes through which people make sense of their worlds through close readings of archival material, examinations of contemporary texts, interviews, and even survey data, to name just a few methods. What matters most is *how* scholars approach the material gathered from these sources – that is, paying attention to the political meanings embedded in these materials. Moreover, the fact that a variety of scholars with a variety of sources can successfully approach their research with an ethnographic sensibility is precisely why we think the arguments made here are important for political scientists broadly. When political scientists incorporate meaning into their arguments – including all of the ambiguity and contradictions that these processes entail – they can potentially offer new understandings of well-traveled terrain or encourage new lines of inquiry, as the examples we discuss suggest.

SHIFTING HOW WE THINK ABOUT COMPARISON

Approaching comparison with attention to meaning creates a mode of analysis that is useful for political science but would require rethinking the goals and object of comparative research designs. Instead of approaching comparison with the goal of exerting control over variables, the comparative approach we propose entails incorporating meaning-making practices at work in the cases. Such attention would entail three core shifts in how we think about and employ comparative methods. The shifts are relevant not only to research designs but also to how scholars formulate questions and collect and analyze data.

First, an ethnographic sensibility requires that we recognize the limitations of efforts to control for theoretically relevant variation (Sewell 2005, chap. 3; Yanow 2014). These efforts create unnecessary analytical binds by requiring that researchers make several problematic assumptions: first, about what might be theoretically relevant; second, that they can see and measure everything of theoretical relevance; third, that the same empirical phenomena work in the same way in different times and places; and, fourth, that these phenomena are independent of one another.[1] Furthermore, efforts to control via case selection can push scholars to put very different social and political practices into similar categories, thus creating the illusion of having "controlled" for a potentially relevant phenomenon. An interest in identifying similarities and differences among cases in an effort to enhance comparative analysis need not force scholars to ignore important contextual complexities. Scholars can and should go into the field or enter the archives with what they think might be relevant similarities and differences in mind. But designing a research project so that potentially relevant factors could be dismissed through control would be inappropriate for scholars approaching research with an ethnographic sensibility: control would be seen as foreclosing opportunities to understand how context-specific nuance might have important implications for the research question. Instead, they would want to understand and incorporate relevant meanings at work in the cases at hand by seeing a political phenomenon through the eyes of their informants, whether they are living human subjects or historical figures found in archives.

For example, when we control for variables such as levels of ethnic self-identification to eliminate them as potential explanations, we assume that ethnicity does the same work across time and space or that it means the same thing in one place as it does in another. We must also assume that the meanings of ethnicity or the processes through which ethnic self-identification takes place can be abstracted away from the political and social context in which they exist. If we are conducting a controlled comparison, we take these similar abstracted levels of ethnic self-identification in two cases where outcomes differ and say with confidence that ethnic self-identification cannot explain the divergence. Yet adopting an ethnographic sensibility suggests that we can say no such thing. Ethnic self-identification may do very different political work in the two cases because ethnicity might mean something very different to actors on the ground – even if the level of identification is the same – and could thus still play a role in shaping the political dynamics at work in the cases.[2]

Because the contexts in which people identify with various ethnic categories may play an important role in the political phenomenon under study, categorizing all instances of self-identification as the same encourages us to create general categories that obscure important differences. In her discussion of scholarship on Islamist politics, for instance, Jillian Schwedler (2015a) finds

---

[1] George and Bennett (2005, 155) identify three slightly different assumptions: a deterministic causal relationship that is either necessary or sufficient, the identification of all causally relevant variables prior to analysis, and the cases represent all possible causal paths. We do not disagree with the importance of these assumptions but argue that even if met (a highly difficult condition), the additional concerns we outline here must be considered.

[2] Sewell (2005, chap. 3) has made a similar point about the problems of controlling for alternative explanations in historical sociology research. See Madrid (2012) for a good example of how ethnic identification can do different work across time and place.

that this inclination to create group categories limits our understandings of political practices; the application of an ethnographic sensibility would minimize these tendencies.[3] Finally, ethnicity should not be conceived as independent from the political systems in which it is produced, suggesting that *ethnic self-identification* and *system of government* cannot be treated as separate independent variables (Laitin 1986; Wedeen 2008). Bringing an ethnographic sensibility to these kinds of studies would push us to incorporate the complexities of seemingly obvious categories into the comparisons themselves. Of course, much of the most highly regarded work in the qualitative comparative tradition already demonstrates a commitment to context.[4] However, comparison with an ethnographic sensibility does more than simply bring context into comparison; it allows us to compare the ambiguous and shifting meanings at work in the political worlds under study. Through explicit attention to meaning-making practices like the political language people use, the symbols they deploy, or the rituals in which they participate (to name a few), comparison informed by an ethnographic sensibility adds unique analytic leverage to even the most context-attentive studies.

This explicit incorporation of meaning into our comparative research designs is the second core shift we outline. When case study comparisons require scholars to live and work in particular field sites, they often cannot help but observe what political practices mean in particular contexts. As a result, attention to meaning may implicitly be incorporated into their analysis of even the most positivist accounts of political behavior. However, positivist comparative practices do not *require* that scholars do so; in some cases, the assumptions on which these studies are based produce "objects of inquiry that are incommensurable with interpretivist social science" (Wedeen 2002, 717). The effect is that more often than not, both at the design and at the analytic stages, scholars categorize political phenomena while ignoring the meanings that words or practices take on and how those meanings shape politics.

By paying attention to how the people we study – whether they are research participants, figures who appear in archival materials, or the authors of texts – understand their worlds, an ethnographic sensibility adds depth to our understanding of politics beyond the incorporation of context. Ethnographers ask questions about what that context means and how it shapes actors' understandings of their worlds. Scholars employing the comparative method with an ethnographic sensibility would not control for levels of indigenous self-identification because the method itself requires an investigation of what those social facts *mean* to political actors on the ground and the roles those meanings play in shaping social processes. This form of comparison does not take the

---

[3] Notably, Schwedler (2015b) says we would "do well to ... make different kinds of practices and processes as our objects of analyses."
[4] See, for example, Locke and Thelen's (1995) discussion of contextualized comparisons.

relevance of a particular variable for granted (how could we possibly meet the requirement of Mill's method of agreement that before we conduct a study we know what the relevant variables are?) but inductively problematizes both its role and meaning in context. Explicitly calling on scholars to compare the work that meanings do in apparently different times and places and bringing an ethnographic sensibility to comparison offer a way out of the analytical binds created through the illusion of control.

Applying an ethnographic sensibility to comparative research radically alters the objects and goals of comparison – a third core shift we advocate. Where political scientists typically compare similar or dissimilar outcomes, ethnographically oriented comparison highlights political processes – the dynamics and practices that shape political life – as the proverbial outcome of interest. By advocating for attention to meaning making, we encourage scholars to understand political phenomena as constantly evolving, often in relationship to contingent events in local contexts, rather than as mechanical phenomena with relatively predictable outcomes.[5] The objects of a social scientist's inquiry are never fixed, frozen, or static – and, therefore, they need to be understood through the lens of political processes. This suggests a move away from the language of variables to one that allows scholars to incorporate fluid and potentially contradictory political processes into their analyses.

In sum, by bringing an ethnographic sensibility to comparison, scholars can rethink what comparison means and the kinds of insights it can produce. They can engage critically with what attempts to control for alternative explanations are actually able to tell about political processes, encourage a focus on the political effects of practices as opposed to outcomes, and allow fieldwork or archival research to define the relevant points of comparison. Adopting this approach would also help scholars refine theoretical models and challenge taken-for-granted conceptual categories, a process we describe in greater detail in the next section by advocating that political scientists shift the goals of their research from a logic of generalization to one of translation.

RETHINKING THE GOALS OF COMPARISON: FROM GENERALIZABILITY TO TRANSLATION

If adopting an ethnographic sensibility can shift how scholars think about the practice of comparative research, it can also shift the goals of that research. The current gold standard for comparative research is to develop an argument that can be generalized. As Przeworski and Teune (1970) famously argued, the goal of comparative social science should be to eliminate proper names from one's analysis, so that one's theories are not bound by the particulars of any specific

---

[5] We thank an anonymous reviewer for pushing us to clarify this point.

case and can therefore approach universal explanation.[6] More recently, comparativists oriented to small-n research have modified this view to focus on how causal mechanisms work similarly across cases (Grzymala-Busse 2010; Imai et al. 2011; Ahram 2013; Saylor 2018; Slater and Ziblatt 2013; see also Hirschman and Reed 2014), focusing on the ways in which arguments travel or are portable to different contexts – goals that have a family resemblance to the goals of generalizability outlined by Przeworski and Teune (1970) (see also King, Keohane, and Verba 1994).

Yet even as they use different languages, both logics are essentially ones of mechanical reproduction. Like the inner workings of a watch, mechanisms should work the same in similar environments. Ironically, though, for small-n researchers, the emphasis on discovering such mechanisms as the standard by which a qualitative study should be judged may have the effect of effacing the importance of context, which qualitative scholars often argue is the value of their methods.

Still, the goals of generalizability, travelling, and portability remain powerful as both intellectual ideals and intellectual habits that discipline the production of political scientific knowledge. How many job talks have collapsed or journal submissions have been rejected when a candidate or author has been ill equipped to respond to a questioner or reviewer who demands to know, "But can your argument explain what happened in Country X?" The implication of such questions is typically twofold. First, because the mechanisms derived from Country Y do not obviously travel to Country X, the arguments are at best of interest only to scholars of Country Y. Second (and worse), that the arguments do not travel to Country X might suggest that the arguments are wrong even relative to Country Y from which they were derived in the first place! To limit the likelihood of such possibilities, scholars typically limit the scope of their argument, suggesting that their findings should only work under certain conditions – a practice that has the dual effect of placing their causal claims on somewhat firmer ground while necessarily limiting what they can claim elsewhere.

To think of comparison with an ethnographic sensibility, though, is to think differently about the goals of comparison and how arguments derived from different places might speak to political processes that occur elsewhere. Typically, political scientists use optical metaphors to describe the purpose of their work – their case provides a "lens" onto a bigger problem or the "scope" of their argument sets limits on how widely one can see. Given the interest in meaning that drives much ethnographic study, though, it may be more useful to switch to linguistic metaphors to understand what our work achieves.

To that end, we propose a logic that is also built on a linguistic foundation: translation (see also Friedman 2013, 39–42; Longxi 2013, 56–59; Von Soest

---

[6] During our own graduate training, we recall one prominent scholar teaching his graduate students that the quality of an argument was based on how much of the world it could explain.

and Stroh 2018, 71–73; Cheesman, Chapter 4, this volume).[7] Much like translation of a word or text, the logic of methodological translation assumes that ideas, practices, or processes are comprehensible across different contexts but that they may not work in precisely the same manner. A word in translation, for instance, may not carry exactly the same meaning as its cognate in another language, but the meaning is typically still understandable and interpretable. That is, there is typically a family resemblance between meanings across cultural contexts that can facilitate communication and understanding.

We suggest something similar may be true with the comparison of political processes, practices, or meanings. Looking for such family resemblances (Wittgenstein 2010; see also Boswell, Corbett, and Rhodes 2019) in politics across contexts can help us see political commonalities and how ideas derived from one place may be graspable elsewhere. For instance, as Von Soest and Stroh (2018, 72) note, patron-client relationships are described differently by area specialists of Africa, Latin America, and Asia. Africanists typically refer to patrimonial relationships, Latin Americanists discuss *caudillismo*, and Asianists may describe bossism. Each term refers broadly to the distribution of patronage in exchange for political support, even as each also comes with its own nuances in meaning. *Caudillismo* and bossism do not translate directly, yet there are important similarities; if we overlook them, we lose important opportunities for insight. Indeed, the differing terminology means that area scholars often talk past one another, missing opportunities to unearth common patterns because of a failure to translate ideas that have a family resemblance across context.

At the same time, if we understand them to translate directly, we run the risk of treating patronage politics as if it works identically everywhere. The logic of translation may thus allow scholars to draw parallels between political practices that are often quite similar across space but may be considered differently because of the balkanization of academic subdisciplines or the separation of area specialists from one another. In this sense, to focus on the similarities in meaning across context is not to assume that there is no possibility of mistranslation.[8] Indeed, even seemingly minor differences in meaning can have profound consequences depending upon the context. Who has not bungled a social interaction when using a foreign word whose seemingly slight difference in meaning entirely changes the premise of the conversation? Such mistranslations need not necessarily be negative, though. In fact, they are often generative of new insight and understanding – about both the context

---

[7] We thank Richard Beth for suggesting this term during a discussion of early versions of these ideas at a panel during the 2014 Annual Meeting of the American Political Science Association.
[8] In this regard, our interest in translation differs somewhat from that of Von Soest and Stroh (2018, 71–73). Where they focus primarily (though not exclusively) on the ability to develop universal arguments through conceptual translation, we would encourage scholars to simultaneously think about the limits of translation. Indeed, the frictions of translation may reveal as much about the concepts or processes that interest a scholar as the ideas that carry over.

with which one is only partially familiar and the assumptions that inform one's own world.

As with the logic of family resemblance, the logic of mistranslation can also be useful for understanding politics. Here, we might think of the ways in which a concept has some friction when translated across context as a means for clarifying one's own thinking. One example is Fred Schaffer's (1998) work on concepts of democracy in Senegal. Schaffer seeks to understand what French-speaking Senegalese and Wolof-speaking Senegalese mean when they use the word "democracy" (*democracie* in French and *demokaraasi* in Wolof) and what effect the meanings have for political practice. He finds that each group has a different sense of democracy. For French speakers, *democracie* means something akin to the political science idea of free and fair elections, while Wolof speakers use *demokaraasi* to mean something like social and economic equality. These different meanings affect political practice within each group, as they have different ideas for what goals leaders should pursue and how citizens should hold leaders accountable. In other words, the friction in meaning across the two areas allows Schaffer to show how the "standard" model of democracy used by political scientists – free and fair elections – is limited in its ability to apprehend democracy globally. The upshot is Schaffer's attention to issues of (quite literal) translation opens a conversation about divergent meanings of democracy across cultural contexts with the effect of enriching how political scientists can understand democracy well beyond Senegal.

To go further with the metaphor of translation, though, may require thinking very differently about how our arguments are constructed. At a basic level, discussing how arguments derived from one context illuminate politics elsewhere would involve describing how our arguments translate to other places by describing what patterns we expect to be comprehensible across contexts, what patterns we expect to take on a different meaning in new contexts, and how we think our arguments would take on a different inflection. Similarly, we might think of questions of timing and sequencing as parts of an argument's "syntax." That is, much like the order of words in a sentence, the ways in which political patterns are arranged can produce wildly varying meanings and wildly different political consequences.

The overall goal of such research may not strictly be to tell a causal story, though. Rather, one might think of research as a means for producing different "grammars" that enable understanding across time and place. Much as Schaffer (2015; see also Schaffer, Chapter 3, this volume) argues about work that is concept seeking rather than cause seeking, one might try to uncover how people think of political ideas similarly or differently across space and with what effects. One might also consider how any time we talk about effects, we are, in fact, telling a causal story. It just looks a bit different from the kind of causality that one strives for through identification.

In the remainder of the chapter, we describe two such research projects – one on mobilization in Latin America and one on vigilantism in South Africa – that

Comparisons with an Ethnographic Sensibility 241

use ethnographically informed comparison to make arguments that explicate politics in their respective field sites, even as the arguments derived from those sites translate to other contexts.

CREATING NEW CATEGORIES THROUGH ETHNOGRAPHICALLY ORIENTED COMPARISONS

In her ethnographic study of mobilization in response to marketization in Bolivia and Mexico, Erica Simmons (2016) is able to expand her category of analysis through comparison, showing that subsistence goods that are at the center of daily life might work to produce similar political effects when threatened by markets. Simmons's claims are only possible because of how she is able to identify similar processes at work in two cases when two decidedly different material goods were at stake. By examining mass mobilizations in response to the privatization of water in Bolivia and the rising price of corn in Mexico, she makes the argument that market-driven threats to subsistence goods can help bridge salient cleavages and forge understandings of common grievances that create the conditions of possibility for broad-based, widespread mobilization. The analysis thus sheds light on processes of political resistance and on how identifications are mobilized and groups are formed by theorizing the connections among subsistence, markets, and social mobilization.

The meanings that water took on played a critical role in the ways in which protest events unfolded in Cochabamba, Bolivia. It is impossible to understand the dynamic growth and broad-based composition of the movement that emerged to oppose water privatization in Cochabamba without taking into account the ways in which water worked to symbolize community for Cochabambans across social and economic classes, and how, as a result, privatization could be perceived as a threat to communities as small as neighborhoods and as large as the Bolivian nation. Highly localized perceptions of water intersected with insecurities rooted in marketization to help generate political resistance. To threaten access to water in Cochabamba was to create perceptions that ancestral *usos y costumbres* (roughly translated as "customary uses") were at risk. This threat also tapped into a legacy of cultivation and regional scarcity, undermined irrigation and water collection practices – as well as the community organizations that had developed to maintain these practices – and challenged a pervasive belief that water belonged to "the people." What water meant to Cochabambans and, in particular, the ways in which it indexed different, sometimes overlapping communities throughout the region mattered in the mobilization process. An ethnographic sensibility allowed Simmons to see how water's meanings shaped the communal identifications that played a central role in the protests.

Had the Cochabamba case been the only protest event in the analysis, Simmons could have offered important insights into the potential relationships among water, conceptions of community, and the insecurities produced through privatization. However, she would have been unable to explore the ways in which the processes at work might appear in other times and places, and how they might work similarly when different goods were at stake. As a result, scholars might have understood the analysis as limited to processes of water privatization, and potentially broader patterns in the relationship between subsistence goods and social mobilization would have gone unexplored.

Incorporating a comparison with protests against rising corn prices in Mexico City, Mexico, allowed Simmons to develop broader theoretical claims. By examining a case of protest around a different, technically substitutable good, in this case corn, Simmons demonstrated how two materially different goods could actually take on similar meanings and ultimately have similar causal effects when threatened by markets. In Mexico, tortillas (and corn more generally) are a cornerstone of both urban and rural diets; they are included in well-known myths, serve as a centerpiece of daily ritual and social interaction, and are a part of how many citizens conceive of themselves as Mexican. In each of their respective contexts, to threaten water or corn was to threaten not only a material relationship with a material good but also perceptions of community.

By comparing the processes she observed in Cochabamba to processes at work in Mexico, as well as how those processes play a role in contentious episodes, Simmons advances our understandings of the relationships among subsistence, markets, and resistance more broadly than she could have by looking at the Bolivian case alone. It was only through the analytic process of tacking back and forth between cases – Bolivia and Mexico, water and corn – that Simmons was able to develop an argument that was not specific to free trade and corn, or to privatization and water; rather, she offered broader theoretical insights into the kinds of insecurities produced through marketization, and how those insecurities manifest themselves in social mobilization (Simmons 2014). The work encourages us to understand the meanings that staple material goods take on in different times and places and to theorize connections among markets, subsistence goods, and social protest.

There are multiple ways that the insights Simmons develops might translate to other times and places. While we are unlikely to see events unfold elsewhere exactly as they did in the cases she studies, various aspects of the mechanisms and processes she identifies are most certainly at work. Most generally, Simmons's proposition that we should study grievances as materially and ideationally constituted is broadly applicable not only to the study of social movements and contentious politics but also to any context in which we study the processes and outcomes of claim making. More specifically, her argument that the ideas with which some claims are imbued are more conducive than others to motivating political resistance is applicable to any study that seeks to explain and analyze dynamics of contention (for more on these points, see Simmons 2014).

But Simmons also offers a number of insights that might be relevant to scholars who study processes that do not involve social mobilization. For example, her analysis shows relationships with subsistence goods will be textured and nuanced in ways that produce different kinds of communities across time and place. The meaning-making processes she identifies will not work in precisely the same way in other contexts. Yet her argument that goods that have formed a critical part of the material life and livelihood for particular populations over long periods of time – goods she calls "subsistence goods" – are likely to have also become central to semiotic practices translates easily to a variety of contexts. Understanding these goods as potentially imbued with community-related meanings – either imagined or quotidian – could help us better understand any number of political processes including elections, provision of welfare services, and the development and functioning of political parties.

Simmons's argument also draws attention to the ways in which meaning making and perceptions of markets might be connected. These insights can potentially help scholars better understand responses to markets in a variety of conditions. By encouraging us to think about perceptions of markets as not only rational and strategic but also produced by the meanings with which markets themselves, as well as the goods they regulate, are imbued, her arguments help shed light on everything from the positive public perceptions of free trade throughout Latin America, to recent protests in Brazil and Chile in response to transportation rate hikes, to violent responses to the elimination of food subsidies in Sudan in early 2019. Critical to the value of Simmons's contribution is that we do not simply pick up the entire argument and expect it to work in other times and places precisely as it does for the cases she studies. Instead, we must see how each of her theoretical contributions – individually or in combination – might translate to the questions, times, and places that motivate our own research interests and questions.

USING ETHNOGRAPHICALLY ORIENTED COMPARISON TO CHALLENGE DOMINANT THEORIES

If Simmons's work shows how an ethnographic sensibility helps us incorporate processes into our analysis and generates opportunities for the creation of new categories of analysis, Nicholas Rush Smith's (2019) study of vigilantism in South Africa shows how bringing an ethnographic sensibility to case comparison can help complicate existing explanations, refine categories of analysis, and develop arguments that are translatable to other cases. Smith seeks to explain why vigilantism is prevalent in post-apartheid South Africa despite a celebrated transition to democracy, a lauded constitution, and massive reforms of the state's legal institutions following democratization. In contrast to standard accounts, which portray vigilantism as a response to state failure or civic breakdown, Smith shows that vigilantism is a response to processes of democratic state formation and is fostered by dense civic ties. Specifically, vigilante citizens contest the extension of rights, particularly to criminal suspects (see also Smith 2015), arguing that rights to due process produce insecurity because alleged criminals may be released into their neighborhoods following arrest and continue to prey on residents. In other words, citizens interpret the technical success of legal institutions – the arrest and subsequent release of suspects on bail or the withdrawing of charges if there is insufficient evidence to convict – as state *failure*. In South Africa's townships, where the suspect might be one's own neighbor (see also Cooper-Knock 2014) and is therefore a "known criminal," dense civic ties reinforce these meanings and the emotions attached to them, enabling a collective response.

In developing these arguments, Smith deployed at least three types of ethnographically informed comparisons. The first was a geographic comparison across townships that each experienced vigilantism despite being institutionally, ethnically, and politically different. This allowed Smith to anticipate existing explanations while recognizing how these control variables still impacted social practice. For example, that high rates of crime would lead to vigilantism is likely the most common and certainly the most intuitive explanation for vigilantism. Yet crime rates across the townships where Smith conducted his work are dissimilar, suggesting crime alone cannot be a primary cause of vigilantism. Does this mean that crime is irrelevant? No. But what has to be asked is *how* crime matters. By working across field sites, Smith found that infrequent major crime or frequent petty crime carried out by one's neighbors could lead to heightened feelings of insecurity, even within relatively safe areas. That is, the insecurity produced by crime could be experienced similarly across areas, despite different probabilities that one would experience violent victimization. The effect was that if accused criminals were arrested but released on bail back into the neighborhood, residents could feel insecure. Although the arrests and subsequent legal proceedings may have technically represented success, to some residents, such releases meant that the state was failing and citizen action like vigilantism was sometimes necessary to "correct" the state. By comparing geographically across townships with an eye to understanding local meanings, Smith was able to anticipate existing explanations, identify similar understandings of crime and policing across institutionally different places, and connect such meanings to acts of vigilantism.

Comparison across geographic sites enabled Smith to identify conditions of possibility by centering the meanings that institutions hold to individuals, while a second ethnographically informed comparison helped him refine conceptual categories. The complicated relationship between crime and vigilante violence suggests how important it is to explore the meanings of the variables that we are trying to control. This became readily apparent in the case of crime statistics, where comparison across his field sites raised the question of what the statistics actually represented. At first glance, crime statistics seem to offer an ideal, objective measure of safety or insecurity at the local level. However, because they are tabulated from crimes reported to the police, such statistics fail to capture crimes that are not found in legal statutes but nevertheless cause insecurity. Witchcraft, a feared practice in South Africa, is not illegal. However, some residents see it as a mortal threat, and it is therefore considered socially and morally to be a crime (Ashforth 2005). By comparing how legal crimes and witchcraft accusations could lead to similar responses (stoning, burning, or ostracism), Smith saw that connecting vigilantism to crime understood in a purely legal sense (as opposed to a social or cultural sense) is analytically flawed because crimes not found in legal statutes could incur sanctions. In comparing the similarities in response to these two types of crimes with attention to how, in local context, they meant a moral threat to local communities, Smith could sharpen his understanding of how the category "crime" related to acts of vigilantism.

While a first comparison was geographic and a second comparison was conceptual, a third ethnographically influenced comparison was about practices. Smith's work initially aimed to understand why South Africans participated in a wide variety of extra-state protection practices that bypassed the state's legal institutions, including participating in gangs, joining civic associations, and using occult powers. Through ethnographic immersion, however, it became clear that vigilantism had distinct logics from these other practices and that he had made a conceptual error in initially thinking of all of these practices as of a similar type. In this sense, an ethnographically situated comparison across practices helped him clarify what vigilantism was in the first place and how it should be studied as distinct from other practices geared toward protection. In fact, Smith learned during his fieldwork that vigilantism may not offer protection at all and may actually create new risks for those practicing it, opening new areas of inquiry, such as why one would participate in vigilantism given the high risks of reprisal. The result of these multiple modes of meaning-attuned comparisons does not only provide an account of the conditions under which vigilantism becomes possible but also questions the analytical categories, particularly state effectiveness and state failure, through which political scientists study politics.

It is on this last point where Smith's arguments about vigilantism in South Africa may translate to other contexts – in terms of both its account about the relationship between rights and vigilantism and its conceptual arguments about the differing meanings of state effectiveness and failure. Specifically, Smith (2019, chap. 4) found that vigilantism occurs with surprising frequency after someone has been arrested, both in South Africa and in elsewhere. Such counterintuitive events suggest that common understandings of state effectiveness – for instance, the successful following of legal or bureaucratic procedures (e.g., Tyler 2006) – may only partially translate to citizens' concepts of state effectiveness. To be sure, many South Africans hold the country's constitution and the rights that flow from it in high regard. But, for many of Smith's interlocutors, the procedures by which a suspect is arrested and tried created the possibility that they might be released if there is insufficient evidence or while awaiting trial, which in local context meant the state was failing to provide the security that citizens prioritized. Even as such activity might be a technically correct application of legal procedure, in local contexts, such acts could mean state failure, leading citizens to feel justified in taking the law into their own hands to correct the "failing" state. In seeing how common academic assumptions about bureaucratic procedures translated unevenly to local contexts, Smith was able to explain the surprising phenomenon of citizens lynching someone under arrest. He was also able to translate back these local concerns to the academic literature by showing that for some citizens, police violence represents a kind of state effectiveness to the degree that they perceive it as producing order, even if such violence is illegal. Put differently, by looking at the translation and mistranslation of a commonly circulating concept to local contexts, Smith was able to see that in practice citizens sometimes hold ideas about what a state should do that are opposed to assumptions in the prevailing literature.

CONCLUSION

What we as political scientists choose to compare and how we make those comparisons fundamentally structures the questions we ask and the knowledge we produce. If we bring an ethnographic sensibility to the formation of our questions, the design of our research projects, and the evaluation of our data, we will be able to ask new questions and improve our contributions to long-standing debates.

Adopting an ethnographic sensibility at the research design stage creates new possibilities for the process of case selection. As illustrated in this chapter, cases need not be selected for their ability to address potential alternatives through control but rather for how elements of their processes speak to one another in theoretically relevant ways. As with most qualitative approaches to comparison, researchers would need to remain flexible – willing to change cases and rethink categories – during data collection. But this adaptation would come not from discovering that a case did not, for example, provide the necessary variation but rather from developing an understanding of what interactions or events mean to the people directly involved. Here the design and analysis stages overlap as scholars redesign their projects in response to new information gleaned during the research process.

Our goal is not to provide a "how-to" guide for bringing an ethnographic sensibility into research projects at each of these stages. Rather, we encourage scholars to think differently about how they view the goals of comparison in the first place by bringing an ethnographic sensibility to their work. Adopting such a sensibility also has the potential to have wide-ranging effects by allowing the viewpoints we encounter through our research to reflect back on and potentially challenge the analytical categories with which we began our research. Moreover, bringing an ethnographic sensibility to comparative research is not reserved for ethnographers. Scholars engaging in comparative historical analysis (e.g., Lawrence 2013), large-N statistical studies (e.g., Beissinger 2002), network analysis (e.g., Wimmer 2013), and even game-theoretic approaches (e.g., Meierhenrich 2008) can – and sometimes do – incorporate meaning into their analyses. When they do, they challenge us to embrace the ways in which meaning shapes political structures and how attention to meaning can produce novel insights into political life.

REFERENCES

Ahram, Ariel I. 2013. "Concepts and Measurement in Multimethod Research." *Political Research Quarterly* 66 (2): 280–91.
Ashforth, Adam. 2005. *Witchcraft, Violence, and Democracy in South Africa*. Chicago: University of Chicago Press.
Beissinger, Mark R. 2002. *Nationalist Mobilization and the Collapse of the Soviet State*. New York: Cambridge University Press.
Boswell, John, Jack Corbett, and R. A. W. Rhodes. 2019. *The Art and Craft of Comparison*. New York: Cambridge University Press.
Cheah, Pheng. 2013. "The Material World of Comparison." In *Comparison: Theories, Approaches, Uses*, edited by Rita Felski and Susan Stanford Friedman, 168–90. Baltimore: Johns Hopkins University Press.
Cooper-Knock, Sarah-Jane. 2014. "Policing in Intimate Crowds: Moving beyond 'the Mob' in South Africa." *African Affairs* 113 (453): 563–82.
Dunning, Thad. 2012. *Natural Experiments in the Social Sciences: A Design-Based Approach*. New York: Cambridge University Press.
Friedman, Susan Stanford. 2013. "Why Not Compare?" In *Comparison: Theories, Approaches, Uses*, edited by Rita Felski and Susan Stanford Friedman, 34–45. Baltimore: Johns Hopkins University Press.
George, Alexander L., and Andrew Bennett. 2005. *Case Studies and Theory Development in the Social Sciences*. Cambridge, MA: MIT Press.
Giraudy, Agustina, Eduardo Moncada, and Richard Snyder, eds. 2019. *Inside Countries: Subnational Research in Comparative Politics*. New York: Cambridge University Press.
Gisselquist, Rachel M. 2014. "Paired Comparison and Theory Development: Considerations for Case Selection." *PS: Political Science & Politics* 47 (2): 477–84.

Grzymala-Busse, Anna. 2010. "Time Will Tell? Temporality and the Analysis of Causal Mechanisms and Processes." *Comparative Political Studies* 20 (10): 1–31.

Hirschman, Daniel, and Isaac Ariail Reed. 2014. "Formation Stories and Causality in Sociology." *Sociological Theory* 32 (4): 259–82.

Imai, Kosuke, Luke Keele, Dustin Tingley, and Teppei Yamamoto. 2011. "Unpacking the Black Box of Causality: Learning About Causal Mechanisms from Experimental and Observational Studies." *American Political Science Review* 105 (4): 765–89.

King, Gary, Robert Keohane, and Sidney Verba. 1994. *Designing Social Inquiry: Scientific Inference in Qualitative Research*. Princeton, NJ: Princeton University Press.

Laitin, David D. 1986. *Hegemony and Culture: Politics and Change Among the Yoruba*. Chicago: University of Chicago Press.

Lawrence, Adria. 2013. *Imperial Rule and the Politics of Nationalism: Anti-Colonial Protest in the French Empire*. New York: Cambridge University Press.

Locke, Richard M., and Kathleen Thelen. 1995. "Contextualized Comparisons and the Study of Comparative Labor Politics." *Politics & Society* 23 (3): 337–67.

Longxi, Zhang. 2013. "Crossroads, Distant Killing, and Translation: On the Ethics and Politics of Comparison." In *Comparison: Theories, Approaches, Uses*, edited by Rita Felski and Susan Stanford Friedman, 46–63. Baltimore: Johns Hopkins University Press.

Madrid, Raúl L. 2012. *The Rise of Ethnic Politics in Latin America*. New York: Cambridge University Press.

McAdam, Doug, Sidney Tarrow, and Charles Tilly. 2001. *Dynamics of Contention*. New York: Cambridge University Press.

Meierhenrich, Jens. 2008. *The Legacies of Law: Long-Run Consequences of Legal Development in South Africa, 1650–2000*. New York: Cambridge University Press.

Pader, Ellen. 2006. "Seeing with an Ethnographic Sensibility." In *Interpretation and Method: Empirical Research Methods and the Interpretive Turn*, edited by Dvora Yanow and Peregrine Schwartz-Shea, 161–75. New York: M. E. Sharpe.

Przeworski, Adam, and Henry Teune. 1970. *The Logic of Comparative Social Inquiry*. New York: Wiley-Interscience.

Saylor, Ryan. 2018. "Why Causal Mechanisms and Process Tracing Should Alter Case Selection Guidance." *Sociological Methods & Research* 49 (4): 982–1017.

Schaffer, Frederic Charles. 1998. *Democracy in Translation: Understanding Politics in an Unfamiliar Culture*. Ithaca, NY: Cornell University Press.

——— 2015. *Elucidating Social Science Concepts: An Interpretivist Guide*. New York: Routledge.

Schatz, Edward. 2009. "Ethnographic Immersion and the Study of Politics." In *Political Ethnography: What Immersion Contributes to the Study of Politics*, edited by Edward Schatz, 1–22. Chicago: University of Chicago Press.

Schwedler, Jillian. 2015a. "Comparative Politics and the Arab Uprisings." *Middle East Law and Governance* 7 (1): 141–52.

——— 2015b. "Why Academics Can't Get beyond Moderates and Radicals." *Washington Post*. 2015. www.washingtonpost.com/blogs/monkey-cage/wp/2015/02/12/why-academics-cant-get-beyond-moderates-and-radicals/.

Sewell, William H. 2005. *Logics of History: Social Theory and Social Transformation*. Chicago: University of Chicago Press.

Simmons, Erica S. 2014. "Grievances Do Matter in Mobilization." *Theory and Society* 43 (5): 513–46.
———. 2016. *Meaningful Resistance: Market Reforms and the Roots of Social Protest in Latin America*. New York: Cambridge University Press.
Simmons, Erica S., and Nicholas Rush Smith. 2015. "Comparison and Ethnography: What Each Can Learn from the Other." Annual Meeting of the American Political Science Association. San Francisco.
———. 2017. "Comparison with an Ethnographic Sensibility." *PS: Political Science & Politics* 50 (1): 126–30.
Slater, Dan, and Erica S. Simmons. 2010. "Informative Regress: Critical Antecedents in Comparative Politics." *Comparative Political Studies* 43 (7): 886–917.
Slater, Dan, and Daniel Ziblatt. 2013. "The Enduring Indispensability of the Controlled Comparison." *Comparative Political Studies* 46 (10): 1301–27.
Smith, Nicholas Rush. 2015. "Rejecting Rights: Vigilantism and Violence in Post-Apartheid South Africa." *African Affairs* 114 (456): 341–60.
———. 2019. *Contradictions of Democracy: Vigilantism and Rights in Post-Apartheid South Africa*. New York: Oxford University Press.
Tyler, Tom R. 2006. *Why People Obey the Law*. Princeton, NJ: Princeton University Press.
Von Soest, Christian, and Alexander Stroh. 2018. "Comparison across World Regions: Managing Conceptual, Methodological, and Practical Challenges." In *Comparative Area Studies: Methodological Rationales and Cross-Regional Applications*, edited by Ariel I. Ahram, Patrick Köllner, and Rudra Sil, 66–84. New York: Oxford University Press.
Walsh, Katherine Cramer. 2009. "Scholars as Citizens: Studying Public Opinion through Ethnography." In *Political Ethnography: What Immersion Contributes to the Study of Politics*, edited by Edward Schatz, 165–82. Chicago: University of Chicago Press.
Wedeen, Lisa. 1999. *Ambiguities of Domination: Politics, Rhetoric, and Symbols in Contemporary Syria*. Chicago: University of Chicago Press.
———. 2002. "Conceptualizing Culture: Possibilities for Political Science." *American Political Science Review* 96 (4): 713–28.
———. 2008. *Peripheral Visions: Publics, Power, and Performance in Yemen*. Chicago: University of Chicago Press.
Wimmer, Andreas. 2013. *Ethnic Boundary Making: Institutions, Power, Networks*. New York: Oxford University Press.
Wittgenstein, Ludwig. 2010. *Philosophical Investigations*. Malden, MA: John Wiley & Sons.
Wood, Elisabeth Jean. 2003. *Insurgent Collective Action and Civil War in El Salvador*. New York: Cambridge University Press.
Yanow, Dvora. 2014. "Interpretive Analysis and Comparative Research." In *Comparative Policy Studies: Conceptual and Methodological Challenges*, edited by Isabelle Engeli and Christine Rothmayr Allison, 131–59. New York: Palgrave Macmillan.

EPILOGUE

13

Theory and Imagination in Comparative Politics
An Interview with Lisa Wedeen

Erica S. Simmons
University of Wisconsin–Madison

Nicholas Rush Smith
City University of New York–City College

September 30, 2019
Chicago, Illinois

Simmons and Smith: You have lectured in the past about how various forms of methods training have disciplined the kinds of knowledge produced by students of political science, mentioning publications like King, Keohane, and Verba's (KKV) Designing Social Inquiry. How have such works disciplined political science? Or to put it differently, what kinds of assumptions do they make about how to do political science that continue to undergird the discipline?

Lisa Wedeen: For the most part, I've used KKV in my interpretive methods class at the University of Chicago, not to evaluate whether the book is good or bad, but to illustrate how a Foucauldian discourse analysis can help us study the historical conditions of possibility that enabled a particular phenomenon's emergence, such as, in this case, an exceptionally influential book. And, can give us the tools to analyze how the text works.[1]

When I refer to the "work" performed by a text – or in a more ambitious study by a set of discourses – I refer to both specific logics and their political effects. In other words, the work a discourse does is two-pronged. Let me explain by focusing on the narrow exercise of analyzing KKV in this way. First, in terms of the logic of the text itself, I enjoin students to analyze the text's implications. How do concepts relate to each other? What are the book's citational practices? What gets foreclosed in our thinking by using quantitative understandings of causal inference and applying them to qualitative research? What are the book's underlying assumptions? Second, "work" indexes the book's effects. What kinds of debates has it prompted? How does it get cited? What sorts of institutional arrangements has it helped change over time? What are its enduring legacies?

This mode of inquiry about the work KKV does is different from other kinds of critical engagements with the text. Even the important critiques of KKV (Brady and Collier's

---

[1] King, Gary, Robert O. Keohane, and Sidney Verba. 1994. *Designing Social Inquiry: Scientific Inference in Qualitative Research*. Princeton, NJ: Princeton University Press.

Rethinking Social Inquiry comes to mind) remain engaged with the virtues and deficits of the text itself.[2] A discourse analysis is not like a book review. It brackets those kinds of judgments and looks at the implications and ramifications the book has for the ongoing conversations in which it intervenes. By studying the book's logics, we can grasp how words and concepts make sense in specific contexts. Their intelligibility comes from language and institutions being embedded in a social world of iterative actions and performative practices. By studying the book's effects, which is admittedly trickier than arguing pros and cons or, for that matter, analyzing the book's logics, we can consider how the text and its dissemination have shaped debate or occasioned new standards for evaluating what counts as a good research design.

It could be argued that the further we get from when the KKV text was actually written, the more its efficacy becomes attenuated or weakened – KKV clearly doesn't have the same kind of direct impact that it had before. But in some ways, it doesn't need to be read as a primary text to remain influential because so many of its assumptions have come to seem self-evident in the discipline at this point.

S&S: In what ways do you see it continuing to influence political science training today? What do you see as the enduring legacies of texts like KKV?

LW: Well, I suggested a partial answer already, but let me elaborate. You could make the argument that the cadre that has recently become powerful in certain political science departments (around, say, survey experiments, computational modeling, big data, or machine learning techniques) represents an especially prominent part of the KKV legacy. But more generally, the emphasis on research design, the celebration of multi-method research, the notions of data transparency currently in vogue in the discipline are all beholden to the book – as well as to other writings in a similar vein. More fundamentally, we can recognize common features across a series of transformations, from pre–World War II through behaviorism and on to King, Keohane, and Verba. One of these features is what might be termed "objectivist reductionism," that is, that the world exists "out there," as a collection of facts to be apprehended and analyzed, independent of the values of the scholars who study it, and that complex phenomena are to be explained in terms of elements that all phenomena of a given category share in common. Perhaps most importantly, with KKV comes the epistemological primacy of method, entailing procedures of social scientific inquiry that must be public and subject in principle to repetition, i.e., validation, by other practitioners. This is a point nicely summarized by KKV when they insist on page 9 that "the content is the method." A striking assertion.

S&S: What are the most important forces you see disciplining political scientists today?

LW: I would say that the DA-RT [Data Access and Research Transparency] initiative is one key effort to discipline the discipline. I think that DA-RT, which is not simply sponsored by quantitative folks but by a number of qualitative scholars, is fundamentally an effort to take a quantitative view of what counts as evidence, as well as how evidence is gathered and impose it on forms of qualitative social science that are not amenable to it. Proponents of DA-RT tend to uphold the principles of objectivist reductionism

---

[2] Brady, Henry E., and Collier, David, eds. 2004. *Rethinking Social Inquiry: Diverse Tools, Shared Standards*. Lanham, MD: Rowman & Littlefield.

Theory and Imagination in Comparative Politics

I invoked in response to your last question. They also insist that the procedures of social science must be public and subject in principle to repetition. This anxiety about replication tends not to be based on varied and importantly contested philosophical understandings of cultural reproduction or iteration, but instead on the rather naïve understanding of data as "raw," easily extractable, and unmediated.

The metaphor of data extraction is deeply problematic for some types of qualitative scholarship. It implies that data is inert, ready to be mined, unmediated from the get-go. It suggests a kind of objectivity that is independent of analysis. It also implies that replication requires reproducing the very same encounter in, say, successive interview situations. No one would think that marrying the same person a colleague used to be married to results in the same relationship. But we do learn that the practice of marriage is iterative, that, like other social practices, it is reproduced over and over. The claim I am making is not that generalizing is impossible, but that while individual interview encounters are not strictly replicable, they can be fruitfully understood as iterative, just as all social practices are iterative. Moreover, so much of qualitative work is not confined to interviewing. Gathering ethnographic evidence requires a profound immersion in one's sources – and a long-term commitment to places and people, to the pleasure and difficulties of being attuned to what is iterative and what is evolving in ongoing interpretive encounters.

The term "replication" likewise raises questions of general import that the data-extraction view overlooks. What does replicability tell us about the phenomenon being researched? How do researchers' priors inform their construction of evidence? The added value that comes from considering alternative understandings of replication is also ignored. Instead, we have here another example of the way the discipline tends to restrict what kinds of questions it is acceptable for political scientists to ask and what kinds of answers are deemed cogent. And this emphasis on DA-RT and replication is part of how the current narrowing is taking place. There is a lot more to be said about this, but I shall stop here for now.

S&S: This might be a great moment to turn to your research specifically, because your work pushes back against a variety of methodological conventions. We want to invite you to think about some of the methodological choices that you've made in all of your writing, but particularly we want to ask you about your most recent book, Authoritarian Apprehensions, *and your second book,* Peripheral Visions.[3]

Specifically, in both books, you examine "exemplary events," putting them into conversation with each other to generate broader insights about the places and processes that are subjects of the book – Syria *in* Authoritarian Apprehensions, Yemen *in* Peripheral Visions. *We want to ask you in the next several questions how you chose the events you considered exemplary in each book, to place those choices in broader methodological*

---

[3] Wedeen, Lisa. 2019. *Authoritarian Apprehensions: Ideology, Judgment, and Mourning in Syria.* Chicago: University of Chicago Press; Wedeen, Lisa. 2008. *Peripheral Visions: Publics, Power, and Performance in Yemen.* Chicago: University of Chicago Press.

terms, and to explain how considering the events allows you to make new, general claims about politics.

We want to begin with the concept of an "exemplary event." Quite simply, what do you mean when you say that? How do you know that an event is exemplary? How do you know what an event is exemplary of?

LW: I mean exemplary as an example of, an instantiation of, as characteristic of its kind. So, not exemplary in a good sense (as a desirable model) and not exemplary in a bad sense (such as serving as a deterrent). Just an example. In some ways, my own training matters here. When I was an undergraduate at Berkeley, Michel Foucault was on campus. It was very much in the style of his approach to think about the historical conditions of possibility that generated X, X being the phenomenon under scrutiny, and then seeing how X works. He often chose events that were exemplary in the sense of being examples of. Now, there is a tweak on exemplary that I would want to suggest is common in Foucault's work. For him, an example is often a dramatization. That is to say, something exemplary might not be simply an instantiation but could be something that dramatizes the phenomenon being studied. Think about the way Foucault opens *Discipline and Punish*, with the punishment of the regicide Damiens.[4] The execution, the very public spectacle of that event, instantiates and dramatizes a form of sovereign power that is very different from what he treats in the rest of the book as the judicialization of politics and the emergence of what he calls the carceral state, the latter being the way modern power is hidden in plain sight. As the last execution of its type, the scene exemplifies a convergence of sovereignty and spectacle that then disappears. That opening is memorable because it both encapsulates the convergence and marks an important shift away from the sovereign power of the king toward what Foucault saw as the more diffuse mechanisms of social control characteristic of modern power.

S&S: If exemplary events are instantiations and/or dramatizations of broader processes, how does one choose such an example?

LW: For me, choosing these events requires a lot of fieldwork, a lot of immersion in worlds. I could not parachute into a place or skim an archive and know what was exemplary or not. Beyond immersion as an initial step, though, there are different ways to choose. Some events have to do with impact and what people are discussing – the buzz around the event. What is being talked about in various influential circles? How is it being referred to? What kind of "shelf life" does the event have?

For example, in my recent book on Syria, *Authoritarian Apprehensions*, I write about a series of television comedy episodes.[5] I chose some that were obviously well known and

---

[4] Foucault, Michel. 1977. *Discipline and Punish: The Birth of the Prison*. New York: Pantheon Books.

[5] In Chapter 2 of *Authoritarian Apprehensions*, Wedeen examines forms of "humor in dark times." Examining several comedy skits – some wildly popular, some less so – she argues that "comedy both reproduces and places [ideology] at risk, operating through the forms of immanent critique that are powerful because they are internal and proximate to the objects of (ir)reverence while also achieving a degree of clear-sighted detachment from them" (49). Amidst authoritarian rule, Wedeen argues, comedy is politically effective because it can induce "alternative solidarities that

Theory and Imagination in Comparative Politics

popular. Some cultural products or events so perceptibly have traction that you can't help but notice them. People are talking about them. They cause scandals that get refracted in other public sphere venues. They become cultural references for various kinds of people and diverse demographic constituencies. They have staying power over time. You get the idea. Thinking about how they "work" (in the two-pronged sense I noted earlier) becomes incumbent on the researcher. Other skits, though, to go back to Syria, had very little impact, but for me they opened up a way of thinking about authoritarianism. They were exemplary of the phenomenon (because, for example, they dramatized the ways in which compliance was secured), independent of their reception.

We can understand some events or cultural artifacts as exemplary because of the questions they provoke. Something like the execution of the regicide in Foucault's *Discipline and Punish* seems to me to be almost by definition a rare-ish event. But it was an event that speaks to a broader set of concerns – indicative of a logic (of sovereign power's reliance on spectacle). Film studies and literary criticism are excellent fields for exploring interpretation of this sort. When Fredric Jameson writes about the experimental novels of George Gissing in *The Political Unconscious*, he hasn't chosen them because they were popular or because there were so many of them, but because they are exemplary of the ways in which novels of the late nineteenth century worked ideologically to contain social antagonisms and showcase *ressentiment*. Even when he analyzes the popular movie *Jaws*, the point is not to understand reception but to explicate the logic of the film – what the shark stands in for and why that might matter in analyzing American politics. To stand in for something is another way of saying "exemplary," that it is illustrative of something more general.

In the case of an alleged serial killer I discussed in *Peripheral Visions*, my book on nationalism in Yemen, his capture and arrest were arguably unique.[6] This was not an instance of a larger phenomenon of serial killing. It was exemplary because it brought into bold relief the anatomy of citizen contestation and the regime's jockeying for control. It helped me see how national sentiments were expressed in the absence of a strong state. And it was a visible instance of the regime's precariousness. The brouhaha around his arrest allowed me to think more generally about the images a fragile state is able to convey. They are intermittent and transient – hints of political possibility. Appeals to the corporate identity of "a people," uses of the "we" to speak of fellow Yemenis, and desires for a strong state capable of protecting the community are all

---

counteract the atomization and isolation fostered by powerful mechanisms of social control" (50). Nonetheless, it can also reproduce domination, she argues, because authoritarian rule relies on external obedience and comedy can "advertise and reproduce a self-consciousness of routinized civic obedience, drawing attention to the ways in which many citizens lack conviction but are nevertheless willing to act as if they have it" (50).

[6] In *Peripheral Visions* (Chapter 2), Wedeen looks at three events that are exemplary of the processes through which Yemenis experience nationalism – the country's first presidential election, a celebration of ten years of the country's unification, and the public scandal surrounding the arrest of the country's first serial killer. In the case of the serial killer, Wedeen shows that the arrest, rather ironically, produced public discussion that allowed Yemenis to complain about the ways in which the state is usually absent because of its inability to provide order on a daily basis.

instances of nation-ness, of feelings of collective belonging in which, in the case of the serial killer, the state became the addressee for citizens' grievances *in the very breach of its authority*. Citizens used the idioms of national belonging to demand more than episodic exercises of state protection, performing national attachment by voicing longings for security in the form of a state capable of ensuring it. And this made me think about how nation-ness or nationalism requires ongoing work. That the state, sometimes by its very absence, helps to produce this kind of political imagining, etc.

To be sure, in this event there was a real observable impact. Discussions of the serial killer completely overwhelmed conversations in different parts of the country, newspaper reports, and the like. It was a moral panic in a very wide-ranging and discernible way. But as I suggest, the public sensation created by the arrest and prosecution of a man touted as Yemen's first bona fide serial killer was only part of what interested me about the event. It also opened up my thinking about the paradoxical relations of state and nation, the ways in which nationalism can be intensified even at times *because* the state is weak or absent.

S&S: So, this leads to a subsidiary question: How do you know whether or not these instantiations hang together? It sounds like part of your method is to put these instances into conversation with other scholars or thinkers that then allows you to speak about whatever it is that you've become interested in and what these events are instantiations of in that moment.

LW: Right. It is a kind of tacking back and forth. Theorists like Ludwig Wittgenstein or Hannah Arendt help me think about what I'm observing. But what I'm observing also helps me rethink the theoretical insights from Wittgenstein and Arendt. So, there is constantly that kind of tacking. Or, to use a non-sailing metaphor, I allow theory and events to chafe against one another, where events also rub up against one another in a way that generates new thinking. Indeed, by looking at selected exemplary events, putting them alongside one another while also putting relevant thinkers into conversation with each other, I hope to open up fresh ways of approaching abiding, perennial issues of central importance to politics.

This is not to suggest focusing primarily on theorists from the Western canon. *Authoritarian Apprehensions*, in particular, makes a serious effort to use Syrian films, videos, television serials, comedies, and other artistic works by regime- and opposition-oriented cultural producers, not simply as evidence for a point, but also as a way of thinking with and through their cultural products. In other words, I treat some Syrian artists as political theorists in their own right, interlocutors rather than informants, so their artifacts expand the space of the interpretive encounter to help diagnose (and see ways out of) current impasses – collectively. I take conversations with artists and filmmakers who are exploring ways to open our thinking about, for example, political judgment or how ideological interpellation happens, and put them into conversation with scholars like Arendt and Wittgenstein (in the case of judgment), or Marx, Althusser, Butler, Jameson, and Žižek (in the case of interpellation).[7] Now, is Wittgenstein well known in Syria? No. But does he have something to say about how political judgments

---

[7] In *Authoritarian Apprehensions* (Chapter 4), Wedeen examines in depth three Syrian films that struggle with the challenges that arise for political judgment amid the intensified emotional context of large-scale war and mass mourning.

Theory and Imagination in Comparative Politics

are made that is relevant to Syria? Yes. So, there are different ways to use evidence or work with texts, and not all of them are simply evidence or affirmations of a theory. They can also be specific encapsulations of or pathways into broader questions.

S&S: *Now that we have a better understanding of the tacking back and forth between theory and event, can you help us better understand how the events you choose come together to help you make broader claims? Specifically, can you talk us through how the three exemplary events you discuss in chapter 2 in* Peripheral Visions *hang together? Why did you choose to put Yemen's first serial killer, presidential elections, and the reunification celebrations into conversation with one another? Why these three events? And how does analyzing them together help us better understand relationships between state power and citizenship?*

LW: Ah, I see that I didn't really answer the question you asked me before. I was thinking more about the relationship between theorists and the events I highlight. In chapter 2 of *Peripheral Visions*, I take three of what I call exemplary events and show how they work together to prompt important insights about the performative character of national belonging, democratic citizenship in the absence of a democratic regime, and state formation. I chose them in part because they were all happening simultaneously; they were all dramatic instances of political life in Yemen at that moment; and they helped me explore three counterintuitive notions of the relations among state sovereignty, democracy, and nationalism.

All three events betrayed a note of irony, and two posed important puzzles. The election was widely touted as "the first free direct presidential election" ever held in Yemen, and yet the ruling party, on dubious legal grounds, barred the opposition's jointly chosen challenger from the race and appointed its own nominee. President 'Ali 'Abdullah Salih had the chance to win what the world would have regarded as a fair and free election but chose instead to undermine the process, using the democratic form of elections to foreclose democratic possibilities. The unification ceremonies required the regime to introduce state-like practices such as garbage collection and street cleaning, making apparent to citizens the ways in which such services were usually absent. And the revelation that a shocking series of murders had taken place inside the state-run university produced communities of argument in which people found themselves sharing a sense of belonging to a nation the existence of which was imputed by the state's failure to protect its citizens.

The first two events posed a puzzle, one arguably common to poor dictatorships: Why would a regime that was widely expected to win a fair and free election choose to undermine its credibility unnecessarily? And in the case of the unification ceremonies, why spend tremendous amounts of money in a country with a per capita income of less than $300 (or whatever it was at the time), when state coffers were drained and the IMF was pressing for austerity? The serial killer event differs from the first two in that it occurred independently of state officials' intention. But like the other two, the publicity surrounding the arrest and the ensuing discussion exemplified the ways a political community can be formed by the shared experience of events – which, with the grisly revelations of body parts being found in the campus morgue, was really the shared experience of talking about a well-known event. And importantly, unlike the other two cases, the publicity attending the arrest, rather than exaggerating the presence of state institutions, advertised their absence. Exploring this third event allowed me to see how, in their awareness of the simultaneous and common character of their anxieties and moral entitlements – even in the absence of functioning state institutions – inhabitants of a common territory found themselves experiencing a shared sense of connection to it.

So the three counterintuitive notions went something like this: first, whereas some influential literature suggests that contested elections require "strong" states and national cohesion of some sort, other forms of democratic activity (such as widespread political activism and lively public deliberation) may exist because state institutions are fragile and affective connection to nation-ness, where evident, is not cohesively supportive of regime practices. Second, common experiences of moral panic can be more effective than state spectacles in generating a sense of passionate belonging to the imagined community of the nation. And third, experiences of national belonging might be shared in the breach of state authority, as I noted earlier, in the episodic expressions of national identification brought to the fore by an event, such as the serial killing, that dramatized collective vulnerability.

S&S: In capsule form, then, how would you describe the practice of knowing what events are exemplary and how one would go about choosing them?

LW: Typically, the process begins with a set of theoretical concerns about the world. In the case of *Authoritarian Apprehensions*, my question was about authoritarian resilience and the creation of neoliberal subjects. So, I think about this abstract question in relation to specific places – Syria in this case. Then answering the questions requires a lot of immersion – going to these places with Marx, Althusser, Žižek, Wittgenstein, Arendt, and Berlant in mind – and observing how, at different moments, people in Syria were being interpellated or addressed as specific kinds of subjects (e.g., as loyalists or the ambivalent middle or opposition activists) in the context of extraordinary political change. Through my immersive fieldwork I was able, for lack of a better way to put it, to collect data. The ambivalence many Syrians expressed about the regime, for instance, could not have been known prior to this immersion, especially amidst the rapid transformations on the ground in 2011. And, importantly, my findings challenged some of my prior assumptions. I had initially imagined exploring the forms of generational change that were both a product of and a driver of market openings. I had envisaged researching the new aesthetic imaginaries accompanying Syria's embrace of consumption in the decade before the uprising and the shift away from Soviet-era styles of insularity and asceticism. And I wanted to think about the palpable support Bashar al-Asad seemed to be garnering from communities that previously had withheld it from the regime.

Then came the uprisings in Tunisia, Egypt, Yemen, Libya, Bahrain – and Syria in March 2011. I was living in Damascus as the events unfolded and stayed until May 21. After that, my research became multi-sited, with significant fieldwork done in Beirut, Istanbul, on the border of Syria and Turkey, in Paris, Berlin, Budapest, and even in my hometown of Chicago. With my informants dispersed to these varied contexts, certain exemplary events and forms of cultural production appeared in ways that allowed me to reflect on and at times challenge my prior theoretical interests. I came to realize that I needed a more sophisticated understanding of ideology, and an understanding of humor that moved beyond my former framework of domination and resistance. I wanted to capture the array of Syrian responses to the uprising in order to say something theoretically motivated about the seductions of authoritarianism and the heady days of revolutionary exuberance – that is, to specify the fantasy investments, political ambivalences, and incoherencies that ultimately helped a flailing regime survive. Neoliberalism remained part of that story, but the "good life" it initially promoted was about more than aspirations to economic prosperity. It also involved fantasies of multi-sectarian accommodation and a secure, ordered, pride-inducing sovereign state. The pleasure in status quo conventionality, the forms of political paralysis that attended the uncertainties of "fake news," the internet's "high-speed eventfulness," as I put it in chapter 3, and the devastations of war further compelled me to rethink the importance of political judgment in times of overwhelming turmoil – and to grapple with the genres of unbearability that citizens of various stripes made use of in doing the hard work of mourning. The aim became not only to grasp what was happening in Syria, as important as my commitments to the Middle East are, but also to repurpose the concept of "ideology" more generally for the present.

S&S: *In* Authoritarian Apprehensions, *it seems that you not only focus on how events rub against abstract theory but also examine the ways in which events rub against one another. We're thinking here of your discussion of the consequences of information overload that you discuss relative to the killing of Qashush, the suspected singer of a liberation song, and the confusion about the Asad regime's reported use of chemical weapons in 2013. How did you see these two events as working relative to each other?*

LW: I used these two exemplary events to undermine a common conception of authoritarianism, according to which it is the withholding of information that enables domination. Syria demonstrates how an excess of information and accelerated conditions of dissemination can be exploited for authoritarian political gain. I also wanted to invite a renewed exploration of the fragile relationship between truth and politics. In the case of Qashush, it was the controversy that arose concerning the mystery of who might have been responsible for the murder of a prominent local singer that interested me. That controversy entailed investigating the story's twists and turns, including revelations that it wasn't Qashush who had been murdered at all, or that if it was Qashush, he wasn't the revolutionary singer. The process of sowing doubt that the story's twists and turns suggested was my central focus. The event of finding a corpse with its larynx removed by the banks of the Orontes River in Hama, and the subsequent narratives associated with it, marked a very important turn in the uprising, when it became evident that activist expressions of revolutionary exhilaration, crystallized in the song's uptake in many parts of Syria, were beginning to encourage forms of rhetorical overreach, exaggeration, and a willingness to rush to judgment.

The story has many permutations that are exemplary of revolutionary exuberance, the hopes for countryside solidarity, outrage, and creativity. It also brings to our attention how polarized positions can be generated based on only the murkiest of facts – and how over time a generalized atmospherics of doubt can take phenomena such as the revolutionary singer's playful lyrics and the popular solidarity they generated and quash them. The curious lack of follow-up by activists initially so invested in the song and the purported singer's purported murder was also of interest. And although that could be chocked up to journalistic failings, I think it would be ungenerous to do so. More interesting and relevant is the way the story evolved. The intense outrage that

Qashush's alleged murder initially engendered, followed by the uncertainty caused by rumors he had been sighted on Facebook in Turkey, followed by doubts that Qashush was the revolutionary singer or that the revolutionary singer was even dead could be seen as symptomatic of reading and writing habits cultivated in conditions of what I call high-speed eventfulness and information overload. And the silence about new revelations that the revolutionary singer was alive (and that Qashush himself was an informant and therefore presumably not murdered by the regime after all) was in striking contrast to the brouhaha caused by the initial discovery of the corpse by the river. That silence spoke volumes – about the attenuation of revolutionary enthusiasm, the collective disappointment from the uprising's ongoing-ness, the dying out of exhilaration over time. As one activist put it, "the idea of Qashush had already been assassinated" long before the revelations that it wasn't Qashush who sang the songs and that the revolutionary singer, whose name was actually Rahmani, was alive and well in Madrid. The story crystallized the ways in which the opposition regularly overplayed its hand and how the regime, itself flailing, was able to take advantage of these circumstances of epistemic murk.

The chemical weapons attack is in some ways easier, and in others harder. As with Qashush's killing, it was a local event, but it was also a global event, because it was so important to international decision making, with Obama having declared that the regime's use of chemical weapons in the civil war was crossing a "red line." Even though one can say now that most people are pretty sure that the regime was responsible for the chemical weapons attack, the widely broadcast Qashush killing laid the ground or produced conditions of possibility for confusion, which were there to be exploited in the wake of the chemical weapons attack.

Both events allowed me to explore three key points, which helped me dilate the book's focus on ideology and its relationship to judgment. Let me summarize these points here: First, too much information can generate the very uncertainty that circulating it is intended to allay. Second, as scholars of American politics have pointed out, information overload and the accompanying uncertainty may induce people to seek out opinions reaffirming their own, and this tendency toward balkanization can lead to polarization, or what I call "siloed publics." Third, and this may be the most original point, conditions of generalized uncertainty make it easy for people to find alibis for avoiding commitment to judgment at all. In circumstances of information oversaturation, uncertainty can provide a compelling rationale for inaction, for the suspension of judgment in situations where action might otherwise have seemed morally incumbent. Granted, in the circumstances of intensifying violence, reasons for hunkering down and staying safe overwhelm. But in the beginning this recourse to nonjudgment mattered. It put what came to be referred to as the "gray people" – moderates, or those occupying the ambivalent "silent middle" – at odds with activists, and ultimately with the project of political transformation.

S&S: Still, when seen from the positivist point of view so many political scientists take from their training, the Qashush event and the Syrian chemical weapons attack look like very different types of things. We would like to hear more about what warrants your comparing them to each other such that you were able then to gain insights that helped you understand what was unfolding in Syria.

Theory and Imagination in Comparative Politics 263

LW: I'm not sure if I would say that I'm comparing them, exactly, at least not if we think about comparison in the way the term is conventionally used by political scientists. But, as you were talking, I began thinking that these two exemplary events might be more like nested dolls, where in some ways the connection between the little one, the local Qashush killing, and the big one, the chemical weapons attack, make them all of a piece. Seeing the big doll, the expectation is that the little one and the others are there. There's a relation. They can be treated as discrete events sharing some important mutual reference, or they can be seen as integral to one another.

S&S: *To push the metaphor a bit, though, nested dolls sit comfortably inside of one another. Part of what seems interesting about these two events is the friction between these things that's potentially useful to think through. In other words, although the Qashush killing is independent of the chemical weapons attack, there is also a friction in the ways that the politics of information, the way in which judgment works, that these things are not wholly independent cases necessarily, and therefore potentially not comparable. So, even as they are related to each other, they also have a useful friction in both their similarities and differences.*

LW: Yes. I think of them as having a lot of friction, but I didn't put them together because of the friction they produce. Rather, they're put together because at both a local level and a grand level, they demonstrate the conundrums of judgment I want to bring to the fore, the ways in which ideology works, and the sorts of opportunities for representative thinking that such events enable. Now, why these two events? They do seem incommensurable. But they were both momentous; they generated conflicting accounts that mattered for prevailing conversations about fake news, post-truth, and questions of judgment. Bringing the two examples together allowed me to see in events local and world historical – events of different scales – the ongoing reproduction of what I call in the chapter an "affective and epistemic insecurity," the operation of which conduced to the favor of the beleaguered Asad's regime's counterinsurgency project – and to that extent its survival.

S&S: *There's something scalar about this particular example from your work. The Qashush events could be described as very local or national while the chemical weapons attack had a direct impact on local, national, and international conversations. Do you think the nesting doll metaphor works as well for the comparison you make in* Peripheral Visions *when you put Yemen's first serial killer, the presidential election, and the reunification celebrations into conversation with one another to produce broad insights about how nationalism works?*

LW: Those events are certainly more on the same scale. But they also scale up, both in how I use them to talk about nationalism and in how they are each national events for some of the reasons I noted earlier – they are shared events, widely publicized, refracted through mini publics that generate the larger national public sphere, in which the "we" of the imagined community is invoked as a specifically Yemeni one. It could be that the serial killer example is more local than the others, but it produced a moral panic that was avowedly national, in which anonymous citizens, unknown to one another, imagined themselves as sharing experience with a broader world of Yemenis. In this way the event, restricted to a university in the capital, becomes a national event, while the presidential election and the reunification celebrations are national by definition. Even when social media wasn't the force that it's become, there was still the possibility of something small and local becoming much broader. Going viral, if you will. At the same time, the peculiarity of the social-media generation is that these much broader events can still work to produce siloed publics.

S&S: The question here about scaling ties to generalizability and how one knows that something is representative of broader kinds of issues – judgment, in the case of Authoritarian Apprehension. *It seems that you, as a scholar, are making judgments about the representativeness of these events for broader questions about political judgment. So, we're curious for you to talk about the scholarly judgment that allows you to do that.*

LW: Well, I think it's the obligation of all scholars, really, to exercise judgment and defend choices. In the best sense of our work, we try to practice what Hannah Arendt called "representative thinking." With representative thinking there's an invitation to imagination, or what Kant called an "enlarged mentality." Arendt is explicitly not referring to what she describes as counting noses and joining a majority. Nor is she referring to the act of narcissistically putting yourself in another's place, as if there were no difference remaining. It's not a kind of overreaching empathy, in other words. Rather, it is to be yourself in a place where you are not.

That seems to me to be what a scholarly enterprise is about at its best. It's an interest in imagining multiple standpoints that I think guides some of my intuitions in the field, as well as the sorts of objects I choose for inquiry, and then the ways I try to think against myself and anticipate my audience and the objections my addressees might raise. Often, when we think of political science, it's with the emphasis on the science part, and we construe science as a kind of technocratic enterprise involving procedures and methods or, we could say, one with a managerial focus. I've always been much more attracted to the arts and to politics in a more imaginative register, the "it could have been otherwise" of politics, for it seems things so rarely work out the way that is wanted. That otherwiseness is, I think, what many of the films I talk about in *Authoritarian Apprehensions* are getting at – they are examples of interpretive generosity working creatively with hypotheticals and imagining a multiplicity of standpoints. They challenge us to envisage our political worlds differently. So, the kind of political science I engage in is as much an imaginative enterprise as a technocratic one. By which I do not mean, by the way, that it isn't rigorous. Indeed, all forms of political science to the degree that they engage in comparison and generalizability involve an imaginary leap.

S&S: Let's talk specifically about Peripheral Visions *and the ways you generated broad theoretical insights not only about nationalism but also about public spheres and conceptions of democracy. In chapter 3, you discuss* qat *chewing as a practice that can be examined to understand democracy as both a concept and a practice in other places. Can you speak more about how you go from local* qat *chews to understanding public spheres and democratic practices?*

LW: I did not go to Yemen thinking I was going to talk about *qat* chews.[8] I didn't even know that *qat* chewing was as important or as widespread a practice as it was. It was

---

[8] In Chapter 3 of *Peripheral Visions*, Wedeen examines the pervasive practice of *qat* chewing in Yemen. Such events, Wedeen argues, constitute an important Yemeni public sphere where

Theory and Imagination in Comparative Politics

only in being in Yemen that I realized I couldn't do interviews in the afternoon because people were preparing to chew. That required going to the market for *qat* and making sure there would be food on the table, because the leafy stimulant is better ingested on a full stomach. The world of the office tended to stop and another kind of world of social gathering commenced. It would have been easy to dismiss *qat* chews. But they so overwhelmed social life in the afternoon in a variety of contexts – rural, urban, etc. – that it became very difficult to ignore them. I love that about fieldwork. I love it when something you learn makes it impossible to stay moored to the position you were committed to at the beginning of your research.

So, being in Yemen made me focus on how important this practice was and inspired my thinking about democratic practices in the absence of a democratic regime. When I arrived, my thoughts had been much more about nationalism. But I would go to these chews and ask my questions about Yemeni identity, and we would end up having long conversations that had an altogether different character than, say, a structured interview or even just hanging out. A typical *qat* chew consisted in a series of monologic performances that built on one another and became sort of dialogic or polyphonic in the context of the event itself. And because this was a routine practice, it forced me to think about the ordinary. The conversations can be about very quotidian sorts of practices and were not always the most compelling part of my fieldwork – hours spent talking about date palms come to mind. But some were much more about major events, like when the serial killings happened, and the national discussions in newspapers and mosque sermons about these killings got refracted in *qat* chew conversations. In both the ordinary and the extraordinary I could see how these mini publics actually work in tandem to produce a broader national public.

Thinking about the *qat* chews pushed me to reread works in democratic theory. It also prompted me to return repeatedly to Yemen and follow up with people about questions and concerns that hadn't originally animated the fieldwork at all. In some ways, the most successful chapter of that book is also the one that emerges the most out of the fieldwork itself. That isn't to say it's inductive. I came to the field with a certain understanding of Habermas and public sphere theory, which I engage in the chapter, but I didn't actually know Habermas all that well when I got there. So, I went back and did more reading and then returned to what I was seeing in the field with insights generated by his work and others commenting on it. But being in Yemen also prompted me to consider some problems that arise for social science and democratic theory from thinking about public spheres in the way Habermas does. That's where the chafing and the friction come into play.

What that made me realize in this case was the need for a dialogic approach – that is, assuming that you don't already know what's important but have to discover it – which was critical to the development of my argument. I would not have identified the practice of chewing *qat* as something that would help me develop insights into democracy were it not for having to attend chews in the first place to keep in contact with my interlocutors.

democratic politics are practiced through public discussion. She suggests such practices reveal the limits of prevailing procedural understanding of democracy in political science that reduce democracy to free and fair elections, as democratic publics like those at *qat* chews can exist even under an authoritarian regime.

Of course, my theoretical training was also important to helping me think about what insights into democratic practice could be prompted by the chews. Having had the advantage of studying under political theorists such as Hanna Pitkin who were committed to scholars like Hannah Arendt was very helpful. It gave me a range I wouldn't have had otherwise.

Since we're thinking about fieldwork, I want to take a minute for a quick aside about how we talk about the people with whom we engage in the field. Social scientists often use the label "informants" when they discuss their fieldwork. For me it's an ugly word. Its implications are creepy. But it's also very inaccurate. I prefer to talk about "interlocutors." It's not about equal footing. As many of my colleagues have written about, there are a variety of ways in which asymmetrical power relationships operate in the context of fieldwork. But it's also not "you're either in power or outside of power." The *qat* chew was an iterative practice that dramatized how Goffman's concept of footing works.[9] People were renegotiating their status relationships constantly, within structures inherent to the chew itself that enabled a modicum of equality, and this was part of the democratic practice I ended up theorizing in the chapter.

S&S: Let's turn to talking about a similar set of issues in Authoritarian Apprehensions *as they relate to people's desire for autocracy. Work on* Authoritarian Apprehensions *began prior to the civil war. You initially planned it to be a book about neoliberal autocracy and how it is sustained. It also seems that both your earliest assumptions about looking at this in Syria and the way in which the desire changed as the war unfolded help us understand the appeal of autocracy in other times and places, including in contemporary liberal democracies. Can you say a little bit about how Syria helps us understand desires for autocracy elsewhere?*

LW: With all of my work, the effort is to take questions and concerns of a perennial or abiding nature and rethink them in contexts that are both familiar and not so familiar to my readers. The Syria book had to change to retain any kind of fidelity to the worlds that were changing with it. And this means grappling with grief, my own as well as that of others much closer to the hopes and the violence than I was. It also meant figuring out how to write about a devastating situation in ways that maintained fidelity to my social scientific commitments without either sensationalizing them or seeming insensitive.

So, in some ways, it was very much a foray into a different kind of knowledge production that had to be especially flexible to keep up with changing moods and circumstances. I wanted to be faithful to my interlocutors. I wanted to make an intervention into what Marxist cultural theorists call ideology critique. And I wanted to highlight the stakes involved in understanding ideology's relation to matters of political judgment.

So my theoretical concerns had to be combined with efforts to study events that were moving very rapidly. As you say, I went to Syria with the idea of thinking about the traction of neoliberal autocracy. Then both the neoliberal and the autocratic were fundamentally unraveling (and recomposing) with the uprising. And all of this was happening in the context of my research and writing. So, I had to take a step back and ask some questions: How exhaustive is neoliberalism? Or how totalizing is it? How

---

[9] Goffman, Erving. 1979. "Footing." *Semiotica* 25 (1/2): 1–30.

Theory and Imagination in Comparative Politics

potent is the autocratic? What work is ideology doing both in sustaining the autocratic and in potentially providing openings for it to be challenged? And in thinking about ideology in this context, I realized I needed to learn a lot more from scholars who emphasized the materiality of ideology and who focused not simply on its content but also on its form.

It became a much less rote project as events unsettled any assumptions about either neoliberalism's potency or the resilience of autocracy. But aspects of neoliberalism and much about autocracy have proven resilient, even seductive. And, as you say, this is not unique to Syria. It seemed initially that the Arab uprisings heralded a move toward liberal democratic governments. Then it turned out that their defeat is of a piece with new forms of authoritarianism emerging worldwide. Liberal democracy likewise seems to be unmaking itself in the United States and parts of Europe, where we find civil rights being curtailed and forms of ultranationalist populism emerging with little regard for due process or pluralism. *Authoritarian Apprehensions* is part of a scholarly shift toward paying more attention to authoritarian retrenchment in asking why authoritarianism appeals to citizens – why it's not only autocrats who are attracted to autocracy but ordinary people as well. I also wanted to speak both to the moment we're in and to the broader workings of ideology as form and how the latter relates to the possibilities for and limitations of political judgment.

S&S: Let's talk a little bit about how you write and research something that is unfolding and changing as quickly as things were in Syria as the uprising began and during its early stages. How have you thought about putting events into conversation with one another that may have been only months apart but took place in such different contexts vis-à-vis the uprising? And how did you think about researching Syria and the experience of Syrians when you had to leave the country in May 2011 and were unable to return?

LW: For several years, I spent most of the summers in Beirut. For a period, I was gone five, maybe six times a year visiting Beirut. Now I'm spending time in Turkey. So, by this point I've met more Syrians outside of Syria than I did when I was there. Part of that had to do with the way many people were freed up during the heady days of the initial uprising to talk a bit more. But as things devolved into much more violent forms of protest and conflict, people seeking refuge went into exile in places like Beirut. I was living there in the summer of 2012 when another signature event occurred – the bombing of a regime headquarters in downtown Damascus. At that moment, everything became uncertain, and an estimated 50,000 Syrian citizens came over the border in a single week. There were folks who clearly identified with the opposition and others who were pro-regime. And I met even more representatives of that ambivalent middle that became so important to the arguments about ideology that *Authoritarian Apprehensions* ended up making.

As a result, being there at that time in Lebanon provided an extraordinary opportunity, a heart wrenchingly tragic and exceptional opportunity, to meet people. Being the author of *Ambiguities of Domination* was no small thing.[10] People in the opposition wanted to meet me because it had become an influential text in the context of the uprising itself.

---

[10] Wedeen, Lisa. 1999. *Ambiguities of Domination: Politics, Rhetoric, and Symbols in Contemporary Syria*. Chicago: University of Chicago Press.

I was quite surprised by that. By then many Syrians were saying they had overcome their fear threshold, and they were eager to talk about the book and meet its author. Being a minor celebrity made it possible to meet lots of people I wouldn't have met otherwise. Because I was more of a researcher than an activist, I know I disappointed some of them. I got to know an array of young people, many of whom were devoted to the uprising early on. I stayed in contact with some, witnessing how their political stances changed over time. Having access to their views, as a result of ongoing conversations; their social media posts; their creative output; their decisions to, say, go back to school or their lives in refugee camps – it just made the project much less localized, and very intense.

All of this was true for loyalists and folks in the ambivalent middle, too. Many researchers did not have access to these two political demographics. But my experiences living in the dorms in the late 1980s, my long-standing friendships, some going back to the 1980s – and some who turned out to be more regime-identified than I could have imagined – gave me broad access to Syrians' experiences and views. My work in Damascus in the 2010–11 period, immediately preceding and in the early days of the uprising, with members of Syria's new professional managerial elite was also revelatory. In part, because of the catastrophe itself, I was able to carry on these relationships and sustain new ones through multi-sited ethnographic work.

S&S: This unfolding series of events touches on a key methodological question about how to consider the places where you have conducted your work. On the one hand, your cases might be considered single cases – two books on the apparently single case of Syria, for example. But the conditions under which you conducted your research in Syria across your two books were radically different. Could you speak about how doing work in Syria across two radically different authoritarian contexts changed and what it means to think of a case in a single sense?

LW: The two books deal with three different forms of compliance inducement – and three different Syrias. *Ambiguities* captured the conditions of a durable autocracy whose reliance on single-party rule, an omnipresent security apparatus, and flagrantly fictitious claims had come to seem brittle and outmoded in ways that were apparent to researchers and participants alike. *Authoritarian Apprehensions* examines two additional modes of compliance inducement. The first decade of Bashar al-Asad's rule ushered in an avowedly upbeat, modern, internet-savvy authoritarianism. Both in terms of institutions and rhetoric, this decade relied more on increasingly sophisticated cultural products, created by an emerging technocratic elite, along with regime-organized, market-inflected civil society organizations that tapped into a spirit of youthful voluntarism. And then there was the second decade and the emergence of a civil-war autocracy.

But the point you're making is that the comparisons are not contained within the uprising. I am looking at a much longer *durée*. And that matters. It was a lot easier to do fieldwork under a stable situation than in one that was constantly changing – even on the level of crafting sentences where the tenses make sense. But there is also not wanting to make predictions or end up having otherwise compelling voices from the opposition cause me to misjudge the potency of status quo conventionality.

So, I do think that the two Syrias are very different circumstances. But the fact that I had been related to Syria in one way or another for thirty-five years definitely mattered. At

Theory and Imagination in Comparative Politics

first, I was worried that since *Ambiguities of Domination* was banned, I wouldn't be allowed in. But then by the time I did apply for a visa, it was not a problem, perhaps because the Syrian regime had decided to promote tourism in the country. And, indeed, right before the uprising started, Syria was showcased in the *New York Times* as an especially desirable tourist destination.

It did appear that things had really changed by 2010, both in terms of market opportunities and in terms of the kinder, gentler version of autocracy the regime attempted to project. That image, obviously, turned out to be a very thin veneer. But it was an image that activists also bought into, at least to some extent. Some of those early protests were organized in the spirit that the regime would be different and listen to their pleas, or that the endlessly deferred reforms could no longer be delayed once people were in the streets.

One thing that struck me going back to Syria after having been away for a long time was just how much the market had come to influence everyday life, and how Syrian aesthetics had been transformed from the drab, ascetic '80s and '90s to have a much shinier surface in the context of new forms of market-oriented politics. So, that was very different. Also, going back made me think differently about support, because the first book answers a narrow question, really dealing only with a very small slice of the regime's discourse and asking a targeted question about it. It was focused on Hafiz al-Asad's cult of personality, the flagrantly fictitious and the rituals of obeisance that were transparently phony.[11] *Authoritarian Apprehensions* is more ambitious. It asks how the regime was able to bear the brunt of the numerous challenges raised against it, and what the Syrian example tells us about the seductions of authoritarian politics more generally.

I approached this orienting puzzle by identifying novel modes of what Louis Althusser called "ideological interpellation," in other words, new ways of "hailing" citizens into Syria's autocratic system. From various angles, the book investigates the complicated, varied, often incoherent forms of address that secured the citizen buy-in the regime needed to survive.[12] I argue that ideology works through seduction, arousing fantasy content while simultaneously defusing it and smoothing out contradictions. It plays a role in managing collective anxieties and sociopolitical incompatibilities by providing a way for dissonances to be contained, displaced, and disavowed. In the sense of containment, ideology operates by making what are essentially social and historical anxieties seem natural and inevitable, and by gratifying desires largely to the extent that they are kept in check. As displacement, ideology makes it possible for people to relocate unbearable fears onto a new object, allaying anxieties by transferring unacceptable attributes onto a fantasy Other. The regime operates ideologically in encouraging people to displace their fears by identifying "terrorists" as the cause of Syria's problem. Disavowal comes in all kinds of variations. "I know very well and yet nevertheless" is an ideological locution that distances judgment from accountability, with implications for politics: "I know very well that the regime is incorrigibly corrupt, and yet nevertheless we

---

[11] In *Ambiguities of Domination*, Wedeen asks why the regime of Hafiz al-Asad invested heavily in making transparently phony public claims about him and his regime's greatness – a common practice in regimes built on apparent cults of personality.

[12] Althusser, Louis. 1971. "Ideology and Ideological State Apparatuses (Notes Towards an Investigation)." In *Lenin and Philosophy, and Other Essays*, trans. Ben Brewster, 127–86. New York: Monthly Review Press.

can build government-sponsored civil society organizations that truly empower citizens." Or "I know very well that there is 'no going back' to the way things were before the war, and yet everything will resolve itself." "I know very well there *are* violent Islamic militants [among the opposition], but nevertheless they are not really a problem so I can act as if they don't exist." Disavowal goes beyond denial in that the problem calling for judgment is actually posed, so that subjects are hailed into a position where the realities that can no longer be denied can still be dismissed. In this sense, disavowal expresses the contradiction it simultaneously repudiates.

S&S: *This raises what is arguably a perennial tension in ethnographic work – using discrete events from specific places with complicated, often messy local politics to make broader theoretical claims about other times, places, and events. We would like to talk about this challenge with specific reference to your arguments about ideology under the Syrian autocracy. How does your recent work on Syria shed light on the operations of ideology elsewhere?*

LW: The book had that ambition from the get-go, but it faced a perennial challenge: How do you master the messiness enough to tell a generalizable story without riding roughshod over the complications of what is actually occurring on the ground? I think this is always a challenge for interpretive social science, which necessarily wants to engage in clear, theoretically motivated, and elegant storytelling without either being parsimonious or fetishizing the local complications. That took a lot of time. I'm not sure it's entirely elegant or clear, but it does reflect an effort to master the messiness to the extent possible, without doing violence to the complications.

More generally I would make three points, two theoretical and one methodological. First, because *Authoritarian Apprehensions* is a book about ideology – that is, designed to think about ideology as form, about how ideology structures lifeworlds and is materialized in social activity – my claims are abstract enough to travel. They're very portable. Second, the book is deeply concerned with political judgment and possibilities for representative thinking. That, I think, also travels well. Third, I want to think methodologically about the artistic practices I study in the book not simply as evidence to underscore a point but as theoretical openings that come about by placing interlocutors in conversation with other theorists to imagine roads not traveled. This is what I noted before about capturing the elusive political otherwiseness to how things are – considering alternatives that challenge conventional ways of thinking and being in the world. Those three things – the effort to repurpose ideology for the present, the concern with political judgment and the possibilities for representative thinking, and the treatment of Syrian cultural production as political theory in its own right – these interventions, I think, have general portability both conceptually and methodologically.

With that said, certain aspects of the book that might be portable are still time sensitive, like the seductions of autocracy, like the ways in which neoliberalism waxes and wanes. Has neoliberalism become less important than it used to be? If so, what are the lasting effects? How do we see its traces over time? What versions of marketization are with us for the near future? What's the difference between the neoliberal and capitalism? These questions, which I explore in the book, are time constrained. But, as a general proposition, I don't think you're ever going to have a social world that doesn't include ideology: there will always be discourses undergirded by fantasy investments that take a consistent

Theory and Imagination in Comparative Politics 271

form, independent of specific (and important) content. To put it differently, the form of ideology is general and expansive, but the specific conditions and contours of neoliberal autocracy are of the moment.

S&S: *This raises questions about what political scientists typically call "scope conditions." How would you think about the scope conditions of your recent book's arguments? How would you respond to the phrase "scope conditions" as a description of the limits your book's arguments?*

LW: The patterns I identify should be relevant to a number of cases of neoliberal autocracy, including, among others, China, Vietnam, and Russia, and even what's happening in parts of Eastern Europe. That's not exactly a set of scope conditions; that's more like the relevance of the arguments to comparativists studying neoliberal autocracies in different places.

Now, if I'm going to think about scope conditions, which is really not my language, I would resist the imposition of a priori boundaries. You could certainly say, "Oh, this is a book about only neoliberal autocracies." But that reproduces a certain self-satisfaction about democracy in the United States that I think not even the most conservative of political scientists these days can succumb to, given the fact of the Trump administration. The book shows how the ideological form through which a desire for authority is produced has relevance beyond what are, as it were, officially recognized autocracies. It says, pay attention to the efforts to arouse and contain social antagonisms such as ones based on race or gender or class. Think about the consistent, structurally reproduced efforts to displace anxieties onto the Other – for the United States, the immigrant, the communist, the welfare queen.

And most interesting (to me) is thinking about the politics of disavowal, the "I know very well, and yet nevertheless ..." that informs so much of what we humans say and do. People can be aware of contradictions between their beliefs and actions and still act in ways that preserve the contradictions. This ideological form is not unique to Syria, obviously. One of the reasons Žižek is of help here is that, seen through this lens, ideology isn't to be reduced to a doctrine or a party platform or a worldview, and ideological effects such as ambivalence can be extraordinarily efficacious politically. For Žižek, neither ideology nor belief is about an intimate purely mental state but implies ritualized practices, habits, and thoughts that are "materialized in our effective social activity." Ideology isn't opposed to structure but structures our lived experience. There is no operating outside ideology. What would it mean if there were? So, to talk about the scope of ideology as form doesn't make sense, just like the scope of air doesn't make sense. Or to think more politically, the scope of power.

To follow up on the scope metaphor: political scientists typically use it to imply a narrowing of the field of vision. It seems to me that the emphasis on scope conditions is the result of a disciplining of the discipline with the effect of limiting inquiry. Thinking that some objective set of scope conditions is somehow preliminary to scholarly inquiry may mean not allowing the researcher to wonder what other kinds of conditions might be there to be seen, if perhaps not so readily. When we ask scholars to say "my argument applies under X specific conditions" and to obsess over causal identification strategies, what reason is there not to think we are limiting their ability to generate important theoretical insights about politics? I would suggest that we should rethink both the concept of scope conditions and the metaphor of a scope before applying it too broadly. What is always true for me is that whatever question I take on – big or small, capacious and unwieldy or narrow and targeted – there's always an effort to ground the question in the empirical world, in what comparativists would call a case. And as one case always suggests another, the effort is to speak to concerns that are broader than the specifics of the case itself.

So, while, in a strict sense, the scope conditions of *Authoritarian Apprehensions* are neoliberal autocracies under challenge, I don't want to operate with the language of scope, because I want people who are interested in Donald Trump's America, people who are concerned about populism in Eastern Europe, and people who want to help theorize ideology to read this book. If the scope conditions limit the audience or presume a narrow set of addressees from the get-go, it's not helpful to my work as a theorist trying to contribute to theory. Metaphors in general are creative in taking something that is unfamiliar and making it familiar, but they also function as containers, ruling out other ways of imagining a given research project. There are always different ways of seeing a problem. They're not only about how the question is asked, although that matters, but also about how the question directs your attention in relationship to your interests, how you navigate whatever leaps you can make, what kind of relationship you have to language – even to revision.

Some of the questions you've posed seem to presume a John Stuart Mill–like version of comparison or agreement. That is, "if two or more instances of a phenomenon under investigation have only a single circumstance in common, the circumstance in which all the instances agree is the cause or effect of the phenomenon." Or some current variation on this way of thinking: compare cases deemed similar, which only differ in the dependent variable, on the assumption that this makes it easier to find independent variables that explain the presence or absence of the dependent variable. Or examine cases that are deemed fundamentally different, except on the political outcome of interest, i.e., on the dependent variable. Despite having been trained as a political scientist, that has never been my project and I have increasingly moved away from thinking in terms of variables at all. Some phenomena are more amenable to this kind of thinking than others. Ideology is not a variable – or not in any meaningful way. Just as air and power aren't variables.

S&S: This suggests that there is something importantly imaginative about scholarly work and particularly comparative work. Part of your work as both an analyst and as a scholar is to do the imaginative work of formulating this narrow question that can be answered in connection with a larger concern about legitimacy. In your current book, you answer a narrow question about desires for autocracy amid collapse while connecting it to broader concerns about the transportability of ideological form. So, it seems that in your work you forefront the intersection between analysis and imagination. Can you speak to that?

LW: I am not sure I think there is something particularly imaginative about comparative work, however one construes the term "comparison." I do think political science would benefit from a greater exercise of imagination than what is currently on offer. Here I am thinking of the technocratic fixation with replication in a very narrow sense of that term. Instead, my baseline insistence would be on creativity, in terms of both how we construct and use theories and how they are grounded in worlds that are made by imagining hypotheticals forking out in sensible directions, considering the promising roads not taken and the fruitful ways others have imagined those roads.

S&S: *This discussion of the necessity of imagination brings us to our final set of questions, which is about the advice you would give to a political science graduate student. They're arguably the sites of the most intensive disciplining, in a Foucauldian sense, precisely because they are being disciplined by the (disciplined) discipline of political science to think in certain ways and to develop specific intellectual habits. So, what advice would you give to a graduate student who is interested in questions that don't lend themselves to either the languages or disciplinary methodological practices in which they're likely to be trained?*

LW: First of all, if you don't have passion for your project, you might as well go work for one of these technology giants. They have way better working conditions, frankly. So, that's not why we're in this profession. For me, it's a vocation. It's not a career. If it's my vocation, then I'm going to pursue my passions. I really think that passion is more important now than ever before, especially with the kind of retrenchments and reorganizations we're seeing of the university system.

Second, you do need to be well educated. What does that entail? Imagine the viewpoints of those who don't share your assumptions. In the context of prevailing norms of mainstream political science, that means reading the APSR [*American Political Science Review*] and reading the AJPS [*American Journal of Political Science*], developing a sense of what the trends are, what the styles of reasoning are, what kinds of underlying assumptions are being made, and being able to anticipate objections to your work from those points of view. It also means becoming versed in the theoretical worlds and debates you want to embrace. So, being educated is about having multiple audiences in your head at the same time. It means imagining the objections of a positivist political scientist, as well as having enough of a foundation in, say, Arendt or Wittgenstein or Žižek or Marx or whomever you find enlivening and helpful, to be able to make a proactive argument that holds water and gets some sort of purchase or traction in studying politics. So, I think that being widely and deeply educated is very important and, again, goes back to the first point: you had better have passion for this, because we are talking a tremendous amount of time and effort.

The third thing I would say is, be pragmatic. What do I mean? Don't think that people necessarily already share your view or that they're idiots for not doing so. Maybe this is just another version of suggestion number two, but it's about how to both offer a cogent critique and move forward to do something creative in its own right. That is, in part, about being educated and being able to keep lots of voices in your head at all times.

But it's also about a certain kind of humility. Part of how I keep learning to do this is by working for other people. By subtitling films, for example. Teaching in schools. Offering up services – where I'm sure I'm getting way more than I'm giving – but also not necessarily having to be the one with the expertise. Similarly, taking classes. You're never too old to take a class. I realized when I was writing the comedy chapter in *Authoritarian Apprehensions*, I just didn't know enough to move outside the framework of domination and resistance that informed my first book. I just kept coming back to the question of whether the comedies I was looking at were shoring up the regime or mounting resistance. I was talking to Lauren Berlant, one of the world's experts on comedy at this point, and she said, "Well, you should just take my class." So, I did, and it was a revelation for me. So, if it's hard to be humble, put yourself in structural conditions that humble you. If it's hard to be confident, put yourself in structural conditions that also enable you to become more confident.

Thanks for asking such thought-provoking questions. I hope my answers did them justice.

Index

9/11, and the dangers of perspectival comparison, 60

Afghanistan, 60
alternative modes of comparison, development of justifications for, 8–9
Ambiguities of Domination (Wedeen), 269
analytic generalization, 41, 89
Anderson, Benedict, 6, 13, 64
 comparison of bound and unbound seriality, 69–70
 comparison of Java and Europe, 7, 8, 65
 Imagined Communities, 13, 69, 79
 influence in the formulation of unbound comparison, 64–5
 interest in the explanatory potential of comparison, 64
 on Sukarno's apparent admiration for Hitler, 19, 68
 The Spectre of Comparisons, 19, 69, 79
 writing style, 77
antiglobalization movement, 172
April 6, 182
Arab uprisings, Wedeen's thinking, 260, 267–9
Arab uprisings study, 17, 176
 Bahrain's uprising, 179–82
 comparative framework, 176
 constructing an encompassing comparison, 187
 context, 172–4
 Egypt's uprising, 182–4
 encompassing comparisons methodology, 176–9
 Jordan's uprising, 184–5
 terminology, 173

value of an encompassing approach, 186–7
 See also encompassing comparisons.
archival research
 advantages for comparative analysis of complex cases, 16, 130, 139–41, 149
 classification process, 139–40
 engaging the archive as a "subject," 141
 layering process, 140–1
 Tuttle's account of the Chicago Race Riot, 141–7
 understanding the causes of race riots through, 147–9
 See also Chicago Race Riot study.
area studies
 Anderson's association with, 66
 Cheesman's exploration, 22
 consequences of placing in a comparative framework, 9
 second-class status, 9
 shortcomings, 72
 unbound comparison and, 66
Arendt, Hannah, 53, 264, 266
Aristotle, 6
Auguries of Innocence (Blake), 88
Authoritarian Apprehensions (Wedeen), 255, 256, 258, 260, 261, 264, 266–7, 268–9, 270, 272, 273
axes of comparison, Bartlett and Vavrus's description, 8

Bahrain, uprising, 179–82
Battle of Seattle, 173
Ben Ali, Zine El Abidine, 174, 178–9
Beyond Regimes (Duara & Perry), 220

275

Big Structures, Large Processes, Huge Comparisons (Tilly), 176
billionaires
  problems of comparison, 4
  Seawright's paired comparison study, 20, 36–8
biological metaphors, value of for political theorizing, 156
Blake, William, 88
Bolivia
  comparison of anti-market protests in Mexico and, 232–3, 241–3
  water privatization, 241
  water wars, 241–2
bound comparison
  causal inference and, 70
  knowledge claims, 70
  unbound comparison vs., 69–70, 72, 73–6
Brazil, 6, 103, 197, 243
"butterfly effect," 58, 133, 137

Carbon Democracy (Mitchell), 119
carceral state, Foucault's concept, 256
case selection
  context selection vs., 196–7
  controlled comparison approach, 231
  cross-national comparisons, 223–5
  first step of, 114
  nominal approach, 88–93
  realist approach, 85–8
  strategy recommendations, 193–4
  value and limitations of the "human element," 198–9
case studies
  advantages and limitations, 114
  concepts available for study, 90
  conventional approach, 112–17
  falsification and, 115
  Gerring's influential definition of a case study, 86
  nominal approach to case selection, 88–93
  nominal vs. realist approaches, 85, 88, 90, 91
  ostensible bias toward verification, 115
  problems with case-centered analyses, 173
  realist approach to case selection, 85–8
  traditional approach, 84
cases
  alternative types of, 12
  concept of, 84
casing a study
  nominal approach, *see* nominal approach to casing

Soss's concept, 14, 196
casing vs. siting
  Brubaker's ethnic identity study, 116
  canonical usages of "case," 107
  concept of "siting," 107
  conventional approach to single-case studies, 112–17
  criteria for site selection, 120–1
  history of the comparative method, 109–12
  siting and re-siting the global renewable energy transition, 117–20
  See also lithium extraction in Chile study.
causal homogeneity, 36
causal inference
  as primary research goal of the comparative method, 112
  bound comparison and, 70
  failure of qualitative comparison for purposes of, 31
  KKV's idea that comparison is geared toward, 193
  value of controlled comparisons, 136,
  See also qualitative comparisons for causal inference.
causation
  alternative perspectives on the nature of, 32–3
  contemporary theories of, 42
  traditions of thought about, 32
chaos theory, 133, 137
chemical weapons, Asad regime's reported use of, 261–3
Chicago Race Riot study
  context, 141
  findings, 147
  national cross-sectional analysis, 144–7
  terminology, 142
  understanding collective violence through, 147–9
  use of archival sources, 143
  See also archival research.
Chile
  lithium mining, 17
  See also lithium extraction in Chile study.
  protests in, 243
China
  comparative work on a wide-ranging selection of phenomena, 209
  comparison with the United States, 217
  cross-national comparisons involving, 209
  See also cross-regime-type comparisons.
  lithium ion battery production, 17

Index

methods of comparison with other states, 17–18
most-similar-systems comparisons, 210–11
Chinese soldiers, Hundman's study of, 155
coevolution and emergence, concepts of, 134–5
Colombia, 197
comparative analysis
  role in theory development, 197
  Tilly's four types, 176
comparative area studies, 9
comparative method
  as cornerstone of political enquiry, 64
  bifurcated view, 1
  central components, 12
  controlled vs. uncontrolled, 5–7
  dubious history, 5
  foundations for expansion, 7–11
  genealogy of, 109–12
  rethinking the practice of comparison, 16–18
  rethinking the purposes of, 18, 22
  rethinking what is compared, 13–16
  textbook approach, 66
  two types of, 47
comparative politics
  foundational works, 6
  kinds of divergences and convergences available for analysis, 13
comparative racial politics, as example of the theoretical payoff of comparative work, 197–8
comparative research design
  balancing theoretical and practical concerns, 198–9
  case selection vs. context selection, 196–7
  discrepancy between teaching and conduct of, 190
  misperceptions about, 190–1, 192–9
  sources of theoretical inspiration, 197–8
  testing theories as goal of, 192–4
  variation in research design, 194–5
"compare," definition, 47
comparison
  as discursive strategy, 64–5, 77
  forms of, 19
  value for political science, 16
  value for research, 204
  value for theory development, 190
complex comparisons, understanding collective violence through, 147–9
concept development, role that small-n comparisons can play in, 20

concept formation, concept of, 50
concepts in comparative politics, Sartori's observations, 208
conceptual comparison, Htun and Jensenius's concept, 18, 20, 192
conceptual stretching
  importance of avoiding, 86
  in Wedeen and Pachirat's work, 92–3
  propensity of cross-regime-type comparisons to, 208
  Sartori's critique, 208, 209, 212, 226
  ways of avoiding, 209
  welfare participation study as, 94
conflict, analytic utility of, 120
contextualized comparison, 9
controlled comparison
  approach, 231
  assumptions required, 35
  contributions to political science, 3–5
  criticisms, 193
  critique of inferential capabilities, 4
  development of justifications for alternatives, 8–9
  difficulties involved in and techniques to cope, 136–7
  external validity and, 40
  KKV's promotion of, 192
  limitations, 3–4, 234–236
  textbooks' emphasis on, 193
  ubiquity of the strategy in qualitative comparative research, 3
  uncontrolled comparison vs., 5–7
  usefulness, 231
  uses and limits, 130, 136
  value for theory development, 194
"Creole states," Anderson on the emergence of nationalism in, 13
cross-case comparisons, fall in esteem, 31
cross-regime-type comparisons
  analytical requirements, 209–10
  benefits of an ethnographically sensitive approach, 239–40
  case selection, 223–5
  China and India, 213–14, 220–1
  China and Taiwan, 216, 219–20, 223
  conceptual fit, 212–13, 218, 222–3
  dissimilar political systems, 210–13
  foci of comparison, 214–18
    comparable institutions, 214–16
    comparable sociopolitical process, issue, or conundrum, 216–17
    selecting and defending, 217–18

cross-regime-type comparisons (cont.)
  methodological lessons, 226
  methodology, 213–14
  potential benefits, 210, 226–7
  purposes and benefits, 218–25
    concept development, 222–3
    explaining substantive phenomena, 218–20
    insights on political regimes, 220–1
    scope and framing, 223–5
  reasons for emergence of research on China, 225–6
  Sartori's critique, 208–9, 212
  state-backed neighborhood organizations, 219–20
  United States and China, 217
  urban preservation, 216–17, 219
  workers' fate under globalization, 219
cross-regional comparisons, potential contribution, 18

DA-RT (Data Access and Research Transparency) initiative, 254–5
democracy
  American English metaphors, 59
  container metaphor, 57–8
  ways of thinking about, 55
  Wedeen's translation of the concept onto everyday practices, 21
dependent variables
  case selection and, 112, 196, 272
  potential significance, 218
  research design and, 195
  suitability for single-case studies, 112, 113
  value of qualitative comparisons and, 39
descriptive inference, 8, 9, 194, 195
Designing Social Inquiry (King, Keohane, & Verba), 112, 192, 203
  Wedeen's use of in teaching, 253–4
Discipline and Punish (Foucault), 256, 257
discursive strategy, comparison as, 64–5, 77

economics, Samuelson's thermodynamics analogy, 54
Ecuador, 112
Egypt, uprising, 182–4
El Sisi, Abdel Fattah, 183, 184
emergence and coevolution, concepts of, 134–5
encompassing comparisons, 17, 176–9
  definition and function, 177
  locating the Arab uprisings in, 178–9
  Tilly's notion, 176, 177
  variation-finding comparisons vs., 177
  See also Arab uprisings study.
equifinality, 113, 137
ethnic violence, use of controlled comparison to shed light on, 3
ethnographically oriented comparisons
  benefits and requirements of adopting an ethnographic sensibility, 231, 233–4, 246–7
  benefits of the approach for cross-context comparisons, 239–40
  Bolivia-Mexico anti-market protests, 232–3, 241–3
  challenging dominant theories through, 243–6
  comparative analysis of vigilantism in South Africa, 22, 71, 233, 243–6
  concept of "ethnographic sensibility," 231
  creating new categories through, 241–3
  enhancement of comparison through, 231
  generalizability vs. translation, 237–40
  implications for the goal of comparison, 232
  projects under study, 232–3
  rethinking comparison and, 234–7
Europe, Anderson's comparison of Java and, 7, 8, 65
expanded comparative method, building foundations for, 7–11
external validity, 40, 72
  analytic generalization and, 41–2
  bound comparison vs. unbound, 72
  causal capacity and, 43
  qualitative comparison and, 40, 42

Family Romance of the French Revolution, The (Hunt), 56
Flaming Womb, The (Andaya), 79
foreign actors, involvement in regional domestic politics, 178
Foucault, Michel
  concept of the carceral state, 256
  Discipline and Punish, 256, 257
  influence on Wedeen, 256–7
  reaction to Borges's Chinese taxonomy of creatures, 67–8, 79
  The Order of Things, 67
Foundations of Economic Analysis (Samuelson), 54

Geertz, Clifford, 51, 56, 88
gender discriminatory laws

Index

cross-national study, 191
See also women's empowerment research project.
generalizability
  as gold standard for comparative research, 237
  as gold standard for political science work, 20
  large-scale social phenomena and, 133
generalization, rethinking understanding of, 21
German coffee houses, comparison with Yemeni *qat* chews, 21
Gerring, John, 77, 86
global renewable energy transition, siting and re-siting, *See also* lithium extraction in Chile study.
globalization, cross-national comparisons of workers' fate under, 219
green energy revolution, 17
Gulf Cooperation Council (GCC), 179–81, 182, 185, 187

Huntington, Samuel, 6, 13

Imagined Communities (Anderson), 13, 69, 79
immersive inquiry, virtue of, 107
impunity, Haberkorn's hypothesis, 71–2
In Friction: An Ethnography of Global Connection (Tsing), 57
incorporated comparisons, 117
India
  comparisons with China, 213–14, 220–1
  Jensenius's work on marginalized communities in, 199
indigenous mobilization, use of controlled comparison to shed light on, 3
individualizing comparison, as tool for studying the Arab uprisings, 176, 180, 183, 187
Indonesia, Geertz's comparison of historical development of Islam in Morocco and, 51
inferential strategies, design based, 131
intelligibility, as criterion for good writing and argumentation in social science, 77–9
interdependency issues, large-scale social phenomena, 131–2, 133
International Monetary Fund, 186
international relations, 6
inverted telescope, Anderson's trope, 19, 65, 68
Iraq, 60, 179
Islam Observed (Geertz), 51
Israel
  Arab states establish full diplomatic relations with, 184
  Palestinian armed activity against, 162
  See also Palestinian refugee camps study.
  US aid, 183, 185

Japan, 191, 201
  Leheny's study of local impacts of transnational reform, 101–2
Java, Anderson's comparison of Europe and, 7, 8, 65
Jordan, 181, 187
  uprising, 184–5
juxtapositional comparison
  Anderson's interest in the explanatory potential of, 64
  concept of, 47
  examples of, 49, 51
  familiarity, 19
  historical comparison as, 51
  in the social sciences, 50–2
  methodological advice, 50–1
  perspectival comparison vs. 47–50, 190

Kaplan, Abraham, 86, 93
Kifaya, 182
Knowing the Enemy: Jihadist Ideology and the War on Terror (Habeck), 60
Koch, David, paired comparison with John Menard Jr., 36–44

language
  relationship with the social world, 54–5
  Taylor on, 55
large-scale social phenomena
  advantages of historical archives for study of, 130, 139–41, 149
  See also archival research.
  challenges for comparative analysis, 129
  controlled comparison, uses and limits, 130–6
  emergence and coevolution, concepts of, 134–5
  examples of, 129
  generalizability and, 133
  implications of multi-level social processes for comparative analysis, 134–5
  interdependency issues, 131–2, 133
  interdependent and multi-level comparisons, 136–9
  scaling processes, West's analysis, 134
  social revolutions, 132–6

Latin America
　Collier and Collier's study of labor parties and regimes, 43
　mobilization in, 22
　See also individual countries.
Le Chatelier's Principle, 54
Lebanon, 179
　Palestinian refugee camps, 5
　See also Palestinian refugee camps study.
Leviathan (Hobbes), 54
Libya, 175
Lindsay, Nicholas Vachel, 49
lithium extraction in Chile study
　casing and re-casing process, 118
　comparative framework, 118
　context and hypothesis, 118
　site selection process, 120–1
　siting and re-siting dynamics, 119–20
　unexpected connections, 119
Logic of the Moral Sciences (Mill), 50

machine-based metaphors, vs. biological, 156
matching, 33–4
Menard, John, Jr., paired comparison with David Koch, 36–44
metaphor
　as usual means of conceptualizing the world, 56
　Burke on comparing dissimilar things, 48
　cumulative effect of misplaced metaphors, 78
　new ways of thinking and, 78
　perspectival comparison and, 19
　potential for selection bias, 78
methodological training, KKV's influence, 192–3, 204
Mexico, comparison of anti-market protests in Bolivia and, 232–3, 241–3
Middle East, security situation, 17
Mill's methods of agreement and difference, 7, 36, 44, 50, 51, 153, 209, 232
Moral Economy of the Peasant, The (Scott), 79
Morsi, Mohammad, 183
MSDO (most-similar-different-outcomes) approach, 152–3, 159–60
Mubarak, Hosni, 178–80, 183
multi-level comparisons
　addressing, 136–9
　implications of, 134–5
Muslim Brotherhood, 182–4

nationalism
　Anderson's thesis, 6, 13, 69
　Wedeen's thinking, 258, 259, 263, 264
Negro in Chicago, The (Chicago Commission on Race Relations report), 143
Neyman-Rubin counterfactual model, 131
nominal approach to casing
　as a product of earlier intellectual and political activity, 90
　as ongoing research activity, 88
　benefits of, 103–4
　"bucket of objects," 98–9
　dialogic approaches, 102
　examples of innovation through, 101–2
　examples of the use of nominal strategies, 102–3
　Fredrickson on nominal strategies in historical comparison, 102
　importance of distinguishing casing from positioning within a site, 91
　intersection with theme of rethinking comparison, 101–4
　new casings of familiar social kinds, 90
　Pachirat's casing of action at a local slaughterhouse, 92
　potential for reframing, 89
　re-casing, 92
　roots, 85
　Seigel on the value of for insight, 103
　Soss's study into welfare participation, 93, 94–101
　Wedeen's casing of *qat* chews in Yemen, 92
non-controlled comparison
　benefits of understanding the value of, 11–13
　riskiness of work reliant on, 10
　See also uncontrolled comparison.
Norway, 191, 201

Obama, Barack, 180
Occupy movement
　inspiration, 186
　origins and model, 172
omitted variable bias, 112
Operation Decisive Storm, 182
Order of Things, The (Foucault), 67
organized crime, Tilly's thesis on war making and state making as, 71

paired comparison
　billionaires, 36–8
　causal inference and, 34–5
　comparative politics' historical emphasis on, 173
　procedure, 34

Index

renewed interest in, 2
Palestinian refugee camps study
  initial research design, 152–3
  issues with standards of "representativeness" and "non-bias," 158–9
  modes of comparison, 164–7
  MSDO requirements, 159
  neuroscience-based perspectival comparison, 163–4
  re-casing process, 160
    challenges, 161–4
  relational focus, 154
  theoretical and empirical approach, 154–8
pattern matching, 41
Peninsula Shield Force (PSF), 179
People's Republic of China (PRC)
  location of much research, 208
  See also China.
Peripheral Visions (Wedeen), 255, 257, 259, 264
perspectival comparison
  assessment criteria, 54–8
  concept of, 47, 49
  dangers, 58–60
  disciplining power, 153
  examples of, 19, 53–4, 55
  examples of good social science perspectival comparisons, 56–8
  in the social sciences, 52–4
  "insider" and "outsider" perspectives and, 199
  juxtapositional comparison vs., 47–50, 190
pluralism, 2
political participation, welfare claiming as
  See also welfare participation.
political science
  rethinking comparison and, 2–11
  revival of qualitative methods, 2
Political Unconscious, The (Jameson), 257
populism
  comparisons of in Thailand and United States, 73–4, 76
  Cramer's study, 73
postcolonial theory, 1, 4
Power and Humility: The Future of Monitory Democracy (Keane), 57
process tracing, 7, 8, 9, 52, 87, 153
public pressure, billionaires and the causal role of, 36–8
purposes of comparison, rethinking, 18, 22

Qashush, Wedeen on the reported killing of, 261–2

qat chews in Yemen
  as demonstration of groups engaging in democratic practices, 21
  comparison with German coffee houses, 21
  nominal approach to casing in Wedeen's study, 92
  theoretical insights about nationalism and democracy, 264–6
Qatar, 181–2
qualitative comparison
  advantages, 40
  contribution to conceptualization and measurement, 39, 44
  revival of the method, 2
  use of in comparative historical literature, 43
qualitative comparison for causal inference
  billionaires and the causal role of public pressure, 20, 36–8
  implausibility of assumptions required, 31
  modest differences, 35
  no differences between cases, 35
  paired comparison, 34–5
  small-group comparisons, 33–4
  value of comparison, 38–44
  value of the qualitative approach, 32–6

race riots in the United States, challenge of studying, 16
racial classification, comparison of countries in the Americas, 197–8
racism, comparative histories of in the United States and South Africa, 102
Ragin, Charles, 64, 84, 85, 88
random assignment, causal inference and, 33
randomized controlled trials, as "gold standard" for causal explanation, 131
realist approach to case studies
  case selection, 85–8
  defining classes of cases, 86
  positioning of the researcher, 85
  risks of misclassification, 86
  role in the logic of controlled comparison, 87
  selection of sites as cases, 91
  taken-for-granted status, 85
rebel organizations, Staniland's work on cohesion and fragmentation in, 154
re-casing, 92, 103, 118, 153, 160, 168
  challenges of adjusting research design while conducting the research, 161–4
  procedure, 160

regression analysis, allowance for causal inference, 34
relational comparison, micro-level change and macro-level process, 154–8
relational plasticity, concept of, 15, 157
research design, KKV's approach to, 114
rethinking comparison
  building foundations for an expanded comparative method, 7–11
  comparison and political science, 2–11
  controlled vs. uncontrolled comparison, 5–7
  critique of controlled comparison, 3–5
  rethinking the practice of comparison, 16–18
  rethinking the purposes of comparison, 18, 22
  rethinking what is compared, 13–16
revolutionary tactics, worldwide shift in, 172
revolutions
  classification, 134
  value of juxtapositional comparison for study of, 51, 52
  value of perspectival comparison for study of, 52–3
  See also Arab uprisings study; social revolutions.

Salih, Ali Abdullah, 182
Sartori, Giovanni, 208
Saudi Arabia, 181–2, 183–4, 185–6, 187
seriality, Anderson's comparison of two types, 69
shadow cases, 112, 121
simile, 48
Simmons, Erica S., 22, 87, 241, 242, 243
  comparison of anti-market protests in Bolivia and Mexico, 232–3, 241–3
single-case studies
  casing vs. siting, 122
  concept of, 115
  KKV's approach to research design, 114
siting
  casing vs., 117 see casing vs. siting
  concept of, 15, 115
Skocpol, Theda, 51, 132
small-n comparison, 3, 20, 34, 112, 192, 238
  potential role in concept development, 20
Smith, Nicholas Rush, 22, 71, 243
  comparative analysis of vigilantism in South Africa, 22, 71, 233, 243–6
social movements in Latin America, 6
social network-based approaches
  examples of, 154–5

neuroscience-based perspectival comparison, 156–7
Staniland's work on cohesion and fragmentation in rebel organizations, 154
use of in international studies research, 154–5
social phenomena, large-scale, see large-scale social phenomena
social relationships, "relational plasticity," 15, 157
social revolutions
  interdependency issues, 132–6
  Skocpol's comparative analysis, 132
Social Science Methodology (Gerring), 77
social sciences
  Giddens's "double hermeneutic," 56
  juxtapositional comparison in, 50–2
  perspectival comparison in, 52–4
South Africa
  comparative analysis of vigilantism in, 22, 71, 233, 243–6
  comparative histories of racism in the United States and, 102
Spectre of Comparisons, The (Anderson), 19, 69, 79
state capacity, use of controlled comparison to shed light on, 3
state formation, 6
state violence in Thailand, Haberkorn's history of, 71–2
state, Hobbes's and Tilly's perspectival comparisons, 19
subnational comparisons, 1, 2, 4
Sudan, 243
Sukarno, 19, 68
Supreme Council of the Armed Forces (SCAF), 183
Syria, 175, 179, 182, 183–4, 186

Tahrir Square, 183
Taiwan, comparisons with China, 216, 219–20, 223
taxonomy, Foucault's reaction to Borges's Chinese taxonomy of creatures, 67, 68, 79
Thailand
  comparisons of populism in the United States and, 73–4, 76
  Haberkorn's history of state violence in, 71–2
  politics of resentment in, 76
thermodynamics, as analogy for economics, 54
Think Global, Fear Local (Leheny), 101

Index

Tilly, Charles, 6, 13, 19, 71, 176–7
traditional comparisons, new ways to approach, 17
translation, logic of colonial expansion and, 75
transversal comparison, function, 8
Tricks of the Trade (Becker), 98
Tunisia, 174, 178, 179, 181, 182
Turkey, 179, 182, 260
Type II error, 112

unbound comparison
  Anderson's influence in the formulation of the idea, 64–5
  area studies and, 66
  bound comparison vs., 69–70, 72
  desirability argument, 79–80
  Foucault's reaction to a Chinese taxonomy of creatures, 67–8
  functions, 22, 73–6
  location-based approaches and, 66, 69–73
  logic of, 22, 65–6, 71, 75, 79
  populism in Thailand and the United States, 73–4, 76
  relationship of equality and distinctiveness, 76
  social hierarchy in England and India, 74
  textbook approach to comparative enquiry and, 66
  value of good writing, 77–9
unbounding, consequences, 9
uncontrolled comparison
  Anderson's use of, 65
  saturation of the Western canon, 6
  See also controlled comparison; non-controlled comparison.
United Arab Emirates (UAE), 179, 181–2, 184
United States (US)
  Arab uprisings and, 180–1, 183, 185
  challenge of studying race riots, 16
  comparative histories of racism in South Africa and, 102
  comparison with China, 217
  comparisons of populism in Thailand and, 73–4, 76
  racial identity in, 197
  relations with Jordan, 185
  relations with Saudi Arabia, 186
  war in Yemen and, 182
units of analysis, rethinking, 13–16
universalizing comparisons, 176

Unwanted Claims (Soss), 94
urban preservation, cross-national comparisons, 216–17, 219
Useful Adversaries (Christensen), 217

variation-finding comparisons
  as tool for studying the Arab uprisings, 175–7, 180, 186, 187
  encompassing comparisons vs., 177
verification, bias of research toward, 112, 115
vigilantism in South Africa, Smith's comparative analysis of, 22, 71, 233, 243–6
Voice and Equality (Verba, Schlozman, and Brady), 99
vote buying, metaphors for, 59

Wallerstein, Immanuel, 6
"war on terror" metaphor, general acceptance of, 60
We Are All Khalid Saeed, 182
Wedeen, Lisa, 6, 21, 92
  advice for students, 273–4
  Arab uprisings, commentary on, 260, 267–9
  casing across different contexts, 268–70
  choosing exemplary events, 256–9
    comparing events of different scales, 262–3, 264
    events in *Authoritarian Apprehensions*, 261–2
    events in *Peripheral Visions*, 259–60
    judgments about representativeness, 264
    tacking back and forth between theory and event, 258–9
    the process, 260–1
  comparative work and imagination, 272–3
  forces disciplining political scientists today, 254–5
  Foucault's influence, 256–7
  KKV's influence on political science, 253, 254
  methodological choices, 255–6
  researching Syria and the experience of Syrians, 267–8
  scope conditions, 271–2
  theoretical insights about nationalism and democracy, 264–6
  understanding ideology through the study of discrete events, 270–1
  understanding the desire for autocracy through a Syrian lens, 266–7
  Wittgenstein's and Arendt's influence, 258

welfare participation
  recognition as a kind of political participation, 98–101
  Soss's study, 93, 94–101
  Verba, Schlozman, and Brady's measurement of, 99
  With Us and Against Us: How America's Partners Help and Hinder the War on Terror (Tankel), 60
women's empowerment
  challenges, 200
  Htun and Jensenius's research, 18, 20
  principal driver of, 200
women's empowerment research project, 191
  comparative approach, 201–2
  conceptual comparison, 192
  evolution of the project, 199–201
  fieldwork contexts, 191
  methodology, 200–1
  multicultural approach to context selection, 202–3
  starting concept, 191
World Bank, 186
World Social Forum, 173
world systems theory, 6

Yemen, 181, 182, 183–4, 186, 259
  Wedeen's analysis of *qat* chews in, 21, 92, 264–6

Printed in the United States
by Baker & Taylor Publisher Services